Praise for *Chilean Cinema in the Twenty-First-Century World*

"*Chilean Cinema in the Twenty-First-Century World* is an excellent and important contribution to the emerging field of Chilean film studies and to the broader one of Latin American film studies."
—Juan Poblete, University of California, Santa Cruz, co-editor of *Humor in Latin American Cinema*

"While many film studies books deal with large film industries such as Mexico, Brazil, and Argentina, there are few systematic treatments of Chilean film in English, and none that so effectively treat the question of internationalization at a crucial moment of rearticulation/reinvention of Chilean cinema."
—Ignacio López-Vicuña, associate professor of Spanish, University of Vermont

"This volume is a long-awaited homage (in English) of the cutting edge, innovative work coming out of Chile during the past two decades. An excellent resource for everyone from faculty through undergraduates on the ways in which Chilean cinema has attracted global audiences through fresh, heterogeneous directorial voices, fierce networking on the film festival circuit, and bold marketing strategies. This volume is indispensable to those interested in contemporary Chilean cinema."
—Tamara Falicov, author of *Latin American Film Industries*

"Chilean cinema has flourished in the twenty-first century and reached global audiences, and this is an essential book to chronicle and analyze this success story. Written by experts in their field, this book provides an excellent and comprehensive critical guide."
—Deborah Shaw, professor of film and screen studies, University of Portsmouth, and editor of *Transnational Screens*

"Effectively navigating between the national and the transnational, this comprehensive collection offers a much-needed critical account of Chilean contemporary cinema. Unique in its scope—ranging from music videos to horror, from documentary to martial arts, from queer to 'global art' films—this book opens up exciting new lines of inquiry for the study of Chilean cinema."
—Elizabeth Ramírez-Soto, assistant professor, School of Cinema, San Francisco State University, and author of *(Un)veiling Bodies: A Trajectory of Chilean Post-Dictatorship Documentary*

"This refreshing approach to national cinemas addresses the recent Chilean film production taking into account the tensions between the global dialogues it has established and the achievements and constraints of a local film scene. An essential overview of Chilean Cinema and the cultural, political, and economic transformations of the new century."
—Catalina Donoso Pinto, co-author of *El cine de Ignacio Agüero: El documental como la lectura de un espacio* and *(Des)montando fábulas: El documental político de Pedro Chaskel*

CHILEAN CINEMA IN THE TWENTY-FIRST-CENTURY WORLD

Contemporary Approaches to Film and Media Series

Series Editor

Barry Keith Grant
Brock University

A complete listing of the advisory editors and the books in this series can be found online at wsupress.wayne.edu.

CHILEAN CINEMA IN THE TWENTY-FIRST-CENTURY WORLD

EDITED BY VANIA BARRAZA AND CARL FISCHER

Wayne State University Press
Detroit

© 2020 by Wayne State University Press. All rights reserved. No part of this book may be reproduced without formal permission.

ISBN 978-0-8143-4682-2 (paperback)
ISBN 978-0-8143-4681-5 (printed case)
ISBN 978-0-8143-4683-9 (e-book)

Library of Congress Control Number: 2020943221

Wayne State University Press
Leonard N. Simons Building
4809 Woodward Avenue
Detroit, Michigan 48201-1309

Visit us online at wsupress.wayne.edu

Cover image copyright Fábula. Used with permission.

Subventions from the University of Memphis and Fordham University helped defray publication costs.

CONTENTS

Acknowledgments   ix

Introduction: Chilean Filmmaking in the World:
Scattered Industry, Politicized Intimacy, Global Aesthetics   1
Vania Barraza and Carl Fischer

Mapping Theories of Chilean Cinema in the World

1. Learning to be "Global": Chilean Filmmakers at
   International Film Festivals   33
   María Paz Peirano

2. Centrifugal Cinema: Updating and Rereading Chilean
   Feature Films   51
   Carolina Urrutia Neno

3. Political and Affective Shifts in the Contemporary
   Chilean Documentary   71
   Paola Lagos Labbé
   Translated by Patrick G. Blaine and Carl Fischer

On the Margins of Hollywood: Chilean Genre Flicks

4. The Reach of Genre: The Emergence of Chilean
   Horror Cinema   107
   Jonathan Risner

5. The Latin Dragon Going Global: Marko Zaror,
   Martial Arts Films, and Stardom   129
   Moisés Park

Other Texts and Other Lands: Intermediality and Adaptation beyond Chile(an Cinema)

6. *Il Futuro* by Alicia Scherson: Film and Cross-Cultural (Af)filiations   159
   María Angélica Franken

7. Video Built the Cinema Star: Alex Anwandter's *Nunca vas a estar solo*   177
   Arturo Márquez-Gómez

8. Intimacies and Global Aesthetics in *Vida de familia* by Alicia Scherson and Cristián Jiménez   199
   Vania Barraza

Migrations of Gender and Genre

9. A House without Limits: Framing Camila José Donoso's *Casa Roshell* through Disidentification and Disappropriation   221
   Mónica Ramón Ríos

10. The International (Un)intelligibility of Chilean Trans* Film   245
    Carl Fischer

Politicized Intimacies, Transnational Affects: Debating (Post)memory and History

11. Filmmakers to the Rescue of Chilean Memory: Representations of Chile's Traumatic Past in Contemporary Documentary   269
    Claudia Bossay

12. The Life of Things: Materiality and Affectivity in *Atrapados en Japón* by Vivienne Barry   293
    María Constanza Vergara Reyes
    Translated by Elsa Maxwell

13. Displacement, Emplacement, and the Politics of
    Exilic Childhood in Sergio Castilla's *Gringuito*   313
    Camilo Trumper

14. Films on Loss and Mourning: Bridging the Personal
    and the Collective   339
    María Helena Rueda

    Index   359
    Contributors   373

ACKNOWLEDGMENTS

We first talked about the idea of this book at a café in the Barrio Lastarria, in Santiago, during the LASA-Southern Cone Symposium in 2015. Since then, we've managed to carve out other in-person meetings during conferences in Montevideo, New York, Barcelona, and Portland, but so much of this project has taken place over email and especially Whatsapp. Working together has been such an enriching experience for both of us.

We would like to express our gratitude and appreciation to the editors at Wayne State University Press. Marie Sweetman, Kristin Harpster, and Barry Grant trusted in our project and provided incredible editorial support, making the editorial process an exceptional experience. Sandra Judd also played a key role sharply copyediting the manuscript. Rachel Lyon did a great job indexing the book. Thank you all for your dedication.

Thanks also to Fábula Producciones, and particularly Alejandra Undurraga, for granting us permission to use the cover image (gracias totales).

VANIA

This book has been possible thanks to significant support provided by the University of Memphis. The Marcus W. Orr Center for the Humanities (MOCH) selected me as a Catherine and Charles Freeburg Fellow recipient, a program that allowed me not only to edit this book but to write, and research the content of my own chapter, in the spring semester of 2018. This fellowship was an outstanding experience due to the leadership of Deborah Tollefsen and my peer-fellows.

William Thompson, chairperson, and Monika Nenon, interim chairperson at the Department of World Languages and Literatures have been critical mentors for the completion of this book. They have always endorsed my research in Film Studies and assisted with the publication of this volume. I would like to acknowledge my gratitude for their generosity and collegiality.

Finally, a grant from my university's Division of Research and Innovation allowed us to accomplish the final stage of production of this publication. Overall, I want to thank the University of Memphis for giving me so many opportunities to complete this project.

I thank colleagues at the Adolfo Ibáñez University in Chile who kindly invited me to present a preliminary version of my chapter for this book in the summer of 2018. Comments and feedback from faculty and students from the graduate program in Comparative Literature helped me polish my theoretical approach to the chapter. A special word of thanks to María Angélica Franken, Cynthia Francica, and Claudia Darrigrandi Navarro. I take responsibility for errors found in the chapter.

To Pamela Gómez and Rodrigo Márquez, who welcomed me at the Festival de Chile Chileno (FECICH) to support the film festival programming and who became excellent sources for my research—thank you for your expertise and for introducing me to film festival culture.

I have to thank my dearest Iván Ortega Santos and Eduardo Barraza. From their amazing intellectual advice to helping with little Amelia so I could do the editorial work, they have been critical mentors, companions, and supporters. My gratitude, love, and admiration for you.

Finally, I want to dedicate this book to Laura Toledo. Laura and I started watching international cinema in the early 1990s, when Chile was leaving behind a dark dictatorship. We became devotees of Chilean cinema in the early 2000s and kept going to the theaters over the next decade. I vividly remember our enthusiastic discussion about the last two movies we watched together: *Mala junta*, by Claudia Huaiquimilla, and *El diablo es magnífico*, by Nicolás Videla. Unfortunately, Laura was unable to see this book finished; she departed when we were editing the first draft of the manuscript. Dear Laura, although you did not read in English, you would have been so proud of me, mamita querida. Gracias por enseñarme a ver el mundo. Miss you.

CARL

New York City is a great place to see and discuss Latin American films, and I'm thankful to an enthusiastic cadre of critics and thinkers alongside whom I've been able to develop my own ideas about cinema. The main forum for this has been the Encrucijadas series of symposia, and I have the multitalented and ingenious jack-of-all-trades Juana Suárez to thank for spearheading the creation of that space, and for welcoming me into it. Bruno Guaraná, Adrián Pérez-Melgosa, María Ospina, Javier Guerrero, Paul Julian

Smith, and Carlos Gutiérrez have been other key members of this group, and I'm thankful to them as well. A particular shout-out, in this sense, goes to José Miguel Palacios: a proper *consejero* and tireless sounding board and a profound thinker of Chilean cinema.

I would like to also thank my colleague Cynthia Vich at Fordham, with whom I have been able to exchange countless ideas and opinions about Latin American cinema and film criticism (among many other things) over the past eight years, and whose forthcoming book on Peruvian cinema, coedited with Sarah Barrow, will undoubtedly make an excellent companion volume to this one.

As Vania and I have gone through the long process of editing this book, many people have been instrumental in helping us along the way. I'd like to thank the brilliant Elizabeth Ramírez-Soto for pointing me to some helpful resources as I was writing my article in this collection, and for her wisdom about the field of cinema studies in Chile; Patrick Blaine, for his generous translation work; Claudia Bossay, for helping us with historical and statistical questions; Ian O'Sullivan, at the British Film Institute's Reuben Library, for research help; my colleague Jackie Reich at Fordham, for looking over an early version of the proposal for this book and giving me crucial advice; and Ignacio López-Vicuña, for pointing us to Wayne State University Press (and thanks to him and Andreea Marinescu for paving the way for us there, with their excellent volume on Raúl Ruiz).

Thanks to Fordham University's Office of Research and Department of Modern Languages and Literatures for providing crucial monetary support for the project. As ever, I'm grateful to my colleagues at Fordham University (in Modern Languages and Literatures, Women's, Gender and Sexuality Studies, and Latin American/Latinx Studies) for being such tireless interlocutors and *compañerxs de ruta*. Other such *compañerxs* include colleagues in Chile and around the world—in cinema studies, cultural studies, and literature—whom this project has given me the opportunity to converse with and learn from. Thanks to Cecily Raynor, Carey Kasten, Lise Schreier, Francesca Parmeggiani, Arnaldo Cruz-Malavé, Audrey Evrard, Brian Reilly, Yiju Huang, Miguel García, Andrew Clark, Ronald Méndez-Clark, Ruth Halvey, Arturo Márquez-Gómez, Michael Lazzara, Cristián Opazo, Catalina Donoso, Coti Vergara, Macarena Urzúa, Gero Bauer, Regina and Thom Quinn, Daniela Gutiérrez and Stephen Sabetti, Angie Franken, and Sarah Thomas.

I also want to celebrate fellow *cinéfilxs* whom I've seen films with over the years in Santiago and New York, including Coti Vergara, José Miguel

Palacios, Juana Suárez, Javier Uriarte and Fernando Loffredo, Jens Andermann, Cynthia Vich and Alberto Medina, Jeff Lawrence, Rafael Albarrán, Edgar Rebolledo, Mario Riquelme and Emma Budwig, Tibor Gutiérrez, Bernardita Llanos and Fernando Blanco, and César Barros and Ángeles Donoso. Thanks as well to my family: Mark, Bridget, David, Zhi-Ning, Lilah, and Paul.

The work I've put into editing this collection would be meaningless, and also pretty much unbearable, if it weren't for the support and love of Corey McEleney, who has been there for me at every step of this project, from idea to execution. This book is dedicated to him, and also to my aunt Kathleen Lynch, who made so much possible for me growing up.

Introduction
CHILEAN FILMMAKING IN THE WORLD

Scattered Industry, Politicized Intimacy, Global Aesthetics

Vania Barraza and Carl Fischer

Recounting the 1988 plebiscite to decide whether to remove the dictator Pinochet from office, Pablo Larraín's film *NO* (2012) was the first Chilean feature to be nominated for an Oscar for best foreign-language film, and it generally opened to wide acclaim. Its representation of the campaign against Pinochet was hailed by many critics throughout the world as a self-aware commentary on "freedom" as a sincere political value, but also as the triumphant, savvy entrée of Chilean cinema onto the world stage. However, within Larraín's native Chile, it was read by many scandalized critics as the cynical reduction of a grassroots political movement against the dictatorship to little more than a calculated marketing strategy. Larraín had calibrated the film for foreign audiences, who were likely less interested in the exact details of the NO campaign than in the more universal questions it brought up. Those questions included the extent to which capitalism blunts the edges of political activism, the multifaceted aspects of "choice," and the blurred boundaries between archival material and the visual innovations of feature film (*NO* was shot with rebuilt vintage Sony U-Matic video cameras). Critics within Chile were understandably much more concerned with the local aspects of the story, such as the mass mobilizations of the Left in the run-up to the plebiscite, and the "social experience" (Olea 2012) of those who suffered under dictatorship, but for Larraín these concerns were provincial (Palacios 2012).

He, like other directors who have been successful abroad (such as Sebastián Lelio and Sebastián Silva), sought to universalize the narratives of his films, even if doing so came at the expense of addressing more local concerns.[1] The essays collected in this book are written within the disjuncture between the foreign and domestic reception of Chilean films with international orientations similar to that of *NO*: What choices do Chilean auteurs make to render their films, which often deal with very local domestic issues, intelligible to broader global audiences? What are the implications of these choices for the structure of Chile's film industry? What can Chile's experience with this teach us about other national cinemas from small countries? What spaces remain for these auteurs to make political interventions in their films, aimed at either Chilean or non-Chilean audiences, or both?

When the Pinochet dictatorship ended in 1990, Chile underwent an unprecedented period of neoliberal economic opening. The result of drastic structural reforms undertaken by the regime, and then a flood of foreign investment once Chile returned to democracy, this opening had major implications for Chilean cinema. Just two national feature films were released in the country from 1973 (the year of the coup) until 1989 (Trejo 2011, 84); meanwhile, databases estimate that, since 2010, an average of twenty-four Chilean films premiered domestically each year (CAEM 2019, 17). Meanwhile, through free-trade agreements, diplomacy, and a rigorous internalization of Washington Consensus–era policies, Chile has made a concerted effort to integrate itself with the world. The nationalism often associated with *caudillos*, revolutionary projects, and closed economies—and, indeed, often rhetorically brandished (if not practiced) by the dictatorship—waned. This led to the possibility of Chilean film embracing a more global aesthetic, in the way Tamara Falicov (2016) describes many Latin American films doing: "producers have been asked to make their films look more 'authentic' . . . and examine a kind of 'global art house aesthetic' that Global South filmmakers may conform to" (218). Yet, at the same time, and indeed because of the foreign capital that flooded the country, investments were made that allowed the incipient film industry to consolidate itself. These investments are multiple: the creation of film schools; the establishment of public subsidies; new educational programs; regulations for the production, distribution, and exhibition of national films under Chile's 2004 Film Law; the proliferation of digital video; the rise of multiplex cinemas; and the reduction of production and distribution costs.[2] Although it would be difficult to argue that the Chilean film industry has reached the size of the large, established film industries elsewhere in Latin America during the twentieth century—partly because these other film industries were heavily unionized, and anti-union practices persist throughout Chile[3]—this growing professionalization of, and in, Chilean film has led to the consolidation of a local (if not nationalist) aesthetic as well.

Although this volume will deal less with Larraín's work specifically—which has already been widely studied—than with the aesthetic and social tensions that inform the insertion of Chilean film into the global marketplace in a more general sense, the anecdote of *NO* is instructive. Indeed, it leads us to ask how Chilean cinema mediates between local identities and global cinematic trends, all the while staying true to both. In what ways has cinema produced in Chile been affected by the trends of global cinema? Can it be said that Chilean cinema is particularly open to the incorporation of global trends because of its economic openness?

CHILEAN CINEMA IN THE WORLD: A BRIEF HISTORY

Cinema has been linked to the phenomena of globalization since it first arrived in Chile. The earliest films of the Lumière brothers were shown in Santiago's Unión Central Theater on August 26, 1896, just eight months after they were first shown in Paris, and around the same time that they were shown in other Latin American capitals, including Mexico City, Buenos Aires, and Montevideo (Mouesca and Orellana 2010, 12–13). The earliest Chilean-made films, by the photographer Luis Oddó Osorio, were first exhibited in May of the following year in the northern city of Iquique (Jara Donoso 2002, 26). Iquique, which had passed from Peruvian to Chilean control just eighteen years earlier, was then a key port for the exportation of nitrates and other natural resources mined inland, and an important commercial and political center closely connected to the global flow of transnational capital. So it made sense that Iquique would be at the forefront of global innovations like filmmaking; indeed, Chilean nitrate was one of the raw materials that went into the manufacture of celluloid, as Michael Chanan (1976, 6–7) has stated. The arrival and circulation of cinema was thus a key benchmark of Chile's integration with world markets and global culture.

Jacqueline Mouesca and Carlos Orellana (2010) have the most definitive history of the development of Chilean cinema during the twentieth century, but thinking about this history in global terms, there are several key aspects worth mentioning here. One is the fact that the country was a key hub in the development of the militant, committed New Latin American Cinema that took hold throughout the region in the 1960s. This was thanks to Héctor Ríos's formation at Rome's Centro Sperimentale de la Cinematografia (Mouesca and Orellana 2010, 113); Aldo Francia's travels to Paris, where he first saw Vittorio de Sica's *Bicycle Thieves*; and a critical mass of other brilliant young filmmakers. Miguel Littin, Raúl Ruiz, Helvio Soto, Pedro Chaskel, and Patricio Guzmán, along with Ríos, Francia, and others, were highly motivated to create political responses to the upheavals of the period (Mouesca and Orellana 2010, 114). Two film festivals, held in the coastal town of Viña del Mar in 1967 and 1969, were key incubators of the engagé aesthetic of Latin American cinema at the time, showing films from around the region that further awakened Chileans to the possibilities of the medium.[4] Enriched by these exciting moments of international exchange, Chilean filmmakers created important, militantly political films themselves.

In 1970, the socialist Salvador Allende was elected to the presidency of the country, and these filmmakers were key to documenting Allende's ascent. Working in an exciting institutional environment, thanks to the establishment of new laws in 1967 aimed at stimulating domestic film production, Guzmán, Littin, and Ruiz, in particular, made important films that gave a uniquely Chilean spin on the aesthetics of New Latin American Cinema. The Department of Experimental Cinema at the University of Chile was also an important training ground for these filmmakers, as Claudio Salinas Muñoz, Hans Stange Marcus, and Sergio Salinas Roco (2008) have pointed out. Guzmán's *El primer año / The First Year* (1972) conveyed the radical potential of Allende's ideals as it documented the first year of his term in office; so did Littin's *Compañero Presidente* (1971). Ruiz's *Tres tristes tigres / Three Trapped Tigers* (1968), which won a prestigious award in the Locarno Film Festival, depicted and denounced poverty and marginality in the country, as did Littin's *El chacal de Nahueltoro / The Jackal of Nahueltoro* (1969). The political program of the *Unidad Popular* (Popular Unity, or UP), Allende's coalition, called for the nationalization of Chile's natural resources, better working conditions, and novel antipoverty and pro-education programs; many films from this period echoed this program at an aesthetic level. In 1970, eight out of twelve of the film distribution companies operating in Chile were US-owned, and when these American companies hostile to Allende's policies sought to put pressure on the *Unidad Popular* government by restricting the supply of films (Chanan 1976, 17), the domestic film industry found new spaces in which to thrive. Not only was this period well documented on film; the process of filming was an important formative time for filmmakers like Guzmán, Carlos Flores, and Angelina Vásquez, among others (Mouesca and Orellana 2010, 138).

Unfortunately, the work of these filmmakers had to continue in exile for some years, because on September 11, 1973, Allende's presidency was interrupted by a coup d'état led by Chile's military. The country's armed forces, with the backing of its oligarchy (threatened by the expropriations that the UP had undertaken) and foreign interests including the CIA (as Peter Kornbluh [2003] has amply documented), quickly dismantled the advances made under Allende. General Augusto Pinochet took over as head of the *junta militar*, and then as "president" of the country itself. The violent changes the military dictatorship instituted—which resulted in torture, arrests, and disappearances—extended to Chile Films, the government film production company established in the 1940s that later distributed the films of many of the country's best-known filmmakers.[5] Chile Films had come to compete for viewers alongside foreign distributors (Chanan 1976, 18–19), and it came to be known as a hotbed of leftism and anti-imperialism, particularly following the publication, in 1972, of the "Manifesto of the Cineastes of the Unidad Popular." Its offices were ransacked by the military on the very day of the coup (Mouesca and Orellana 2010, 145). Thanks to the rich production of Chilean films made abroad throughout the 1970s and 80s by a huge diaspora that ensued, however, the memory of Allende's ideals remained alive. The work of Guzmán stands out, in this sense: his three-part *La batalla de Chile / The Battle of Chile*, which chronicled the months leading up to the coup and then the coup itself, was edited in Cuba after the footage was smuggled out of the country. It was then shown in the late 1970s and early 1980s throughout Europe and the United States, and spread the message of protest against the injustice of the coup and the abuses committed under dictatorship. As multiple critics have documented in their important reconstructions of Chilean cinema made around the world in this period,[6] the rich reflections on the condition of exile constitute a key part of Chile's film patrimony. This is another key aspect of Chilean cinema's place "in the world" and an important precursor to our project here.

Some critics have written about the period under Chile's dictatorship as an *apagón cultural*, that is, a time of "cultural outage," in which quality, critical cultural production—including cinema—was disincentivized or even impossible, due to the "brain drain" of artists living in exile. However, the dictatorship, which lasted from 1973 until early 1990, was actually a time of rich cultural production. As stated above, very few films were released during the period, but a number of critics have shown that it was a time of exciting developments in film, television, video, and video-art production in Chile.[7] Filmmakers, artists, and videographers such as Flores, Chaskel, Lotty Rosenfeld, Ignacio Agüero, Juan Downey, Carlos Leppe, Eugenio Dittborn, and Gloria Camiruaga all created important work within Chile that defied the limitations (and some of the repression) of the dictatorship's institutional frameworks.

Although the dictatorship was a time of violence, fear, and death, the government's policies of repression occasionally entered into tension with the radical openness of the economic system it had put in place. A series of neoliberal policies were implemented by the dictatorship: aided by a group of Chilean economists trained under Milton Friedman at the University of Chicago, known as "Chicago Boys," the government applied "shock doctrine" (Klein 2007) tactics that decimated Allende's social welfare programs, undid agrarian reform policies, and allowed for the massive importation of goods and services. While this new economic "openness" devastated local industry, which found itself having to compete with foreign goods on unequal footing, it facilitated the entry into the country of digital recording material. Moreover, it led to debates about the relationship between consumer choice (which had proliferated) and political choices (which were circumscribed). The military regime's tight grip on the flow of information began to loosen amidst the new ideas that flooded into the country unimpeded by any sort of government regulation on imports.

Many Chilean intellectuals who had lived in exile during the dictatorship began to trickle back into the country in the mid-1980s. They had gained valuable knowledge and education while abroad, and put their know-how to use to rebuild their country. The clever publicity campaign in favor of the NO vote during the plebiscite was one manifestation of these new ideas. Indeed, the postdictatorship period was a time of major economic growth for Chile, a time during which investors increasingly flocked to the country, which was no longer a pariah state, to take advantage of its neoliberal macroeconomic policies. Although the policies instituted by the Chicago Boys mostly continued in place, as Tomás Moulián has pointed out (2002), they came to be moderated somewhat by social welfare programs.

The decade following the end of the dictatorship brought a gradual rebirth of local cinema. Poverty rates declined. Even though only twenty-seven films premiered between 1990 and 1999, some of them provided Chilean cinema a certain visibility within the international circuit (Estévez 2005, 27). Little statistical information is available in terms of spectatorship during this decade, but from 1990 onward, the state was able to grow, and eventually put more and more investment into the stimulation of film production through tax abatements, subsidies, and competitive funding for artistic projects.[8] Silvio Caiozzi's *La luna en el espejo / The Moon in the Mirror* (1990), Gonzalo Justiniano's *Caluga o menta / El Niki* (1990), Ricardo Larraín's *La frontera / The Frontier* (1991), and Gustavo Graef Marino's *Johnny 100 Pesos* (1993) received nominations and awards in prestigious international film festivals. This restored interest in and enthusiasm for domestic cinema. However, contrary to a general perception of Chilean cinema of the period as overly political, particularly in Chile's right-wing, mainstream media (Estévez 2005, 52–53), only a few films actually addressed the military regime and its effects. *La frontera, Johnny 100 Pesos*, and *Archipiélago / Archipelago* (1992), by Pablo Perelman, depict the dictatorship and the return to democracy indirectly, and *Amnesia* (Gonzalo Justiniano, 1994) and *Los náufragos / The Shipwrecked* (Miguel Littin, 1994) focus directly on Pinochet's political repression. Instead, a spate of mediocre, local comedies and crime thrillers that received limited international attention were the dominant industry trend in the 1990s. Auteurs including Cristián Sánchez (*El cumplimiento del deseo / "A Wish Comes True"* [1995],[9] *Cuídate del agua mansa / "Watch out for Calm Water"* [1995], and *Cautiverio feliz / The Happy Captive* [1998]), Tatiana Gaviola (*Mi último hombre / My Last Man* [1996]), and Claudio Sapiaín (*El hombre que imaginaba / "The Man Who Used to Imagine"* [1998]) maintained an experimental and independent style, however.

Around the end of the millennium, by producing movies that were more visually and thematically appealing to general audiences, filmmakers started developing a new relationship with the public. Sergio Castilla's *Gringuito* (1998), which Camilo Trumper analyzes in this volume, was the most-seen Chilean film in the year it was released, and it marked a new era in domestic filmmaking. Andrés Wood's first and second films, *Historias de fútbol / Soccer Stories* (1997) and *El desquite / Revenge* (1999), respectively, announced a new generation of younger Chilean filmmakers. In terms of genre film, the blockbuster comedy *El chacotero sentimental / The Sentimental Teaser* (Cristián Galaz, 1999) exemplified the improved production quality and more professional output that would become the norm in the twenty-first century.

CHILEAN CINEMA IN THE WORLD: THE TWENTY-FIRST CENTURY

Since the 1990s, Chilean cinema has opened itself up to the world, positioning itself "as a high-quality export commodity similar to the country's successful wine and fruit exports" (Falicov 2019, 47). There have been four principal currents of cinema during this period: first, genre film (comedies, action films, and horror), some of which have had political undertones, though many have not. Second, a young group of filmmakers—named the *Novísimos* (Cavallo and Maza 2011), Generation 2000 (Parada Poblete 2012), or the Generation of 2005 (Kemp 2010)—has brought a notable aesthetic and industrial renovation to Chilean cinema. Their interest has largely been in narrating intimate stories about themes such as love, solitude, estrangement, or abandonment. Third, we can identify a current of filmmakers who approach social and political issues or historical topics in their feature films, albeit from a more personal, noncollective point of view. These filmmakers—some of whom are part of the *Novísimo* Generation, and shifted from largely apolitical to more political films later in their careers, as Carolina Urrutia Neno discusses later in this volume—have been able to pinpoint the universal aspects of very local issues, in order to position their films for global audiences. And fourth, we can find a number of films—particularly documentaries—that have explicitly dealt with highly political topics. The main such topic is that of memory—that is, the "labor" (Jelin 2002) of coming to terms with the impact that the dictatorship had on the lives of the Chilean people. In what follows, we will outline how these different currents of contemporary Chilean cinema have positioned themselves globally.

Genre film, mainly comedy, horror, and action, has become a relevant product with significant repercussions not only at the local level but also on the international circuit. Cult filmmaker Patricio Valladares's gore cinema—rarely distributed in Chile—has received broad international attention, for example. The remake he directed in English of his horror film *En las afueras de la ciudad* (2012), titled *Hidden in the Woods* (2014), launched Valladares's career abroad: he filmed *Nightworld* (2017) in Bulgaria and *Vlad's Legacy* (2017) in Turkey. Lucio Rojas's work has also been little distributed in Chile, yet his recent work *Trauma* (2017) deals with issues that are extremely relevant in Chilean politics and, indeed, in the film industry today: the "rape and revenge" subgenre of horror films that Rojas works with are considered by some to be feminist, given that their female characters, after suffering horrible sexual assaults, exact revenge against their aggressors, some of whom have ties to the dictatorship. Jonathan Risner's chapter in this volume addresses some of the political aspects of these horror films, and Moisés Park's chapter addresses the political aspects of Chilean action films, particularly those of the Chilean-Palestinian actor-director Marko Zaror. Other filmmakers, however, such as those affiliated with the production company Sobras, have preferred to make mass-market horror and comedy films that are completely unconnected to Chile's politics. Some of those films, such as Nicolás López's popular comedies *Sin filtro / No Filter* (2016) and *Hazlo como hombre* (2017), have been remade abroad and have had success on streaming platforms like Netflix.[10]

The *Novísimo* Generation is a term originally coined by Ascanio Cavallo and Gonzalo Maza (2011) to refer to a group of filmmakers who all premiered feature films around the same time: Alicia Scherson, Matías Bize, Sebastián Lelio, and the author Alberto Fuguet. All four had films at the Valdivia International Film Festival in 2005, and all were considered resolutely apolitical, at least at the time. Matías Bize's single-set movie *En la cama / In Bed* (2005), about two strangers who spend the night together at a love motel, brought the young director local and international recognition,[11] and is perhaps the most paradigmatic example of the *Novísimo* Generation. Bize's apolitical aesthetic won him great notoriety abroad: *La vida de los peces / The Life of Fish* (2010), an exploration of personal trauma and broken relationships also set in a limited time-space, garnered him a Goya Award in Spain.

This second tendency in contemporary Chilean film—a focus on personal malaise, often of upper-class characters, rather than on topics considered to be more politically urgent—has met with harsh criticism. Ximena Póo, Claudio Salinas, and Hans Stange (2012) argue that these films about individual subjectivities are more conservative than subversive (10), despite their significant formal innovations. Roberto Trejo (2009, 2011) and Carlos Saavedra (2013) agree with this interpretation, stating that the "disenchanted" poetics of the *Novísimos*, indeed, is no more than a reflection of the globalized and neoliberal system.

Contrary to these readings, however, scholars such as Antonella Estévez (2010, 2011, 2017), Catalina Donoso Pinto (2007), and Carolina Urrutia Neno (2010, 2013) suggest that although many of these new features cannot be related to an explicit ideological discourse due to their primary focus on intimacy and everyday life, their representation of estrangement, alienation, and melancholy reflects a political feeling of unease. Vania Barraza (2018), meanwhile, has identified more overtly political agendas certain feature films, particularly when they address contemporary social issues. Examining how allegorical narratives of social and political discontent subtly emerge in this new cinema, she shows that Chilean auteurs articulate a confluence between aesthetics, political detachment, and a social reflection upon neoliberalism. When crafting a different way of displaying the effects of the past on the present, then, they offer an oblique social critique.[12] Urrutia Neno's analysis of "centrifugal cinema" makes use of Deleuze's idea of the "time-image" to identify a turn inward in these films, whose impressionistic "atmosphere, tension, latency . . . [and] ductile and sonorous configuration . . . expose the artifice of the *mise-en-scene* itself" ["una atmósfera, una tensión, una latencia . . . [y] la configuración plástica y sonora . . . pon[en] en evidencia el artificio propio de la puesta en escena"] (2013, 56).[13] Albeit in subtle dialogue with the explicit, "centripetal" realism of militant New Latin American Cinema, Urrutia Neno finds that even when the films she analyzes address real-life topics, they maintain a subjective turn. Curiously, although the *Novísimos* distanced themselves, at least initially, from the political activism of previous militant generations of filmmakers, they do share with them a sense of projection beyond national boundaries.

A third tendency in contemporary Chilean feature film has also made major inroads in the world film festival circuit: a more politicized look at social issues previously unaddressed in Chile's social arena. These include the dictatorship, but also other issues such as aging, gender identity, indigenous struggles, and urban gentrification and displacement. Lelio's and Scherson's later work, and also the work of Andrés Wood, Pablo Larraín, Cristián Sánchez, and Alejandro Fernández Almendras, are typical in this sense, narrating local political issues and packaging them for international audiences. While Larraín's trilogy on Pinochet's dictatorship moved from the dark *Tony Manero* (2008) and *Post Mortem* (2010) to the more inspiring *NO* (2012), Fernández Almendras maintains a more experimental, hermetic, art house style: his *Matar a un hombre / To Kill a Man* (2014) and *Aquí no ha pasado nada / Much Ado About Nothing* (2016) both address deeply entrenched issues of national injustice and power. The latter film, in particular, deals with how certain Chileans with outsized privilege seek to skirt the justice system, although it does not make a larger, collective critique of that system. Pepa San Martín's *Rara* (2016), a fictional account of the case of Judge Karen Atala, who lost custody of her children when she came out as a lesbian, also addresses this abuse of political power through an oblique lens, by focusing on the perspective of the children. Arturo Márquez-Gómez's article in this volume focuses on Alex Anwandter's film *Nunca vas a estar solo / You'll Never Be Alone* (2016), which examines homophobia in its representation of the 2012 murder of Daniel Zamudio. Feature films taking an affective, aestheticized look at the country's dictatorial past, such as Andrés Wood's *Machuca* (2004) and *Araña / Spider* (2019), Marcela Said's *Los perros / The Dogs* (2017), and Dominga Sotomayor's *Tarde para morir joven / Too Late to Die Young* (2018), also continue to be of great interest to foreign audiences.

Finally, filmmakers have focused on documentary as a way of addressing political issues on a more affective, personal level: this focus on generational memory and what Marianne Hirsch called "postmemory" (2012) is the fourth major tendency of contemporary Chilean cinema. As Michael Lazzara (2018b) points out, the "study of memory within Latin America has really taken root since the 1980s, and more so throughout the 1990s and 2000s, as postdictatorial or postconflict societies have struggled to forge democracies and negotiate the complex meaning of the past" (15). This trend has roughly coincided with the increase of film production in these same countries, particularly Chile (Ramírez-Soto 2019). Memory posits a broader, more affective, and indeed more activist approach to the past than the discipline of history. Memory studies has been a key axis of debate about postdictatorship Chilean cultural studies and has been an important way for Chilean cultural production, in general, to enter into larger debates about memory and history taking place in Europe, South Africa, and elsewhere in Latin America, as Claudia Bossay's chapter in this volume shows. Chilean filmmakers have sought to come to terms, in their work, with the effects of the dictatorship, addressing issues such as trauma, family separation and exile, antidictatorship activism, reparation, complicity and responsibility, human rights, and mourning (María Helena Rueda's chapter in this volume focuses on the latter subject).

These issues are often quite personal to filmmakers, a fact that increases the stakes of the narrative, making it more dramatic for audiences. Patricio Guzmán's more recent documentaries, in this sense, have addressed the role of Guzmán himself in the traumatic events of the dictatorship, lending them a more personal dimension than his earlier, more militant films. Carmen Castillo's *Calle Santa Fe* (2007), too, personalizes the struggle against the dictatorship by examining the aftermath of the filmmaker's love affair with militant activist Miguel Enríquez, who was killed by the military in the early period of the dictatorship. Meanwhile, Macarena Aguiló's *El edificio de los chilenos / The Chilean Building* (2010) explores the effects of the decisions made by adults who left their children behind, in exile, to return to Chile clandestinely and resist the dictatorship. Its focus on how these decisions affected the next generation makes it, in this sense, a "postmemory" documentary, inasmuch as Aguiló reckons with what her parents did: were they heroes in struggle, or did their decision to leave their children behind constitute abandonment? María Constanza Vergara Reyes's chapter in this volume, on Vivianne Barry's film *Atrapados en Japón / Trapped in Japan* (2015), also addresses these generational reckonings. Often working in dialogue with the political commitments of New Latin American Cinema, these documentaries work through the legacy of the dictatorship, and other forms of loss that went along with it, in a personal way. Moreover, as Paola Lagos-Labbé's chapter in this volume shows, many of these documentary filmmakers use this affective, sensorial lens to affiliate political struggles in Chile today with past struggles, to bolster the credibility and legitimacy of those movements.

CHILEAN CINEMA IN THE GLOBAL ECONOMY: IS NATION-BASED CRITIQUE STILL RELEVANT?

Although we have been talking about Chilean film production, it is also necessary to ask whether it is still worthwhile to use national lenses, in general, to examine Latin American cinema. Gabriela Copertari and Carolina Sitnisky (2015) take up this issue head-on, pointing to the delicate balance that must be struck when examining the intersections between cinema and nation in Latin America. They note that although national cinemas have always been traversed by global and transnational phenomena and practices (11) in Latin America—particularly because of global capital funding of national productions—the state continues to be "crucial for the appreciation of cultural capital" ["crucial para la valorización del capital cultural"] (16), because it is an organizing factor in terms of the distribution and consumption of cinema. They thus propose reconceptualizing the essentialist definition of the national state, in order to refer to *national state cinemas* (a category coined by Stephen Crofts, who worked to distinguish the state from the nation(s)) rather than national cinemas, particularly given the complicity of states in suppressing ethnic, religious, and cultural differences (13). In this way, cinema from a particular country can be conceived of as less associated with the state, while still remaining intelligible as the expression of a national culture.

Other thinkers have problematized the relationship between cinema and the nation in different ways. Paulo Antonio Paranaguá (2003) combined an early examination of Latin American film production with a historical approach, paying attention to exhibition and distribution of the cinemas of the region (17–19). Lisa Shaw and Stephanie Dennison (2005) introduced a theoretical and cinematic debate on national film industries by connecting modernity, globalization, gender, and national identity in the scenario of the new century. Nayibe Bermúdez Barrios (2011) expanded the discussion of current transformations in identity construction and the desire for community, the crisis of the nation-state, and transnationalism. In turn, Laura Podalsky (2011) interprets Latin American transnational cinema through the prism of gender, affects, and emotions rather than through specific nations; in this sense, her approach to transformations in the Latin American film industries is more along affective than economic lines. Focusing on Argentinean cinema, Tamara Falicov (2007) notes a displacement from a definition based on nationhood narratives to a conception centered on the economic and political conditions around a national cinema. Ana López and Dolores Tierney (2014) and Deborah Shaw (2013, 2017) have also addressed the tension between the national and the transnational. Some recent scholarship on Latin American cinema in English has been moving away from an emphasis on any particular nation, however, which would seem to indicate that more regional approaches are increasingly relevant.[14] As John King (2009) points out, "nobody working in Latin American film offers an essentialist reading of national cinemas, since there is a clear awareness that these cinemas, from their inception . . . are a blend of national and transnational elements" (17). This work speaks to an overall tradition, in Latin American film and cultural studies, to read the continent together, in the spirit of a political project of regional integration.

The work of Falicov on film festivals, in this sense, is key. Following SooJeong Ahn's assertion (2011) that film festivals are increasingly acting as "cultural intermediaries" (111–12) by "helping to shape the kinds of films they think will show promise" (209), Falicov identifies several characteristics of "festival films," that is, films that circulate internationally (often, although not exclusively, in Europe and the United States) but not necessarily commercially. For Falicov, these films follow "particular aesthetic and narrative conventions for an educated audience and from a higher socioeconomic class stratum" and "are generally not fast-paced action genre films" (2016, 213). Moreover, these films are often tied to the "brand" that their director confers upon them: certain auteurs have long-standing partnerships with certain film festivals, and the director's name, over time, becomes something of a "seal of approval" for the film (Falicov 2016, 214–15). In this sense, the "festival film" that Falicov describes is one that incorporates themes favored by global festival funding structures, while also bearing the brand of a particular nation—often in cooperation with official state boosters. María Paz Peirano's chapter in this volume provides further context on this in the Chilean case.

Yet scholarly approaches to single national cinemas have hardly been rendered irrelevant. Such studies usually focus on the countries in Latin America with the largest film industries: Argentina, Brazil, and Mexico.[15] Cuban cinema is also a frequent object of study, due to its size and historical development and the persistent state support for it since 1959. Although Juana Suárez's studies of Colombian cinema (2010 and 2012) have also constituted important contributions, movies from nations with less cinematic output and smaller (or nonexistent) industrial footprints, such as Chile, remain relatively understudied in the Anglophone world. The recent English-language studies of Latin American film that have centered on one or two particular countries in the region have not looked to Chile at all, despite the recent developments in the industry there. Chilean film has been featured in many of the studies of cinema in the larger region, but has rarely itself been the focus, with the exception of one brief volume by Michael Chanan in 1976,[16] and a volume on documentary by Elizabeth Ramírez-Soto (2019).

However, several recent monographs published in English have focused exclusively on Chilean cultural studies, often with at least a partial focus on cinema.[17] It therefore seems imperative to address this gap in the scholarship, particularly in light of the recent and growing interest in Chilean cinema, for Anglophone readers. The books on Chilean cinema that do exist (all but Chanan's and Ramírez-Soto's are in Spanish) are primarily focused on aesthetics,[18] the *Novísimo* Generation,[19] and historical approaches to cinema.[20] Other books are more focused on "rescuing" domestic film patrimony or specific authors than on dealing with Chilean cinema in a global context.[21] Indeed, Chilean film criticism is experiencing a similar disjuncture to the one experienced by Chilean film itself: should it read Chilean films based on their global impact, or based on how they dialogue with local issues?

How, then, has Chilean cinema been navigating these contradictory currents between the national and the transnational? How do these films mediate among the (sometimes conflicting) desires and motives of the Chilean state, global festival funders, art house audiences abroad, and Chilean audiences at home?

LOCAL AUDIENCES, GLOBAL PROJECTIONS

Currently, as debates continue about how to best classify the principal political and aesthetic currents of Chilean film today, the field of Chilean cinema continues to evolve. Its industrial footprint is growing, with new public and private agencies working to promote Chile as a filming location for foreign productions and boost the profiles of Chilean films abroad,[22] partnerships between Chilean production companies and foreign producers like HBO and Netflix, and Chilean directors like Lelio and Larraín directing English-language films for major US studios. When Lelio won an Academy Award for his 2017 film *Una mujer fantástica / A Fantastic Woman*, it seemed to signal an unprecedented level of visibility for Chilean film in the world. In any case, the history of Chilean film shows that its "expanding field," as Valeria de los Ríos (2018) calls it, has always been closely tied to its place in the global economy. The fact that Chile has so often been seen, for better or worse, as a model of economic development in the world (Fischer 2016) means that the globalization of its cinema is relevant for other national cinemas, and for cinema studies as a whole.

Chile's organization of multiplex exhibitors (known by its Spanish acronym CAEM) reports that, since 2001, domestic cinema has represented a yearly average of approximately 4 to 7 percent of the domestic market (CAEM 2019, 16); 85 to 90 percent of films that premiere in Chile are foreign productions, mainly from Hollywood. Chile's film industry is made up of heterogeneous, scattered, nonsystemic means of production and distribution (Larraín 2010). Independent production companies linked to specific directors—Larraín's Fábula, Andrés Wood's Wood Producciones, and Valladares's Vallastudio—have coexisted in this incipient field alongside other less commercial production models.[23] National productions are mainly exhibited in a few art theaters and limited movie theatre chains, or, more recently, distributed through independent channels funded by CNCA (Chile's National Council of Culture and Arts) grants (Miradocs, Red de Salas de Cine en Chile, and ondamedia.cl). Some companies have been able to position their films abroad: Fábula in particular has managed to become an important force behind Chilean "prestige" films that make their way around the global art house and film festival circuit. However, Chile's own productions can almost never sustain themselves economically solely through domestic box office receipts.

Except for some specific titles, mainly comedies, local productions do not appeal to massive audiences (following a general trend found in other Latin American cinemas). For this reason, many Chilean films, even when they address extremely local and personal topics, prioritize their distribution abroad, in film festivals and global film grants and programs, which has sometimes meant ignoring the domestic commercial market. The case of Sundance is, in this sense, paradigmatic. Although some awardees there were box office hits in Chile,[24] other films that appeared in Sundance were met with a tepid response from the Chilean public.[25] There is hardly a guarantee, then, that Chilean films shown in festivals abroad will have any kind of impact on the Chilean market.

Most young (and experienced) directors are moving beyond solo state funding of films to complete their projects through international grants and funds.[26] Indeed, local coproductions receive both state tax incentives and subsidies from international treaties, renewing questions about national and continental frameworks.[27] In this sense, Chilean cinema occupies a contradictory place as both a "peripheral cinema" (Elena 1999) and a global trendsetter.

Peirano has examined the internationalization and cultural commodification of Chilean cinema at an economic and sociological level, but what impact has this internationalization had on Chilean film aesthetics? Falicov (2016) explores the neocolonial dimensions that underlie the power structure that exists between international film funds and festivals and the filmmakers and films they support, often from the so-called global south: filmmakers may feel the need to carry "the 'burden of representation' . . . to write storylines about marginalization for the benefit of wealthy viewers or what has been deemed 'poverty porn (*pornomiseria*)'" (218). Much of the Chilean cinema that has circulated outside the country, particularly feature films, has avoided these themes by not making poverty and marginality its focus. Still, it is worth noting that this avoidance can also be the result of the very same "burden of representation" that Falicov points out. When deciding to portray a version of Chile to foreign viewers that is free of marginality, certain filmmakers have still chosen to make a politicized intervention in the way Chilean cinema relates to the world. Are the apolitical poetics—or, alternatively, the more subtly politicized narratives of social discontent—of Chilean cinema simply the inevitable outcome for *all* films produced in globalized, neoliberal economies? This volume aims to respond to these questions by surveying a series of recent Chilean films—documentary, fiction, and hybrids between the two—that have explicitly placed themselves in dialog with global filmmaking currents. In this way, it will explore how the country's insertion into the global marketplace since 1990 has impacted, particularly at an aesthetic level, the content of its cinema.

The act of looking, so central to cinema, has been at the center of the so-called *estallido social* (social explosion) that hit Chile in October 2019 in response to widespread, recalcitrant social inequality. Given that police repression of the protests resulted in many people being partially or totally blinded—due to the *Carabineros* police aiming rubber bullets and teargas cannisters at protesters' eyes—being able to witness and denounce these (and other) abuses, in Chile and from abroad via social media, has taken on increasing importance. At the same time, the global impact of the performance "Un violador en tu camino" ("A Rapist in your Path," also known as "The Rapist Is You") created by the feminist collective Las Tesis, which women have carried out with blindfolds on, indicates new ways of thinking about the gaze. The highly mediated nature of the protests and performances has offered yet another connection between seeing, protesting, and Chile's global exposure.[28] Cinema, historically allied with social protest in the country, has thus been an arena where such protests have been anticipated and addressed, and it is also a means for getting news of those protests to circulate globally. Watching Chilean cinema allows progressive audiences around the world to create bonds of solidarity with contemporary protestors: it is a form of spectatorship that, in this case, draws attention to the power of looking itself.

CHILEAN CINEMA AS RESEARCH AND PRACTICE: BRIDGING NORTH AND SOUTH

This book is divided into five sections. The first section, "Mapping Theories of Chilean Cinema in the World," puts traditional analysis of film content and historical perspectives aside for a moment in favor of research on the market for, distribution of, exhibition of, and consumption of Chilean film at the regional and global level. Based on ethnographic work in international markets and industry hubs from Chile to Cannes and Berlin, María Paz Peirano's chapter, "Learning to Be 'Global': Chilean Filmmakers at International Film Festivals," tracks the increasing presence of local film production in the international film festival circuit. Focusing on productions since 2005, Carolina Urrutia Neno's stylistic analysis of rhythm, temporality, self-reflexivity, and the relationship between center and periphery as part of a filmography built around intimacy, small stories, and minimal narrations came to be a major focus of debate about Chilean cinema. Her chapter, "Centrifugal Cinema: Updating and Rereading Chilean Feature Films," revises her previous arguments to take into account the ways in which Chilean filmmakers, despite becoming more internationally and domestically established, have maintained "peripheral" narrations made of experimental forms and audiovisual language. Paola Lagos Labbé's chapter, "Political and Affective Shifts in the Contemporary Chilean Documentary," shows how the country's documentaries dialog with the militant aesthetics of documentaries from the 1960s and 1970s, but also take on a more affective, self-reflective sensibility.

The second section of the book, "On the Margins of Hollywood: Chilean Genre Flicks," focuses on what Chilean horror and martial arts cinema—which have received little study—show us about humor, Orientalism, indigenous conflicts, and masculinities in the nation, and about transnationalism as a whole. In "The Reach of Genre: The Emergence of Chilean Horror Cinema," Jonathan Risner studies a growing Chilean horror cinema community to demonstrate how this movement inserts itself into a larger transnational horror film culture. Risner observes that Chilean horror films formally replicate and differ from horror cinema from elsewhere in accordance with national, cultural, and ideological particularities. Moisés Park, meanwhile, takes up star theory in "The Latin Dragon Going Global: Marko Zaror, Martial Arts Films, and Stardom" to posit that the Chilean-Palestinian martial arts actor's performance is a metonymy for current Chilean filmmaking entering the global scene. By examining these transnational exchanges between Chile and Hollywood, we hope to map the ways in which Chilean directors have approached and achieved "crossover success," in terms of casting, coproduction, location, and writing.

The third section, "Other Texts and Other Lands: Intermediality and Adaptation Beyond Chile(an Cinema)," examines how Chilean filmic texts have taken on "lives of their own" in adaptation, beyond Chile and beyond the medium of film itself. In "*Il Futuro* by Alicia Scherson: Film and Cross-cultural (Af)filiations," María Angélica Franken draws together the transnational strands of Alicia Scherson's 2013 film, an Italian coproduction, with a Dutch star, based on a novel by a Chilean author (Roberto Bolaño) who lived most of his life in Spain. Arturo Márquez-Gómez, in "Video Built the Cinema Star: Alex Anwandter's *Nunca vas a estar solo*," examines the parallels between Anwandter's 2016 film—loosely based on the 2012 murder of the Chilean gay man Daniel Zamudio—and Anwandter's 2016 album *Amiga*, whose songs narrate the film and deal with the same topics. The film and the album, produced outside of Chile, indicate the extent to which, for Márquez-Gómez, music and film work together to re-elaborate Chile's strong tradition of protest music and expose the fissures of the Chilean neoliberal prototype. Finally, Vania Barraza's article, "Intimacies and Global Aesthetics in *Vida de familia* by Alicia Scherson and Cristián Jiménez," examines how the codirected film *Vida de familia* (2017), adapted from a short story by Alejandro Zambra, negotiates the apolitical aesthetics of recent Chilean film by indirectly addressing sensitive topics related to collective and national interests.

In the fourth section, "Migrations of Gender and Genre," we focus on how Chilean cinema has intervened in larger, transnational debates about sexual difference and dissidence. Mónica Ramón Ríos's essay "A House Without Limits: Framing Camila José Donoso's *Casa Roshell* through Disidentification and Disappropriation," examines Donoso's 2017 docufiction about a place where men can rent a kit to transform themselves into women and then meet other "straight" men who come to the club looking for sexual dalliances. The film, made in Mexico, bridges nations and genres, departing from documentary into fiction, and also harks back to another work of queer Chilean cultural production, José Donoso's novella *El lugar sin límites*, itself written (and adapted into a film) in Mexico. In "The International (Un)intelligibility of Chilean Trans* Film," meanwhile, Carl Fischer contrasts *Una mujer fantástica*, which is more intelligible to liberal, international audiences because it advocates for particular political rights for trans* people, with Donoso and Nicolás Videla's *Naomi Campbel*, which offers a more local representation of trans* life, albeit with less international success and visibility. This essay explores the extent to which an internationally intelligible representation of trans* identity and its concomitant political claims makes for a more palatable, but less pluralistic, international image of the trans* experience in Chile.

The final section of the book, titled "Politicized Intimacies, Transnational Affects: Debating (Post)memory and History," focuses on Chilean filmmakers whose work deals with memory. Documentary film has been one of the most important arenas where Chilean artists have reckoned with the dictatorship. With this in mind, Claudia Bossay begins this section with an overarching discussion of six documentary films that have systematically cautioned against the dangers of forgetting Chile's past, in "Filmmakers to the Rescue of Chilean Memory: Representations of Chile's Traumatic Past in Contemporary Documentary." In "The Life of Things: Materiality and Affectivity in *Atrapados en Japón* by Vivienne Barry," María Constanza Vergara Reyes reckons with the large body of scholarly work about "filiation narratives": dialogues, in South American documentaries, between the director and an (often lost or disappeared) relative of his or hers. By examining Vivienne Barry's documentary in this context, Vergara examines how such dialogues can work haptically, through objects lost and found. In "Displacement, Emplacement, and the Politics of Exilic Childhood in Sergio Castilla's *Gringuito*," Camilo Trumper examines the film *Gringuito*, which chronicles one child's experiences of "exilio" and "retorno" after coming "home" to his parents' country, a nation unknown to him. Finally, in "Films on Loss and Mourning: Bridging the Personal and the Collective," María Helena Rueda examines four films where collective memory struggles function in tension with more personal, individualized ones, in ways that fight oblivion through forms of mourning.

Chilean film has taken on a global reach, and so criticism of it should do so as well. By bringing more of the wealth of information about Chilean cinema to Anglophone readers and examining it in depth—with contributors from both Chile and the United States—this book thinks about Chilean cinema in the context of its own national development, even as it also addresses the ways in which it has positioned itself internationally. Meant for both researchers and students in cinema studies and Latin American studies, it expands on the ways in which we think about politics—both affective and militant—following both the fall of the Chilean dictatorship and Chile's negotiation of its place in a post–Berlin Wall world. The volume also evaluates an active and emergent film movement that has yet to receive sufficient attention in global cinema studies. Furthermore, we expand the debate concerning recent political and economic transformations occurring in contemporary Latin American countries and introduce this research field to the US academy in order to see how the Chilean film industry compares with how other national cinemas are negotiating their place on the world stage. What are the aesthetic implications for a small national cinema that has to negotiate between these local and global demands?

NOTES

1. María Paz Peirano (2018) examines the controversy surrounding *NO* at length, pointing out how, dating back to the 1960s, cinema in Chile has been a tool of leftist political critique (145), which left *NO* in a somewhat ambiguous position for Chilean film professionals. On one hand, the success of *NO* brought welcome attention to Chilean cinema in the global marketplace, which benefited them. On the other hand, though, they viewed the film's success abroad not as a result of "its quality, but . . . as a demonstration of how the film 'sold' Chile's recent history to a global market dominated by the United States, turning the trauma of the dictatorship into a commodity for the international film market, exploited by the elite" (143).

2. To date, there is little systematic study of how the Chilean film industry has developed, particularly in terms of the impact of these changes to film distribution and exhibition in the country. Statistical information from Chile's Chamber of Multiplex Exhibitors (CAEM) and the National Council of Culture and the Arts (CNCA) mainly focuses on the growth of the industry (see the Catholic University's series "Panorama del Audiovisual"). Certain scholarly studies have advocated for the relevance of developing public policies to stimulate production (Bettati 2012), but they have yet to systematically address the effects of these factors on contemporary filmmaking. Antonella Estévez (2005, 60; 2011, 77) and Roberto Trejo (2011, 88) have referenced some of these changes, but more work needs to be done to study their impact.

3. For a detailed sociological and historical analysis of the Chilean labor movement, see the work of Peter Winn (2004), and Carolina Bank Muñoz's (2017) discussion of workers' rights in the country over the past fifty years. Her focus is on workers at Walmart, a large employer in Chile since 2009, but her discussion of the structural challenges to labor organizing in Chile, particularly in her second chapter, is relevant for all industries in the country, including cinema.

4. These included films by the Bolivian Jorge Sanjinés, the Argentinians Octavio Getino and Fernando Solanas, the Cubans Tomás Gutiérrez Alea and Humberto Solás, and the Brazilian Glauber Rocha (Mouesca and Orellana 2010, 117).

5. For more information about Chile Films, see Peirano and Gobantes (2015).

6. See Jacqueline Mouesca (1988), Verónica Cortínez (2001), José Miguel Palacios (2016), and Elizabeth Ramírez Soto and Catalina Donoso Pinto (2016).

7. These critics include Sebastián Vidal (2012), Jorge Morales and Gonzalo Maza (2012), Andrea Chignoli and Catalina Donoso (2013), Valeria de los Ríos and Catalina Donoso (2015), Claudia Aravena and Iván Pinto (2018), and Claudio Lagos Olivero (2019).

8 Arts and culture were highly relevant for Patricio Aylwin's administration (1990–1994), the first government after the military dictatorship. In addition to soft loans for the completion of film projects early in the decade (eventually, the program did not succeed because film productions failed to develop adequate distribution and marketing plans), the National Fund for the Development of Culture and the Arts (Fondart) was created in 1992 with the aim of promoting arts and culture. The fund played a key role in developing the postdictatorship cinema industry, financing 466 projects (films, documentaries, short films, and videos) between 1992 and 2002 (Estévez 2005, 75). The National Council of Culture and the Arts (CNCA) was founded in 2003, and the CNCA was replaced by the Ministry of Cultures, Arts and Heritage in 2018. Fondart is now the name of the ministry's grant program.

9 When a Chilean film is distributed in an English-language market and its title has been translated by the distributor, we initially provide the English-language title in italics. Otherwise, we translate the original titles into English and enclose them in quotation marks. In those cases in which only one title in English or Spanish appears in italics, the film's title is the same in Spanish- and English-language markets.

10 However, there have been multiple sexual harassment accusations against López, one of the principals of Sobras.

11 *En la cama* was so successful that it was remade several times: in Brazil as *Entre Lençóis / Between the Sheets* and in Colombia as *Entre sábanas / Between the Sheets* (both directed by Gustavo Nieto Roa in 2008), in Spain as *Habitación en Roma / Room in Rome* (directed by Julio Medem in 2010), and in the Dominican Republic as *En tu piel / 7:20 Once a Week* (directed by Bize in 2018).

12 The phenomenon of a generation not sharing a group identity or a common discourse is the result of what Barraza has called "the politics of detachment" of the Chilean postdictatorship, in order to distinguish it from a total political detachment. Although an apparent lack of interest in social issues prevails among the *Novísimos*, Barraza explores how this cinema reframes the debate between public and private spheres, criticizing and expressing apprehension regarding sociopolitical conditions in contemporary Chile (see also Barraza 2012, 2013, 2014, and 2015).

13 This, and all other translations from Spanish here, are our own.

14 See, among others, Glickman and Huberman (2018), Lerner and Piazza (2017), Roberts-Camps (2017), Arenillas and Lazzara (2016), Schroeder Rodríguez (2016), Venkatesh (2016), Poblete and Suárez (2016), Castillo and Lema-Hincapié (2015), Navarro and Rodríguez (2014), Podalsky (2011), Burton (1986, 1990), Pick (1993), and Chanan (1983).

15 For example, Andermann and Fernández Bravo (2013) have focused on Argentine and Brazilian cinemas in comparison; Risner (2018), Stites Mor (2012), and Aguilar (2008), among others, have focused on Argentine film. Meanwhile, studies of Mexican film, including Luna (2018), Smith (2017), Lahr-Vivaz (2016), Ramírez Berg (2015), and Sánchez Prado (2014), among others, have placed recent cinematic developments there in the context of the long development of that country's national industrial cinema apparatus. The same can be said for studies of Brazilian cinema, such as Brandellero (2013) and Marsh (2012). Although she questions the idea of a uniform national identity, Joanna Page (2009) posits that a national framework (and national state support) is still essential in the case of the Argentinean cinematography. Cacilda Rêgo and Carolina Rocha (2011) also review national and transnational funding along with the transformations in citizenship and gender in Argentine and Brazilian cinema.

16 Chanan's volume, titled *Chilean Cinema*, is an intriguingly heterogeneous compilation. It includes a historical introduction to Chilean cinema; interviews with certain Chilean directors (Ruiz, Soto, and Littin) and with the Belgian sociologist Armand Mattelart; an English translation of the UP Cineastes' Manifesto; a useful bibliography of texts about Chilean cinema and a filmography listing Chilean films made between 1959 and 1976; and reprints of news articles (from *Variety*, *Ercilla*, and the British socialist newspaper *The Morning Star*) about the state of Chilean cinema under the *Unidad Popular* and in its aftermath.

17 See, for example, Lazzara (2006 and 2018a), Trumper (2016), Fischer (2016), and Gómez-Barris (2009 and 2018), among others.

18 See Donoso Pinto (2007), Urrutia Neno (2010 and 2013), Corro (2012), and Estévez (2017).

19 See Trejo (2009), Cavallo and Maza (2011), Saavedra (2013), and Barraza (2018).

20 See Estévez (2005), Barril and Santa Cruz (2011), Salinas Muñoz and Stange Marcus (2008 and 2017), and Mouesca and Orellana (2010).

21 See Verónica Cortínez and Manfred Engelbert's work on Alejo Álvarez, Germán Becker, Álvaro Covacevich, Aldo Francia, Patricio Kaulen, Miguel Littin, Raúl Ruiz, and Helvio Soto (2014), Andrea Chignoli and Catalina Donoso Pinto's work on Pedro Chaskel (2013), Mónica Villarroel and Isabel Mardones's study of Chilean silent film (2012), Valeria de los Ríos and Catalina Donoso Pinto's study of Ignacio Agüero (2015), Catalina Donoso Pinto and Elizabeth Ramírez Soto's study of Angelina Vásquez, Marilú Mallet, and Valeria Sarmiento (2016), Valeria de los Ríos and Iván Pinto's work on Raúl Ruiz (2015), and Ignacio López-Vicuña and Andreea Marinescu's study of Raúl Ruiz (2017), among others.

22 Within the National Council of Art and the Audiovisual Industry (CAIA), and in collaboration with public and private entities, Film Commission Chile (FCCh) has sought, since 2011, to promote Chile internationally as a filming destination, attracting productions to the country and facilitating the development of national productions throughout the country. Cinema Chile, which "is an active office that facilitates the exporting and internationalization of film and every format of audiovisual production, both for companies that are consolidated in the international circuit, as well as those who are beginning to forge their paths abroad," was created in 2009 by Chile's Film and TV Producers Association (APCT) and ProChile. See their English-language websites: www.filmcommissionchile.org/en/ and www.cinemachile.cl/en/.

23 Such models are more collaborative and less commercially driven, and include Perut+Osnovikoff, run by documentary filmmakers Bettina Perut and Iván Osnovikoff, Mitómana Producciones, Carolina Adriazola and José Luis Sepúlveda's production company, and MAFI (*Mapa Fílmico de un País*, or the "Filmic Map of the Country").

24 Examples of films that received enthusiastic responses both at Sundance and at the domestic box office include *La nana / The Maid* (2009) by Sebastián Silva, *Violeta se fue a los cielos / Violeta Went to Heaven* (2011) by Andrés Wood, and *Joven y alocada / Young & Wild* (2012) by Marialy Rivas.

25 Examples of films with this fairly modest reception include *Crystal Fairy & the Magical Cactus* (2013) by Sebastián Silva and *Matar a un hombre* (2014) by Alejandro Fernández Almendras. The same can be said for other Chilean Sundance releases, including *Gatos viejos / Old Cats* (2010), *Magic Magic* (2013), and *Nasty Baby* (2015) by Sebastián Silva, *Il futuro / The Future* (2013) by Alicia Scherson, *Aquí no ha pasado nada / Much Ado About Nothing* (2016) by Alejandro Fernández Almendras, or *Vida de familia / Family Life* (2017) by Cristián Jiménez and Alicia Scherson.

26 These include Ibermedia, Latin America Media Arts Fund—TFI (Tribeca), Hubert Bals Fund—HBF (Rotterdam), World Cinema Fund—WCF (Berlinale), Cinema in construction (San Sebastián), NHK International Filmmakers Award (Sundance), the Global Film Initiative, Fonds Sud Cinema, and others.

27 Ďurovičová and Newman (2010), Tierney (2013), and Dennison (2013) have studied the structural impacts of transnational funding on Latin American film.

28 Peirano (2018, 142) has observed this link from an anthropological perspective, and Marcelo Morales (2019) has compiled an interesting list of some of the films that have denounced the issues that those participating in the estallido social have protested against ("12 películas"). Since the *estallido*, a number of filmmakers have been actively working in solidarity with members

of the media, particularly photographers, who have been affected by police brutality ("*Conforman colectivo*"), and have facilitated meetings (*cabildos*) to allow filmmaking professionals to voice their opinions about the possible new constitution.

WORKS CITED

Aguilar, Gonzalo. 2008. *Other Worlds: New Argentinean Film*. Translated by Sarah Ann Wells. New York: Palgrave MacMillan.

Ahn, SooJeong. 2011. *The Pusan International Film Festival: South Korean Cinema and Globalization*. Hong Kong: Hong Kong University Press.

Andermann, Jens, and Álvaro Fernández Bravo, eds. 2013. *New Argentine and Brazilian Cinema: Reality Effects*. New York: Palgrave MacMillan.

Aravena, Claudia, and Iván Pinto. 2018. *Visiones laterales: Cine y video experimental en Chile (1957–2017)*. Santiago de Chile: Ediciones Metales Pesados.

Arenillas, María Guadalupe, and Michael Lazzara. 2016. *Latin American Documentary Film in the New Millennium*. New York: Palgrave MacMillan.

Bank Muñoz, Carolina. 2017. *Building Power from Below: Chilean Workers Take on Walmart*. Ithaca: Cornell University Press.

Barraza, Vania. 2012. "Chilenos en Barcelona: entre el deseo, lo (a)político y el olvido en *199 recetas para ser feliz*." In *Capital Inscriptions: Essays on Literature, Film and Urban Space in Honor of Malcolm Alan Compitello*, edited by Benjamin Fraser, 195–211. Newark: Juan de la Cuesta.

———. 2013. "De cine, lucha y representación en José Luis Sepúlveda y Carolina Adriazola." *Cinémas d'Amérique Latine* 21: 130–38.

———. 2014. "Reviewing the Present in Pablo Larraín's Historical Cinema." *Iberoamericana*. 13 (51): 159–72.

———. 2015. "From Sanhattan to Nashvegas: The Aesthetics of Detachment in Alberto Fuguet's Filmmaking." *Hispania* 98 (3): 442–51.

———. 2018. *El cine en Chile (2005–2015): Políticas y poéticas del nuevo siglo*. Santiago de Chile: Cuarto Propio.

Barril, Claudia, and José M. Santa Cruz. 2011. *El cine que fue: 100 años de cine chileno*. Santiago de Chile: Editorial ARCIS.

Bermudez Barrios, Nayibe, ed. 2011. *Latin American Cinemas: Local Views and Transnational Connections*. Calgary: University of Calgary Press.

Bettati, Bruno. 2012. *WHY NOT? Política industrial para el audiovisual chileno*. Santiago: ebooks Patagonia.

Brandellero, Sara, ed. 2013. *The Brazilian Road Movie: Journeys of (Self) Discovery*. Cardiff: University of Wales Press.

Burton, Julianne, ed. 1986. *Cinema and Social Change in Latin America: Conversations with Latin American Filmmakers*. Austin: University of Texas Press.

———. 1990. *The Social Documentary in Latin America*. Pittsburgh: University of Pittsburgh Press.

CAEM. (Cámara de Exhibidores Multisalas de Chile A.G). 2019. "El cine en Chile en el 2018." (June). http://caem.cl/index.php/informes-anuales/item/28-el-cine-en-chile-en-el-2018.

Castillo, Debra, and Andrés Lema-Hincapié, eds. 2015. *Despite All Adversities: Spanish-American Queer Cinema*. Albany: State University of New York Press.

Cavallo, Ascanio, and Gonzalo Maza. 2011. *El novísimo cine chileno*. Santiago de Chile: Uqbar Editores.

Chanan, Michael, ed. 1976. *Chilean Cinema*. London: British Film Institute.

———, ed. 1983. *Twenty-Five Years of the New Latin American Cinema*. London: British Film Institute.

Chignoli, Andrea, and Catalina Donoso Pinto. 2013. *(Des)montando fábulas: El documental político de Pedro Chaskel*. Santiago de Chile: Uqbar.

"Conforman colectivo de audiovisualistas y trabajadores de las comunicaciones, ante abusos y lesiones en movilización social." 2019. *Edición Cero* (November 8). http://edicioncero.cl/2019/11/conforman-colectivo-de-audiovisualistas-y-trabajadores-de-las-comunicaciones-ante-abusos-y-lesiones-en-movilizacion-social/.

Copertari, Gabriela, and Carolina Sitnisky. 2015. "Introducción." In *El estado de las cosas: Cine latinoamericano en el nuevo milenio*, edited by Gabriela Copertari and Carolina Sitnisky, 11–19. Madrid/ Frankfurt: Iberoamericana/Vervuert.

Corro, Pablo. 2012. *Retóricas del cine chileno: Ensayos con el realismo*. Santiago: Cuarto Propio.

Cortínez, Verónica. 2001. *Cine a la chilena: Las peripecias de Sergio Castilla*. Santiago: RiL Ediciones.

Cortínez, Verónica, and Manfred Engelbert. *Evolución en libertad: El cine chileno de fines de los sesenta*. Santiago de Chile: Cuarto Propio, 2014.

de los Ríos, Valeria. 2018. "Contemporary Chilean Cinema: A Provisional Cartography of an Expanding Field." *Senses of Cinema* 89 (December). http://sensesofcinema.com/2018/latin-american-cinema-today/contemporary-chilean-cinema-a-provisional-cartography-of-an-expanding-field/.

de los Ríos, Valeria, and Catalina Donoso Pinto. 2015. *El cine de Ignacio Agüero: El documental como la lectura de un espacio*. Santiago de Chile: Cuarto Propio.

de los Ríos, Valeria, and Iván Pinto. 2015. *El cine de Raúl Ruiz: Fantasmas, simulacros y artificios*. Santiago de Chile: Uqbar.

Dennison, Stephanie. 2013. *Contemporary Hispanic Cinema: Interrogating the Transnational in Spanish and Latin American Film*. London: Tamesis Books.

Donoso Pinto, Catalina. 2007. *Películas que escuchan: Reconstrucción de la identidad en once filmes chilenos y argentinos*. Buenos Aires: Corregidor.

Donoso Pinto, Catalina, and Elizabeth Ramírez Soto. 2016. *Nomadías: El cine de Marilú Mallet, Valeria Sarmiento y Angelina Vázquez*. Santiago de Chile: Metales Pesados.

Ďurovičová, Natasa, and Kathleen E. Newman. 2010. *World Cinemas, Transnational Perspectives*. New York: Routledge.

Elena, Alberto. 1999. *Los cines periféricos: África, Oriente Medio, India*. Barcelona: Paidós.
Estévez, Antonella. 2005. *Luz, Cámara, Transición: El rollo del cine chileno de 1993 a 2003*. Santiago: Radio Universidad de Chile.
———. 2010. "Dolores políticos: Reacciones cinematográficas. Resistencias melancólicas en el cine chileno contemporáneo." *Aisthesis* 47: 15–32.
———. 2011. "Joven cine chileno: En la movilización de los márgenes." In *El cine que fue: 100 años de cine chileno*, edited by Claudia Barril and José M. Santa Cruz, 75–83. Santiago de Chile: Arcis.
———. 2017. *Una gramática de la melancolía cinematográfica: La modernidad y el no duelo en cierto cine chileno contemporáneo*. Saarbrücken (Alemania): Editorial Académica Española.
Falicov, Tamara L. 2007. *The Cinematic Tango: Contemporary Argentine Film*. New York: Wallflower Press.
———. 2016. "The 'Festival Film': Film Festival Funds as Cultural Intermediaries." In *Film Festivals: History, Theory, Method, Practice*, edited by Marijke de Valek, Brendan Kredell, and Skadi Loist, 209–29. New York: Routledge, 2016.
———. *Latin American Film Industries*. London: The British Film Institute (BFI) and Bloomsbury, 2019.
Fischer, Carl. 2016. *Queering the Chilean Way. Cultures of Exceptionalism and Sexual Dissidence, 1965–2015*. New York: Palgrave Macmillan.
Glickman, Nora, and Ariana Huberman. 2018. *Evolving Images: Jewish Latin American Cinema*. Austin: University of Texas Press.
Gómez-Barris, Macarena. 2009. *Where Memory Dwells: Culture and State Violence in Chile*. Oakland: University of California Press.
———. 2018. *The Extractive Zone: Social Ecologies and Decolonial Perspectives*. Durham: Duke University Press.
Hirsch, Marianne. 2012. *The Generation of Postmemory: Writing and Visual Culture After the Holocaust*. New York: Columbia University Press.
Jara Donoso, Eliana. 2002. "¿Cien años de cine chileno?" *Patrimonio Cultural: Revista de la Dirección de Bibliotecas, Archivos y Museos* 7, no.25 (Fall–Winter): 26.
Jelin, Elizabeth. 2002. *Los trabajos de la memoria*. Madrid: Siglo XXI Editores.
Kemp, Leah Harmon. 2010. "*Citizenship in Chilean Post-dictatorship Film, 1900–2005*." PhD diss., University of California Los Angeles. ProQuest (AAT 3451050).
King, John. 2009. "Latin American Film Scholarship in the UK: Mapping the Field." *LASA Forum* 40 (1): 16–18.
Klein, Naomi. 2007. *The Shock Doctrine: The Rise of Disaster Capitalism*. New York: Picador.
Kornbluh, Peter. 2003. *The Pinochet File: A Declassified Dossier on Atrocity and Accountability*. New York: New Press.
Lagos Olivero, Claudio. 2019. *Cine chileno en el Santiago del apagón cultural*. Santiago de Chile: Editorial Universidad Finis Terrae.

Lahr-Vivaz, Elena. 2016. *Mexican Melodrama: Film and Nation from the Golden Age to the New Wave.* Tucson: University of Arizona Press.

Larraín, Carolina. 2010. "Nuevas tendencias del cine chileno tras la llegada del cine digital." *Aisthesis* 47: 156–71.

Lazzara, Michael. 2006. *Chile in Transition: The Poetics and Politics of Memory.* Gainesville: University of Florida Press.

———. 2018a. *Civil Obedience: Complicity and Complacency in Chile since Pinochet.* Madison: University of Wisconsin Press.

———. 2018b. "The Memory Turn." In *New Approaches to Latin American Studies: Culture and Power,* edited by Juan Poblete, 14–31. New York: Routledge.

Lerner, Jesse, and Luciano Piazza. 2017. *Ismo, ismo, ismo: Cine experimental en América Latina.* Oakland: University of California Press; Los Angeles: Los Angeles Filmforum.

López, Ana, and Dolores Tierney. 2014. "In Focus: Latin American Film Research in the Twenty-First Century." *Cinema Journal* 54 (1): 112–42.

López-Vicuña, Ignacio, and Andreea Marinescu. 2017. *Raúl Ruiz's Cinema of Inquiry.* Detroit: Wayne State University Press.

Luna, Ilana Dann. 2018. *Adapting Gender: Mexican Feminisms from Literature to Film.* Albany: State University of New York Press.

Marsh, Leslie. 2012. *Brazilian Women's Filmmaking: From Dictatorship to Democracy.* Urbana: University of Illinois Press.

Morales, Jorge, and Gonzalo Maza. 2012. *Idénticamente desigual: El cine imperfecto de Carlos Flores.* Santiago de Chile: FIDOCS.

Morales, Marcelo. 2019. "12 películas online que sirven para entender el estallido social chileno." *Cinechile* (November 7). http://cinechile.cl/criticas-y-estudios/12-peliculas-online-que-sirven-para-entender-el-estallido-social-chileno/.

Mouesca, Jacqueline. 1988. *Plano secuencia de la memoria de Chile: Veinticinco años de cine chileno (1960–1985).* Madrid: Ediciones del Litoral.

Mouesca, Jacqueline, and Carlos Orellana. 2010. *Breve historia del cine chileno: Desde sus orígenes hasta nuestros días.* Santiago de Chile: LOM Ediciones.

Moulián, Tomás. 2002. *Chile actual: Anatomía de un mito.* Santiago de Chile: LOM.

Navarro, Vinicius, and Juan Carlos Rodríguez, eds. 2014. *New Documentaries in Latin America.* New York: Palgrave MacMillan.

Olea, Raquel. 2012. "NO . . . La perversión de la verdad en la película." Radio Tierra.

Page, Joanna. 2009. *Crisis and Capitalism in Contemporary Argentine Cinema.* Durham: Duke University Press.

Palacios, José Miguel. 2012. "The Problems of Fiction: Pablo Larraín with José Miguel Palacios." *Brooklyn Rail,* November 6.

———. 2016. "Resistance vs. Exile: The Political Rhetoric of Chilean Exile Cinema in the 1970s." *Jump Cut* 57 (Fall). www.ejumpcut.org/archive/jc57.2016/-PalaciosChile/2.html.

Parada Poblete, María Marcela. 2012. "Cine chileno en dos tiempos: La operación visual sobre el cuadro-encuadre teatral-cinematográfico." LASA Conference, San Francisco, CA, May 23–26.

Paranaguá, Paulo Antonio. 2003. *Tradición y modernidad en el cine de América Latina*. México: Fondo de Cultura Económica.

Peirano, María Paz. 2018. "Larraín's *No*: A Tale of Neoliberalism." In *Contemporary Latin American Cinema: Resisting Neoliberalism?*, edited by Claudia Sandberg and Carolina Rocha, 135–52. New York: Palgrave MacMillan.

Peirano, María Paz, and Catalina Gobantes, eds. 2015. *Chile Films: El Hollywood criollo*. Santiago de Chile: Cuarto Propio.

Pick, Zuzana M. 1993. *The New Latin American Cinema: A Continental Project*. Austin: University of Texas Press.

Poblete, Juan, and Juana Suárez, eds. 2016. *Humor in Latin American Cinema*. New York: Palgrave MacMillan.

Podalsky, Laura. 2011. *The Politics of Affect and Emotion in Contemporary Latin American Cinema: Argentina, Brazil, Cuba, and Mexico*. New York: Palgrave Macmillan.

Póo, Ximena, Claudio Salinas, and Hans Stange. 2012. "Políticas de la subjetividad en el 'novísimo' cine chileno." *Comunicación y Medios* 26: 5–11.

Ramírez Berg, Charles. 2015. *The Classical Mexican Cinema: The Poetics of the Exceptional Golden Age Films*. Austin: University of Texas Press.

Ramírez-Soto, Elizabeth. 2019. *(Un)veiling Bodies: A Trajectory of Chilean Post-Dictatorship Documentary*. Cambridge: Legenda.

Rêgo, Cacilda, and Carolina Rocha, eds. 2011. *New Trends in Argentine and Brazilian Cinema*. Bristol and Chicago: Intellect.

Risner, Jonathan. 2018. *Blood Circuits: Contemporary Argentine Horror Cinema*. Albany: State University of New York Press.

Roberts-Camps, Traci. 2017. *Latin American Women Filmmakers: Social and Cultural Perspectives*. Albuquerque: University of New Mexico Press.

Saavedra, Carlos. 2013. *Intimidades desencantadas: La poética cinematográfica del dos mil*. Santiago de Chile: Cuarto Propio.

Salinas Muñoz, Claudio, Hans Stange Marcus, and Sergio Salinas Roco. 2008. *Historia del cine experimental en la Universidad de Chile, 1957–1973*. Santiago de Chile: Consejo Nacional de la Cultura y las Artes Fondo de Fomento Audiovisual.

———. 2017. *La mirada obediente: Historia nacional en el cine chileno*. Santiago de Chile: Editorial Universitaria.

Sánchez Prado, Ignacio. 2014. *Screening Neoliberalism: Transforming Mexican Cinema, 1988–2012*. Nashville: Vanderbilt University Press.

Schroeder Rodríguez, Paul. 2016. *Latin American Cinema: A Comparative History*. Oakland: University of California Press.

Shaw, Deborah. 2013. "Deconstructing and Reconstructing 'Transnational Cinema.'" In *Contemporary Hispanic Cinema: Interrogating the Transnational in Spanish and Latin American Film*, edited by Stepanhie Denisson, 47–66. London: Tamesis Books.

———. 2017. "Transnational Cinema: Mapping a Field of Study." In *The Routledge Companion to World Cinema*, edited by Rob Stone, Paul Cooke, Stephanie Dennison, and Alex Marlow-Mann, 290–98. Milton Park: Routledge.

Shaw, Lisa, and Stephanie Dennison. 2005. *Latin American Cinema: Essays on Modernity, Gender and National Identity*. Jefferson: McFarland.

Smith, Paul Julian. 2017. *Queer Mexico: Cinema and Television Since 2000*. Detroit: Wayne State University Press.

Stites Mor, Jessica. 2012. *Transition Cinema: Political Filmmaking and the Argentine Left Since 1968*. Pittsburgh: University of Pittsburgh Press.

Suárez, Juana. 2010. *Sitios de contienda: Producción cultural colombiana y el discurso de la violencia*. Madrid: Iberoamericana/Vervuert.

———. 2012. *Critical Essays on Colombian Cinema and Culture: Cinembargo Colombia*. New York: Palgrave MacMillan.

Tierney, Dolores. 2013. *Contemporary Latin American Cinema: New Transnationalisms*. Edinburgh: Edinburgh University Press.

Trejo, Roberto. 2009. *Cine, neoliberalismo y cultura: Crítica de la economía política del cine chileno contemporáneo*. Santiago de Chile: Arcis.

———. 2011. "El cine chileno en la primera década del siglo XXI: El agotamiento ideológico de una estrategia de desarrollo material." In *El cine que fue: 100 años de cine chileno*, edited by Claudia Barril and José M. Santa Cruz, 84–101. Santiago de Chile: Arcis.

Trumper, Camilo. 2016. *Ephemeral Histories: Public Art, Politics, and the Struggle for the Streets in Chile*. Oakland: University of California Press.

Urrutia Neno, Carolina. 2010. "Hacia una política en tránsito: Ficción en el cine chileno (2008–2010)." *Aisthesis* 47: 33–44.

———. 2013. *Un cine centrífugo: Ficciones chilenas 2005–2010*. Santiago de Chile: Cuarto Propio.

Venkatesh, Vinodh. 2016. *New Maricón Cinema: Outing Latin American Film*. Austin: University of Texas Press.

Vidal, Sebastián. 2012 *En el principio: Arte, archivos y tecnologías durante la dictadura en Chile*. Santiago de Chile: Ediciones Metales Pesados.

Villarroel, Mónica, and Isabel Mardones. 2012. *Señales contra el olvido: Cine chileno recobrado*. Santiago de Chile: Cuarto Propio.

Winn, Peter, ed. 2004. *Victims of the Chilean Miracle: Workers and Neoliberalism in the Pinochet Era, 1973–2002*. Durham and London: Duke University Press.

MAPPING THEORIES OF CHILEAN CINEMA IN THE WORLD

1

LEARNING TO BE "GLOBAL"

Chilean Filmmakers at International Film Festivals

María Paz Peirano

Chilean cinema is an emergent field of film production that has flourished on the international scene in the last decade, positioning itself as a promising "global" cinema that includes outstanding internationally successful films such as the award-winning *NO* (Pablo Larraín, 2013), *Gloria* (Sebastián Lelio, 2013), and the recent Oscar-winning *Historia de un oso / Bear Story* (Gabriel Osorio, 2014) and *Una mujer fantástica / A Fantastic Woman* (Lelio, 2017). The expansion of Chilean film production is intertwined with radical transformations in Chilean cinema over the last decade, particularly its growing professionalization and a deepening of its internationalization policies. Both aspects have contributed to a noticeable increase in film production (almost threefold in comparison to previous decades), an increase in international audiences, which exceed local ones by a factor of three (CinemaChile 2016), and an unprecedented positioning of Chilean cinema in the international film festival circuit, where films have gained critical recognition and multiple awards. Chilean filmmakers have benefitted from their participation in the festival circuit, learning new models of production and transnational networking that contribute to their international success and shape some of their films into "global" cinema.

Drawing from in-depth ethnographic interviews with filmmakers and participant observation in the main international markets and industry hubs at major film festivals—including Cannes, Berlin, the International Documentary Film Festival Amsterdam (IDFA), and San Sebastián—in this chapter I give an account of the various social and cultural processes that have contributed to the formation of a new corpus of Chilean cinema with global pretensions, that is to say, national films that also target international audiences as forms of "global art cinema" (Galt and Schoonover 2010). The chapter analyzes how these processes have inspired the production of this kind of auteur cinema with a cosmopolitan vocation, considering that film festivals, showcases, industry sections, and marketplaces have served as training grounds for Chilean filmmakers to learn how to produce this form of cinema.

Film festivals are considered here as global "territorialised assemblages" (Collier and Ong 2005, 4), where the global intersects with the personal experiences of everyday life. Festivals are transnational hubs, where filmmakers experience the globalization of the film industry in daily international social interactions and cultural negotiations. Thus, festival spaces can be seen as the interstices of global cultural production, with a strong impact on the personal and professional experiences of filmmakers who learn to work in this increasingly interconnected international environment. Their learning processes include making sense of these spaces, building their subjectivities (their professional outlook and artistic persona, for example), and negotiating both image-making and business practices based on their training. I argue that the increasing participation of a Chilean network of filmmakers and producers in the film festival circuit has allowed them to accumulate symbolic, cultural, and social capital, and therefore contribute to an unprecedented position in the international field of film production. Aiming to increase their cultural value in the world of alternative cinema by combining their films' local flavor with the political and aesthetic expectations of the international circuit, Chilean filmmakers have reshaped their production and circulation strategies, contributing to the ongoing internationalization of Chilean film production.[1]

A SMALL NATIONAL COMMUNITY WITH GLOBAL ASPIRATIONS

The Chilean film industry is a small one, relatively marginal to global film production. Mette Hjort and Duncan Petrie have used the term "cinema of small nations" (2007) to refer to the production of small national industries like Chile's in the context of globalization. The size of these industries, in their telling, is proportional to a relatively small volume of production and a high level of state subsidy, rather than to the actual size of the country. In the Chilean case, for example, around forty national films are premiered every year in local cinemas, meaning that Chilean films have a very low market share in their own country, in terms of audience and total revenues, relative to films from other countries.[2] Most of these films receive some funding from the Chilean state, thanks to the *Fondo de Fomento Audiovisual* (Fund for Audiovisual Development) and the *Corporación de Fomento de la Producción* (CORFO, or Production Development Corporation). The "cinemas of small nations" tend to be "peripheral"—that is to say, they are films "encoded on the margins of the dominant modes of production, distribution and consumption" (Iordanova, Martin-Jones, and Vidal 2010, 9) of global cinema, even when the hierarchical relationship between center and periphery is not necessarily straightforward, with the center always seeking to subsume its margins. Given their position, small cinemas often aspire to internationalize their production and expand outside their limited domestic markets (Lorenzen 2007). International film festivals offer this opportunity, since they tend to crave films from what they consider "novel" regions, that is, films from non–Western European and North American nations (with the exception of Mexico) that do not normally get international distribution. Curating this type of cinema contributes to film festivals' prestige as genuine international hubs that promote cultural diversity, and it builds a certain level of interdependence between peripheral art cinema and the festival circuit.

Considering Latin American cinema's transnational connections, several scholars have explored the creative freedom and new possibilities apparently opened up by globalization (Shaw and Dennison 2005), along with the chances to supplement both small internal film markets and national states' endorsement of local film industries. Thinking about national cinemas transnationally is based on a recognition of the particular conditions of filmmaking on the periphery, which are increasingly connected with international circulation channels, transnational film practices, and the emerging narratives enabled by these productions. From this point of view, agencies other than the nation-state and the individual aims of particular filmmakers can be considered, in order to understand the dynamism of contemporary cinema.

During my research, I have observed how the practices and patterns of film professionals' circulation on the film festival circuit have allowed them to be part of the international film industry as a group, under the umbrella of a recent and flourishing "Chilean Cinema" brand. Chilean filmmakers, including the aforementioned Oscar winners and nominees, were able to internationalize their films because they integrated local, national, and global perspectives in their interpretations of international cinema, engaging in various ways with national and foreign films. I suggest that this was made possible by the ways in which filmmakers assumed a global position, influencing the construction of their specific subjectivities and films. We will see that this process was embedded in social and cultural interactions at film festivals in at least three different spheres: exhibition and circulation, markets, and training hubs. The combined personal and communal experiences at these three different festival spaces allowed filmmakers to learn the ways in which global cinema is produced and exchanged, and to train themselves to perform in the international market.

This internationalized learning process by Chilean film professionals was enabled by social networks that preceded Chilean participation at film festivals, and it has been reinforced during their participation in the circuit in the last decade. In the 1990s and early 2000s, a small professional network was fostered and reinforced at new film schools, workplaces, and Chilean film festivals (Peirano 2016), helping them to both build close relationships among themselves and learn new production and circulation practices from one another. Thus, filmmakers created a growing "community of practice" (Wenger 1998) that further expanded in the 2010s. We can consider this community to be an "art world"—that is to say, a "network of people whose cooperative activity, organized via their joint knowledge of conventional means of doing things, produces the kind of art works that art world is noted for" (Becker 1982, x). As Becker suggests, for Chilean professionals, cooperation is more or less routine, producing patterns of collective activity that affect film production. Filmmakers' practices then rely on a certain rationale according to which artistic activities make sense for the participants, such as the required learning practices that foster creativity and collective aspirations. Social practices also enable certain aesthetic values, and in this case, a shared sense of the worth of films collectively produced under the umbrella of "Chilean cinema" with an artistic and international orientation.

This Chilean "film community," I argue, is the basis of the renovated Chilean "field of cultural production" (Bourdieu 1993), where filmmakers act as key agents of an internationalized field. It is formed by a particular group of Chilean film directors and film producers with cosmopolitan aspirations (Peirano 2018a) who live and work transnationally. Their "cosmopolitan *habitus*," that is, the sets of cultural dispositions grounded in the structure of positions occupied by the agents, is embedded in their professional practices, re-created and reinforced through their circulation in the international circuit. Filmmakers tend to be "cosmopolitan subjects" (Hannerz 1996) who do not think of themselves as only Chilean but also as part of an international community of alternative or art cinema. In the terms of Schneider, they could be considered to be global artists and professionals who are "interfaces" or "nodal points" in the global system (2006, 20), incorporating transnational connections and symbolic references in their work. The dynamic links between artists, artifacts, and artworks result from a global appropriative process (27) where filmmakers can be seen as active agents of transnationalization through their practices.

In the Chilean case, this sociocultural configuration of the field has replaced a purely "national" popular aesthetics in Chilean cinema that was prevalent throughout the 1990s and early 2000s. The cinema of this period aimed to represent collective national images rooted in Chilean popular culture and lower-class characters, focusing on the particularities of Chilean national identity. Up to the 2000s, Chilean cinema followed the tradition of the New Chilean Cinema movement of the 1960s, which understood filmmaking as a social and political duty and aimed to reveal the struggles of the "real" Chilean people by affirming their cultural and political independence. Recent Chilean cinema moves away from these expectations, and national cinema does not seem to be defined by its social role and its cultural specificity any longer. While political and social narratives continue to exist in some films, and are relevant for some filmmakers (even in films that circulate internationally), film directors no longer attempt to produce big social narratives that represent Chilean national identity.[3] "Chilean cinema" is more and more often considered as a group of individual films made by innovative and creative professionals and artists who belong to the globe. Thus, their films tend to be more delocalized, retaining only a few "local" traits in order to look both culturally different and international at the same time. The practices, meaning, and values of this recent "cosmopolitan" Chilean cinema are mainly learned and reinforced at international film festivals.

EXHIBITION AND CIRCULATION IN THE FESTIVAL CIRCUIT

It is possible to identify almost ten thousand film festivals in the world during the last decade, 75 percent of which have been created since the middle part of the first decade of the twenty-first century.[4] They constitute a network of venues to which film professionals from different parts of the world travel every year, forming a dynamic mediascape that incorporates overlapping circuits of production, distribution, and consumption. The increasingly interconnected festival phenomenon has been deemed an autonomous circuit with its own nodes, connections, and tenets (Elsaesser 2005) that plays a fundamental role in the production, circulation, and consumption of contemporary peripheral cinema, functioning as a series of key hubs in a global film network. Festivals are a relatively stable channel of exhibition, allowing for the circulation of nonmainstream films, so they are often seen as a way to establish an alternative circuit that allows for the recognition of independent "foreign language" films and filmmakers (Turan 2002, 8) and "world cinema" (Ďurovičová and Newman 2010). Festivals also establish vital links with different stakeholders and players in the international field of film production, such as states, intellectuals, and city marketers (Valck 2007). They are the main transnational spaces for encounters between international film agents, such as festival programmers, filmmakers, and critics, who gather together, watch, and review new films, and, in sum, decide what will be seen by audiences all over the world; they act as gatekeepers for contemporary world cinema. Thus, festivals can be seen as nodes where film professionals meet in personal micronetworks created by elites in the film world (Peranson 2009), who reconstruct a certain global film culture in these settings (Wong 2011).

The multiple dimensions of film festivals as hubs of world cinema make them key for the process of value-addition to peripheral cinemas such as Chile's. By traveling around the circuit, a film can accumulate symbolic value: the more praise, awards, and buzz a film attracts, the more attention it is likely to receive at other festivals, and likewise with the filmmakers involved in its production. Consequently, filmmakers gain increasing prestige due to the circulation of their products, which in turn become more valuable with the signature of prestigious "authors." For these reasons, festivals are often seen as establishing an alternative circuit that allows the international recognition of independent films and filmmakers at the periphery, as has been the case with the recent globalization of Latin American cinema (Rodríguez-Isaza 2014; Shaw 2007). Thanks to their selection processes, awards systems, authors' retrospectives, and special national sidebars, festivals have performed a fundamental role in showcasing and promoting Latin American auteur cinema.

That has also been the case with recent Chilean cinema, which has become visible on the circuit through film festivals' active sponsorship. Since 2011, the most prestigious international film festivals (mostly the so-called

A-Class festivals),[5] including Cannes, Berlin, San Sebastián, Rotterdam, Venice, Locarno, and Sundance, have increasingly included Chilean films in either their main or their minor competitive sections, and these films have gained generally positive critical reception and a growing number of awards. As a result, Chilean films and filmmakers have received more and more recognition in the circuit thanks to a "snowball effect," a form of prestige that, to a certain extent, is symbolically transferred to other filmmakers and films from the same national film industry. Other secondary and specialized festivals then started to include Chilean films and "Chilean cinema" special sidebars in their programs during the same period, and filmmakers have been increasingly invited to present their work to international audiences at these spaces, taking part in Q&As after the screenings and being interviewed by local press. Thus, "Chilean cinema" has become visible as a group of films necessarily linked by national ascription that also fits into the festivals' category of "Latin American cinema" when grouped with other films from the region.

Despite these national and regional categories that serve to identify, promote, and lend some "exotic" flavor to these films (particularly the non-Western ones), the type of film selected by festivals is consistently a form of global art cinema, understood as a form of a somewhat delocalized, cosmopolitan "auteur cinema." This type of cinema corresponds, in general terms, to the idea of global art cinema suggested by Galt and Schoonover (2010, 7), which encompasses narrative films on the margins of commercial cinema, characterized by a transnational tenor that articulates an ambivalent relationship with their geographical origin. This form of cinema is often thought of as intrinsically cosmopolitan and dislocated from its particular national heritage, even when it appears to retain certain "local flavor" in order to keep its non-Western value.

Given the predominance of this type of cinema in the international circuit, it is also the one Chilean filmmakers gain access to when traveling throughout the circuit. This is an essential part of their learning process that helps them keep up to date with recent forms of international filmmaking while also discovering fellow directors from Europe, Latin America, and other peripheries, who are, like them, often categorized as auteurs. This authorial category is often stressed in the program, in the catalogues, and by the festivals' press, particularly when a filmmaker has become internationally famous, turning more and more into a "global" filmmaker. This is the case for the two most recognized Chilean film directors in the circuit, Pablo

Larraín and Sebastián Lelio, who seem to embody this global aspiration thanks to their recent international film awards and projects. The international films that they have recently directed, such as *Jackie* (Larraín 2016) and *Disobedience* (Lelio 2018), are in English and have international funds, casts, and themes, so by this point Larraín and Lelio could hardly be classified as "Chilean," but rather as simply "global."

Film festivals' interest in promoting this type of auteur Chilean cinema is explained by the historical aims that these events have had since the 1960s of trying to defend and promote a concept of cinema as an "art form" that moves away from the mainstream industrial conditions of film production (Vallejo 2014). Festivals have consistently highlighted non-Hollywood peripheral cinemas with personal points of view, traditionally encouraging a modernist concept of author cinema. As festivals are constantly searching for new international directors providing groundbreaking films that fit these categories, they tend to work as gatekeepers of what they consider to be the latest world quality cinema. As a result, they become the main sites for the reproduction of contemporary world cinema, and "heterotopias" (Sansi 2016, 172) that aim to resist Hollywood's hegemony. Festivals position themselves as hubs for the exhibition and exchange of the newest forms of global cinematic art, reconstructing an international film world that redistributes knowledge, fame, and prestige and allows their participants to accumulate cultural and symbolic capital. As we will see in the following section, these festivals' concerns have also helped to develop a deeper industrial and economic role for the international film world, since they sponsor not only the exhibition and circulation but also the production of world cinema.

MARKETS AND INDUSTRY SPACES AT FILM FESTIVALS

International film festivals have provided a platform for Chilean cinema on the world stage, not only through circulation but also through the active promotion of Latin American film production. Festivals' industrial support has allowed film industries that lack a large domestic market, such as Latin American cinema, to fund national filmmaking (Falicov 2010), helping them to partially overcome their unstable, precarious conditions. This economic support complements festivals' programming strategies and adds to their impact on peripheral cinemas, opening up new possibilities for filmmakers. Thus, recent research on this topic has focused on the different ways in which festivals have provided funding for Latin American cinema at different stages of film production (Ross 2011; Falicov 2010 and 2012), suggesting that festivals have helped not only to exhibit but also to shape the production of recent Latin American cinema. Miriam Ross analyzes, for example, the influence of the Rotterdam Festival's Hubert Bals Fund on Latin American cinema, exploring how grantees become representatives of a "minority film culture" (2011, 267) for international film festival spectators and increase their chances of receiving further funding. Campos (2015) has analyzed the case of San Sebastián's *Cine en Construcción*, highlighting its importance for Pablo and Juan de Dios Larraín's production company Fábula, which has successfully incorporated an international funding scheme in their model of production. There is still more statistical data to be gathered in order to fully assess this impact, but what is undeniable is that festivals' economic aid has shaped peripheral filmmakers' expectations, opening up new paths in their professional careers. Now more than ever, internationalizing their films is an option for filmmakers trying to fit into the market of non-Hollywood cinema, a path that has been articulated with the recent internationalization policies of their home countries, as in the case of Chilean cinema.

Festivals function as the main economic hubs for this "international" film industry. The global rise of industry niches dedicated to art cinema has entailed important transformations of festivals toward commercialization and the "economization of culture" (Valck 2014), and they have increasingly opened up spaces for international market exchanges under a "business model" (Peranson 2009, 25–26), exchanges that have enhanced the number and size of market spaces associated with film festivals (such as the Cannes *Marché du Film*, Berlin's *European Film Market*, and IDFA's *Market*). These are the main sites for encounters between peripheral filmmakers and other global cinema agents, sponsoring "industry" spaces that allow for professional networking, coproduction meetings, work-in-progress events, and pitching forums, as well as formal training opportunities. They thus play a fundamental role in the social constitution of the field, not only as a site of economic exchange but also as a site of knowledge exchange and for the creation of transnational professional networks (Vallejo 2014). Thus, festivals are field-configuring events similar to other cultural fairs (Lampel and Meyer 2008), a fact that has helped them sponsor a global creative industry.

Chilean filmmakers have increasingly attended these spaces as a result of these global trends and the particular transformations of the local field. Due to the neoliberal cultural policies of recent Chilean governments and their interest in developing the audiovisual sector, the state has promoted the participation of Chilean cinema in the international circuit since the mid-2000s, providing funding for traveling to festivals and film markets worldwide (CAIA 2020).[6] In addition, thanks to an alliance with the association of Chilean film producers (APCT) and their sectorial brand CinemaChile, Chile organizes a collective Chilean delegation or "Chilean Mission" that comes together at festivals and markets. This gathering has turned into an institutionalized practice to allow Chileans to congregate at these events, thus becoming the main international marketing strategy of CinemaChile and ProChile (the state's organization for the promotion of national industries abroad). CinemaChile publishes the official annual catalogue of national cinema, offered at the Chilean stand inside the market and funded by ProChile. The stand, which represents "Chilean Cinema," functions as a marketing spot that promotes delegates' films and film projects, and is also the place where the Chilean Mission can congregate and have business meetings. In addition, CinemaChile organizes cocktail parties and other social events designed to help Chileans' professional networking and self-promotion, reinforcing "Chilean cinema" as a "lived brand" that is experienced in these events. Using all of these strategies, Chilean organizations have managed to position "Chilean Cinema" at film festivals as a collective brand.

This strategy has helped Chilean film directors and producers learn how to be more involved in the international field, while also helping them gain further recognition as both artists and business professionals. It is no coincidence, for example, that Fábula has also been behind Lelio's films, from *El Año del Tigre / The Year of the Tiger* (2011) onward. The company is responsible for the only two Chilean feature films nominated to the Oscars so far (*NO* and *Una mujer fantástica*), since film producers and directors associated with the company have been learning the art and business of the international film industry together, traveling around the circuit for more than a decade and accumulating experience, international partners, and prestige.

Chileans' constant circulation at industry spaces and markets has helped them secure the attention of interested audiences and encounter the most suitable international business partners, not only for their already-made films but also for their new projects. As I describe in more detail elsewhere (Peirano 2018a), at these spaces filmmakers can "pitch" and develop new ideas and learn the business. Chilean film professionals have also met new people at these spaces (international film producers to coproduce, film directors to work with, festival programmers interested in their films, and distributors that can acquire those films), which in time has facilitated the building of partnerships and ensured more productive and stable relationships. International professional relationships are weak ties that need to be rekindled through constant interactions at different festivals, in order to foster the necessary trust and reliability among colleagues. Hence filmmakers require constant circulation to develop these social bonds over time, an eventuality that has been ensured principally by the Chilean state's funding scheme. This circulation, along with the branding strategies developed by CinemaChile, has added to film directors' and producers' cultural and social capital, helping them create vital transnational social networks while also reinforcing the idea of belonging to an "international film community."

TRAINING HUBS

In addition to their traditional role as exhibition spaces and their more recent role as industry hubs, film festivals have also become one of the most relevant sites for the education of global filmmakers. Besides the informal learning process developed at different festival spaces, formal training has become one of the main attractions for young Chilean film directors and producers, who have increasingly participated in festival educational programs (summer schools, academic residencies, creative laboratories, and industry workshops). These programs, which aim to educate future film auteurs and young businessmen and women in the international film world, concentrate on the training of film directors, producers, and other creative professionals. Training spaces combine the artistic and industrial aspirations of contemporary film festivals, and are sites where filmmakers can develop their own artistic projects as well as create professional networks.

The number of such training programs has noticeably increased in recent years. In the 1990s, following the Sundance *Filmmakers' Lab* (1981) for project development, European events started to multiply the spaces for encounters between emerging talents and experts. Since the creation of Europe's most prestigious program, the Cannes *Cinéfondation* (1998), other key events emerged during the 2000s, noticeably the Berlinale *Talents* (formerly the Talent Campus, 2003), the *Rotterdam Lab* (2005), and the *Torino FilmLab* (2008). By 2010, the tendency had spread among other European festivals (for example, the *IDFA Academy Summer School* in 2010), and the model has also been replicated in peripheral regions, in both regional labs (for example, the

AustraLab, which until 2017 worked in association with FicValdivia in Chile) and programs that mirror European hubs, such as the *Talents*, taking place in Buenos Aires, Argentina (2006) and Guadalajara, Mexico (2008). There are now hundreds of such events taking place each year that are open to filmmakers from small and peripheral countries, whose participation is encouraged by festivals' selection of their projects and sponsorship of their trips.

Training hubs aim to position festivals in the global market. According to the organizers, by opting to participate in the festivals' selection processes, filmmakers tap into the festivals' role as cultural gatekeepers and influential nodes in the circuit. Festivals aim to promote the kind of niche cinema they rely on, by professionalizing the global field and trying to ensure the production of internationalized "quality" or "art" cinema. As Cindy Wong has suggested (2011, 100), festivals support the learning process by reinforcing the meanings and performance of authorship, actively scouting for new talents to exhibit, in addition to training emerging filmmakers (Ostrowska 2010). Festivals devote entire sections to students' films, provide scholarships, and sponsor multiple training possibilities for selected young talents, who later show their films (and hopefully win awards) at the film festivals that sponsored them. In turn, festivals benefit from the prestige of having discovered the new key names in the international film world. Moreover, training programs work as global spaces for social interaction and international networking, contributing to the creation of an international artistic community with similar values. For instance, the Berlinale tries to use Talents not only to connect filmmakers but also to foster loyalty to the so-called Berlinale family by supporting filmmakers at an early stage of their career.

These training programs also seem to match festivals' institutional shift into industrial nodes, aiming to contribute to an internationalization strategy that could be seen as closer to a Hollywood paradigm instead of a sign of cultural difference. Noticeably, the training explosion coincides with the sponsorship of these events by the European Commission's Creative Europe program (Valck 2013, 128),[7] which has turned to the neoliberal ideal of "cultural entrepreneurship," reflecting an ambition to be a more competitive "knowledge economy," which is an idea that dominates creative industries worldwide. These training hubs also foster world cinema and global film culture, since as Valck (2013, 127) has suggested, training programs might be considered to be "sites of initiation" that transcend national borders and are the main nodes for the intense movement toward the internationalization of the industry.

In the Chilean case, we can see an increasing number of film professionals participating in these events, starting in the 2010s with Cannes' exclusive *Cinéfondation*, where several Chilean directors studied until 2012 (Cristián Jiménez, Fernando Guzzoni, and Dominga Sotomayor in 2010, René Ballesteros and Christopher Murray in 2011, and Jairo Bosier in 2012) and more recently with both *Talents Berlin* and *Talents Buenos Aires*, where at least forty other Chilean directors have participated. In addition, film projects by these directors increasingly participate in laboratories in festivals in Europe and Latin America. Their participation has helped enhance Chileans' international social connections, creating transnational social networks and reinforcing some of the filmmaking and business practices developed in other festival spaces, including their sense of belonging to a "global" film culture.

CONCLUSIONS: A "GLOBAL" FIELD OF CULTURAL PRODUCTION

We have seen how the institutional and economic transformations at both the national and global levels have helped restructure the Chilean field of film production, enabled the "global" self-perception of filmmakers and producers, and produced striking changes in contemporary Chilean cinema, including its increasing professionalization and internationalization. The learning process of Chilean filmmakers at the exhibition, industry, and training spaces of international film festivals highlights the ways in which directors and producers have complemented their formal education in Chile, internationalizing their practices and professional networks. The flow of persons and the exchange of films have reaffirmed Chilean filmmakers' agency in film production, legitimizing and expanding their possibilities in the international sphere. Thus, the group of Chilean filmmakers participating in the international circuit has taken up a position in the global field while also transforming the local one, which has itself progressively become a globalized cultural space.

I have suggested that the contemporary Chilean field of film production has been mainly constituted by the accumulation of social, cultural, and symbolic capital by a particular group of Chilean filmmakers, in the form of transnational social networks, film knowledge and education, and international prestige, all of which they have acquired by circulating in the film festival circuit. Social capital has been understood as the sum of the resources that accrue to an individual or group "by virtue of possessing a durable network of more or less institutionalized relationships of mutual acquaintance and recognition" (Bourdieu and Wacquant 1992, 119), such as the transnational professional networks of the international film world that are fostered at film festivals. This accumulation of social capital is intertwined with the accumulation of both cultural and symbolic capital. The first refers to the knowledge and skills that can be objectified in institutionalized forms, such as the educational qualifications given by the festivals' training hubs. The second is understood as prestige that, even when it has not yet been converted into much economic capital (most Chilean filmmakers and producers are not rich, even when they tend to be part of the upper middle class), has been accumulated by Chilean film professionals who have managed to position themselves in the festival circuit, transforming the most recognizable recent Chilean cinema into a global art cinema.

The process has not taken place without some tensions. As Bourdieu suggests, agents are engaged in a permanent struggle to occupy or maintain legitimate positions in artistic fields, and the recent internationalization of Chilean filmmakers' positions, practices, and narratives has opened ongoing debates in the Chilean field. As Chilean professionals move toward internationally oriented narratives and audiences, they are perceived by some journalists and critics as being detached from local audiences, or they are accused of being too focused on elite intellectual audiences with a taste for art cinema. On the other hand, scholars have largely focused on the ambiguous role of international film festivals in the production of this new international Chilean cinema. As "Western" festivals continue to provide cultural legitimization for the acceptable world cinema, and Euro-American funding and training models have a strong influence on international productions, we could ask to what extent peripheral cinema continues to be a global "alternative," and to what extent "international" cinema models shape peripheral production, when filmmakers need to accept the rules of the film festival circuit.

The answer is not straightforward, especially if we believe in filmmakers' agency and deem them to be active learners who can resist and negotiate those structures, even as they benefit from them. Assuming that filmmakers and professionals are not only passive subjects assimilating dominant forms of film production, they can be seen as reflexive participants in the global process who could eventually challenge dominant forms, incorporate local trends in their work, and transform the field. Filmmakers' circulation in the international circuit has allowed them to capitalize on social and cultural resources and professionalize the Chilean field, learning new practices of film production and circulation. How they will use their new capital and collective position to further develop Chilean cinema in the future remains an open question.

NOTES

1. One could also argue that Chilean cinema, like other world cinemas, has influenced the festival circuit as well, by contributing cultural and linguistic diversity to the existing landscape of international cinema. However, in this chapter I focus on the ways in which Chilean filmmakers have been influenced by international patterns, which seems to be the clearer trend in local filmmaking so far.
2. For a detailed analysis of Chilean film production in the last decade, see Ministerio de las Culturas, el Arte y el Patrimonio and Consultora 8A (n.d.), available from www.estadisticascine.cl.
3. For a further analysis of these changes in recent Chilean cinema, see the case of the local reception of the film *No* (Larraín 2012) in Peirano (2018b).
4. See Follows (2013), as well as Turan (2002) and Iordanova and Rhyne (2009).
5. International film festivals that have been accredited by the FIAPF (*Fédération Internationale des Associations de Producteurs de Films*, or International Federation of Film Producers Associations).
6. See https://www.fondosdecultura.cl/wp-content/uploads/2020/01/audiovisual-festivales-2020.pdf for more information about the Chilean government's programs to support the country's filmmakers' participation in international programs.
7. Formerly the MEDIA and Culture Programmes (2007–13) by the European Union's EACEA (Education, Audiovisual and Culture Executive Agency).

WORKS CITED

Becker, Howard. 1982. *Art Worlds*. Berkeley: University of California Press.
Bourdieu, Pierre. 1993. *The Field of Cultural Production: Essays on Art and Literature*. New York: Columbia University Press.
Bourdieu, Pierre, and Loïc Wacquant. 1992. *An Invitation to Reflexive Sociology*. Cambridge: Polity Press.
CAIA, Consejo del Arte y la Industria Audiovisual. 2020. *Fondos de Cultura: Programa de Apoyo para la participación en Festivales, Premios, e Instancias*

Competitivas Internacionales. Santiago: Consejo Nacional de la Cultura y de las Artes. Accessed February 26, 2020. https://www.fondosdecultura.cl/wp-content/uploads/2020/01/audiovisual-festivales-2020.pdf.

Campos, Minerva. 2015. "Film (Co)Production in Latin America and European Festivals." *Zeitschrift Für Kulturmanagement* 1 (1): 95–108.

CinemaChile. 2016. *Audiencias Globales del Cine Chileno 2013*. Santiago de Chile. https://issuu.com/cinema.chile/docs/metricas_2016.

Collier, Stephen, and Aihwa Ong. 2005. "Global Assemblages, Anthropological Problems." In *Global Assemblages: Technology, Politics, and Ethics as Anthropological Problems*, edited by Aihwa Ong and Stephen Collier, 3–21. Oxford: Wiley-Blackwell.

Ďurovičová, Nataša, and Kathleen E. Newman. 2010. *World Cinemas, Transnational Perspectives*. New York: Routledge.

Elsaesser, Thomas. 2005. *European Cinema: Face to Face with Hollywood*. Amsterdam: Amsterdam University Press.

Falicov, Tamara. 2010. "Migrating from South to North: The Role of Film Festivals in Funding and Shaping Global South Film and Video." In *Locating Migrating Media*, edited by Greg Elmer, Charles Davis, Janine Marchessault, and John McCullough, 3–21. Lanham: Lexington Books.

———. 2012. "Programa Ibermedia: ¿Cine Transnacional Iberoamericano o Relaciones Públicas para España?" *Revista Reflexiones* 91 (1): 299–312.

Follows, Stephen. 2013. *How many film festivals are there in the world?* https://stephenfollows.com/many-film-festivals-are-in-the-world/.

Galt, Rosalind, and Karl Schoonover. 2010. *Global Art Cinema: New Theories and Histories*. Oxford: Oxford University Press.

Hannerz, Ulf. 1996. *Transnational Connections: Culture, People, Places*. London: Routledge.

Hjort, Mette, and Duncan Petrie. 2007. *The Cinema of Small Nations*. Edinburgh: Edinburgh University Press.

Iordanova, Dina, David Martin-Jones, and Belén Vidal. 2010. *Cinema at the Periphery*. Detroit: Wayne State University Press.

Iordanova, Dina, and Ragan Rhyne. 2009. *The Festival Circuit*. St. Andrews: St. Andrews Film Studies.

Lampel, Joseph, and Alan Meyer. 2008. "Field-Configuring Events as Structuring Mechanisms: How Conferences, Ceremonies, and Trade Shows Constitute New Technologies, Industries, and Markets." *Journal of Management Studies* 45 (6): 1025–35.

Lorenzen, Mark. 2007. "Internationalization vs. Globalization of the Film Industry." *Industry and Innovation* 14 (4): 349–57.

Ministerio de las Culturas, el Arte y el Patrimonio and Consultora 8A. n.d. *Estudio Oferta y Consumo en Chile 2017*. Accessed January 26, 2019. www.estadisticascine.cl.

Ostrowska, Dorota. 2010. "International Film Festivals as Producers of World Cinema." *Cinema & Cie* 10 (14–15): 145–50.

Peirano, María Paz. 2016. "Pursuing, Resembling and Contesting the Global: The Emergence of Chilean Film Festivals." *New Review of Film and Television Studies* 14 (1): 112–31.

———. 2018a. "Film Mobilities and Circulation Practices in the Construction of Recent Chilean Cinema." In *Envisioning Networked Urban Mobilities: Art, Performances, Impacts*, edited by Aslak Aamot, Sven Kesserling, Peter Peters, and Kevin Hannam. 35–47. New York: Routledge.

———. 2018b. "Larraín's No: A Tale of Neoliberalism." In *Contemporary Latin American Cinema Resisting Neoliberalism?* edited by Claudia Sandberg and Carolina Rocha, 135–52. London: Palgrave Macmillan.

Peranson, Mark. 2009. "First You Get the Power, Then You Get the Money: Two Models of Film Festivals." In *Dekalog 3: On Film Festivals*, edited by Richard Porton, 23–37. London: Wallflower, 2009.

Rodríguez-Isaza, Laura. 2014. "De 'gira' por los festivales: Patrones migratorios del cine latinoamericano." *Secuencias: Revista de Historia del Cine* 39: 65–82.

Ross, Miriam. 2011. "The Film Festival as Producer: Latin American Films and Rotterdam's Hubert Bals Fund." *Screen* 52 (2): 261–67.

Sansi, Roger. 2016. "Afterword: After Utopias." *Cadernos de Arte e Antropologia* 5 (1): 169–75.

Schneider, Arnd. 2006. *Appropriation as Practice: Art and Identity in Argentina*. New York: Palgrave Macmillan.

Shaw, Deborah. 2007. *Contemporary Latin American Cinema: Breaking into the Global Market*. Lanham: Rowman & Littlefield.

Shaw, Lisa, and Stephanie Dennison. 2005. *Latin American Cinema: Essays on Modernity, Gender and National Identity*. Jefferson: McFarland.

Turan, Kenneth. 2002. *Sundance to Sarajevo: Film Festivals and the World They Made*. Berkeley: University of California Press.

Valck, Marijke de. 2007. *Film Festivals: From European Geopolitics to Global Cinephilia*. Amsterdam: Amsterdam University Press.

———. 2013. "Sites of Initiation: Film Training Programs at Film Festivals." In *The Education of the Filmmaker in Europe, Australia, and Asia*, edited by Mette Hjort, 127–45. New York: Palgrave Macmillan.

———. 2014. "Film Festivals, Bourdieu, and the Economization of Culture." *Revue Canadienne D'études Cinématographiques / Canadian Journal of Film Studies* 23 (1): 74–89.

Vallejo, Aida. 2014. "Industry Sections: Documentary Film Festivals between Production and Distribution." *Iluminace: Journal of Film Theory, History, and Aesthetics* 26 (1): 65–82.

Wong, Cindy. 2011. *Film Festivals: Culture, People, and Power on the Global Screen*. New Brunswick: Rutgers University Press.

Wenger, Ètienne. 1998. *Communities of Practice: Learning, Meaning, and Identity*. Cambridge: Cambridge University Press.

2

CENTRIFUGAL CINEMA

Updating and Rereading Chilean Feature Films

Carolina Urrutia Neno

In October 2005, at the Valdivia International Film Festival in Chile, four Chilean films premiered, all representing a radical transformation of the national cinematic landscape. These were works by young directors, many of whom had undertaken formal film studies, who established a generational turnover and renewal in relation to the filmmakers from the nineties. The films featured in that edition of the competition were: *Play* (Alicia Scherson), *En la cama / In Bed* (Matías Bize), *Se arrienda / For Rent* (Alberto Fuguet), and *La sagrada familia / The Sacred Family* (Sebastián Lelio).[1] Their tendency toward a type of cinema that incorporated experimental forms, with unstable, open narratives, a careful recording of temporal flows, and a watchful eye on both the social and political environment and the subjectivity of the characters, has only consolidated itself since then. The *Novísimo Cine Chileno* ("Newest Chilean Cinema"), as some critics called it, was the category into which an increasing number of premieres fit each year.[2] These films had a strong presence in film festivals and premieres in the country, both in commercial theatres and in the independent exhibition circuit; in some cases they received international distribution as well.

This article stems from the observation of certain decisive changes that have emerged regarding what I called "centrifugal cinema" in 2013 (Urrutia Neno 2013): there are several symptomatic elements that account for these metamorphoses (some more evident, others less so) in the Chilean cinema of the past decade. Aesthetic and narrative strategies in fiction films have gone largely unchanged; however, in the plots, I identify more and greater complexities in the films' relationship with the social realm and with the political demands of Chilean citizens. In what follows, I would like to address the changes in Chilean cinema that have taken place since I first used the term "centrifugal cinema," by reviewing the academic and critical publications on the *Novísimo Cine* and by considering the deviations and transformations in current fiction films vis-à-vis those premiered during the first decade of the new millennium.

THEORIES OF CHILEAN CINEMA

The past decade has generated an unprecedented amount of film criticism, led by a group of researchers within the Chilean audiovisual scene who study productions from different fields and perspectives (such as aesthetics, history, literature, philosophy, anthropology, gender studies, communications, and cinema studies itself). Together, these writings cover virtually every period of national cinema, from silent films to the *Novísimo Cine Chileno*. The so-called *Nuevo Cine Chileno* (New Chilean Cinema), made in the sixties and early seventies in dialogue with the larger movement of the *Nuevo Cine Latinoamericano* or New Latin American Cinema, is probably the period that has been written about the most.[3]

There have been many theoretical, critical, and aesthetic studies published in Chile over the past ten years about the *Novísimo Cine Chileno*, this new wave of Chilean filmmakers. In these studies, authors analyze each film's formal techniques and material devices while also examining them from a social and political point of view, particularly in terms of the emergence of new types of characters immersed in profound states of crisis, both internal and external. Critics identify in these films a sort of "fresco" representing today's Chile, in all its political, cultural, and economic difficulties and conflicts, which contextualizes the subjectivity typical of the contemporary world. These critics have analyzed a cast of characters whose emergence has been marked not only by their surroundings (for example, their dealings with their neighbors and others) but also by their subjectivities, desires, frustrations, and affects.

Here, I will briefly focus on four relevant publications from Chile about the country's cinema during the first decade of the millennium, in order to examine how this field of *Novísimo* filmmakers has developed alongside a burgeoning field of critical studies of their films. First of all, the filmmaker and academic Carlos Flores Delpino's master's thesis, published as *Excéntricos y astutos* (2007)[4] anticipated all the studies to come. In his own words: "The hypothesis is that we are standing before a generation that has a notion of the materials it uses; that works on a material. Unlike other, more adult generations, which had a notion of content, this is a generation that works on the material, making it meaningful" ["La hipótesis es que estamos ante una generación que tiene noción de los materiales que usa, que trabaja sobre un material. A diferencia de otra generación más adulta, que tenía noción de los contenidos, esta es una generación que trabaja sobre el material, haciendo que el material tenga sentido"].[5] Flores was the founder and director of the Escuela de Cine de Chile, an institution that trained several filmmakers from this "new wave," including Matías Bize, Sebastián Lelio, Elisa Eliash, and Marialy Rivas. Therefore, the author has privileged the productive and creative processes implicit to the audiovisual medium and the directors that are part of the "B side"[6] of Chilean cinema (a term used by Flores himself), whose unique narrative approaches are organized based on their films' forms and material construction.

Another publication worth mentioning is Carlos Saavedra's *Intimidades desencantadas: La poética cinematográfica de los 2000* (2013).[7] The author selects films he considers to be representative of the time, including *La vida de los peces / The Life of Fish* and *En la cama*, by Matías Bize; *La buena vida / The Good Life* by Andrés Wood; *Se arrienda* by Alberto Fuguet; *Play* by Alicia Scherson; and *Navidad* by Sebastián Lelio. In his research, Saavedra suggests that the cinema made during the first decade of this century displays the Chilean society of the time, immersed in a neoliberal economy that narratively and stylistically lends itself to the characters' inward-lookingness and disenchantment. The author contrasts contemporary Chilean cinema, for which his dislike is obvious, with the films of the seventies, in which "the subjects sense the presence of a collective history and refuse to be indifferent to it." Meanwhile, "the current works have a more skeptical view about this issue, showing that turning inward is not a solution or a valid response, since the characters have neither goals nor models" ["los sujetos sienten la presencia de una historia colectiva y no son indiferentes a su marcha. . . . las obras actuales nos plantean una mirada escéptica sobre esta cuestión y a la vez, muestran que el repliegue personal no es una solución o respuesta, pues es notorio que los personajes no tienen referentes ni proyectos"] (Saavedra 2013, 18). The disenchantment implicit in this title is not only a reference to the state of the characters; it also has to do with the author's attitude toward the films he has chosen to study.

In 2017, Antonella Estévez published *Una gramática de la melancolía cinematográfica: La modernidad y el no duelo en cierto cine contemporáneo* (2017),[8] which takes up *Lucía* (2010) by Niles Atallah, *Il futuro / The Future* (2013) by Alicia Scherson, *Sentados frente al fuego / By the Fire* (2011) by Alejandro Fernández Almendras, and *Las cosas como son / Things the Way They Are* (2012) by Fernando Lavanderos. Here, she analyzes the second or third films of some of the directors whose first productions came out in 2005, to examine how they have followed up on their initial work. Estévez does this by using the concept of melancholia that, in her opinion, manifests itself in their movies in a grammatical (rather than plot-related) way. She writes: "It seems to me that many of the films made in the past decade have certain melancholic resources in their construction, but the four chosen here are good examples of films built from narrative motifs that we will recognize as melancholic" ["Me parece que muchas de las películas desarrolladas en la última década poseen recursos melancólicos en su construcción, pero que las cuatro escogidas dan buenos ejemplos de películas que están armadas a partir de motivos narrativos que reconoceremos como melancólicos"] (17). Subsequently, she stipulates that melancholy is understood as "an exit strategy for the unmentionable, for something we cannot talk about, for that which is elusive, which is a product of the superficiality of our social relationships, and which finds an outlet using cinematic methods" ["una estrategia de salida para aquello innombrable, aquello de lo que no se puede hablar, lo inasible, que es producto de la superficialidad de nuestras relaciones sociales y que encuentran posibilidades de salida a través de estas maneras cinematográficas"] (18).

Another fundamental publication is by Pablo Corro, who writes about Chilean cinema's "poéticas débiles" ["weak poetics"]. His book *Retóricas del cine chileno: Ensayos con el realismo* (2012)[9] focuses on films where the scale of representation drops to an everyday level, and where there is, in the words of the author, "a progressive interest in trifling storylines, of insignificant affairs" ["un interés progresivo por los argumentos de menudencias, de asuntos insignificantes"] (217). This is a short yet important text for understanding certain defining categories of contemporary national cinema in the context of Latin American film production. It is an essay that, unlike the rest, not only attends to fiction films but also to documentary, and to films that carve out an intermediate space between both formats.

Finally, in *Un cine centrífugo: Ficciones chilenas 2005 a 2010* (Urrutia Neno 2013),[10] I chose a corpus of fourteen Chilean feature films—including, but not limited to, the work of Alicia Scherson, Cristián Jiménez, José Luis Torres Leiva, José "Ché" Sandoval, Alejandro Fernández Almendras, and Pablo Larraín—in order to map the national cinematic landscape. My analysis was based on four categories: *Margin and Periphery, The Misalignments of Memory, Urban Poetics*, and *Subject and Territory*. I studied a corpus of Chilean films that propose a particular poetics for approaching the world. First, I defined the theoretical guidelines at the foundation of the concept of "centrifugal cinema." This cinema is different from mainstream filmmaking, understood as Hollywood productions whose scripts are often governed by action and reaction, cause and effect, and clear character motivations. Our film corpus was instead characterized by the banishment of "certain narrative, storyline and aesthetic assumptions made by the Chilean cinema of the nineties, in order to settle into new, unexplored territories that, in our opinion, are poetically, aesthetically and linguistically rich" ["ciertos presupuestos narrativos, argumentales y estéticos que instituyó el cine chileno de los años 90, para instalarse-en la actualidad-en territorios nuevos, inexplorados y, a nuestro parecer, poética, estética y lingüísticamente, enriquecidos"] (Urrutia Neno 2013, 13). Within this framework, the two volumes of Deleuze's *Cinema* (1986, 1989) were useful in establishing a contrast between the movement-image, used for understanding classic films, and the time-image, and the influence of this contrast on contemporary Chilean cinema of a more personal, essayistic, and experimental nature. These spatial and temporal categories, always blurred in the films of Torres Leiva, Fernández Almendras, Sepúlveda, and Adriazola, meant that the forms of realism that these directors used were constructed—to use the characteristics of the "centrifugal"—through a direct, although more inward-looking, relationship with the formal coordinates that some directors from the New Latin American, and particularly Chilean, cinemas had already proposed. Like the aforementioned studies (carried out over less than a decade, albeit with somewhat divergent perspectives), *Un cine centrífugo* observed the representation and visibility of the affects, which seemed omnipresent in cinematic spaces, contexts, and scenarios from 2005 onward. These affects tinge the films with melancholia and disenchantment (to use the terms of Estévez and Saavedra), charging the atmosphere with an opacity that allows the progressive alienation of the characters to be staged vis-à-vis the social dynamics of the country; this representation of the affects seems to operate as a walled-in landscape that is permanently on the verge of collapse.[11]

In synthesis, we observe that in aesthetic terms, *Novísimo* Chilean cinema is defined in opposition to the previous cinematographic period—the cinema of the transition to democracy[12]—which developed during the nineties and extended into the first years of the twenty-first century. This cinema which can be characterized, in broad strokes, by an aesthetic linked to the field of advertising, given that many of the director had come from the advertising world. These earlier films also adhered to more classical narrative codes usually inscribed in genre cinema (mainly action, suspense, and comedy), and many featured marginal characters and criminals such as thieves and drug dealers.[13] As a detour from this trend, the new generation of *Novísimo* filmmakers created a more contemplative, more intimate, and more aesthetically and narratively experimental cinema. This cinema, according to the various aforementioned authors, included a turn toward the intimate, without clear plotting. Its representation of social conflicts was largely dormant, and when it did address sociopolitical issues, it did so from a sidelong perspective, or placed them largely in the background.

At present, however, we note a transition in the poetics of the *Novísimo* generation, toward a much more explicit focus on the social and political situation of contemporary Chile. The work of two Chilean filmmakers in particular, Alejandro Fernández Almendras and Pablo Larraín, illustrates this shift from a conventionally *Novísimo* cinema (contemplative, intimate, and only obliquely related to current events), to one that focuses on current social issues, tensions with the past, and a reflection upon persistent social ills in our country. This shift is evident in Alejandro Fernández Almendras's *Huacho*, from 2009, and *Sentados frente al fuego*, from 2011, and Pablo Larraín's trilogy *Tony Manero*, *Post Mortem*, and *NO*, made between 2008 and 2012. In these films, Larraín brings the era of the military dictatorship back to the present, using formal strategies to represent the collective imagination of a traumatic past and efficiently display the ruins left by the dictatorship in the country. These directors establish a transition toward contemporary cinema, redirecting their previously inward-facing gaze toward the (real) social sphere. Their work no longer addresses the world in which it is inserted in a centrifugal manner, but rather addresses it from a centripetal and central perspective, by engaging with the present and documenting the problems and crises of contemporary Chile.

NOVÍSIMO FILMMAKERS AFTER THE NOVÍSIMO: MATAR A UN HOMBRE

In the context of Chilean filmmaking today, I believe that Alejandro Fernández Almendras is central.[14] His work is illustrative of a possible transition from *Novísimo* Chilean cinema—a category in which his films *Huacho* and *Sentados frente al fuego* would seem to fit—to a more political cinema made in dialogue with the issues of the day. His film *Aquí no ha pasado nada / Much Ado About Nothing* (2016) is paradigmatic of the latter. Here, I will discuss an earlier film, *Matar a un hombre / To Kill a Man* (2014), and the ways in which it directly appropriates current social and political conflicts in anticipation of a more realistic project. The film, Fernández Almendras's third, begins with a close-up that introduces a suspenseful atmosphere. A melody with threatening tones can be heard, and we see a leafy forest, dramatically illuminated by the sun that shines through the treetops, articulating a poetic play between light and shadow (Figure 1). In the center of the landscape, we see the figure of a man walking away with his back turned to us. The sequence is built from a fixed shot where the only movement is that of the man walking slowly, until he is lost in the thickness of nature. Then the shot is interrupted, and we see the credits. Taking up the whole screen, they announce the title: *Matar a un hombre* ("To Kill a Man").

In the film, Fernández Almendras introduces us to Jorge (Daniel Candia), a married father of two teenage sons. The story starts out by showing Jorge's daily routine (his diabetes treatments, his daily commute, and his stop at the supermarket to buy a birthday cake). This is synthesized in the opening minutes, only to be interrupted by Jorge's mugging by a group of

Figure 1. Light and shadow in *Matar a un hombre / To Kill a Man* (Alejandro Fernández Almendras, 2014).

violent criminals who live in his neighborhood and intimidate, rob, and rape its residents while under the influence of alcohol and drugs. That starting point will forever disturb the story of Jorge and his family: the affective ties that bind them, their everyday life, and their evolution. It throws him into an absolute state of vulnerability that no institution can help. Although he reports the abuses, society seems to abandon him and his family, leaving them helpless and humiliated. They must await a solution from the judicial system and the police. The camera stays with the family, insistently recording their waiting and their fears. It makes spectators uncomfortable, establishing a point of view where violence is not visually or psychologically enjoyable (as it might be portrayed in other films) but rather full of conflict and aggression. We accompany the main character and his family in this permanent state of physical and psychological suffering. I thus propose that *Matar a un hombre* bridges two types of poetics of contemporary Chilean cinema, moving from a formal realism to another kind of realism anchored in the social issues of today's Chile. Indeed, Fernandez's next film, *Aquí no ha pasado nada*, abandons conventional realism (which can be seen in the three earlier films) in favor of a realism that becomes evident only through explicit references to the news story that the film represents and reflects upon.

Fernández Almendras maintains the same aesthetic and concerns throughout his four movies. Still, he seems to be slowly distancing himself from the pure realism that characterized his debut feature, *Huacho*, which was structured around extensive shots that followed nonprofessional actors through southern Chile, fictionalizing their lives and their stories. In contrast, *Aquí no ha pasado nada*, which premiered in 2016, was inspired by a real event that was extensively covered by the media.[15] Here, he uses professional and well-known actors and shifts the focus away from the popular classes and onto the wealthiest people in the country, effectively showing the ways in which children repeat their parents' vices.

On the whole, Fernández Almendras's filmography reflects upon the social ills of this century in a country marked by class conflicts. All of his films present an interesting meditation on what is "real" through the representation of news and facts, the politicization of forms, and the strains of unavoidable, rampant social inequality in terms of both reality and representation. Fernández Almendras thus brings a critical, reflexive view to a sector of Chile that has otherwise been forgotten by social representation. In this way, his work goes hand in hand with social protests that reconfigure an increasingly politicized and multitudinous society. This is characteristic of how Chilean filmmakers, particularly since 2012, have been making fiction out of the real, taking overarching themes and situations that are present in the country's political and journalistic agenda and using them to construct a cinema that is anchored in the real.

The shift toward the subjective that occurred within the context of a more nihilistic and melancholic *Novísimo Cine Chileno* developed a new twist around 2012. We might call this a return to realism, not necessarily in the sense in which the theory of cinema has historically understood it, but rather vis-à-vis a *reintegration* with realism shaped by news events and television reports. Indeed, narrative films moved from a state of malaise and discontent to a strong degree of outrage infinitely reproduced through social media. These features do not completely deviate from the disenchantment of the first *Novísimo* movement, nor from the poetics identified as centrifugal. Rather, they distance themselves from direct confrontation with viewers through their plots and through storylines that reflect the historical conflicts of Chilean society (and in many cases, Latin American society as well) even as they maintain a decentralized aesthetic and a narrative approach. Thus, an important corpus of films has emerged in which the categories proposed for reading the centrifugal or *Novísimo* cinema seem insufficient. The current trend powerfully echoes what we might call "social reality": aside from being inspired by current topics and events, it reflects upon the present, analyzing it but also mirroring it, without abandoning the subjective gaze proper to the filmography initiated in 2005.

NEW REALISMS IN CONTEMPORARY CHILEAN CINEMA: ON *RARA* AND *JESÚS*

The concept of realism is complex and perhaps not completely adequate for my purposes here, considering that it largely surpasses the field of cinematography, to philosophy, fine arts, and literature. If we limit ourselves to realism in film studies, we would have to mention André Bazin, a theorist of Italian neorealism who refers to an "adhesion to reality," a sort of participation in it that allows for the configuration of an ontological realism.[16] Then we would have to subsequently expand to other theorists, both European and American, such as Siegfried Kracauer, Jens Andermann, Ángel Quintana, and Bill Nichols, the latter of whom focuses on the documentary.

Here, I will speculate about the possibility of a new realism in contemporary Chilean cinema by updating the discourses of the subject, that is, by preliminarily defining a realism that contemplates some of the formalisms, stylistic resources, and operations of realist cinema. These strategies include the use of the sequence shot and depth of field, the depiction of real cities, and the use of nonprofessional actors in order to show the "common man." I will stretch this concept in order to address an important trend in Chilean cinema: the narration of cases inspired by actual events, the likes of which we have continued to observe since *Aquí no ha pasado nada*. These recent and outrageous national developments are covered in the news media and are the object of many opinions in social media. As "political events," they have resulted in the great social movements and mobilizations that have taken place in Chile in the second decade of this century.[17] Chilean filmmakers now have a greater personal engagement with the present, and their work addresses particular events and political, social, and environmental conflicts. They offer new ways of representing violence and tensions, and of reinterpreting the past by filtering what overflows into the present. In the preface of his book, Corro writes that

> the filmmakers are the ones who rehearse realism. Their practices result from the conscious and unconscious appropriations of formal schemas for treating the current and immediate historical reality, from the exhibition of subjectivity as a reality of biography, to forms of argumentation, to resources for simulating external events of collective stimulation, to inner experiences of consciousness, to ailments of corporeality, to dominant figurations of the landscape or the natural world. [son los cineastas los que ensayan con el realismo. Sus prácticas resultan de las apropiaciones conscientes o inconscientes de esquematismos formales para el tratamiento de la realidad histórica actual e inmediata, de la exposición de la subjetividad, como realidad de la biografía, de formas de argumentación, de recusos de simulación de acontecimientos exteriores de estimulación colectiva, de vivencias interiores de consciencia, de padecimientos de la corporeidad, de figuraciones dominantes del paisaje o del mundo natural.] (2012, 15–16)

Corro's take is relevant because, in this corpus, we can observe not one but many ways of "rehearsing" realism in the context of Chilean cinema.

These contemporary fiction films deviate somewhat from the topics established in the filmography initially designated as "centrifugal," in order to address certain topics that concern our current society, while showing points of view and specific situations in a socially and politically realistic and reflective way. To quote Fredric Jameson (1990), realism here implies the possibility of knowledge: "We may expect, therefore, the moment in which this conviction of the possibility of aesthetic knowledge appears (however we decide to evaluate it) to have something significant and symptomatic to tell us about its own unique historical opening and situation, which is evidently no longer our own" (158). Meanwhile, Giorgio Agamben (2008) asks what it means to be contemporary, and what we are contemporaries *of*. He thinks of contemporary subjects in relation to how they insert themselves in a particular era and how they are inscribed in the present: "[t]he contemporary is he who firmly holds his gaze on his own time so as to perceive not its light but rather its darkness. All eras, for those who experience contemporariness, are dark" [el contemporáneo es aquel que percibe la oscuridad de su tiempo como algo que le concierne y no deja de interpelarlo, algo que, más que toda luz, se dirige directamente a él. Contemporáneo es aquel que recibe en pleno rostro el haz de tiniebla que proviene de su tiempo] (3). This position of cohesion with the contemporary seems to be embedded in the "darkness" dragged along by the present, which manifests itself in different ways in the various periods of Chilean cinema. We suggest that in current Chilean cinema there is a certain taste for that darkness, in a configuration of the contemporary that sifts through the past with a permanent and growing discomfort. The contemporary aspect of this cinema is held in the possibility of representing the present from a perspective that has captured the trajectory of a turbulent history.

From another perspective, we could also speak about Mark Fisher's "capitalist realism" (2008) and see some of the signs described by the author as being present in a certain global cinema that is mostly disconnected from more classic models of representation.[18] Indeed, "realism" may not be the most appropriate term, particularly when thinking about it from the perspective of Bazin, for describing this ever-evolving corpus of films. However, it is possible to articulate, based on the concepts and theorists mentioned here, a form of realism that manifests itself in Chilean film in particular. While this approach contains certain formal aspects of historical realism, it is also related to the intention of observing reality to problematize it, nuance it, and ask questions about it, particularly vis-à-vis the ways in which Chileans live on a day-to-day basis.

We can observe a shift of emphasis in Chile's growing cinematographic field, with the *Novísimo* filmmakers now premiering their third, fourth, or fifth films, all increasingly internationalized and part of a progressively consolidated film industry.[19] Although in formal terms the aesthetics in place since 2005 remain present (staging the figuration of a personal, subjective imagination that seeks to become collective), it is in the area of subject matter where the films are transforming, in order to directly allude to conflicts inherent to our society. When I initially analyzed centrifugal Chilean cinema in 2013, I observed a stripped-down aesthetic that took over the forms and topics, completely dissociating them from the filmography of the nineties. Before that, it had been easy to find moralizing or didactic perspectives for the spectator. For example, films like *Caluga o menta / El Niki* (Gonzalo Justiniano, 1990) and *Johnny 100 pesos* (Gustavo Graef Marino, 1993) portrayed the social crisis in Chile following the end of the military dictatorship in a clear, obvious way. Conversely, the *Novísimo* filmmakers dealt with the political realm as an off-camera phenomenon that led, for example, to their characters' discontentment and apathy. Everyday life was represented through the recording of routines, wanderings, transits, moments of leisure, and contemplation. That is the case, for example, in films like *Turistas / Tourists* (Alicia Scherson), *La sagrada familia* (Sebastián Lelio), *Huacho* (Alejandro Fernández Almendras), and *Lucía* (Niles Atallah). All of these films outline, as we suggested in *Un cine centrífugo*, a shift from the political toward a subjective place of enunciation where social crises were part of the story lines but did not constitute their core.

Today, however, the trend[20] in contemporary cinema is to observe reality by using fictional forms (or sometimes by hybridizing documentary techniques with those of fiction cinema), from the personal perspectives of directors, and project a collective conflict. This is not a form of denunciation (as one might say about the New Latin American Cinema) but rather it takes place using a complex subjectivity that tries to poetically appeal to the political universe of the spectators. Here, we are referring not only to *Aquí no ha pasado nada* but also to *Rara* (Pepa San Martín, 2016), *Volantín cortao / Kite Adrift* (Aníbal Jofré and Diego Ayala, 2013), *El club / The Club* (Pablo Larraín, 2015), and *Jesús* (Fernando Guzzoni, 2016).[21] These films are all inspired by various recent real-life situations and social conflicts. Respectively, they address: the case of a judge denied custody of her daughters by the Chilean state for being a lesbian (*Rara*); the case of inhumane conditions and abuses in Chile's SENAME, the National Service for Minors (*Volantín cortao*); the case of a group of priests from the Catholic Church who have committed abuses (*El club*); and the case of a gay adolescent who was brutally beaten to death by a group of drunk youngsters in a Santiago park (*Jesús*).[22] Although the true stories on which these films are based are local, they represent situations that unfortunately are hardly unique to Chile. Discrimination, homophobia, and priest sexual abuse are all international issues, and these films appeal to a global imaginary as much as to a local one. Indeed, this tension between the local and the global is what has made these films successful in different film festivals around the world.

Even though documentaries have always been able to record political events and social changes, fiction cinema—following a trajectory that begins with Italian neorealism[23]—is strongly capable of reflecting on the real. In light of Ángel Quintana's proposal that "[i]f we consider film as a fictional discourse with fundamental importance as a testimony of its time, we can start to ask ourselves a series of fundamental questions about how the different crises of thought have defined the discourses of fiction in a specific period" ["Si consideramos el cine como un discurso de ficción que posee una importancia fundamental como testimonio de su tiempo, podemos comenzar a plantearnos una serie de cuestiones fundamentales sobre el modo en que las diferentes crisis del pensamiento han determinado los discursos de ficción en un determinado periodo"] (2003, 265), we can reflect on fiction film. It transforms, adjusts to our time, mirrors and reflects different perspectives and emphases, and educates the eye in its modes of seeing, imagining, and critically considering past and present history.

To take up the poetics established in the *Novísimo* Chilean Cinema once again, the cinematographic accounts seem to operate from a logic of subtraction; the forms of realism are considered pensive and propositional, without adhering to specific discourses, but rather as expanded, open possibilities for reading. In contemporary films, even if a defined, centripetal core exists (in which the plot revolves around the particular event summoned by the movie), the plot itself becomes lost in trivialities, idle moments, observations, and transits that do not necessarily coincide with the development of the action.

The aforementioned films and filmmakers intervene in a reality that has also been modified by the media. As spectators, we do not know exactly how things really happened; the version proposed by the media is the starting point. That which is turned into fiction is not reality but rather always already a representation of it; a fiction of the fiction is a way of entering the contextualized reality. For example, *Jesús* is inspired by true events: a young gay man, Daniel Zamudio, was beaten by a group of drunken young people in a central Santiago park; he was left unconscious and died a few days later. The case that inspired this film was particularly notorious, not only due to the brutality of the act and the prominence it obtained in the Chilean press and public opinion but also because it enabled the passage of a national antidiscrimination law.[24] These films, interestingly, do not attempt to capture a particular reality so much as they simply nuance one that already exists. Unlike feature films that maintain a documentary aesthetic to remain in the realm of the real, these films propose a critical representation of reality from a clearly political dimension, given that they can potentially influence laws, popular opinion, and the agenda of the media.

There are two films that illustrate this tendency toward what we might call a "new realism" in Chilean cinema today, both post-*Novísimo* and postcentrifugal. It is necessary to reflect on the point of view chosen by the filmmaker in *Jesús*, where the main character is not the victim but rather one of the aggressors. Something similar happens with the film *Rara*: the main character is not the lesbian judge whose children are taken from her by an extremely conservative state and her ex-husband but, on the contrary, the oldest daughter, a twelve-year-old who feels "rara" (strange or different), not because her mother is a lesbian but because she herself is entering puberty. Her body is changing, and her desires and her vision are changing along with it. The film enters the conflict from a child's perspective, a world that unfolds on a different scale, in which no caption or initial explanation is presented that might cue us in to a specific context and problem, but rather we remain on the edge of the perceptual, the subjective, the emotional, and the ordinary.

These are films in which reality overflows, not from an objective camera that records a particular event but rather by entering into specific, recognizable stories, surpassing the possibilities for enunciating concrete realities. The events that trigger the films are central yet also tangential. There is an emphasis on subjective shots, where affects and emotions interweave with the events of the story (on or off camera). Just like in the *Novísimo Cine Chileno*, something intimate and private is displayed. In the case of *Jesús*, what happened in 2012 is only the starting point of the film. However, the beating overflows into many other topics that are just as important: the institution of the family, sexual identity, popular culture, emptiness, and banality. The filmmaker takes on what is dark in the story, not to make it clearer but to insist on its darkness. There are no possible answers. Nothing is clearly explained. The centrifugal component of the narrative thus remains: the action is omnipresent throughout the story, but the narration does not conclude or close. The endings are left open, the conflicts unresolved, and the characters end up in a place similar to where they were at the beginning.

Rara is analogous to *Jesús* in this sense: the final shot of the film embraces a profound melancholy that makes us think about the end of childhood. The mother rides in the front seat of the car with her girlfriend, and the two sisters ride in the back with the cat, the suitcases and everything else piled up. They are on their way to the father's house, where the daughters are now going to live, and there is silence. The mother cries while she drives. When the camera focuses on the main character looking out the window as the car stops outside the father's house, the film is interrupted, and the credits begin (Figure 2). It is a sad ending, and spectators unaware of the case that inspired the filmmaker might think that this is the beginning of a relatively brief period of separation. However, the press reports tell us that the family's fracture will be permanent: the mother will not get her daughters back until they are adults, and the relationship, intimacy, and complicity of that particular family is permanently broken.

Figure 2. Melancholy and the end of childhood, in *Rara* (Pepa San Martín, 2016).

These are not feature films in the most conventional sense (if a distinction between fiction and documentary is still worth making at this point). The documentary and its intermediate formats (experimental films, for example)[25] also resort to speculation about the social realm in order to aesthetically reconfigure the world and narrate politics differently, powerfully seizing upon the social changes that Chile is undertaking (albeit too slowly).[26] If centrifugal cinema was about discontentment, contemporary cinema is outraged by a disgraceful present, representing the ways in which events affect or disrupt the everyday life of the people experiencing them. In response, they adopt a state of suspicion, violence, and darkness, with no apparent exit. So when carefully analyzing the new films of Chilean cinema, we see that the centrifugal forces become centripetal and the conflicts that were prominent in theorizations of the *Novísimo Cine Chileno* are now presented as powerful centers of gravity.

NOTES

1 When a Chilean film is distributed in an English-language market and its title has been translated by the distributor, I initially provide the English-language title in italics. Otherwise, I translate the original titles into English and enclose them in quotation marks.

2 The *Novísimo Cine Chileno* was the term for a group of feature films that came out in Chile around the year 2005. It comes from the eponymous book, edited by Ascanio Cavallo and Gonzalo Maza (2011), in which twenty-one film scholars and critics wrote about twenty-one filmmakers whose work was, in their opinion, characteristic of the new millennium. Other *Novísimo* filmmakers profiled included Pablo Larraín, Cristián Jiménez, José Luis Sepúlveda, Carolina Adriazola, Elisa Eliash, Christopher Murray, and Pablo Carrera, among others. The criteria for selecting the filmmakers in the book was based on the generational turnover they enacted, as well as on the fact that their work was more auteurist. The *Novísimo* filmmakers whose work was considered most experimental and removed from the bounds of classical narration were Niles Atallah (*Lucía*, 2010) and José Luis Torres Leiva (*Verano*, 2011). On the other hand, the *Novísimo* filmmaker most associated with a markedly genre cinema, aligned with classical models of representation, was Ernesto Díaz Espinoza (director of films such as *Kiltro*, *Mirageman*, and *Tráiganme la cabeza de la mujer metralleta / Bring Me the Head of the Machine Gun Woman*).

3 Regarding this topic, I recommend two studies: "Mapa de los estudios de cine en Chile (2005–2015)," a research study led by Marcela Parada, a faculty member at the Catholic University of Chile (available at http://www.estudiosencine.cl),

and the article "Escritos sobre cine chileno. Un estado del asunto" by Carolina Urrutia Neno, published in *VI Panorama del audiovisual chileno* (available at http://comunicaciones.uc.cl/wp-content/uploads/comunicaciones/2017/12/VI-Panorama-del-Audiovisual-Chileno-ilovepdf-compressed-2.pdf).

4 This title roughly translates as "Eccentric and Astute."

5 See www.artes.uchile.cl/noticias/42035/carlos-flores-editara-su-tesis-excentricos-y-astutos. Unless otherwise noted, this and all other translations here are my own.

6 He said this in an interview conducted in 2007, before the success experienced by filmmakers like Sebastián Lelio and Matías Bize, who underwent a gradual process of internationalization that is presently culminating with the Oscar awarded to Lelio's film *Una mujer fantástica / A Fantastic Woman* for Best Foreign Language Film. Therefore, it is interesting how this "B side" turns into an "A side" in just a few years. A crop of B movies that came out in Chile during the first decade of the twenty-first century was made in opposition to a more commercial, genre-based cinema being made at the time, with films such as *Sexo con amor / Sex with Love* (Boris Quercia, 2003), *Los debutantes / The Debutantes* (Andrés Waisbluth, 2003), and even *Machuca* (Andrés Wood, 2004).

7 This title roughly translates as "Disenchanted Intimacies: The Cinematic Poetics of the 2000s."

8 This title roughly translates as "A Grammar of Cinematic Melancholia: Modernity and the Refusal to Mourn in Contemporary Cinema."

9 This title roughly translates as "Rhetorics of Chilean Cinema: Rehearsing Realism."

10 This title roughly translates as "A Centrifugal Cinema: Chilean Fiction Films from 2005 to 2010."

11 In *Un cine centrífugo*, I suggested that the film that most clearly anticipated this model of representation born in 2005 (in terms of style, experimental narrative, and the hybridization of fiction with documentary) was *Y las vacas vuelan / And Cows Fly* (Fernando Lavanderos, 2004). The story inserts reflective moments—through a voice-over in which the main character externalizes the flow of thought of a European foreigner, who describes and questions how contemporary Chileans inhabit and engage with what's around them—but also the self-reflectiveness of cinematic work, given that it proposes the filming of an impossible short film within the film after the main character leaves the set halfway through production.

12 See Cavallo, Douzet, and Rodríguez (1999).

13 These films include *Caluga o menta / El Niki* (Gonzalo Justiniano, 1991); *Johnny 100 pesos* (Gustavo Graef Marino, 1993); *Taxi para tres / A Cab for*

Three (Orlando Lübbert, 2001), and *Los debutantes / The Debutantes* (Andrés Waissbluth, 2003).

14 See my article (2019) on Fernández Almendras's body of work.

15 The film refers to the case of Martín Larraín, the son of a right-wing, conservative senator, who ran over and killed a pedestrian while driving drunk on a highway in southern Chile. Following two trials, Larraín was acquitted of all charges.

16 For more discussion of Bazin, see Casetti (2005).

17 The first administration of president Sebastián Piñera, which began in 2010, brought about large-scale political protests, particularly among students, who demanded free, quality education as a way of remediating the country's major social inequalities. Although these had begun as student protests in 2006, these demonstrations returned in 2011 and then reached their apex in late 2019, focusing on issues that ranged from the social to the ecological, economic, and political. My contention is that the transformations in the cinema of this period are reflective of the social convulsions underway in the country.

18 "The power of capitalist realism derives in part from the way that capitalism subsumes and consumes all of previous history" (Fisher 2008, 4).

19 I say this based on quantitative growth in the number of films produced and increasing recognition of Chilean films in international markets and film festivals.

20 We are facing a tendency among possible ways of producing local cinema: there is a diverse corpus of films, and those identified here represent only a fragment of the total number of fiction films and documentaries premiered each year, both in movie theaters and in national and foreign festivals.

21 We mention a small handful within a greater corpus that includes around twenty feature films that premiered from 2012 until the present.

22 We insist that the corpus of premiered films, inspired by real events and conflicts, exceeds the ones mentioned here. Just to name some films that appear adversarial and in conflict with the present: *La visita / The Guest* (Mauricio López, 2015); *El bosque de Karadima / "The Parish of Karadima"* (Matías Lira; 2015); *Mala junta / Bad Influence* (Claudia Huaiquimilla, 2016); *Una mujer fantástica* (Sebastián Lelio, 2017); *El Tila, fragmentos de un psicópata / Inside the Mind of a Psychopath* (Alejandro Torres, 2015); *Princesita* (Marialy Rivas, 2017); *Niñas araña / Spider Thieves* (Guillermo Helo, 2016); and *Naomi Campbel* (Camila José Donoso and Nicolás Videla, 2013).

23 By the late 1960s, Italian neorealism had become a major ethical and aesthetic reference point in Latin America. It modeled ways of representing poverty,

24   misery, hunger, and social inequality in the different countries of the region. See, for more information, León Frías (2013).

24   The Daniel Zamudio case inspired two feature films (*Nunca vas a estar solo / You'll Never Be Alone*, by Alex Anwandter [2016], and *Jesús*, by Fernando Guzzoni [2017], as well as a TV miniseries: *Solos en la noche*, by Ignacio Sabatini [2017]). Another case relevant to this discussion is the fact that *Una mujer fantástica* by Sebastián Lelio won Chile's first Foreign Language Film Oscar in March 2018, at the same time that the law on gender identity became a central focus of political discussion in the country after languishing in obscurity for quite a while.

25   These include films like *11 de septiembre* (Claudia Aravena, 2002), *Undocumented* (Edgar Endress, 2004), and *El vals de los inútiles / The Waltz* (Edison Cajas, 2013), among other various examples.

26   In the documentary field, the shift from autobiographical documentaries "by the children" (Macarena Aguiló's *El edificio de los chilenos / The Chilean Building*, 2010) to documentaries where the authors are the relatives of aggressors (Orlando Lübbert's *El color del camaleón / The Color of the Chameleon*, 2017, and Lizette Orozco's *El pacto de Adriana / Adriana's Pact*, 2017) is interesting.

WORKS CITED

Agamben, Giorgio. 2008. "¿Qué es lo contemporáneo?" Translated by Ariel Pennisi. Fundación Paiz. https://archive.org/stream/agamben-que-es-lo-contemporaneo/agamben-que-es-lo-contemporaneo_djvu.txt.

Casseti, Francesco. 2005. *Teorías del cine*. Madrid: Cátedra.

Cavallo, Ascanio, and Gonzalo Maza. 2011. *El novísimo cine chileno*. Santiago de Chile: Uqbar.

Cavallo, Ascanio, Pablo Douzet, and Cecilia Rodríguez. 1999. *Huérfanos y perdidos: Relectura del cine chileno de la transición 1990–1999*. Santiago de Chile: Uqbar.

Corro, Pablo. 2012. *Retóricas del cine chileno: Ensayos con el realismo*. Santiago de Chile: Cuarto Propio.

Deleuze, Gilles. 1986. *Cinema 1: The Movement-Image*. Translated by Hugh Tomlinson and Barbara Habberjam. Minneapolis: University of Minnesota Press.

———. 1989. *Cinema 2: The Time-Image*. Translated by Hugh Tomlinson and Robert Galeta. Minneapolis: University of Minnesota Press.

Estévez, Antonella. 2017. *Una gramática de la melancolía cinematográfica: La modernidad y el no duelo en cierto cine chileno contemporáneo*. Santiago: Editorial Radio Universidad de Chile.

Fisher, Mark. 2008. *Capitalist Realism: Is There No Alternative?* Alresford, U.K.: Zero Books.

Flores Delpino, Carlos. 2007. *Excéntricos y astutos*. Santiago: Ediciones Universidad de Chile.
Jameson, Fredric. 1990. *Signatures of the Visible*. New York and London: Routledge.
León Frías, Isaac. 2013. *El Nuevo Cine Latinoamericano de los años sesenta: Entre el mito político y la modernidad fílmica*. Lima: Fondo Editorial.
Parada, Marcela. 2016. *Mapa de los estudios de cine en Chile (2005–2015)*. At http://www.estudiosencine.cl.
Quintana, Ángel. 2003. *Fábulas de lo visible: El cine como creador de realidades*. Barcelona: El acantilado.
Saavedra, Carlos. 2013. *Intimidades desencantadas: La poética cinematográfica de los 2000*. Santiago de Chile: Cuarto Propio.
Urrutia Neno, Carolina. 2013. *Un cine centrífugo: Ficciones chilenas 2005 a 2010*. Santiago de Chile: Cuarto Propio.
———. 2017. "Escritos sobre cine chileno, un estado del asunto (2000 a 2017)." In *VI Panoramas de audiovisual*, 121–38. Santiago de Chile: Facultad de Comunicaciones, Pontificia Universidad Católica de Chile.
———. 2019. "Variaciones del realismo en el cine chileno contemporáneo: Las películas de Alejandro Fernández Almendras." *Comunicación y medios* 39 (1): 98–108.

3
POLITICAL AND AFFECTIVE SHIFTS IN THE CONTEMPORARY CHILEAN DOCUMENTARY

Paola Lagos Labbé
Translated by Patrick G. Blaine and Carl Fischer

The author would like to thank Dr. Pablo Piedras and Dr. Andrea Molfetta, both researchers at CONICET, for their generous collaboration and suggestions on contemporary Argentine and Brazilian documentaries mentioned in this chapter.

The historical, political, and social trajectory of Chile in the second half of the twentieth century resulted in the relationships between documentary filmmaking and politics being dominated less by concerns about narrative content than by the crises in the very systems of representation and aesthetic regimes out of which the films were arising. For decades, in Chile and much of Latin America, the term "political documentary" was associated with combat, belonging, social commitment, situations of misery and underdevelopment, and political activism. Amidst a postmodern crisis of *grandes récits*, however, cinema—alongside other disciplinary fields such as history, sociology, psychology, literature, the arts, and human sciences in general—has turned to memory and subjectivity in the late twentieth and early twenty-first centuries.

In this context, a major point of inflection has emerged in Latin American and Chilean documentary films, which have shifted toward a more subjective, introspective gaze, narrating intimate, private realities, even as they have built on the militant techniques of their predecessors. The gesture of turning the camera "inward" to create a cinematographic *mise-en-scène* of subjectivity has led to the sustained and indeed increasing production of hybrid and intimate models of filmmaking, such as film essays, first-person documentaries, autobiographies, self-portraits, filmed diaries, and epistolary documentaries. In the second decade of the twenty-first century, such expressions have become more common around the world, ratifying what Michael Renov said about how subjectivity has been the determining trend of contemporary nonfiction cinema (2004, 176). In this period, critics have focused on the role of affects, emotions, and feelings in the so-called affective turn. Authors such as Brian Massumi (2002), Sara Ahmed (2015), and Laura Podalsky (2011, 2018) have developed theoretical and methodological reflections on how affective issues strain conceptions of individual and collective memory; their work has political implications as well.

By exploring the subjective strategies exercised by contemporary Latin American and Chilean documentarians, we will find a series of sensorial dynamics that highlight affects and their epistemic possibilities as an alternative way of generating knowledge about memories of the recent traumatic past in the region. In fact, the importance of analyzing the subjective and affective turn as a privileged stage of representation for contemporary Chilean documentary also involves a resistance to hegemonic knowledge, expanding how we understand the political dimensions of the real.

The ways in which sensory experiences—as cultural, social, and political forces—are lived and embodied can lead to new political mobilization; they can also lead to innovative ways of representing traumatic experiences. For example, the representation of missing and tortured people from the Chilean military dictatorship[1] and the inscription of those traumas on bodies through violence, pain, and suffering shift viewers' affective and emotional sympathies.[2] This can lead to what Jane Gaines (1999) calls "political mimesis," in "which radical documentaries 'produce' a similar 'almost voluntary' imitation in sympathetic audiences" (90) such that they react—possibly through political action—to what they see on-screen. Nowadays, other embodied experiences on-screen, such as those of female bodies that have experienced rape or abortion, or transgender bodies, may also affect the sphere of politics in ways that question traditional militant political stances. All of this contributes to a complex understanding of the political and aesthetic dimensions of documentary, which in turn leads to the production and reception of major sociocultural processes.[3]

This chapter will thus outline the potential of subjectivity and affective narrative elements in contemporary Chilean documentary to shift the representation of the political. In the films I will discuss here, embodiment and the sensorial become a means of knowledge, highlighting experiences—both individual and collective—and their circulation in Latin American and global cinema. The provisional set of categories for contemporary Chilean documentaries that I offer here is a way of showing how an emphasis on subjectivity and the affects will not only heighten understanding of previous documentary productions in the twentieth century; it will also map out new ways of connecting political documentaries to direct political action.

PROVISIONAL TAXONOMIES

Following the return to democracy in 1990 and the arrival of the new millennium, Chilean documentary underwent a transition from the paradigm of "camera-fist" ["cámara-puño"] to one of "subject-camera" ["sujeto-cámara"] (Valenzuela 2011). The sustained surge in works produced in the first person—following a period of militant documentary by supporters of deposed President Salvador Allende and his *Unidad Popular* (Popular Unity) government and then a period of relative silence in Chilean filmmaking—is often linked to the processing of traumatic experiences in the aftermath of the 1973 coup d'état. These films investigate unresolved past experiences in recent history from the standpoint of fractured or problematic affective identities.

This affective turn within Chilean documentary at the cusp of the twenty-first century has led to transformations not only of the political, historical, and economic conditions of production but of rhetorical strategies as well.

Documentaries today can largely be distilled into four categories:[4]

1. Works that take up the traditional critical function of the documentary as a means of sociopolitical exposé, but this time questioning the capitalistic, neoliberal systems of the present. These works are situated in a macropolitical framework and continue to mobilize activism on major ideological and social issues.
2. More personal narratives not necessarily linked to national history, but reflecting intimate and affective memories of social taboos hidden from, or ignored by, the dominant culture. These,

in turn, are situated in a micropolitical framework and confront more subjective issues related to visibility and diversity.
3. Collaborative cinematic practices that innovate in method, form, technology, or tools of production in the contemporary documentary. These are situated in a collective framework, and this type of production operates as a motor of social transformation through a community-based conception of cinema, while emphasizing the ways in which the social fabric is bound more by emotional/sensory/affective drives than rational factors when reacting to particular political ideologies.
4. Works that play on the tension between cinematic representation and reality, establishing a novel relationship between images and their affective and political power. These films are situated in a (self-) reflective framework within which they contest hegemonic paradigms, whose representations of the real explore new modes of expression that look critically upon the relationship between ethics and aesthetics.

I will examine the linkage between these documentaries, affects, and political action in dialogue with, among others, the ideas of the French philosopher Jacques Rancière (2004, 2005, 2011, 2012). To understand the multiple exegetical possibilities offered by the confluence between subjectivity, affection, emotions, and politics, Rancière examines the emergence of unforeseen, alternative, and disruptive political interpretations of spaces and times. The author has called for a "sharing of the sensible" (2004) precisely to allow for unconventional, sense-based approaches to political praxis. Subjective and affective turns become points of inflection that resist hegemonic approaches to political representation.

This "sharing of the sensible" has implications for the aforementioned categories of contemporary Chilean documentary, because it allows for a redefinition of the links between experience and memory. For Rancière, the work of images involves the distribution of the senses as a common ground upon which subjects relate to each other, organizing and transforming the space where the images operate politically. Given that these films are recovering, interpreting, and interpellating the political in its most intimate dimension, Rancière's ideas offer a framework for examining the sense-based dimensions of their narrative, visual, and sound strategies:

What links the practice of art to the question of the common is the constitution, simultaneously material and symbolic, of a determined space/time, of an uncertainty in relation to the ordinary formulas of the sensory experience. In the first place, art is not political because of the messages and feelings that it transmits about the order of the world. It is also not political because of the form in which it represents societal structures, conflicts, or identities of social groups. It is political because of the distance that it keeps in relation to these functions, for the type of time and space it establishes, and for the manner it divides this time and populates this space. [Lo que liga la práctica del arte a la cuestión de lo común, es la constitución, a la vez material y simbólica, de un determinado espacio/tiempo, de una incertidumbre con relación a las fórmulas ordinarias de la experiencia sensible. El arte no es político en primer lugar por los mensajes y los sentimientos que transmite sobre el orden del mundo. No es político tampoco por la forma en que representa las estructuras de la sociedad, los conflictos o las identidades de los grupos sociales. Es político por la distancia misma que guarda con relación a estas funciones, por el tipo de tiempo y espacio que establece, por la manera en que divide ese tiempo y puebla ese espacio.] (Rancière 2005, 17)[5]

Rancière's reflections indicate a shift from the question of *what images are* to the question of *how images operate politically*. Therefore, for Rancière, it is not as necessary to inquire *about* images as it is to inquire *with* and *among* them, since their political value lies much more in the positioning of the enunciation than in the content being enunciated. It is from those interstitial spaces that images resist, question relationships between domination and emancipation, and interrogate categories of action and production. The political process of cinema is thus turned on its head, insofar as "it is not so much the revelation of mechanisms of domination as the examination of the aporias of emancipation" ["El proceder político cinematográfico volcado en lo sucesivo no tanto a la revelación de los mecanismos de dominación, como al examen de las aporías de la emancipación"] (Rancière 2012, 107). Documentary is not political just because it is part of the documentary genre.

The means by which images (trans)form reality are profoundly political, in that they modify not only the configuration of images themselves but also the larger world. For Rancière, the resistance of images comes out of the application of relational processes of contradiction that are mobilized toward the creation of countercultural forms and images that reformulate established and accepted notions in the universe of the sensory, proposing new relationships at the expressive level.

Contemporary Chilean documentaries presuppose the politicization of the aesthetic experience and the critical subversion of certain social and narrative categories in the relationships between dominance and subordination. Decolonized and insubordinate images force us to reflect upon dominant practices in order to deconstruct them, encouraging shared thinking that proposes new relationships and shifts in meaning, as well as constant confrontations with, and transformations of, reality.

Rancière's ideas shed light on the four aforementioned categories of documentary because they show us how images based not on explicitly militant themes but rather on more obliquely sensory experiences can still help effect political change. Micropolitical practices of collaboration and reflection, as well as more traditionally political themes on-screen, can all contribute to a new understanding of the ways in which documentaries are linked to real, activist interventions, beyond the realm of representation.

HISTORICAL NOTES: FROM THE ACTIVIST DOCUMENTARY TO THE SUBJECTIVE TURN

Like the rest of Latin America, Chile was not immune to the effects of the Cuban Revolution. Milestones such as the 1955 creations of the Film Institute within Chile's Catholic University (by the priest Rafael Sánchez) and the Cinema Club of the University of Chile (by filmmakers Pedro Chaskel and Sergio Bravo) cemented the origins of a socially and politically committed documentary there. In 1957 Chaskel and Bravo founded the Experimental Film Center of the University of Chile, an entity that produced many of the most iconic documentaries of the period.[6] By the 1960s, the openly activist documentary was gaining strength: "Inasmuch as the political radicalization of the filmmakers was transformed into activism, documentaries made in Chile began to acquire a combative character similar to the cinema produced in other Latin American countries in the 1960s" ["En la medida en que la radicalización política de los cineastas se transformaba en militancia activa, el cine documental realizado en Chile iba adquiriendo un carácter combativo similar al del cine que se producía en otros países latinoamericanos durante los años 60'"] (Valjalo and Pick 1984, 36).[7] Some significant moments in the emergence of the "New Chilean Cinema" in the 1960s were the first and second Amateur Film Festivals (1963 and 1964), which became the Chilean Film Festival in 1966 and occasioned the first Chilean Filmmakers Conference. In 1967, the first New Latin American Film Festival was organized by the Viña del Mar Film Club, founded in 1962 by Aldo Francia. It featured the participation of the Cubans Santiago Álvarez and Humberto Solás and the Bolivian Jorge Sanjinés. Another event was the creation, in 1965, of the Board for the Promotion of the Cinema Industry by then-President Frei Montalva. In 1967 Frei also signed the Law for the Promotion of National Cinema.

Beginning in 1970, with the *Unidad Popular* running the government, the documentary thrust of the *Cine de Allende* (Bolzoni 1974) focused on consolidating the "Chilean road to socialism." These documentaries chronicled the lived political process and exalted in the enthusiasm of the *pueblo*. The documentary thus became a medium to raise consciousness and ensure the adherence and active participation of the workers in the process of emancipation, while giving voice to the marginalized and exploited classes.[8]

According to Jacqueline Mouesca (2005), the army ransacked the offices of Chile Films and burned thousands of meters of film after the coup, resulting in a terrible loss for the country's cinematographic patrimony. This destruction was exacerbated by the closure of university film departments and schools and the exile of dozens of filmmakers, artists, and intellectuals whose work and lives were truncated by the dictatorship. This was one of the most difficult periods for the production of cinema and culture in Chile.[9] Outside Chile, however, exiled Chilean filmmakers produced 178 films between 1973 and 1983 alone (Mouesca 2005, 94). Of these, more than 100 were documentaries,[10] many of which heightened the justifiably combative political stance that was already palpable in those years. Others sought to make the suffering of the Chilean people known around the world and denounced human rights abuses, thereby appealing to international solidarity for the abolition of the dictatorship, the restoration of a democratic order, and justice for the families of those who were tortured, detained, and disappeared.

Chilean documentaries of this period—from the "cinema of Allende" to the cinema of exile—exhibited the three fundamental characteristics that Octavio Getino and Susana Velleggia (2002) attribute to political film: first, a focus on the film's *political objective*, beyond its subject matter; second, its *intentionality*, whether in the service of a creative treatment of reality or a fictional story; and third, an emphasis on *political institutions* over cinematographic ones in the relationship among the film, the spectator, and *reality*.

In addition to these characteristics, the cinema of exile also contains some reflexive and intimate projects that subjectively represent affective issues, like disconnection and nostalgia, as part of the universal experience of exiles. *Diario inconcluso / Unfinished diary* (1982, Marilú Mallet, Canada) and *Fragmentos de un diario inacabado / Fragments of an Unfinished Diary* (1983, Angelina Vázquez, Finland) are pioneering examples of the self-reflective turn that later characterized the Chilean documentary:

> [B]oth works are notable for being examples of cinema in exile that begin with that premise and interrogate the cinematic condition, not as a means of advancing the reflection, but instead from a sense of instability from which the methodological questioning and the search for a tone ("another tone") from which to make films. This creates an ideological and discursive separation among lines of cinema in exile and relates to the type of link—deepening, continuity, rupture—that films in exile establish with the discursive formation of the 1960s and 1970s; above all this is the case with the combative, militant protest discourses. . . . A cinematographic image from which the disarticulation (rhetorical), the emptying (political), the lyricism, the discontinuity, and a strong emphasis on subjectivity re-signifies iconographies, issues, and aesthetics crystalized in the framework of the relationship between aesthetics and politics. [Me parece que ambas obras destacan por ser ejemplos de un cine del exilio que parte de esta premisa para interrogarse sobre su condición cinematográfica; no como avance en su reflexión, sino, desde la inestabilidad, desde el cuestionamiento metodológico, desde la búsqueda de un tono ('otro' tono) para filmar. Esto separa ideológica y discursivamente líneas de trabajo dentro del cine del exilio y tiene relación con el tipo de vínculo—profundización, continuidad, ruptura—que establecen los filmes del exilio con las formaciones discursivas de la década del sesenta y setenta; sobre todo en relación

a los discursos combativos, militantes y de denuncia. . . . Es, sí, la concepción de una imagen cinematográfica que desde el desajuste (retórico), el vaciamiento (político), el lirismo, la discontinuidad y un fuerte énfasis en la subjetividad, re-significa iconografías, temáticas, y estéticas cristalizadas en el marco de las relaciones entre estética y política.] (Pinto 2012, 216–18)

As much in their formal gestures (the relationship between space and time, poetics, politics of memory, sound and music, voices, the performative) as in the narratives themselves (the representation of exile, the return, detachment, memory, gender roles, the emergence and politicization of a feminist discourse), these documentaries[11] offer a number of different critical and aesthetic approaches to the connection between the affective and the political.

The frequent affirmation that cultural production in general, and cinema in particular, went through one of the most sterile periods of its history during the Chilean dictatorship—a cliché frequently used to describe cultural production in the country in the late 1970s and throughout the 1980s—risks overshadowing the importance of various resistance audiovisual collectives that contributed to renovating the counterculture scene from the early 1980s until the early 1990s. Documentary practices during this period were not only conceived as having combative, denunciatory potential but also created a space for collective work. With electromagnetic video as a political and technological tool, counterhegemonic groups like CADA, Teleanálisis,[12] and ECO Comunicaciones[13] developed methodologies for action based on artistic experimentation, counterpropaganda, and popular communication and education. These were strategies that—despite strong repression and censorship—contributed to political resistance, social transformation, and efforts toward democratization. These collaborative forms came out of the cinema of the *Unidad Popular* when, in the late 1960s and early 1970s, they operated as community-building and didactic instruments with great political potential. The beginnings of these filmmakers are described in the *Manifiesto Político de los Cineastas de la Unidad Popular*, which understands cinema as community work—a revolutionary art "that is born of the collective work of the artist and the united people" ["que nace de la realización conjunta del artista y del pueblo unidos"] (Mouesca 1988, 71–72). Meanwhile, they formed the basis for a number of audiovisual collectives that emerged later on, such as MAFI (an acronym for *Mapa Fílmico de un País*, A Country Mapped on Film), which will be discussed at length below.[14]

With the triumph of the "NO" vote in the national plebiscite of 1988, a new period began for Chilean documentary. Works like those of Carmen Castillo (*La flaca Alejandra / Skinny Alejandra* from 2004 and *Calle Santa Fe / Santa Fe Street* from 2007) and the entire documentary body of work of Patricio Guzmán following *La batalla de Chile / The Battle of Chile* (1973–77), provide a series of self-reflexive, sense-based strategies for reclaiming issues surrounding affective memory and human rights. The subjective positioning that these documentaries adopt emphasizes the fact that one's identity is not necessarily defined by structural conditions of history but rather by how one's uniqueness as a subject can elucidate the inner workings of, and the relationships among, political, social, cultural, or economic structures. These documentaries thus express the personal and emotional connections of the filmmakers to political events that affected them directly—even bodily. Through the recovery of their own words and those of others, the directors become what Dori Laub (1992) refers to as "documentary witnesses" revealing testimony that they feel ethically bound to make heard, recognized, revalued, and recorded:

> This imperative to tell and to be heard can become itself an all-consuming life task. . . . Yet no amount of telling seems ever to do justice to this inner compulsion. There are not enough words or the right words, there is never enough time or the right time, and never enough listening or the right listening to articulate the story that cannot be fully captured in *thought*, *memory* and *speech*. (78, emphasis in original)

In this sense, the entire cinematographic project of Guzmán is emblematic. Through the construction of images and the narration of urgent testimonies, the director of fundamental political pieces such as *Primer año / The First Year* (1971), *La batalla de Chile* (1973–77), *En nombre de Dios / In God's Name* (1987), *La cruz del Sur / The Southern Cross* (1992), *Chile, la memoria obstinada / Chile, Obstinate Memory* (1997), *El caso Pinochet / The Pinochet Case* (2001), *Salvador Allende* (2004), *Nostalgia de la luz / Nostalgia for the Light* (2010), *El botón de nácar / The Pearl Button* (2015), and *La cordillera de los sueños / The Cordillera of Dreams* (2019) has cemented his ethical and aesthetic commitment to memory. This documentary corpus highlights the liberating potential of a narrative capable of restoring the tissues of broken memory and the integrity of broken identities following traumatic events. This happens through what Brian Winston (1988) terms the "documentary victim" (269): a subject emotionally affected by trauma who finds relief, liberation, or at least the ability to channel his or her pain—expressively, through the images—by telling painful stories that until then had not been revealed or discovered.

An additional step on the path toward self-representational introspection is found in documentaries made by a new generation of directors, many of whose parents participated in the left-wing struggles during the dictatorship. This retelling of history is positioned in a framework of "postmemory" (Hirsch 2008 and 2012)[15] and depends upon a reflective, critical viewpoint that interpellates and questions the role of the parents' generation in the development of political events. These films nuance the primarily hagiographic discourse that had prevailed about the period. Thus, this *cine de hijos*, or "cinema of children,"[16] created a crisis and a displacement vis-à-vis the classical rhetoric of political cinema. The decidedly subjective and affective turns that began to gather steam during this period continue to be the preeminent characteristics of the Chilean documentary genre in the present. It is precisely through these self-reflexive and hybridized strategies that they blur the previously fixed divisions between categories like fiction and nonfiction, public and private, and history and memory. They therefore destabilize the hegemonic definition of the political documentary and its relationship with reality.

During the last twenty years there have been many documentaries that—from the first-person perspective—continue not only to re-create the memory of the Chilean people but also to confirm the liberating potential and "restorative function" that Lejeune (2008) attributes to the autobiographical enterprise. These documentaries suggest that repair of the tissues of shattered memories and identities can be achieved through the expressive channeling of experiences that traumatically marked the lives of families. They bridge the gap between "second-generation cinema" (Quílez 2010) developed in Chile and documentaries that, during the same time period, emerged forcefully in other Latin American countries, like Argentina and Brazil, that were also victimized by dictatorial repression.[17]

A TAXONOMIC PROPOSAL FOR THE CONTEMPORARY CHILEAN DOCUMENTARY

I will now explore the four tendencies in Chilean documentaries outlined in the first part of this chapter, in order to show (a) how they mark a degree of continuity with previous documentary films and (b) how they reflect an affective, emotional turn that connects representation to real political issues in new ways. Indeed, these new Chilean political documentaries attempt, in the words of Rancière, "to affix the transformations in the relationship between cinema and politics, and to reflect upon the continuities and ruptures that characterize it today" ["fijar las transformaciones de la relación entre política y cine, y reflexionar sobre las continuidades y rupturas que hoy la caracterizan"] (2012, 107).

The first of these provisional categories is that of documentaries with traditional, macropolitical rhetorics that turn their critical focus onto contemporary issues of neoliberalism; they also mark an affective shift away from the traditional militant documentaries of the past. They have brought to light problems of repression, inequality, underdevelopment, discrimination, migratory crises, and ecological and environmental devastation. All of them attack Chile's image as a neoliberal "model student" disciplined by the dictatorship and sustained by successive democratic governments. These works[18] oppose and question the current system of imperialist capitalism, promoting a transformation toward a more just social order.[19] Toward the end of the 1990s, documentaries such as *Fernando ha vuelto / Fernando is Back* (1998, Silvio Caiozzi) and *El derecho de vivir en paz / The Right to Live in Peace* (1999, Carmen Luz Parot) marked the resurgence of a tradition of politically committed filmmaking through social and political dissent. In the three decades between the return to democracy and today, these works[20] have continued to piece together the remnants of a shattered national memory. Emotion and affect can also play a crucial political, reflective, and critical role in this process (Valdés 2008, 8). By sharing a common sense of indignation, rather than propagating militant haranguing, this type of documentary actually privileges the creation of citizen empowerment and the articulation of a collective voice to demand civil rights threatened by hegemonic powers. These rights include education, health care, decent pensions, abortion, life in an environment free from pollution, and the full integration of groups such as immigrants or the LGBTQ community.

Two documentaries that illustrate how recent productions can echo the militant rhetoric of their precursors while questioning neoliberal structures from an affective-militant dimension are *Venceremos / We Shall Overcome* (1970) by Pedro Chaskel and Héctor Ríos and *Tres instantes, un grito / Three Moments, One Cry* (2013) by Cecilia Barriga (Figure 3). *Venceremos*, the first documentary made in Chile after the victory of Salvador Allende, is characterized primarily by the emotional power of its images that, by way of constant juxtapositions, illustrate the radical differences between the most marginalized classes and the wealthiest in the country. The dialectical montage is reinforced by songs whose vehement lyrics appeal to spectators' emotions. Since the documentary lacks narrative voice-over, dialogue, or any other form of oral narrative, these songs are the only verbal element in the film:

> The parallel montage of the bourgeois frivolity and the destitution of the working class, punctuated by abrupt changes in music, is indicative of the class warfare that was occurring in the country at the time. . . . [T]he dynamic established by the montage [in the final scenes] of the mass celebrations turns the spectator into a participant in a historical moment. [El montaje paralelo de la frivolidad burguesa y del desamparo de la clase obrera, puntuado por cambios abruptos de la música, es significativo de la lucha de clases que se daba en el país. . . . [L]a dinámica establecida [en las escenas finales] por el montaje de las manifestaciones convierte al espectador en partícipe de un momento histórico.] (Valjalo and Pick 1984, 36)

Both *Venceremos* and *Tres instantes, un grito* appeal to the idea of a surging popular voice[21] as a rhetoric that makes certain universal demands questioning the dominant political and economic paradigms of their respective time periods. *Tres instantes, un grito* is constructed around three social explosions rooted in popular dissatisfaction that occur in different latitudes but at the same time. During 2011, Barriga's camera explores the protest of *Los indignados* (the indignant ones) in Madrid's Puerta del Sol, the "Occupy Wall Street" movement in New York, and the actions, marches, and occupations of schools by Chilean secondary and postsecondary students demanding free, high-quality education. While the documentary short made by Chaskel and Ríos focused on Chile, Barriga's feature-length film weaves together movements calling for a deep transformation of the neoliberal system. Both works emphasize the value of citizen voices and the ability of the collective whole to effect social, cultural, and political change. In these films there are abundant messages, chants, and slogans alluding to the *pueblo*, often shouted in mass demonstrations. *Venceremos* and *Tres instantes, un grito* seek to call us to action, situating the social body in protest as the site where rights are reclaimed. The call to citizens and to the spectator is to be converted into action, and because of that, the films often make their appeals using pathos more than logos.

Along this line of reclaiming agency, one could include documentaries that critically expose the struggles of Chile's indigenous people to recover their rights and territory, confronting systematic and historical persecution and repression by the state.[22] These characteristics are often seen in contemporary nonfiction cinema from other Latin American countries with significant First Nations populations.[23]

The second provisional category I will discuss here is that of documentaries centered on more intimate issues. Despite the fact that they are necessarily less focused on monumental events in national history than on sensorial and affective approaches, they are no less political. Often, they are concerned

Figure 3. A man reading during the "Occupy Wall Street" protest movement in New York, in *Tres instantes, un grito / Three Moments, One Cry* (Cecilia Barriga, 2013).

with private or family memories encoded with secrets, absences, traumas, voids, shames, lies, and confessions. In Chile, the political function of these works[24] is to illuminate taboos like adoption, homosexuality, transgender issues, single parenthood, suicide, illness, disability, and rape and sexual and gender violence. These documentaries promote resistance to the homogenizing tendencies of global culture,[25] making political claims for diversity and exposing practices that project a strengthened, pluralistic society, in cultural, social, ideological, ethnic, age, sexual, and gendered terms. Not only does this sort of work make visible events that are commonly hidden or absent from the average Chilean family's life but it also sets in motion processes of identification and empathy that contribute to the acceptance and normalization of stigmatized events and situations, endowing these films with a considerable amount of political meaning. These works shine light onto atomized identities that are still underrepresented in the subjective practices of the Chilean documentary.

A particularly interesting example of how films like these can use the representation of affects and emotions to articulate the political tension between public and private spaces can be found in *Hija / Daughter* (2011), by María Paz González (Figure 4). In this road movie–documentary hybrid, the director and her mother travel from southern to northern Chile, looking for family members whose existences were denied in family lore, supposedly to protect children from the social stigma of *el qué dirán*, or gossip. As a young girl, the director's mother was adopted, separating her from a biological sister whom she barely remembers, and for whom she has been searching her whole life. The physical voyage becomes a metaphor for affective transformation, and for a quest for self-knowledge. It is a device for the revelation of her fractured identity and the closing of loopholes in her familial memory. The movement is shown to be both cartographic and spiritual, as she closes in on her origins. González, the director and titular "daughter," hopes, for her part, to meet her real father, even though he was never interested in getting to know her. María Paz was raised by a single mother who invented a last name, "González," for her, along with the story of an imaginary father who never existed.

Adoption, unplanned pregnancy, and single-parent upbringing—with the attendant consequences of being called a *huacho* (Chilean slang for an illegitimate or unrecognized child)—are topics that cinema tends to represent using serious, melodramatic narratives. *Hija*, however, approaches this expression through humor and irony to draw in the spectator. Moreover, *Hija* offers a refreshing take on the documentary scene in Chile, dispensing with

Figure 4. The voyage of the director with her mother becomes a metaphor for affective transformation and self-knowledge in *Hija / Daughter* (María Paz González, 2011).

typical devices such as voice-over (retrospective commentary) and archival material, in order to firmly situate the search for identity and genealogy in the present. *Hija* projects intimate memories that come out of private space, and weaves together the stray threads of an idiosyncratic national microhistory. In a similar way, albeit through different registers and expressive modalities, these new characteristics of the micropolitical can also be found in the documentary production of Argentina and other Latin American countries.[26]

The third category is that of documentaries whose political substance lies in a community-based conception of cinema, with corresponding innovations in methodology, aesthetics, and technological tools. This change in expression subverts the notion of the documentary as an individual work, in favor of a collective and collaborative filmmaking practice. For Rancière, creation and thought should not be the privilege of the few, but rather a common experience that, in its own way, is the product of greater integration and equity. If, in mainstream cinema, authorship is traditionally vertical and often exclusionary, these new collaborative forms of working presuppose horizontal and participative stylistic and aesthetic decisions. Collective authorship thus represents a strong contrast to the intimate and personal creations of the previously discussed category. As Mateos and Sedeño (2015) point out, "credit attributed to the group is one of the most genuine and solid signs of collective authorship" ["la firma de grupo es una de las formas más genuinas y sólidas de autoría colectiva"], as it announces the "conscious and voluntary formation of anonymity in audiovisual creation" ["formulación consciente y voluntaria del anonimato en la creación audiovisual"] in its erasure of authorial identification (315–21).

One contemporary project that shows a documentary collective politically situating itself as a community and privileging the use of multimedia platforms for the generation and distribution of high-quality, cinematically expressive documentary content is MAFI (Mapa Fílmico de un País, www.mafi.tv). MAFI was born in 2011, thanks to the initiative of a group of young Chilean audiovisual enthusiasts who organized themselves into a nonprofit, independent collective. It formed around a network of about one hundred creators from all over the country who collaborate on microdocumentaries that together make up a web-based map. The activities of MAFI center on three lines of action:

1. The **Film Map**, collected on the group's digital platform. A veritable documentary kaleidoscope, these fragments of reality bring together content from multiple practices and imaginaries related to Chilean identity. There are multiple themes, including politics, memory, ecology, indigenous peoples, technology, and daily life, among others. Apart from their collective authorship, the works use audiovisual language—based on instructions laid out in the "MAFI Shot"[27]—that focuses on the expressive and artistic value of the image as a way of thinking about reality, contributing to the construction of the country's memory and encouraging social reflection.[28]
2. The **MAFI School**, which offers workshops on documentary filmmaking throughout Chile, mostly outside of the capital, and usually in remote areas. The inhabitants of the various towns where the collective works become cocreators of the web-based map, and their contributions—which reflect their own social and identity practices—form part of the audiovisual fabric of the platform.
3. **Feature-length films** made collectively, such as *Propaganda* (2014) and *Dios / God* (2019). Following the 2013 presidential campaign throughout Chile, *Propaganda* integrates work done

by sixteen filmmakers, tracing a new map of the country's territory and diversity in the context of an election that was particularly tense due to growing social instability and discontent in Chile.[29]

Dios (Figure 5), meanwhile, depicts the controversial visit of Pope Francis to Chile in January 2018, amidst the biggest crisis of the Catholic Church in the history of the country—several media outlets even called it his most unsuccessful foreign trip. The institutional church that the Pope found in Chile was in deep crisis, not only due to pedophilia and sexual abuse scandals but also because of the systematic concealment of those crimes by the entire church hierarchy. The film shows people in the streets claiming their rights to free abortion, marriage equality, reparations for the violent repression of the Mapuche people by the Chilean state, and other social demands that the church has opposed. Like *Propaganda*, *Dios* constructs images that institutions would rather hide, and reveals religion as a charade, albeit a captivating, seductive one. The Pope's visit becomes an excuse to generate a series of icons with his image: flags and pins with Francis's face; life-sized cardboard images allowing people to be photographed next to the "double" of the Pontiff; keychains; stickers; and of course the image depicted in newspapers and the

Figure 5. Religious icons and the image of the Catholic Church are examined during the controversial visit of Pope Francis to Chile in January 2018 in *Dios / God* (MAFI, 2018).

mainstream media. With this, *Dios* exposes an operation to whitewash the image of a church increasingly discredited by Chilean society.

In order to take critical stances on Chilean identity in its documentaries, MAFI has developed a particular approach that exposes how society tends to collectively respond much more strongly to emotional/sensory/affective stimuli than to reason and objectivity, particularly when faced with ideological or value-laden issues like politics and religion (Lagos 2019). In both *Propaganda* and *Dios*, we can observe the impacts that sensory dynamics have on bodies that are faced with ideological phenomena. The subjects of *Propaganda* come together, march, clap, sing, and jump in the campaign events of the candidates they support; these physical bodies become, together, a body politic, and a social signifier. In *Dios*, we also see huge groups of bodies coming together to either protest the Pope's visit or simply see him in person. When these groups are protesting in favor of abortion rights, for example, they chant "take your rosaries out of our ovaries," but when they make professions of faith, they also flagellate themselves in religious processions. Power, both ecclesiastical and political, often appeals to people's most visceral emotions, particularly in order to manipulate them. Credos and dogma are made flesh, and in cinematic representations that focus on the senses, they become lenses—and potential cultural and social forces—through which we can understand the complexity of national experience.

Audiovisual collectives have always developed alongside the evolution of technological tools in the hands of amateurs and early-adopters.[30] In the militant cinema of the 1960s and 1970s,[31] it was sixteen-millimeter film; in the resistance against the dictatorship it was electromagnetic media (VHS/Beta); and in the case of MAFI, it is digital video. To quote Domin Choi's prologue to one of Rancière's texts,

> The evidence of the change from analog technology (photography and cinema) to digital technology and its adoption worldwide form the starting point of hypotheses of paradigm changes in perception, consciousness, bodies, and of course subjectivity, together with changes in sociopolitical organization. [La evidencia del cambio de las técnicas analógicas (fotografía y cine) a la tecnología digital y su adopción a escala planetaria hacen que se arrojen hipótesis masivas sobre el cambio de percepción, de conciencia, de cuerpos y por supuesto

de la subjetividad, junto a cambios de organización social y político.] (2011, 18)

Amidst the progressive convergence[32] of film, television, the Internet, and mobile communication, digital cultural production and mass media consumption have diversified and become more complex, and MAFI posits new challenges that distinguish it within the broad field of audiovisual initiatives in Latin America dedicated to collective documentary production.[33]

The fourth provisional category in my discussion seeks to approach how the political documentary in present-day Chile has sought to establish a different kind of interaction between image and political power, complicating the logic of dominant representation and questioning the consensus surrounding its meaning and its link to reality. Such works, which are often aesthetically quite experimental, critique certain aspects of audiovisual language as obsolete, in order to undermine the status quo of the poetic-political dialectic and strengthen the reach of an emancipated gaze.

By emphasizing sensory experience, this type of documentary can also be understood in the terms that Rancière conceives of politics, to accommodate not only social issues of general interest, or the life experiences of those with marginalized or dissident subjectivities, but, above all, a concern for embracing forms of representation that experiment with the visibility of new experiences heretofore unrecognized by hegemonic models:

> A social situation is not sufficient to make political art, nor is evident sympathy for the exploited and disenfranchised. These should be augmented with a mode of representation that makes them intelligible as the effects of certain causes, and that engages them to produce forms of consciousness and affects that might lead to change. Therefore, the formal aspects of the work must be concerned with pointing out these causes and signaling how they should lead to particular effects. [Una situación social no basta para hacer un arte político, como no basta una simpatía evidente por los explotados y los desamparados. De ordinario se considera que debe sumársele un modo de representación que haga inteligible esa situación como el efecto de ciertas causas y la muestre productora de formas de conciencia y afectos que la modifican. Se reclama,

pues, que los medios formales de la obra obedezcan a la preocupación por las causas que deben señalarse a las inteligencias y los efectos que deben producirse sobre las sensibilidades.] (Rancière 2012, 127–28)

The images and sounds of these films work to expose the cinematographic operations through which certain experiences are naturalized and other ones are excluded. With diverse emphases, these works[34] offer an experimental poetics, reflect upon the filmmaking apparatus, and propose interstitial aesthetics to connect the multiple layers of personal experience, critical thought, collective meaning, evidence of the real, the very act of filming, and the relationships between past and present, memory, history, and forgetting.

However, these transits and displacements can be understood not only as the literal physical movements of the filmmakers but also as symbolic operations in which directors cross interstitial spaces—topographic and affective territories that accentuate the idea of flow, of the mutation of forms, that make the invisible appear or alter the appearances of what we see. These flows also extend, as Rancière shows us, to that which we do not see, and that which, due to its complexity, cannot be transfigured in images or well-defined sounds but rather become diffuse, oblique representations of reality.

Following Rancière, this obliqueness results from moving through passages [*passages*] rather than landscapes [*paysages*]—of voyages that, even as they signify a physical movement from one point to another, principally serve to represent cinematic intervals between discrete spaces and times and to permit or obstruct the flow between the thresholds of the real and its representation.

The documentaries of Tiziana Panizza highlight the potential of celluloid, and particularly Super 8, to function as interstitial forms of the image.[35] The use of this format—which corresponds as much to the images that she captures with her S8 Nizo 801 camera as to the found footage that she resignifies in her documentaries—allows Panizza to reflect poetically upon time, impermanence, the relationship between absence and presence, and the relationship between materiality and memory (Lagos 2015). The director takes advantage of montage as an act of creative writing with great political value, establishing critical relationships among images, sounds, sensations, and words. In this way, she generates new formal and discursive associations in which visual and auditory languages "take a position" (albeit without taking "part") vis-à-vis reality, to paraphrase Didi-Huberman (2008).

Tierra sola / Solitary Land (2017), Panizza's latest documentary (Figure 6), was created after finding, resignifying, and ascribing value to thirty-two films shot on Easter Island between the 1930s and the 1970s. The majority of the recovered films are ethnographic documentaries and home movies made by different foreign tourists. Through a refined process of montage, Panizza reflects on these fragments along with a series of sounds (phonographic recordings, songs in the Rapa Nui language, and other found sounds), interspersed with titles from filmmakers who transformed the field of cinematic ethnography, such as Chris Marker or Trinh T. Minh-Ha, or visual anthropologists such as Jay Ruby. To these fragments she adds digital video of the island and its inhabitants, set in the present day. Unlike in her previous work, here Panizza completely dispenses with voice-over to articulate the narrative of this film. Despite that, words—spoken, written, found, and quoted—are very present throughout *Tierra sola*. While the titles mobilize the self-reflective expression of the author, the spoken word is ceded to others. Even as the intimate/subjective tone of the first person persists, self-reference gives way to otherness, and very particularly, to exploring the gaze that the "other

Figure 6. Stereotypical ethnographic images about Easter Island revisited, in *Tierra Sola / Solitary Land* (Tiziana Panizza, 2017).

others"—ethnographic documentary makers—have deployed to construct Rapa Nui. It is an essay about ethnographic cinema, with which Panizza's film shares an exploratory ethos.

Tierra sola possesses at least two profoundly political elements. The first is the deconstruction of colonial stereotypes about Easter Island that have been created over time by ethnographic documentaries. Panizza compiles fragments of the thirty-two documentaries to show how they repeat the same shots over and over, with identical framing and angles, to create stereotypical visual motifs of the Moai. "I've counted more images of Moai stone figures than of people" ["He contado más imágenes de moais que de personas"], she notes in the titles, adding, "My gaze here is at the same time [that of] all of the others. In the films that I look over, I'm searching not for memory, but for patterns. The hand of the person holding the camera" ["Mi mirada aquí, y al mismo tiempo, todas las otras, en las películas que he revisado. No estoy buscando memoria, sino patrones, el pulso de quien sostiene la cámara"] (*Tierra sola*). By reassembling these images to propose new operations of meaning within them, the director allows the found cinematic materials to undo the commonplaces that they themselves construct.

The second political intervention that *Tierra sola* makes is to provide a space to articulate the current demands and resistance of the Rapa Nui people. Panizza reminds spectators that the island's geography and landscape are inhabited by social actors whose history, memory, and folklore form a bridge between the past of the island and its present struggles. In this sense, the documentary bridges other dichotomies, between its representation of the island's jail and the larger question of enclosure in a land surrounded by the ocean, and between the exteriority and interiority of Easter Island and those of its residents. Panizza's titles lay this out explicitly:

> People say that in this place, the distance gives you freedom. But I don't know what the relationship is between being distant and being free. . . . Here, sometimes I think about how if the ocean that separates the island were vertical, it would be a 4,000 km-high wall. An escape would be impossible. Where would a fugitive go on the most remote island in the world? [La gente dice que en este lugar, la distancia te da libertad. Pero no sé cuál es la relación entre estar distante y ser libre. . . . Aquí a

veces se me vienen pensamientos como si el océano que separara la isla, fuese vertical, sería una muralla de 4 mil km., sería imposible escapar . . . ¿Dónde se iría un fugitivo en la isla más remota del mundo?] (*Tierra sola*)

According to Irene Depetris (2018), *Tierra sola* evidences a turn toward the affective at a formal level, associating the exploration of sensorial potentialities—in the visual, textural, and sonorous dimensions—with memory. Depetris resorts to authors such as Katrina Schlunke (2013) to point out the inadequacy of the opposition between objects as tangible and concrete things and the intangible and immaterial world of affects, within which memory works as a kind of "effect" produced "through" and "with" the order of the material. "The performative function of the documentary is enhanced by a gaze that, from the visual, expands in terms of the tactile and the sonorous. The aim is to construct a 'gaze' and an 'ear' that seek to reveal the innumerable effects and affects of the surfaces" ["La función performativa del documental se potencia a partir de una mirada que, desde lo visual, se expande en lo táctil y en lo sonoro. Se trata, entonces, de la apuesta a construir una 'mirada' y una 'escucha' que busca revelar los innumerables efectos y afectos de las superficies"] (Depetris 2018, 115).

Chilean documentaries that can be placed in this fourth grouping typically emphasize symbolic spaces where the sensible and the affective make the contradictions and complexity of reality visible. It is from the conflicts expressed in language that it is possible to construct an interstitial image capable of giving voice to that which belongs more to the order of absence. This type of cinema often represents itself as a never-ending search. In it, the cinematic process is put into relief, and images and sound are employed in a process of trial and error, thereby sharpening the fractures, the fragments, and the ellipses. The ethical and aesthetic displacements of these searches reinforce imprecisions, doubts, and questions, more than certainty and definition. By conceiving of the real as that which is veiled, opaque, and diffuse, these documentary forms seek to uncover the political and cinematic tensions between that which can be represented and that which cannot:

> It is a delimitation of spaces and times, of the visible and the invisible, of speech and noise, that simultaneously determines the place and the stakes of politics as a form of experience.

> Politics revolves around what is seen and what can be said about it, around who has the ability to see and the talent to speak, around the properties of spaces and the possibilities of time. (Rancière 2004, 8)

CONCLUSIONS

These political shifts in the contemporary Chilean documentary indicate a transition from an obsolete conception of the audiovisual image as a "fixed" element, toward a fresh notion of it as an open text, incomplete and dialogic in its attempts to capture the rich political, aesthetic, reflective, and emotional complexity of cinematic language. In these relational operations, the documentary expands its features, using subjectivity and the affective to enrich our comprehension of the real.

Outlining this provisional taxonomy of new Chilean documentaries allows us to focus on the political potential of the affects in cinematic operations such as self-reflexivity, mass mobilization, and collaboration. The subjective relationships between public and private spheres represented in current Chilean documentaries often include an affective dimension of great political and cinematic value. These documentaries are now moving toward a conception of the political that focuses less on explicit, militant politics per se, but rather on the relationships and operations of audiovisual language. In this sense, they are in dialogue with other Latin American documentary traditions, as well as with events going on around the world. Questioning the codes of this language, the inflections of its content and praxis, and the tools and methods through which it raises consciousness are all different ways of connecting ethics and aesthetics.

NOTES

1 On the role of affect in the "management of memory" by postdictatorial regimes, Podalsky points out: "One could say that the turn toward affect began as an attempt to address the complex legacies left by state-sponsored terrorism and/or years of civil war that took place in the late twentieth century in countries from Argentina and Chile to Guatemala, El Salvador and Peru" (Podalsky 2018, 239).

2 Based on a Deleuzian and Massumian conceptual framework, Podalsky distinguishes affect, on the one hand, as the emotional experience within or between

bodies; on the other hand, she examines emotion as the coding of experience within linguistic and social grammars (2018, 250). The distinction between terminologies such as affect and emotion is also discussed by Vinodh Venkatesh and María del Carmen Caña (2016): "To be clear, while the cinema is largely an art of emotions that are both displayed and provoked, what is of interest here instead is its precursor, that is, affect. When we study affect, we examine how it is manifested in intensities, sensations, and impulses that (re)configure and impact the somatic experience of engaging the moving image" (177).

3   Authors like Podalsky (2018) propose an examination of the intersection of affective forces and circulations in relation to politics in contemporary Latin American cinema.

4   Despite the particularities of each of these four tendencies in this provisional taxonomy of Chilean documentary, it is important to recognize that they are similar to descriptions of other national cinemas in Latin America and across the world. Many Latin American countries share a historical, political, cultural, or economic trajectory, having suffered together from the consequences of global capitalism. Their cinemas also share similar attempts to renovate and complicate the ways in which audiovisual language works, expanding its potential and its critical edge.

5   When texts by Rancière have not been available in translation to English, quotes by him have been translated to English from the Spanish translations of his work. In the case of work that has been published in English, the English translations have been quoted directly.

6   These included *Mimbre* / "Wicker" (1957), *Día de los organillos* / *Day of the Organ-grinders* (1959), *Trilla* / *Thresher* (1959), *Aquel Nguillatun* / "That Nguillatun" (1960), and *Amerindia* / *Amerindian* (1962), all by Sergio Bravo; *Aquí vivieron* / *They Lived Here* (1964), *Aborto* / *Abortion* (1965), *Testimonio* / *Testimony* (1969), and *Venceremos* / *We Shall Overcome* (1970) by Pedro Chaskel; *Santa María de Iquique* / "Iquique's Santa María" (1969, Claudio Sapiaín); *Herminda de La Victoria* / "Herminda from La Victoria" (1969, Douglas Hübner); *Desnutrición infantil* / "Child Malnutrition" (1969), *Por Vietnam* / *For Vietnam* (1969), and *Brigada Ramona Parra* / *Ramona Parra Brigade* (1970), all by Álvaro Ramírez; and *Casa o mierda* / *House or Shit* (1969) and *Descomedidos y chascones* / *Insolent and Disheveled* (1972) by Carlos Flores Delpino, among others. Here and elsewhere, when a film is distributed in an English-language market and its title has been translated by the distributor, the English-language title is provided in italics. Otherwise, the original titles have been translated into English and enclosed in quotation marks.

7   Translation of this quote from the Spanish original, and others throughout the essay, are mine unless otherwise indicated.

8   The cinematic processes had to have the support of the members of the political parties that made up the UP, represented on the board of Chile Films. Valjalo and Pick indicate that during the three years of Allende's government, Chile Films supported the production of "more than 100 documentaries that had a political function and a clear propagandistic character" (1984, 36). Among these were: *No nos trancarán el paso / They Won't Block Our Way* (1971, Guillermo Cahn and Héctor Ríos), *Ahora te vamos a llamar hermano / Now We're Going to Call you Brother* (1971, Raúl Ruiz), *Compañero Presidente / Comrade President* (1971, Miguel Littin), *El primer año / The First Year* (1971) and *La respuesta de octubre / The October Answer* (1972), both by Patricio Guzmán, and Flores's *Descomedidos y chascones* (1972).

9   Within the country, some documentaries managed to prove exceptions in evading the dictatorship's censors, including *Recado de Chile / Message from Chile* (1979, directed by Carlos Flores, Pedro Chaskel, and José Román and edited in Cuba), *No olvidar / Not to Forget* (1982, directed by Ignacio Agüero and edited in Sweden and Italy), and *Chile, no invoco tu nombre en vano / Chile, I Don't Take your Name in Vain* (1983, directed by Colectivo Cine Ojo and edited in France).

10 On one hand, there were some who had begun to film in Chile and found their work interrupted by the coup, which is why they were finished in exile. Among these are: *La Batalla de Chile / The Battle of Chile* (1973–77, made by Patricio Guzmán in Chile, France, and Cuba) and *Los puños frente al cañón / "Fists Before the Cannon"* (1972–75, made by Gastón Ancelovici and Orlando Lübbert in Chile and East Germany). On the other hand, there were other documentaries developed entirely in exile, including *Pinochet: Fascista, asesino, traidor, agente del imperialismo / "Pinochet: Fascist, Murderer, Traitor, Agent of Imperialism"* (1974, Sergio Castilla, Sweden), *La historia es nuestra y la hacen los pueblos / "History is Ours and the People Make It"* (1975, Álvaro Ramírez, East Germany), and *¡La canción no muere generales! / "The Song Does not Die, Generals!"* (1975, Claudio Sapiaín, Sweden).

11 A detailed discussion of the work of these filmmakers can be found in the book *Nomadías: El cine de Marilú Mallet, Valeria Sarmiento y Angelina Vásquez* (2016), edited by Elizabeth Ramírez Soto and Catalina Donoso Pinto.

12 The monthly news program *Teleanálisis* (1984–89) chronicled the social movements that contributed to the end of the dictatorship, giving agency to victims of repression. Although its distribution was prohibited in Chile, its reports and documentaries were distributed abroad and circulated clandestinely within the country as well. Its activist practices sought to generate an alternative, independent media platform that could democratize the dictatorship's hegemonic media practices and resist its control over most of the country's mainstream media.

13 The ECO Communications Collective focused on creating community-oriented documentaries. Its leaders offered workshops to teach cinematography to young people, lending them video cameras to record their experiences in the same way that militant Latin American filmmakers had in the 1960s and 1970s with sixteen-millimeter film. ECO worked with different communities to create documentaries that highlighted the marginal discourses and experiences of popular cultures and subcultures, ethnic and urban minorities, the proletariat, students, and other young people.

14 Apart from the rhetorical displacement from a "political subject" ["sujeto político"] to a "collective politics" ["colectivo político,"] MAFI echoes the efforts of audiovisual collectives in the 1980s in its use of narratives in and of dissident spaces, making visible the experiences of marginalized subjects and staging political and creative action in opposition to industrial production.

15 Hirsch's proposals give great importance to the memory constructions of the second generation and—particularly in her book *Family Frames: Photography, Narrative, and Postmemory* (2012)—they suggest that the image is the privileged device to analyze their stories. Although her work focuses on the generation that followed the survivors of holocausts, exiles, and genocides of the first half of the twentieth century, her analyses can be extrapolated to the "generation of children" of Latin American dictatorships and particularly to the cinema of the postmemory. In addition, these considerations may dialogue with the so-called affective turn, since they privilege the representation of traumatic events less than the embodied and sensitive ways of living memory and politics.

16 Among the most notable documentaries of postmemory in Chile—which began at the beginning of the 2000s and continues to the present—are *La hija de O'Higgins / O'Higgins's Daughter* (2001, Pamela Pequeño), *Reinalda del Carmen, mi mamá y yo / Reinalda del Carmen, My Mom and I* (2006, Lorena Giachino), *Mi vida con Carlos / My Life with Carlos* (2008, Germán Berger), *El edificio de los chilenos / The Chilean Building* (2010, Macarena Aguiló), *Sibila* (2012, Teresa Arredondo), *Allende, mi abuelo Allende / Beyond my Grandfather Allende* (2015, Marcia Tambutti), *Venían a buscarme / They Were Coming to Get Me* (2016, Álvaro de La Barra), and *El pacto de Adriana / Adriana's Pact* (2017, Lissette Orozco), among others.

17 These include the Argentinean *Papá Iván / Dad Iván* (2000, María Inés Roqué), *Un tal Ragone: Deconstruyendo a pa / "That Ragone: Deconstructing Dad"* (2002, Vanessa Ragone), *Los rubios / The Blonds* (2003, Albertina Carri), *M* (2006, Nicolás Prividera), and *Perón, mi papá y yo / "Perón, My Dad and I"* (2017, Eloy Martínez) and the Brazilian *Diário de uma busca / Diary of a Search* (2010, Flávia Castro) and *Os dias com ele / The Days with Him* (2013, Maria Clara Escobar).

18 They include *El tesoro de América: El oro de Pascua Lama / America's Treasure: Pascua Lama's Gold* (2010, Carmen Castillo), *Cuentos sobre el futuro / Tales about the Future* (2012, Pachi Bustos), *74 m2* (2012, Tiziana Panizza and Paola Castillo), *Tres instantes, un grito / Three Moments, One Cry* (2013, Cecilia Barriga), *El vals de los inútiles / The Waltz* (2013, Edison Cajas), *Darío en toma / Diary of a School under Siege* (2014, José María González), *Cuando respiro / When Breathing* (2015, Coti Donoso), *Pascua Lama: El llanto de la montaña / Pascua Lama: The Cry of the Mountain* (2015, Rodrigo Insunza), and *Secos / Dry* (2017, Galut Alarcón and Chamila Rodríguez), among others.

19 Political and economic neoliberalism and its impact on film production allow for the tracing of relationships between the Chilean documentary and that of other countries around the world, including those of neighboring countries. The work of the Argentine director Fernando "Pino" Solanas—icon of the militant Latin American documentary since his monumental trilogy *La hora de los hornos / The Hour of the Furnaces* (1968, codirected with Octavio Getino)—has continued more recently: *Memoria del saqueo / Social Genocide* (2004), *La dignidad de los nadies / The Dignity of the Nobodies* (2005), *Argentina latente / Latent Argentina* (2007), *La próxima estación / Next Stop* (2008), *Tierra sublevada I y II / Land in Revolt I and II* (2009, 2010), *La guerra del fracking / The Fracking War* (2013), and *El legado estratégico de Juan Perón / "Juan Perón's Strategic Legacy"* (2016).

20 Among these, some highlights include *La venda /* "The Bandage" (2000, Carmen Gloria Camiruaga), *Estadio Nacional / National Stadium* (2002, Carmen Luz Parot), *I Love Pinochet* (2001, Marcela Said), *Actores secundarios / Secondary Actors* (2004, Pachi Bustos and Jorge Leiva), *El astuto mono Pinochet contra la Moneda de los cerdos / The Clever monkey Pinochet Versus La Moneda's Pig* and *La muerte de Pinochet / The Death of Pinochet* (2004 and 2011, by Bettina Perut and Iván Osnovikoff), *El diario de Agustín / Agustin's Newspaper* (2008, Ignacio Agüero), *El mocito / The Young Butler* (2010, Marcela Said), *País invisible / The Invisible Country* (2015, Anthony Rauld), *Habeas Corpus* and *Guerrero* (2015 and 2017, Sebastián Moreno and Claudia Barril), and *Las cruces / The Crosses* (2018, Teresa Arredondo and Carlos Vásquez).

21 Some examples of this: the slogan "Venceremos" explicitly invokes a plural, a *nosotros* (we/us) that refers to the *pueblo*. At the end of the documentary, there is a shot of a huge ¡*Basta!* ("Enough!") slogan written on a wall, and later we see titles that include "People: The way is open," "Toward the birth of a new man," and "We will overcome." In *Tres instantes, un grito*, we hear similarly protesting crowds in Madrid, fighting against riot control in the Puerta del Sol: "We're not going! We are growing!," or against the politicians: "No! No! You don't represent us!" Occupy Wall Street protesters sing "This 99 of mine, I'm gonna let it shine," referring to the 99 percent of the world that is left out of economic power, and then they emphasize again, "People? Power!"

In Chile, the students sing in their marches, "Let's go, everyone! Put in more effort! Let's head out to the street again! Chilean education can't be sold—it has to be defended!"

22 Among these, see *Newén Mapuche / Newén Mapuche* (2010, Elena Varela), *Calafate, zoológicos humanos / Human Zoo: The Story of Calafate* (2011, Hans Mülchi), *Dungún, la lengua / "Dungún: The Language"* (2012, Pamela Pequeño), *Genoveva* (2014, Paola Castillo), *Surire* (2015, Bettina Perut and Iván Osnovikoff), *Te Kuhane o te tupuna* (2015, Leonardo Pakarati), and *Riu, lo que cuentan los cantos / Riu, What the Songs Tell* (2017, Pablo Berthelon). In this political dimension the Chilean documentary can trace certain parallels between contemporary works and some earlier ones: for example, the search for vindication in *Newén Mapuche* echoes the demands around the restitution of Mapuche lands that were reclaimed forty years before in *Nutuayin Mapu* (1969, Carlos Flores, Antonio Campi, Luis Araneda, Samuel Carvajal, and Guillermo Cahn).

23 In Brazil: *Pachamama* (2008, Eryk Rocha) and *Martírio / Martyrdom* (2016, Vincent Carelli). In Argentina: *Río arriba / Upriver* (2004, Ulises de la Orden), *El país del diablo / The Devil's Country* (2008, Andrés Di Tella), and *Damiana Kryygi* (2015, Alejandro Fernández Mouján).

24 These include documentaries like *Hija / Daughter* (2011, María Paz González), *El Huaso / El Huaso: The Last Rodeo* (2012, Carlo Proto), *Genoveva* (2015, Paola Castillo), *El soltero de la familia / The Bachelor of the Family* (2015, Daniel Osorio), *Atrapados en Japón / Trapped in Japan* (2015, Vivianne Barry), and *Visión Nocturna / "Night Vision"* (2019, Carolina Moscoso).

25 In this respect, it is useful to consult the abundant work of authors like Stuart Hall, Jean-Pierre Warnier, Néstor García Canclini, Jesús Martín Barbero, George Yúdice, and Luis Reygadas, among others.

26 These include *Madres con ruedas / The Mothers on Wheels* (2006, Mario Piazza y Mónica Chirife), *Fotografías / Photographs* (2007, Andrés Di Tella), *Return to Bolivia* (2008, Mariano Raffo), *Familia tipo / Typical Family* (2009, Cecilia Priego), *Los nueve puntos de mi padre / "My Father's Nine Points"* (2010, Pablo Romano), *La chica del sur / The Girl from the South* (2012, José Luis García), and *El padre / The Father* (2016, Mariana Arruti). In Brazil this tendency can be appreciated in works like *Um passaporte húngaro / A Hungarian Passport* (2001, Sandra Kogut) and *33* (2002, Kiko Goifman).

27 The "MAFI Shot" is known for being a fixed shot (without cuts), lasting one to two minutes, with direct sound.

28 Cf. http://mafi.tv/sobre-mafi/.

29 Following Rancière, Adriana Valdés refers to dissent as "a political act that seeks to modify these coordinates: 'one spectacle or tonality that replaces another'"

["un acto político que busca modificar esas coordenadas: 'un espectáculo o una tonalidad que reemplaza a otra'"], and as "a way of reconstructing the relationships between places and identities, spectacles and gazes, proximities and distances" ["una forma de reconstruir las relaciones entre lugares e identidades, espectáculos y miradas, proximidades y distancias"] (2008, 11).

30 "Amateurism is also a theoretical and political position. It is a position that rejects the authority of the specialists by reexamining the way in which the boundaries of their fields are traced in the crossroads of experiences and knowledge. The politics of the amateur affirms that cinema belongs to all those who, in one way or another, have traveled to the interior of the system of distances organized by their name, and that each one can authorize themselves to trace, between one and another point of this topography, a singular itinerary that is added to the film world and its knowledge" (Rancière 2012, 15).

31 This is not the only concomitance between political cinema of the 1960s and 1970s and collaborative contemporary documentary, such as the MAFI collective. Today, certain characteristics of what Isabel Seguí (2018) describes as oppositional cinema (political films that she dates as between 1960 and 1990) may be understood as methodological continuities coming from modes of production that result in aspects directly related to the affective turn, described as one of the characteristics of contemporary Chilean documentary. Friendship as the starting point behind MAFI's collaborative project is one of them. "Personal relationships, regarded as a sensitive subject, have traditionally been considered only fit for gossip and are often overlooked in scholarly work on the history of Latin American film. However, in the context of its precarious mode of production, they cannot be a secondary consideration. Rather, they were the cornerstone of an artisanal film's feasibility. Perhaps in other modes of production with more stable industrial and financial structures, personal bonds of love, friendship, or kinship do not affect production in the same way. However, in the case of Latin American oppositional cinema, they often had a direct impact on production. Emotions such as companionship, enthusiasm, and generosity could turn an impossible film project into a great success" (Seguí 2018, 18).

32 The transformations of the tools and their potential in a context determined by a digital culture of circulation and open content, constant flows, and ever-increasing access on the Internet results in an exponential offering of and demand for content, along with an atomization and diversification of the preferences of the audiences. The public is no longer considered a group of mere receptors, but instead they are seen as active agents that increasingly constitute a participative culture, not only for their interaction on social networks and virtual communities but also in directly uploading their own audiovisual content to the web. With this scenario the challenges do not only appertain to the realm of technology, but also directly commit to a sociopolitical ethic that

adjusts to the mode in which Scolari (2008) characterizes these new forms of communication. Rather than in its mere technique, the political power of digital video is found in its activism and its capacity to produce transformations in the networks of social organization, stimulate citizen participation, and exercise particular modes of inclusive political resistance. For more information about this material, see authors such as Scolari (2008) and Sierra and Montero (2015), among others.

33 These include the Escuela Cultural Comunitaria "El Culebrón Timbal" and the collective "Cine en Movimiento," both in Argentina. For a description of communal audiovisual production in that country, see Andrea Molfetta (2017).

34 See, for example, Ignacio Agüero's recent films (*El otro día / The Other Day*, 2012, *Como me da la gana II / This Is the Way I Like It II*, 2016, and *Nunca subí el Provincia / I Never Climbed the Provincia*, 2019), as well as the trilogy *Cartas visuales / Visual Letters* by Tiziana Panizza (*Dear Nonna: A Film Letter*, 2005; *Remitente: Una carta visual /* "Sender: A Visual Letter," 2009; *Al final: La última carta /* "At the End: The Last Letter," 2012). Panizza's more recent series of dystopian cartographies in the documentaries *Tierra en movimiento / Land in Motion* (2015) and *Tierra sola / Solitary Land* (2017) are also good examples of films that experiment with the sensory, as are José Luis Torres Leiva's *El viento sabe que vuelvo a casa / The Wind Knows that I'm Coming Back Home* (2016) and *Todas las cartas que nunca envié / All the Letters that I Never Sent* (2017).

35 In her trilogy *Cartas visuales*, Panizza's interstitial poetics can be recognized in the intervals traced between the intimacy of her world—a matrix of subjectivity present in almost all of the work of this director—and the exterior world, marked in *Dear Nonna* . . . by the worldwide protests in favor of peace in the context of the U.S.-led Iraq War, and that Panizza registers from London in 2004. In *Remitente* . . . , the public is represented by the streets flooded by celebrations and protests following the death of Pinochet in Chile. In *Al final* . . . , the private is alternated with the student marches demanding free education over the last few years in Chile (Lagos 2015).

WORKS CITED

Ahmed, Sara. 2015. *La política cultural de las emociones*. México D.F.: PUEG.
Bolzoni, Francesco. 1974. *El cine de Allende*. Valencia: Fernando Torres.
Depetris, Irene. 2018. "Mirar, escuchar, tocar: Políticas y poéticas de archivo en *Tierra Sola* (2017) de Tiziana Panizza." *452F, Revista de Teoría de la Literatura y Literatura Comparada* 18: 106–29.
Didi-Huberman, Georges. 2008. *Cuando las imágenes toman posición*. Madrid: Antonio Machado.

Gaines, Jane. 1999. "Political Mimesis." In *Collecting Visible Evidence*, edited by Jane Gaines and Michael Renov, 84–102. Minneapolis: University of Minnesota Press.

Getino, Octavio, and Susana Velleggia. 2002. *El cine de "las historias de la revolución": Aproximación a las teorías y prácticas del cine de "intervención política" en América Latina (1967-1977)*. Buenos Aires: Altamira.

Hirsch, Marianne. 2008. "The Generation of Postmemory." *Poetics Today* 29 (1): 103–28.

———. 2012. *Family Frames: Photography, Narrative, and Postmemory*. Cambridge: Harvard University Press.

Lagos, Paola. 2015. "El Súper 8mm. como imagen intersticial en la Trilogía Cartas Visuales de Tiziana Panizza (Chile, 2005, 2009, 2012)." In *Nuevas Travesías por el Cine Chileno y Latinoamericano*, edited by Mónica Villarroel, 159–67. Santiago: LOM.

———. 2019. "Resistencia política y videoactivismo en colectivos documentales chilenos: El caso de MAFI, Mapa Fílmico de un País." In *Contraculturas y Subculturas en el Cine Latinoamericano (1975-2015)*, edited by Sonia García and Ana María López, 157–79. Valencia: Tirant Humanidades.

Laub, Dori. 1992. "An Event Without Witness: Truth, Testimony and Survival, in Testimony: Crisis of Witnessing." In *Literature, Psychoanalysis, and History*, edited by Shoshana Felman and Dori Laub, 75–92. New York: Routledge.

Lejeune, Philippe. 2008. "Cine y Autobiografía, problemas de vocabulario." In *Cineastas frente al espejo*, edited by Gregorio Martín Gutiérrez, 13–26. Madrid: T&B.

Massumi, Brian. 2002. *Parables of the Virtual: Movement, Affect, Sensation*. Durham: Duke University Press.

Mateos, Concha, and Ana Sedeño. 2015. "Videoactivismo y Autoría Colectiva." In *Videoactivismo y movimientos sociales: Teoría y praxis de las multitudes conectadas*, edited by Francisco Sierra and David Montero, 298–331. Barcelona: Gedisa.

Molfetta, Andrea. 2017. *Cine comunitario argentino: Mapeos, experiencias y ensayos*. Buenos Aires: Teseo.

Mouesca, Jacqueline. 1988. *Plano secuencia de la memoria de Chile*. Madrid: Ed. del Litoral.

———. 2005. *El documental chileno*. Santiago: LOM.

Pinto, Iván. 2012. "Lo incompleto: Desajuste y fractura en dos diarios fílmicos del exilio chileno." In *Prismas del cine latinoamericano*, edited by Wolfgang Bongers, 215–35. Santiago: Cuarto Propio.

Podalsky, Laura. 2011. *The Politics of Affect and Emotion in Contemporary Latin American Cinema: Argentina, Brazil, Cuba, and Mexico*. New York: Palgrave Macmillan.

———. 2018. "The Affective Turn." In *New Approaches to Latin American Studies: Culture and Power*, edited by Juan Poblete, 237–54. New York: Routledge.

Quílez, Laia. 2010. "*La representación de la dictadura militar en el cine documental argentino de segunda generación.*" PhD diss., Universitat Rovira y Virgili, 2010. http://www.tdx.cat/handle/10803/8596.

Ramírez Soto, Elizabeth, and Catalina Donoso Pinto, eds. 2016. *Nomadías: El cine de Marilú Mallet, Valeria Sarmiento y Angelina Vázquez*. Santiago de Chile: Metales Pesados.

Rancière, Jacques. 2004. *The Politics of Aesthetics: The Distribution of the Sensible*. Edited and translated by Gabriel Rockhill. London: Bloomsbury Academic.

———. 2005. *Sobre políticas estéticas*. Barcelona: Museu d'Art Contemporani de Barcelona, Servei de Publicacions de la Universitat Autónoma de Barcelona.

———. 2011. *El destino de las imágenes*. Buenos Aires: Prometeo.

———. 2012. *Las distancias del cine*. Buenos Aires: Manantial.

Renov, Michael. 2004. *The Subject in Documentary*. Minneapolis: University of Minnesota Press.

Schlunke, Katrina. 2013. "Memory and Materiality." *Memory Studies* 6 (3): 253–61.

Seguí, Isabel. 2018. "Auteurism, Machismo-Leninismo, and Other Issues Women's Labor in Andean Oppositional Film Production." *Feminist Media Studies* 4 (1): 11–36.

Scolari, Carlos. 2008. *Hipermediaciones: Elementos para una teoría de la comunicación digital interactiva*. Barcelona: Gedisa.

Sierra, Francisco, and David Montero, eds. 2015. *Videoactivismo y movimientos sociales: Teoría y praxis de las multitudes conectadas*. Barcelona: Gedisa.

Valdés, Adriana. 2008. Preface to *Alfredo Jaar: La política de las imágenes*, edited by Adriana Valdés, 5–15. Santiago: Metales Pesados.

Valenzuela, Valeria. 2011. "Giro subjetivo en el documental latinoamericano: De la cámara-puño al sujeto-cámara." *La Fuga* 12 (April). http://www.lafuga.cl/giro-subjetivo-en-el-documental-latinoamericano/439.

Valjalo, David, and Zuzana Pick. 1984. *Diez años de cine chileno: 1973–1983*. Los Angeles: Ediciones de la Frontera.

Venkatesh, Vinodh, and María del Carmen Caña. 2016. "Affect, Bodies, and Circulations in Contemporary Latin American Film." *Arizona Journal of Hispanic Cultural Studies* 20: 175–81.

Winston, Brian. 1988. "The Tradition of the Victim in Griersonian Documentary." In *New Challenges for Documentary*, edited by Alan Rosenthal, 269–87. Berkeley: University of California Press.

ON THE MARGINS OF HOLLYWOOD: CHILEAN GENRE FLICKS

4

THE REACH OF GENRE

The Emergence of Chilean Horror Cinema

Jonathan Risner

In his recent overview of contemporary genre cinema from Latin American countries, Gerard Dapena cites Mexico, Argentina, and Chile as the primary producers of horror cinema in the region (2018, 158). Indeed, websites devoted to horror cinema in Chile and elsewhere—*Be Afraid* in Chile, *Dread Central* in the United States, *Aullidos* in Spain, and *Scary Movies* in Germany—have alerted readers to particular Chilean films as they enter different production phases, are screened at festivals, and are released in particular national markets. The geographic scope of websites covering Chilean horror cinema intimates that the domestic and transnational orientation of horror parallels that of other genres currently emerging from Chile. The success of Chilean art house / "independent" cinema at A-list film festivals and the 2018 Academy Award given to *Una mujer fantástica* / *A Fantastic Woman* (Sebastián Lelio, 2018)[1] create a transnational calling card of sorts for Chilean cinema. However, horror constitutes a coeval, if relatively minor, national film marker that circulates across the globe.[2] Akin to its more prestigious art house cousin, Chilean horror achieves modest domestic and international success and avails itself of a transnational circuit of distribution and consumption.

Here, I examine how an amorphous and, at times, fractured horror genre cinema community in Chile is constructed via consumption and production. Relying on virtual and material uses of Chilean horror films, I map the coordinates of Chilean horror cinema culture and trace how it interfaces with a larger transnational horror film culture. In addition, I briefly consider how select Chilean horror films formally replicate and differ from horror cinema emerging from elsewhere. Finally, I consider what, if anything, the emergence of horror cinema in Chile divulges about national culture. As I will describe below, critics have often characterized genre cinema, especially horror cinema, as being particularly responsive to national tensions or tragedies. Chilean horror provides a corpus of films through which to broach the dynamics of visibilization and omission of Chileanness, including its historical and contemporary crises.

LATCHING ON AND OUT: HORROR FILM CULTURE IN CHILE AND BEYOND

Mary Douglas and Baron Isherwood consider consumption as a mode of "making visible and stable the categories of culture" (1996, 38). Film can achieve the trappings of a culture via its consumption, and Rick Altman's notion of a "constellated genre community" is instrumental for conceiving how the consumption of horror cinema makes a horror film culture visible in Chile. Though the viewing platform to which he refers is dated, Altman characterizes a constellated genre community as "a selective view of telespectators, all separate, and all facing in the same figurative direction—towards the screen—but implicitly broken into separate groups according to the programme they are watching, and the other spectators they imagine watching the same programme in the same way at the same time" (1999, 161). Furthermore, though a spectator may watch a film alone, an act that seemingly would defy a fundamental tenet of creating a viewing collective (Hanich 2014), "the process of viewing a film generically serves as symbolic communication with other spectators who read the film through the same generic lens" (Altman 1999, 162).[3] As I will detail below, the multiple consumptions of horror cinema in Chile make manifest a horror community that overlaps with other genre communities while folding itself into a larger transnational horror film culture.

Michel de Certeau's notion of production and secondary production fleshes out the notion of how consumption can create a horror film culture. De Certeau considers consumption to be "another production" or "secondary production" that entails how consumers appropriate and use a product (1988, xii–xiii). De Certeau's allusion to television and the need to study "what the cultural consumer 'makes' or 'does' with the images" (31) provides a starting point from which to think about what consumers in Chile do with horror cinema. If a horror film is the basis of production, secondary productions are the ways consumers use a horror film in Chile, such as commenting on a film via social media or attending a screening. Supplementing de Certeau's ideas, I would add that secondary production can occur on different scales and should encompass what larger entities—distribution and production companies, film festival juries and programmers, journalists, and government agencies—do with a film (Risner 2018, xviii). Such entities are composed of individuals, and, albeit lacking the autonomy of a single being, those individuals belonging to an entity *do* things with a film as well.

A conception of Chilean horror cinema culture should not be circumscribed merely to the consumption of domestically produced horror cinema but should also include horror films that circulate in Chile, irrespective of their national or multinational origins, via one or more modes (multiplexes, television, video-on-demand, DVDs, legal and illegal online streaming, informal street markets). Pierre Sorlin defines Italian film culture as "not a set of films which help to distinguish a nation from other nations, [but rather] the chain of relations and exchanges which develop in connection with films, in a territory delineated by its economic and juridical policy" (1996, 10). In other words, Sorlin's analysis of Italian cinema is not limited to films that achieve some authentic expression of Italianness; he also examines how those films circulate within Italy. In the case of Chilean horror cinema culture, commercial and noncommercial relations emerge alongside the transnational horror cinema that circulates through Chile and Chilean horror cinema that circulates in Chile and abroad. In turn, one must account for both the international horror cinema that is consumed in Chile and the Chilean horror films that are consumed domestically and abroad. Although my analysis is largely focused on auteurist approaches that hone in on the Chilean nationality of directors, I will amend Sorlin's approach and insist that Chilean horror cinema can be produced beyond the physical geography of Chile or in languages other than Spanish. Patricio Valladares's *Vlad's Legacy* (2017) and *Nightworld* (2017) and Raúl Ruiz's *La mansión Nucingen / The House of Nucingen* (2008) are films commonly classified as horror. Yet, the films' content and conditions of production complicate the transposition of Sorlin's parameters for Italian film culture onto Chilean horror film culture. *Vlad's Legacy* and *Nightworld* were filmed in Turkey and Bulgaria, respectively, do not have Spanish-language dialogue or a Chilean cast, and draw production support from companies located in the United States, Turkey, and Bulgaria. *La mansión Nucingen* was filmed in Chile with a mostly French cast speaking French, German,

Spanish, and English. To be sure, a film—its content or some facet of its political economy—should not automatically or primarily be scrutinized for its national expression or lack thereof. Valladares's aforementioned two films ostensibly appear devoid of any expression of a Chilean identity. Nevertheless, an expression of Chileanness can happen in films that are more loosely tethered to the physical space of Chile than, say, a film that is produced in Santiago with government and private support from Chile and boasting dialogue rife with *chilenismos*. Critics, such as Zuzana Pick and Ruiz himself, have asserted how Ruiz's films made in exile simultaneously express some aspect of a European culture alongside that of Chilean culture or history (Pick 1993, 161, 176–85). Indeed, an amalgamation of European and Chilean cultures transpires in *La mansión Nucingen*. Steeped in Gothic tropes (i.e., disease, ghosts, incest), Ruiz's foray into horror presents a central European aristocratic enclave anchored in Chile but that is in decline and whose inhabitants regard Chilean culture and the Spanish language as inferior.

Valladares and Ruiz, of course, circulate transnationally as directors for distinct reasons. While Ruiz's filmic works outside Chile were made under the duress of political exile (at least during the dictatorship years), Valladares's productions abroad are symptomatic of how contemporary Latin American horror film directors (e.g., Adrián García Bogliano, Fede Álvarez, Andy Muschietti, and Guillermo del Toro) are able to cross borders and work in different film industries on account of their understanding of the transnational codes of horror. Setting aside these caveats to Sorlin's approach, the relations around the horror films that constitute Chilean horror film culture possess varying connections to Chile, relations that are made visible in production, festivals, online periodicals, and websites. These connections mark the dimensions and forge the creation of a Chilean horror film culture.[4]

Janet Harbord argues for "an understanding of film cultures as institutionally and spatially located" (2002, 39), and a diversity of exhibition spaces abets the creation and maintenance of Chilean horror cinema culture. Commercial cinemas in Chile constitute one such space. Transnational horror hits, such as *Get Out* (Jordan Peele, 2017), *Train to Busan* (Sang Ho Yeon, 2016), and *[Rec]* (Jaume Balagueró and Paco Plaza, 2007), regularly receive widespread theatrical distribution in Chile. And while the overwhelming majority of commercial horror film releases come from the United States,[5] foreign films belonging to the suspense/horror genres captured 5.2 percent of the total domestic box office in Chile in 2015 ("El cine en Chile en el 2015" 2016, 9) and 9.4 percent in 2014 ("El cine en Chile en el 2014" 2015, 9). Evidencing a demand for horror cinema, Chile is a profitable and reliable destination for the distribution of transnational commercial horror cinema. Akin to Altman's notion of genre communities, Charles Acland has examined "the industrial and popular *discourses* about contemporary commercial cinema and its patrons that have become common sense" (2003, 9; emphasis in original). These discourses include a hypothetical conception of a spectator whose filmic tastes transcend a local or national context: "This imaginary cinemagoer might be seen as having similarities with other popular film audiences in assorted geographical locations, sharing elements of pleasure and diversion" (Acland 2003, 11). Distributors of commercial horror cinema in Chile are keenly aware of horror's popularity, and, therefore, globally popular horror films receive domestic theatrical releases.

Although the draw for spectators for these films is decidedly lower, commercial cinemas allow for the exhibition of Chilean horror productions alongside transnational horror. Over the past two decades, there has been a remarkable upsurge in national horror film productions relative to a near absence of horror cinema prior to 2000.[6] Table 1 lists exclusively national horror feature-length films that have been released in commercial cinemas in Chile since 2000. As the table demonstrates, the popularity of Chilean horror films can fluctuate drastically. Moreover, when the box office numbers for Chilean horror films are set against the numbers for popular horror films from elsewhere, one is reminded of domestic audiences' preference for commercial cinema from the United States, a dynamic that is seen elsewhere in Latin America and in the world. In 2014, *Video Club* and *Aftershock* attracted 16,699 and 1,873 moviegoers, respectively. *Video Club* was the fifth best-performing Chilean film released in box offices in 2014, and *Aftershock* occupied the twenty-third position ("El cine en Chile en el 2014" 2015, 12). *Annabelle* (John R. Leonetti, 2014), a U.S. horror film and the most popular horror film at Chilean box offices in 2014, attracted 912,298 spectators ("El cine en Chile en el 2014" 2015, 7). Still, while the box office performance of Chilean horror films ebbs and flows, national horror films continue to be produced at a sustained rhythm, often with the support of government film initiatives, such as Banco del Estado's Programa de Fomento al Cine Chileno.[7]

TABLE 1: CHILEAN HORROR FILMS RELEASED IN COMMERCIAL CINEMAS IN CHILE[8]

Title / Director	Year of release	Number of spectators
Madre (Aaron Burns)	2016	23,395
La maldición / The Stranger (Guillermo Amoedo)	2014	10,233
Aftershock (Nicolás López)	2014	1,873
Video Club (Pablo Illanes)	2014	16,699
Caleuche: El llamado del Mar / "Caleuche: The Call of the Sea" (Jorge Olguín)	2012	62,620
El ejército de los helechos / The Fern's Army (Diego González Durney)	2012	54
Muerte ciega / Zombie Dawn (Lucio Rojas and Cristián Toledo)	2011	227
Baby Shower (Pablo Illanes, 2011)	2011	65,804
Solos / Descendants (Jorge Olguín)	2008	6,997
El huésped (Coke Hidalgo)	2005	data unavailable
Sangre eterna / Eternal Blood (Jorge Olguín)	2002	84,555
Ángel negro (Jorge Olguín)	2000	17,020

The list of Chilean commercial horror films inevitably broaches the topic of what criteria enable a film to achieve a partial or full categorization as "horror." At the essay's start, I drew a distinction between Chilean art house cinema and its horror cinema. Select critics often wield such a distinction in the deployment of the moniker "novísimo cine chileno," or some other designation, to set apart commercial genre film production from films that possess an unconventional or abstract style.[9] Films such as *El club / The Club* (Pablo Larraín, 2015), *La noche de enfrente / Night Across the Street* (Raúl Ruiz, 2012), and Sebastián Silva's *Magic Magic* (2013) and *Nasty Baby* (2015) are four films that often are deemed art house or "independent" productions by critics in different geographies. However, to varying degrees, each film draws upon horror aesthetics via framing, lighting, setting, or narrative. For example, *Nasty Baby* flirts with horror when Freddy stabs the Bishop in the throat in self-defense. Albeit not framed with the same degree of closeness and splatter gore typical of horror films, the violence is framed in a slightly claustrophobic manner and punctuated by nondiegetic metal music. Yet, *Nasty Baby* and the three other art house films are not deemed horror and are excluded from any list of Chilean commercial horror releases. Such an exclusion appears to rest upon the notion of genre consensus. Steve Neale has discussed the "culturally contingent nature of genres" (2000, 18) and how a film's generic classification rests on "a common cultural consensus" (18) among audiences and various other entities, such as critics, exhibitors, film festival programmers, and distributors. Interestingly, a partial consensus exists for *Nasty Baby*'s moment of horror among select critics. Miguel Malermo, for example, touches on how each scene "begins to take on a dark tone that broaches elements associated with different genres of horror" (2016), and the title of Alan Zilberman's review in the *Washington Post* similarly broaches horror's positioning within the film's larger narrative trajectory: "'Nasty Baby' starts out as comedy, but veers into horror" (2015). Malermo's and Zilberman's reviews aside, *Nasty Baby* is, in general, not characterized as a horror film by critics and retail outlets, but instead as a drama and, perhaps surprisingly, a comedy. Matt Hills has described the use of horror motifs by Freud, Marx, and Derrida, among others, as an instance in which the "lines between theory and horror fiction are . . . discursively permeable" (2005, 153) and has discussed how theory acquires "an affective charge" (155) with horror. And though *Nasty Baby* and other art house films may not belong squarely to the horror genre, the films' uses of horror for affective or other purposes signal the occasionally porous relationship between Chilean art house cinema and horror.[10]

Brendan Kredell has characterized film festivals as "the public squares in which hidden audiences gather" (2016, 16). Film festivals and marketing events that feature horror movie screenings constitute other key spaces for the exhibition of Chilean horror cinema and, ultimately, the creation and maintenance of horror cinema culture in Chile. Since 2008, Fixion-SARS: Festival de Cine Fantástico y de Terror in Santiago has screened national short, medium, and feature-length horror film productions alongside international ones. The Santiago Horror Film Festival commenced with its inaugural edition in 2018. Other festivals in or near Santiago include the short-lived FANTEC (Festival international de cine fantástico y de terror) in

Colina, and Fanges, which began in 2018 in Santiago. Screenings of Chilean horror cinema transpire in nonhorror film festivals as well, and the Santiago International Film Festival (SANFIC) has premiered several horror films, such as *Downhill* (Patricio Valladares, 2016). Beyond the capital, Festival Internacional Terror Gore in Valparaíso has been a crucial venue for national and international horror films since 2010, and, likewise, Festival Internacional de Cine de Terror in Valdivia has operated since 2003. Blood Window is a promotional event that originated in Buenos Aires, Argentina, in 2013 and connects film distributors with Latin American directors and producers of genre films, such as horror, science fiction, fantasy, and action. Blood Window has taken place in Buenos Aires since its inception. However, in 2017, a version of Blood Window took place in Santiago and debuted several national productions, including *Gritos del bosque / Whispers of the Forest* (Jorge Olguín), touted as the first national 3D film, and *Wekufe: El origen del mal / "Wekufe: The Origin of Evil"* (Javier Attridge).

Exhibition of Chilean horror cinema occurs on different scales and platforms, all of which are significant in forging a facet of Chilean horror cinema culture that is based around domestic film production. Table 2 lists Chilean horror films that were not released into Chilean cinemas, but instead premiered at festivals or were released straight to DVD.[11] The viewing of Chilean horror cinema here unfolds as private and individualized viewings via DVDs, video-on-demand, and streaming through sites such as Netflix and YouTube and a myriad of illegal sites. While precise data about the extent of viewing of Chilean horror films beyond commercial cinemas is unavailable, the mere presence of these works on the Internet reiterates the visibility of Chilean horror film culture and demonstrates the different fates of particular horror films. In other words, not all Chilean horror cinema circulates equally. Netflix in Chile, for example, enables Chilean horror to circulate at different rhythms and scales. Netflix streams *Aftershock* (Nicolás López, 2012) and *Sendero / Path* (Lucio Rojas, 2015), the first of which was originally released in Chilean cinemas. Given Netflix's range, the two films' availability in over 190 countries provides the films with an incredible breadth of circulation that surpasses that of other national horror productions. Moreover, within Chile, Netflix has agreements with Movistar and VTR, its competitors for streaming content, to make Netflix's content available to Movistar's and VTR's customers. In turn, *Aftershock* and *Sendero* circulate domestically and are more accessible than other horror films that are available via DVD or that have been screened strictly at festivals.

TABLE 2: CHILEAN HORROR FILMS WITHOUT COMMERCIAL CINEMA RELEASE[12]

Title / Director	Year of release
Trauma (Lucio Rojas)	2017
Yo Soy Super Zombie / "I am Super Zombie" (Pablo Villagra)	2017
Wekufe: El origen del mal / "Wekufe: The Origin of Evil" (Javier Attridge)	2016
Sendero (Lucio Rojas)	2015
Perfidia / *Wicked Woods* (Lucio Rojas)	2014
Gritos del bosque / *Whispers of the Forest* (Jorge Olguín)	2014
Apio verde / "Green Celery" (Francesc Morales)	2013
En las afueras de la ciudad / *Hidden in the Woods* (Patricio Valladares)	2012
Humanimal (Francesc Morales)	2010
La mansión Nucingen / *The House of Nucingen* (Raúl Ruiz)	2008 (released in Chile in 2015)
Empaná de pino / "Meat Empanada" (Wincy)	2008
Demencia / "Madness" (David Contreras)	2007
Curriculum (Patricio Valladares)	2006

If we maintain Harbord's previously cited claim that film cultures are "institutionally and spatially located" (2002, 39), the range of viewing platforms and modes of circulation for different films begin to strain any notion of a monolithic horror cinema culture in Chile based around consumption. Commercial cinemas are exhibition spaces that are distinct from horror film festivals and hold out the possibility of creating a fissure between a horror genre fan and a casual moviegoer based on different factors such as the subcultural capital that accompanies particular modes of viewing and exhibition spaces. When asked about the position of horror cinema in Chile within or vis-à-vis mainstream culture, René Weber, director of the Fixion-SARS film festival,[13] draws a distinction between commercial/Hollywood horror cinema that enjoys robust marketing campaigns and independent horror cinema that might lack the production quality of commercial films but nevertheless retains a high level of creative latitude in terms of reworking the horror genre. In turn, horror cinema made in Chile, which is often produced on budgets that pale in comparison to those of commercial horror films made by Hollywood or multinational media corporations, exists in separate cultural spheres. Exhibition spaces put into further relief Weber's remarks. Festivals enable access to horror films that one might not have via commercial cinemas and retail streaming services. A horror film consumer's proximity to a less visible and less mainstream horror cinema culture endows that individual with a certain degree of subcultural capital within Chilean horror film culture that surpasses that of a spectator who strictly views horror films in commercial cinemas. Subcultural capital aside, the consumption of horror still remains common to a constellation of spaces, irrespective of whether a horror film receives a commercial or noncommercial release or is viewed privately or publicly. Horror stands as the common denominator among the medley of exhibition spaces.

Concomitant to an increase in the public and private exhibition of Chilean horror films is increased media coverage of Chilean horror films; this coverage is a vital secondary production that thickens and makes visible Chilean horror cinema culture. There are no publications that exclusively cover Chilean horror cinema. Instead, as noted above, Chilean horror cinema is covered in conjunction with horror cinema from elsewhere and genre cinema from Chile and elsewhere. National newspapers, such as *El Mercurio* and *La Segunda*, occasionally cover horror film releases and festivals. Chilean websites devoted to cinema in general (e.g., *El agente cine*, *La fuga*), genre cinema (e.g., *Be Afraid*), and pop culture (e.g., *Nerdix* and *Plan 9*) all cover Chilean horror cinema to varying degrees. Personal fan pages on Facebook, such as *Bloody Mottel* [sic] and *Cinestro*, also cover Chilean horror cinema alongside horror cinema from elsewhere. Albeit an imprecise measurement, Chilean horror cinema's collective virtual presence lends credence to Altman's notion of a constellated genre community. While there is a measure of interaction among viewers of Chilean horror cinema at festivals, the collective consumption of horror anchors an otherwise atomized genre community.

As touched on above, select horror websites in various countries that cover horror cinema signal Chilean horror cinema's ties to a larger transnational horror cinema culture. There are legions of websites and fan pages based in different countries that are devoted to horror and genre cinema.

Coverage of Chilean horror cinema can operate as a measure of subcultural capital within a horror cinema culture. For instance, Mórbido is a horror and fantasy film festival that currently takes place in Mexico City. Its website has evolved into a sleek storehouse of information covering horror and fantasy film news on an incredibly transnational scale. Among news about horror cinema from Japan, Panama, Italy, Argentina, and Norway, one can find information about any number of Chilean horror film directors and their films, including Lucio Rojas, Jorge Olguín, and Pablo Illanes. Such a registry of information is mirrored on sites in other countries, such as *Horreur.net* in France or *La Zona Muerta* in Spain. Chilean horror cinema, in turn, has a preexisting media circuit that ensures some publicity for its films among horror and genre cinema connoisseurs.

Websites aside, a transnational horror cinema culture is composed of horror and genre film festivals, DVD distribution companies, legal and illegal streaming sites, and websites that cover genre and horror cinema. Chilean horror films insert themselves into this media ecology. *Trauma* (Lucio Rojas, 2017) is an extremely graphic horror film that depicts the violent legacies of Augusto Pinochet's dictatorship in no uncertain terms. Despite lacking a commercial release in Chile, the exhibition trajectory of *Trauma* illustrates how a Chilean horror film can avail itself of festivals and, simultaneously, attract publicity with each festival stop and attain a DVD distribution deal. At Blood Window Pinamar 2018 in Argentina, the distribution rights for *Trauma* were acquired by Artsploitation, a Philadelphia-based distribution company specializing in art house cinema that is often fused with other genres such as horror, gore, exploitation, and science fiction.[14] Prior to and following Blood Window Pinamar, *Trauma* moved through a vast panoply of horror film festivals, such as BIFFF (Brussels International Fantastic Film Festival), Fantaspoa International Fantastic Film Festival in Porto Alegre, Brazil, Mórbido Fest in Mexico City, and Buenos Aires Rojo Sangre in Buenos Aires, Argentina.[15] Festivals serve as value generators for films (Frey 2016, 48) and can attract both moviegoers and distributors. Artsploitation is one of many boutique distribution companies that distribute horror and genre cinema within specific or multiple national markets. In addition to the websites of the festivals and of Artsploitation, genre film and horror fan websites covered select film festival screenings and the distribution deal forged by Artsploitation. Exhibition and media coverage of *Trauma*—both of which are forms of secondary production related to a particular Chilean horror film—attracted viewers' attention at a cultural moment in which the Internet was awash in publicity about audiovisual productions. The media coverage of *Trauma*, which happened on various scales and in different geographies, contributed to a Chilean horror culture on a transnational scale, a dynamic that has been replicated with other particular Chilean horror films.

Returning to de Certeau's notion of secondary production, the production of Chilean horror films can be related to the directors' own consumption of horror from elsewhere. Directors of horror films in Chile were born in the late 1970s and onward. Absent any tradition of national horror cinema, directors invariably allude to films or directors from the United States, England, Italy, and elsewhere as influences. For example, Jorge Olguín has cited U.S. and European cinema as a general influence (Nazarala 2013), Lucio Rojas references John Carpenter, Takashi Miike, Wes Craven, and Guillermo del Toro as cinematic influences (Bustamante 2017), and Patricio Valladares alludes to Robert Rodriguez, Lucio Fulci, Clive Barker, and Sam Peckinpah (Rodríguez 2011). These influences were abetted by a circulation and consumption of horror cinema taking place in Chile and elsewhere initially via VHS tapes, DVDs, and television cable during the 1980s and 1990s. Lucio Rojas, for example, describes being an avid consumer of films from a local VHS rental store in the small town where he grew up (Bustamante 2017). In short, Chilean horror film directors' own consumption, or secondary production, of horror cinema from elsewhere lays the groundwork for national horror cinema production.

Directors' familiarity with horror cinema from elsewhere is readily evident in their films. The Chilean horror films are steeped in an acute awareness of horror cinema's formal construction and possess hallmarks of the genre, such as low-key lighting, ambiguous framing, selective use of subjective and handheld camera work, and editing that induces so-called jump scares. *Downhill* (2016) exemplifies these formal properties. In the film, Joe, a competitive mountain biker, and Stephanie, his girlfriend, have traveled to Chile to participate in a bike race. However, Joe, Stephanie, and various others are captured or killed by a murderous band of occultists who seek to satiate a viral and tentacled creature that infects people who enter a forested area. Much of *Downhill* was filmed at the Termas de Chillán hot springs, and, at particular moments, the camera's positioning and movement behind branches suggest but never confirm the possibility that characters are being watched. At night, lighting schemes shrink the onscreen spaces (Figure 7), and the revelations of a killer virus and occult orgy are depicted with choppy editing and shrill music. A similar awareness of horror's formalism appears

Figure 7. Joe in *Downhill* (Patricio Valladares, 2016) uses the light from a small video camera to illuminate himself as he records a message about being pursued by occultists and being infected with a virus. The scene's lighting and found footage aspect of the scenes reflect the film's awareness of common tropes in horror cinema.

in *Ángel negro*, a slasher/*giallo* film in which Gabriel exacts revenge against high school friends who witnessed the death of his girlfriend, Ángel. A shaky camera communicates the panic of particular characters, the murders frequently transpire in dark, claustrophobic spaces, and the editing can effectively induce a jump scare when the killer attacks.

The Chilean films also evince a thorough awareness of narrative tropes associated with horror. For example, Gustavo Subero notes the salience of horror motifs in *Baby Shower*: the "monstrous" depiction of the pregnant protagonist Ángela (2016, 117–18) and "the isolated and remote 'idyllic' location, the cut-off phone line and the lack of mobile reception that prevent people asking for help, the cult group living next door and its strange leader" (116–17). Likewise, in other Chilean horror films there are informed forays into particular subgenres that enjoy a transnational popularity: vampires (*Sangre eterna*), zombies (*Solos, Muerte ciega / Zombie Dawn, Yo soy Super Zombie*), slasher (*Ángel negro, Demencia*), "redneck" horror (*Sendero, En las afueras de la ciudad*), the occult (*Downhill*), found footage horror (*Wekufe, Downhill, Ángel negro*), torture porn (*Trauma*), trash/queer horror (*Empaná de pino*), and psychological horror (*Apio verde, Ángel negro*). Such engagements with subgenres enable the films to be recognized and received as horror for horror aficionados in Chile and elsewhere and, just as importantly, by distributors and film festival programmers in Chile and elsewhere who inevitably serve as mediators between consumers and film producers.

Yet, akin to the topic of exhibition, Chilean horror films' engagement with other genres, especially trash[16] and queer horror in the case of *Empaná de pino*, holds out the possibility of a fragmentation in Chilean horror cinema via consumption. The low-budget/trash aesthetic and queer content in *Empaná de pino* diverges from most other Chilean horror films that adhere to conventional aesthetics of horror. Often with the help of her lover and slave Perdida, the film's transgender protagonist, Hija de Perra, lures victims to their doom with her "delicious" empanadas that include human body parts, recalling horror films such as *The Texas Chainsaw Massacre* (Tobe Hooper, 1974). After making a Faustian pact with a supernatural figure to revive Caballo, her dead husband, Hija de Perra poisons her friends at a punk rock party and then murders them all by shooting and stabbing. The screen violence largely departs from any measure of realism common to horror cinema. The handheld camera shakily captures the violence at different distances. Some characters are splattered with blood; however, most who are shot by Hija de Perra fall limp after a clearly fake pistol sounds off. Screen violence, histrionic acting, an assortment of queer characters, and trash aesthetics that recall John Waters's films enable *Empaná de pino* to possess a generic hybridity. In turn, the film can be consumed within different genre communities, including horror, queer, and trash cinema aficionados. And while *Empaná de pino* fits under the rubric of horror and is deemed horror by select consumers, a Chilean horror genre community becomes fragmented according to various criteria, like generic hybridity, as well as other factors, such as whether a film receives a commercial release, whether a horror fan's homophobia or transphobia circumscribes the film strictly to a queer or trash mediatic category, and whether a film is distributed on DVD or other platforms.

Though Chilean horror films are thoroughly aware of the formal and narrative properties of transnational horror subgenres, the films are hardly imitations of horror productions emerging from countries with a more established horror cinema tradition. In his analysis of *Baby Shower*, Subero contends that Ángela, the pregnant female protagonist, is distinct from pregnant characters in other horror films in which pregnancy serves as a narrative fulcrum (2016, 117). Other Chilean horror films project Chileanness on a scale that varies with each production, and a film's depiction of Chilean culture can distinguish the film from that of a different national orientation. The urbanscapes of Santiago are readily evident in Olguín's *Ángel negro* and *Sangre eterna*. The Chilean facets of a horror film, however, need not be celebratory. *Wekufe*, for example, invokes Chilote mythology, a system of beliefs belonging to the indigenous inhabitants of the Chiloé Archipelago in southern Chile (Bracho 2017). *Wekufe* thus raises the specter of what remains of Chile's razed and suppressed indigenous cultures. And though the acting in *Apio verde* verges on being excessive, the film provides a harrowing account of debates over abortion that are specific to Chile during the 2000s. Even those films with full or partial English-language dialogue—*Solos, Gritos del bosque*, and *Downhill*—project some cultural or historical facet of Chile.

In closing, it is worth asking what, if anything, the recent uptick in national horror cinema production indicates about Chilean culture. Genre cinema has traditionally been conceived of as a reflection and prime shaper of a culture's values and ideologies (Schatz 1981, 263). A spectatorial expectation that Chilean horror films would depict, either directly or indirectly, national anxieties, especially the country's dictatorial past, can be justified given critical expectations for horror cinema. In his study of select horror films, Adam Lowenstein avers, "The modern horror film may well be the genre of our time that registers most brutally the legacies of historical trauma" (2005, 10). Moreover, most Chilean horror films are low-budget affairs, and critics have often deemed low-budget genres, such as exploitation and gore, as being more responsive toward and embodying of cultural anxieties. Joan Hawkins, for example, alludes to the work of Robin Wood, Carol Clover, and Linda Williams, and states that "low cinematic genres" (2000, 6), such as gore and exploitation, "often handle explosive social material that mainstream cinema is reluctant to touch" (7). Similarly, in her study of the relationship between spectatorship and evolving video platforms, Caetlin Benson-Allot observes that horror films and thrillers, including ones with higher budgets, "were intensely impacted by and reflect upon the technological, political, and economic conditions of their production" (2013, 17).

A primary reason, or suspect, for the rise of horror cinema in Chile may be neoliberalism. In his comments on Chilean documentary cinema, Alessandro Fornazzari contends, "[O]ne of the characteristics of postdictatorship Chile is that the boom in memory becomes indistinguishable from the boom in forgetting" (2013, 68–69), and horror cinema can appear to uphold this tension. With the exceptions of *Curriculum* and *Trauma*, none of the Chilean horror films deal explicitly with the dictatorship. However, the scant number of academic critics who have examined Chilean horror cinema consider national horror films as an allegorical and indirect mode of presenting a tragic past. Vania Barraza Toledo sees *Solos*, a film that prima facie lacks any direct allusion to the Pinochet dictatorship, as enabling an examination of postdictatorial trauma in Chile (2012, 253–54). Walescka Pino-Ojeda, likewise, endows Chilean horror films from the early 2000s with a capacity to depict "a social unease that, despite being centered on individual experiences, serves to exorcise collective anxieties" (2009, 143). Pino-Ojeda alludes specifically to *Ángel negro* and *Sangre eterna* for showing the "social fear and violence that continues to be perceived socially and politically as exclusive to the victims of torture and exile and the families of the disappeared" (143).

Though the question of spectatorial interpretations is a valid one, I prefer to conceive of the emergence of Chilean horror cinemas as evidence that, along with art house cinema, comedies, and documentary, an additional facet of Chilean audiovisual production and culture has tethered itself—via consumption *and* production—to generic mediatic flows that are transnational in scope. With the possible exception of action films, horror cinema is perhaps the most transnational of genres (Och and Strayer 2013, 2). At times, horror aficionados' appetites for horror films, irrespective of their origins, have been conceived as insatiable (Lobato and Ryan 2011, 196). Absent any extensive sociological study, it is impossible to know precisely the motives viewers in Chile have for watching horror, and the motives viewers beyond Chile have for watching Chilean horror cinema. While Chilean horror films evince an awareness of transnational horror genres, the recognition of Chilean horror cinema beyond Chile signals that the flow of horror into Chile is resoundingly not one-way. Chilean directors, such as Javier Attridge, Patricio Valladares, Lucio Rojas, Nicolás López, and Jorge Olguín, among others, commonly appear on horror websites outside Chile, and, as noted above, Valladares has directed abroad. Moreover, the collaborations between U.S. horror auteur Eli Roth and López under the auspices of the now-defunct Chilewood[17] further underscore the transnational breadth of Chilean horror. Chilean horror cinema thus takes its place as a node of horror cinema consumption *and* production that receives and contributes to national cinema and a transnational "slaughterhouse of cinema" (Lobato 2012, 32) in which a seemingly limitless amount of genre cinema circulates over and within national borders.

NOTES

1. When a Chilean horror film is distributed in an English-language market and its title has been translated by the distributor, I initially provide the English-language title in italics. Otherwise, I translate the original titles into English and enclose them in quotation marks. Unless noted, all translations are my own. In those cases in which only one title in English or Spanish appears in italics, the film's title is the same in Chile and in English-language markets.

2. I loosely employ the categories of "art house" and "independent cinema" here, and the monikers hone in on the films' slow pacing and loose cause-and-effect narratological relationship relative to mainstream commercial cinema (Bordwell 1979, 57). In addition to *Una mujer fantástica*, other Chilean films that have featured at A-list festivals, such as Cannes, Berlinale, and Sundance, include *Gloria* (Sebastián Lelio, 2013), *Matar a un hombre / To Kill a Man* (Alejandro Fernández, 2014), and Alicia Scherson's *Vida de familia / Family Life* (2017).

3. It is crucial to note that Altman is keen to acknowledge that a single individual can belong to multiple genre communities at different times (1999, 161). An individual's "membership" in various genre communities aligns with the reality of most spectators who are apt to view a diversity of film genres, as opposed to a 24/7 diet of horror or another genre.

4. While this essay focuses on horror cinema produced in Chile, an examination of horror culture (in lieu of strictly horror film culture) widens the discussion of horror in Chile to include other media, such as horror in television (e.g, *Mea culpa*, *Feroz* / "Fierce" and *Santiago Paranormal* / "Paranormal Santiago") and in literature (e.g., the anthology *Cuentos chilenos de terror*, Editorial Norma, 2010). The character of El Siniestro Doctor Mortis, who has appeared in or on comics, radio, television, and novels from the 1940s through the present, merits special mention for the character's endurance in various media in Chile.

5. According to the 2015 Annual Report published by the Cámara de Exhibidores Multisalas de Chile (CAEM), an industrial group that brings together Chile's primary film exhibitor chains, there were 220 films released in 2015. Of those 220, 133 films were from the United States and accounted for 89.8 percent of the box office attendance. Twenty-five films were produced in Chile, and 62 were from other countries or regions, including Japan, other Latin American countries, and Europe ("El cine en Chile en el 2015" 2016, 9).

6. In the few references to Chilean horror cinema prior to 2000, *La dama de la muerte* / "The Lady of Death" (Carlos Hugo Christensen, 1945), *Hay algo allá afuera* / "There is Something Outside" (Pepe Maldonado, 1990), and *La rubia de Kennedy* / "The Blonde of Kennedy" (Arnaldo Valsecchi, 1995)

are sometimes conceived as horror films that anticipate the current "wave" of Chilean horror. According to René Weber, the director of Fixion-SARS: Festival de Cine Fantástico y de Terror in Santiago (personal communication with author, November 5, 2018), prior to 2000 horror in Chilean cinema did not appear as a genre unto itself. Instead, horror was often combined with elements from other genres, such as comedies, thrillers, or erotic cinema.

7   While there were no prizes awarded in 2005, since 2004 the Banco del Estado de Chile has supported the production of select national films. Horror films that have received support from the Banco del Estado are *Solos* in 2009, *Baby Shower* in 2011, and *Caleuche, el llamado del mar* in 2012. Currently, the film production subsidies from Banco del Estado are being considered for elimination as part of cost-cutting austerity measures taken by the country's Finance Ministry.

8   The majority of box office numbers in Table 1 come from the annual reports of the CAEM, which can be accessed via the organization's website, www.caem.cl. However, the figures for Jorge Olguín's *Sangre eterna / Eternal Blood* and *Ángel negro* come from "Apuntes acerca del audiovisual en Chile" (2003, 23) prepared by the Chilean government.

9   See, for example, Ascanio Cavallo and Gonzalo Maza's introduction to their coedited collection *El novísimo cine chileno* (2011) and Carolina Urrutia Neno's *Un cine centrífugo: Ficciones chilenas 2005–2010* (2013).

10 While a meditation on the moments of horror in art house films is beyond the range of this paper, Sebastián Silva's wariness of *Nasty Baby* being pigeonholed as a queer or a Latinx film could provide a useful starting point to consider how screen violence propels the film beyond a single generic category. In an interview on the Tribeca Film Festival's website, Silva comments on the significance of Freddy and other gay characters who become accessories in the Bishop's murder: "Once you make these characters become murderers, the gay aspect is completely gone" (Martínez 2015).

11 The production and exhibition of Chilean horror cinema also include short films. While the lack of financial backing can operate as an impediment to the production of short films (according to a personal communication I had with Moisés Vilches Quiroz on July 30, 2018), recent short horror films include *Camino al cementerio / "*Road to the Cemetery*"* (Mijael Milies, 2010), *Adentro / "*Inside*"* (Fernando Vuletich, 2012), *Bajo la luna / "*Under the Moon*"* (Enrique Ortega, 2012), *Suegro, su cena está lista / "*Father-in-Law, Your Dinner is Ready*"* (Diego Figueroa, 2013), *Necrolovers* (Víctor Uribe, 2013), and *Hombre / "*Man*"* (Juan Pablo Arias, 2017).

12 *Vlad's Legacy* and *Nightworld* potentially could be included in the table of noncommercial releases. However, given that the films were made outside Chile, cast few, if any, Chilean actors, and have no dialogue in Spanish, fans

and critics appear reluctant to categorize the films as Chilean. As touched on above, the classification of Valladares's two films as Chilean would hinge upon the director's nationality and not the film's content.

13 Fixion-SARS is the Festival de Cine Fantástico y de Terror de Santiago, in Chile.

14 Ray Murray, "Re: Questions about Chilean Horror Cinema," personal communication with author, August 6, 2018.

15 The other festivals in which *Trauma* has featured are too numerous to list here. However, others include the Kew Gardens Film Festival in Forest Hills, New York; the Optical Theater Horror Film Festival in Italy; the Molins de Rei Horror Film Festival in Spain; the Horrorant Film Festival in Greece; Fanges in Santiago; the HorrorHound Film Fest in Cincinnati, Ohio; and Cine de Terror Film Festival in Valdivia, Chile.

16 Trash cinema can be defined as "a rebellion against the hypocrisy, fascism and elitism of art and a glorification of all things anti-art, of the transparently cheap . . . and . . . an anti-intellectual movement, if a purposely vague and ill-defined one" (Stevenson 2003, 125). While I diverge with Stevenson's assessment that trash is inevitably anti-intellectual, his characterizations of "transparently cheap" and rebelliousness are hallmarks of trash cinema.

17 "Chilewood" is a portmanteau for a particular group of filmmakers from Chile who sought to mimic Hollywood's pace of production with genre films either with Spanish or English dialogue. However, Nicolás López, a key figure of "Chilewood," has kept a low profile since 2018, when he was accused of sexual harassment by several actresses who appeared in films he directed. See my 2016 article about López's films.

WORKS CITED

Acland, Charles. 2003. *Screen Traffic: Movies, Multiplexes, and Global Culture.* Durham, NC: Duke University Press.

Altman, Rick. 1999. *Film / Genre.* London: BFI.

"Apuntes acerca del audiovisual en Chile." n.d. Gobierno de Chile: Consejo nacional de la cultura y las artes, 2003, Observatorio iberoamericano audiovisual. Accessed 21 July 2018. www.oia-caci.org/es/.

Barraza Toledo, Vania. 2012. "Cine de terror en Chile (2000–2011): La figura del zombi en el imaginario cultural de la posdictadura chilena." In *Horrofílmico: Aproximaciones al cine de terror en Latinoamérica y el Caribe*, edited by Rosana Díaz-Zambrana and Patricia Tomé, 247–60. San Juan, Puerto Rico: Isla Negra.

Benson-Allott, Caetlin. 2013. *Killer Tapes and Shattered Screens: Video Spectatorship from VHS to File Sharing.* Berkeley: University of California Press.

Bordwell, David. 1979. "The Art Cinema as a Mode of Film Practice." *Film Criticism* 4 (1): 56–64.

Bracho, Alexander. 2017. "Wekufe: El Origen del Mal o cómo hacer que una película de horror chilena, sea necesaria." *Plan 9 Magazine*, November 6. plannueve.net/wekufe-origen-del-mal-una-pelicula-horror-chilena-sea-necesaria/.

Bustamente, Julio. 2017. "Lucio A. Rojas: Veo mal en todas partes." *Espectador Errante*, October 15. http://www.espectadorerrante.com/index.php/2017/10/15/lucio-rojas-veo-mal-todas-partes/.

Cavallo, Ascanio, and Gonzalo Maza. 2011. *El novísimo cine chileno*. Santiago de Chile: Uqbar.

Dapena, Gerard. 2018. "Genre Films Then and Now." In *The Routledge Companion to Latin American Cinema*, edited by Marvin D'Lugo, Ana M. López, and Laura Podalsky, 150–63. New York: Routledge.

De Certeau, Michel. 1988. *The Practice of Everyday Life*. Translated by Steven Rendell. Berkeley: University of California Press.

Douglas, Mary, and Baron Isherwood. 1996. *The World of Goods: Towards an Anthropology of Consumption*. London: Routledge.

"El cine en Chile en el 2014: Informe elaborado por la Cámara de Exhibidores Multisalas de Chile A.G. (CAEM)." April 2015. caem.cl/index.php/informes-anuales/item/19-informe-caem-2014.

"El cine en Chile en el 2015: Informe elaborado por la Cámara de Exhibidores Multisalas de Chile A.G. (CAEM)," March 2016. caem.cl/index.php/informes-anuales/item/23-el-cine-en-chile-en-el-2015.

Fornazzari, Alessandro. 2013. *Speculative Fictions: Chilean Culture, Economics, and the Neoliberal Transition*. Pittsburgh: University of Pittsburgh Press.

Frey, Matias. 2016. *Extreme Cinema: The Transgressive Rhetoric of Today's Art Film Culture*. New Brunswick: Rutgers University Press.

Hanich, Julian. 2014. "Watching a Film with Others: Towards a Theory of Collective Spectatorship." *Screen* 55 (3): 338–59.

Harbord, Janet. 2002. *Film Cultures*. London: SAGE.

Hawkins, Joan. 2000. *Cutting Edge: Art-horror and the Horrific Avant-Garde*. Minneapolis: University of Minnesota Press.

Hills, Matt. 2005. *The Pleasures of Horror*. London: Continuum.

Kredell, Brendan. 2016. Introduction to *Film Festivals: History, Theory, Method, Practice*, edited by Marijke de Valck, Brendan Kredell, and Skadi Loist, 15–17. Abingdon: Routledge.

Lobato, Ramon. 2012. *Shadow Economies of Cinema: Mapping Informal Film Distribution*. London: Palgrave Macmillan.

Lobato, Ramon, and Mark David Ryan. 2011. "Rethinking Genre Studies through Distribution Analysis: Issues in International Horror Movie Circuits." *New Review of Film and Television Studies* 9 (2): 188–203.

Lowenstein, Adam. 2005. *Shocking Representation: Historical Trauma, National Cinema, and the Modern Horror Film*. New York: Columbia University Press.

Malermo, Miguel. 2016. "Nasty Baby: Tintes oscuros." *La Fuga*, no. 18. http://2016.lafuga.cl/nasty-baby/804.

Martínez, Kiko. 2015. "Nasty Baby Director/Star Sebastián Silva Does Not Have Time for 'Gay' and 'Latino' Labels." *Tribeca*, October 29. Accessed October 10, 2018. https://www.tribecafilm.com/stories/nasty-baby-sebastian-silva-movie-interview-lgbt-latino-cinema.

Nazarala, Andrés. 2013. "Así es 'Gritos del bosque', la primera película chilena en 3D." *La Segunda Online*, March 11. www.lasegunda.com/Noticias/CulturaEspectaculos/2013/03/829157/asi-es-gritos-del-bosque-la-primera-pelicula-chilena-en-3d.

Neale, Steve. 2000. *Genre and Hollywood*. New York: Routledge.

Och, Dana, and Kirsten Strayer. 2013. Introduction to *Transnational Horror Across Visual Media: Fragmented Bodies*, edited by Dana Och and Kirsten Strayer, 1–13. London; Routledge.

Pick, Zuzana. 1993. *The New Latin American Cinema: A Continental Project*. Austin: University of Texas Press.

Pino-Ojeda, Walescka. 2009. "Latent Image: Chilean Cinema and the Abject." Translated by Mariana Ortega Breña. *Memory and Popular Culture*, special issue of *Latin American Perspectives* 36 (5): 133–46.

Risner, Jonathan. 2016. "How I Learned to Stop Worrying and Grudgingly Accept Product Placement: Nicolás López, Chilewood and Criteria for A Neoliberal Cinema." *Journal of Latin American Cultural Studies* 25 (4): 597–612.

———. 2018. *Blood Circuits: Contemporary Argentine Horror Cinema*. Albany: State University of New York Press.

Rodríguez, José Miguel. 2011. "Entrevista a Patricio Valladares." *Dioses y monstruos*, May 17. www.diosesymonstruos.com/2011/05/entrevista-a-patricio-valladares/.

Schatz, Thomas. 1981. *Hollywood Genres: Formulas, Filmmaking, and the Studio System*. Philadelphia: Temple University Press.

Sorlin, Pierre. 1996. *Italian National Cinema 1896–1996*. London: Routledge.

Stevenson, Jack. 2003. *Land of a Thousand Balconies: Discoveries and Confessions of a B-Movie Archaeologist*. Manchester: Head Press/Critical Visions.

Subero, Gustavo. 2016. *Gender and Sexuality in Latin American Horror Cinema: Embodiments of Evil*. London: Palgrave Macmillan.

Urrutia Neno, Carolina. 2013. *Un cine centrífugo: Ficciones chilenas 2005 a 2010*. Santiago de Chile: Cuarto Propio.

Zilberman, Alan. 2015. "'Nasty Baby' starts out as comedy, but veers into horror." *Washington Post*, October 29. https://www.washingtonpost.com/goingoutguide/movies/nasty-baby-starts-out-as-comedy-but-veers-into-horror/2015/10/29/3d42c904-7c18-11e5-b575-d8dcfedb4ea1_story.html.

5

THE LATIN DRAGON GOING GLOBAL

Marko Zaror, Martial Arts Films, and Stardom

Moisés Park

> Don't get set into one form, adapt it and build your own,
> and let it grow. Be like water. Empty your mind, be formless,
> shapeless—like water. Now, you put water in a cup, it becomes
> the cup. You put water into a bottle, it becomes the bottle. You
> put it in a teapot, it becomes the teapot. Now water can flow or it
> can crash. Be water, my friend.
>
> <div align="right">Bruce Lee as Li Tsung (<i>Longstreet</i>)</div>

> I have been known by many names. But the one I'm most commonly associated with is the Exterminator. I face you as an equal. With the exception of this blade, we're quite fairly matched.
>
> <div align="right">Marko Zaror as Rastignac (<i>Savage Dog</i>)</div>

SPECTERS OF BRUCE LEE IN CHILE: A CINEMATIC ETYMOLOGY

The most famous quote attributed to Bruce Lee, in the epigraph above, was actually written by Stirling Silliphant for a part in the TV short *Longstreet* (1971–72), where the character states that a fighter must adapt to his surroundings, be flexible, and naturally respond to change. The ghost of Lee, also known as "The Dragon," has haunted action cinema since the early 1970s, with films like *The Big Boss* (1971), *Fist of Fury* (1972), and *The Way of the*

Dragon (1972). His influence can be perceived in American action flicks, whether big-budget superhero Hollywood films with ample action scenes or Rodriguez-Tarantinesque films that are a "postmodern mix of action, humor, and horror and . . . stylish, hyper-violent tributes to 1970s exploitation cinema" (Dapena 2017, 155). Today, Lee's fans remain faithful, idolizing his kicks, his body, and his *kiai*, the unique vocalizations that martial artists produce when fighting. Martial arts is a discipline that has existed in various forms but shares the same principles of "authenticity, tradition, and essence, on the one hand, and inventing, innovation, revolution, and mixing, on the other" (Bowman 2015, 25) that Lee has embodied. Furthermore, Lee's impact on combat sports, method acting, and—for better or worse—the images of East Asian men, is evident.

Marko Zaror, the most famous martial arts actor in Chile and perhaps the only Latin American action star, is following in the footsteps of the Hong Kong–American star. Zaror's character Rastignac in *Savage Dog*, quoted above, is similar to Zaror, in the sense that both have had malleable identities. In the film, Rastignac has been a legionnaire, a torero, and a gambler. Zaror, meanwhile, has played a diverse list of eclectic characters with differing ethnic profiles, including (Palestinian-)Chilean, (Afro-)Colombian, British, French, Russian, and certain mythic characters. The ghost of "The Dragon" is alive and well in Santiago, as evidenced in action films like *Kiltro* (2006), *Mirageman* (2007), and *Redeemer* (2015), which all feature Zaror. In order to argue in this chapter that Zaror, who has been dubbed "the Latin Dragon" by fans and critics, is following in the footsteps of Lee, I examine how the former's filmography, from 2004 to 2018, reflects upon the representations of constructed masculinities in the context of the martial arts genre and theories of "subaltern stardom." First, I argue that Zaror's racial malleability, as well as his varying roles in an increasingly globalized cinema industry, echo Lee's steps toward global stardom and problematize Zaror's status as a "Chilean" film star. Second, I examine how martial arts film can be considered a "body genre," in Linda Williams's terms (1991), in order to explore the link between this genre and masculinity. Lastly, I argue that studying Zaror's filmography will illuminate the relevance of (Chilean) martial arts stardom in global cinema.

STARS AND HEAVENLY BODIES: CAN THE SUBALTERN KICK?

Since 2004, Zaror has played roles that vary in ethnic background, language, and ideology; this has meant not only that Zaror's stardom is less closely associated with nationalistic ideology—unlike, say, Chuck Norris's stardom—but also that Chilean action cinema, such as it is, is also less nationalistic. The Chilean martial artist himself is different from the constructed Pan-American "Latin Dragon" or "exotic" star that is portrayed on the screen. The adjective "Latin" denotes exotic sexuality that the terms "Asian" or "Oriental" lack, especially when referring to males.[1] Like many images in cinema, Zaror's on-screen persona is a combination of previous performers with distinct features (i.e., Bruce Lee, Jean-Claude Van Damme, Sylvester Stallone) that are then imitated and replicated on-screen. Zaror has been in lead roles in eight action films, which themselves are virtually absent in the Chilean "canon," which favors documentaries and dramas.[2] With very few exceptions, the majority of recent commercial Chilean action films are directed and coproduced by Ernesto Díaz Espinoza and feature Zaror. Critic Gerard Dapena describes the Díaz-Zaror duo as a "fetish" that successfully "carved a niche as a director of cult action films" (2017, 155). To this, we could add that the marketability and publicity behind Zaror's stardom is the main fixture in the contemporary Chilean action film genre, regardless of the ethnicity of his characters. Since moving to the United States, Zaror has worked in five projects with Robert Rodriguez, mostly in action films or television (Table 1), establishing him as a recurring cast member in Rodriguez's various lucrative projects with no mention of his ethnic background.

HOW TO CAST A DRAGON: A CLOSER READING OF ZAROR'S FILMOGRAPHY (2005–18)

If we read Zaror's constructed stardom as a "third-world text," that is, to borrow Fredric Jameson's words, as "necessarily allegorical" (1986, 69), we would see that Zaror's stardom mirrors Chile's humble but steadily growing global neoliberalism as a developed country. In 2007, Chile joined the Organization for Economic Cooperation and Development (OECD), an intergovernmental body that includes only countries regarded as "developed." Popular sentiment often recalls this recent membership as an attempt for an "underdog" to become the "Latin Jaguar," emulating the economic flourishing of the "Four Asian Tigers" (Hong Kong, Singapore, South Korea, and Taiwan) since the 1960s.

Ideological commentary in martial arts cinema has increasingly dictated movie plots, where different characters represent various nationalisms and political ideologies.[3] Exotic or legendary animals (jaguars, tigers, and dragons) could be considered metaphors for neoliberal ideology and

Table 1: Zaror's Filmography (2005–18)

Film (Release year)	Character name (Role type)	Character ethnic background and profession	Production company
The Rundown (2003)	(Dwayne Johnson's stunt man)	Samoan-Black-Canadian-American stuntman	USA
Chinango (2005)	Braulio Bo (lead role)	Chinese-Mexican fighter	Mexico
*Kiltro (2006)	Zamir/Zami (lead role)	Arab-Chilean fighter	Chile
*Mirageman (2007)	Marco Gutiérrez (lead role)	Chilean vigilante	Chile / USA
*Mandrill (2009)	Antonio Espinoza (lead role)	Chilean hitman	Chile
Undisputed 3: Redemption (2010)	Raúl "Dolor" Quiñones (main villain)	Colombian fighter	USA
Myths and Legends: The New Alliance (2010)	Marimoto (main villain)	Mythical character	Chile
**Machete Kills (2013)	Zaror (supporting role)	Unspecified hitman fighter and clone	USA
*Redeemer (2014)	Pardo (lead role)	Chilean former hitman, religious vigilante	Chile / USA
**Demi Lovato: Confident (Music Video) (2015)	Unspecified (extra)	Unspecified henchman	USA
Sultan (2016)	Marcus (aka Killing Machine) (supporting role)	British MMA fighter	India
**From Dusk Till Dawn (TV show) (2016)	Zolo (supporting role)	Aztec/Jaguar warrior, trained in hell	USA
Zambo Dendé (2017)	Zambo Dendé (lead role)	Slave and martial artist of Native Amerindian and African ancestry	Colombia

Film (Release year)	Character name (Role type)	Character ethnic background and profession	Production company
Savage Dog (2017)	Jon-Pierre Rastignac (main villain)	Matador/French Foreign Legion	USA
The Defenders (2017) (TV miniseries)	Shaft (supporting role)	Member of the Marvel universe organization Chaste	USA
**100 Years* (2115) [sic]	Bad guy (extra)	N/A	USA
**Alita: Battle Angel* (2018)	Ajakutty (extra)	Based on Japanese manga	USA / Canada / Argentina
Green Ghost (2018)	Drake (supporting role)	Mexican superhero	USA
Invincible (2019)	Brock Cortez (villain)	Technologically enhanced soldier	USA
One Good Thing (TBD)	Main villain	N/A	Indonesia

*Directed by Ernesto Díaz-Espinosa
**Directed by Robert Rodriguez

progressivism. Modern martial arts protagonists subscribe to an ambiguous nationalism that highlights individualism and personal freedom, at times surrounded by explicitly patriotic symbols (e.g., flags, military gear, chants). The villain often embodies excessive sectarian nationalism, bullying, imperialism, and narcissism.

Nevertheless, Zaror's stardom has little nationalistic ideology attached to it; this could be attributed to his heritage as an Arab-Chilean actor who entered the U.S. industry early in his acting career as a stuntman, and to his emergence in a national cinema that neglected the action genre. He downplays his Palestinian heritage on-screen, with the exception of *Kiltro* (2004), where he plays an Arab-Chilean explicitly ("kiltro" in Chilean slang means "mutt," and refers here to his mixed race). He usually accentuates his Chilean or Pan–Latin American identities, and, more frequently, he has assumed a color-blind racial identity within the global market. After all, action flicks supposedly focus on subjects' athleticism and on-camera charisma, rather than line delivery or tear-jerking shots.

Zaror is a subaltern subject, and his film trajectory derives from the double movement, in martial arts culture, of homoerotic emasculation followed by the reinstatement of intense hypermasculinity, as defined by Bruce Lee. This plot is characteristic of martial arts features, where manhood is usually determined by an honorable victory in combat; martial arts films are constructed upon a profound sense that real manliness represents the good that overcomes evil, which tends to be represented as emasculated or excessively hypermasculine. Though he embodies the aesthetics and philosophy of a postcolonial subject, Zaror participates in a film industry that is highly subjected to Western hegemonic patterns of hypermasculinity, while also belonging to Latin American "Third World" otherness.

The Chilean martial artist's trajectory is also reminiscent of Lee's in its detachment from nationalistic ideology in favor of a pan-ethnic subalternity that defies hegemonic hierarchies. Lee allegedly transcended race and was celebrated in many minority circles that claim color blindness, even if most of his roles incorporated his Hong Kong background (Bowman 2015, 69). After settling in the United States in the 1960s, he began a successful career in television and film, further revealing his charisma and self-confidence in several interviews; he had no issues speaking English, as he grew up in British Hong Kong.[4] Kato, the sidekick in the television show *The Green Hornet*, a role Lee played in the 1960s, is an example of a character with a volatile ethnic history. The character has been played by actors from various ethnic backgrounds, and has been identified as Japanese, Chinese, Korean, Taiwanese, and, ambiguously, from the Far East. Although the show was supposed to center around the Euro-American titular character, Lee's rising stardom eclipsed that of the protagonist. He was able to steal the spotlight from the Green Hornet through the spectacle of martial arts; his racial otherness was secondary to his stardom. Transcending race was relative, as Lee's phenotype was not always concealed by the mask of Kato. The black mask symbolizes alterity, an emblem that would tap into the exploitation market. Arguably, the rise of Jim Kelly and 1970s blaxploitation flicks is a direct result of Lee's success in a market that demanded minority representation in lead cinematic roles.[5]

Richard Dyer's *Stars* (1979) and *Heavenly Bodies* (1986) do not mention Bruce Lee or any martial artist, but his theories are relevant to address Zaror's "crossover" into global celebrity. One of Dyer's main points is that a star is a construction. The media industry, the market, and society *make* stars together (1986, 2–3). Furthermore, the star is a commodity: casting is an investment, and the star's image or persona can be replicated for consumption, merchandising, and profit (5). Finally, stars represent ideology, and "articulate what it is to be a human being in contemporary society" in indirect and complex ways (8–9). According to these three points, Zaror can be considered a "local" star with aspirations to global fame. He maintains a bankable presence in Chilean action films, but with marginal profit, particularly when compared to dramas and comedies, which continue to be the only genres that enjoy sizable profits in Latin America.

Zaror's acrobatic athleticism, particularly when featured in social media, has gained a cult following that indicates he has niche stardom. Dyer suggests that there are two characteristics to the "paradox of the star." First, the star must be both ordinary and extraordinary, and second, the star is simultaneously present and absent. Zaror's background identifies him as a member of a "developing country" or a "recently developed country," but also as a Latin American—that is, from a region with vast internal economic differences, and until recently, few ties to recognized "national" martial arts (with the exception of Brazil). However, Zaror's extraordinary skills in fighting and bodybuilding position him among the very few Latin American actors who appear in action films, and as the only one to successfully launch a career in martial arts films internationally.

Zaror was introduced to a large Chilean audience as the stunt double of World Wrestling Federation superstar and actor Dwayne Johnson (aka the Rock) in *The Rundown* (2003) as part of the marketing of his debut film, *Kiltro* (2006). Indeed, Zaror launched his early film career in the United States by supplanting with his own body that of the WWE wrestler, an already athletic actor, in a highly acrobatic performance. Zaror's powerful athleticism is superior, as seen in the most important shots of the Rock's action flick. What is interesting to note here is that Zaror's image was projected on many big screens in Chile, but in an "absent" role—that is, without Chileans knowing that they were already witnessing Zaror's body and talent instead of the Rock's.

The paradox of the star is not only maintained by being both ordinary and extraordinary but also highlighted by his subaltern status. Beyond having a physical resemblance to a 6′5″ WWE superstar, the 6′4″ Zaror soon proved to be able to kick like Bruce Lee in spite of his height. Along with Steven Seagal, Zaror is among the tallest martial arts actors in the industry. Nonetheless, Chilean martial arts films are positioned outside the dominant hegemonic discourse, reiterating postcolonial subalternity. Zaror's ability to successfully mimic Lee's physique and athleticism still reformulates hegemonic paradigms, however. Lee became a global phenomenon once he triumphed in the U.S. film industry, and he was viewed less as an outsider and increasingly more as an American lead actor, playing roles that acknowledged his racial hybridity. Lee's combined Asian-American subaltern identity challenged hegemonic expectations, adapting his otherness as a "sub-hegemonic" authority in martial arts culture. Likewise, Zaror's recent projects in India (i.e., *Sultan* and *One Good Thing*) have relatively increased his celebrity, tapping into the second-largest filmmaking industry in the world.

Additionally, Lee's filmography created a niche where the East Asian male was no longer an exotic, emasculated character: "[w]ith his tough kung fu image, Bruce Lee re-masculinized the Chinese male body in the early 1970s, yet he has not been able to redeem the common asexual screen presence of Chinese men" (Yu 2012, 128–29). As actress and martial artist Diana Lee Inosanto bluntly put it, Lee "put balls on Chinese men" (*I am Bruce Lee*, 2012). Becoming a stereotypical male sex symbol in the 1970s, Lee drastically changed expectations of Oriental masculinity (Chan 2000, 372–73). He quickly created a new type, that of the angry Asian male martial artist, and directly contested certain hierarchies of manhood by introducing a new hypermasculinity. In *The Way of the Dragon* (1972), Lee famously defeats Chuck Norris's character, but *he* simultaneously catapulted Norris to stardom, reversing postcolonial power dynamics. Lee was a transcultural icon that surpassed racial boundaries, demolishing expectations of the East Asian emasculated cartoon male characters, such as Mr. Yunioshi, played by white comedian Mickey Rooney in *Breakfast at Tiffany's* (1961).

Lee had native fluency in English, unlike martial arts superstars Jet Li and Jackie Chan and French-accented Belgian Jean-Claude Van Damme. The 1971 "Lost Interview" from *The Pierre Berton Show*, rediscovered in 1994, revitalized Lee's mythic persona, as it showed viewers an unfiltered martial arts philosophy and a charisma beyond his on-screen performance. Without a doubt, given an increasing demand for a social media presence in a market dominated by English, fluency in the language is instrumental to replicating Lee's path to stardom.

Zaror's entrance into the global market is related to silencing his voice on camera. He is quite fluent in English and he has had some roles with lines, but they are often overshadowed by his ability to defy gravity and showcase his musculature.[6] Moreover, he has an active social media presence, following Lee's footsteps to become a star, entering the American market with confidence and charisma. He has profiles as an actor, as a martial artist, and as CEO and cofounder of Ki-Way, a dietary supplement and nutritional product company. He shares links to images, interviews, movie reviews, fan-edited compilations, film trailers and teasers, nutritional advice, and other mundane activities. Celebrity social media confirms Dyer's idea of the star paradox, since it creates an immanent passive presence in thousands of subscribers, as fans follow or search for the star, and receive updates and notifications on the star's whereabouts, as he is increasingly playing roles outside Chile.

Zaror's place in Chilean national cinema has diminished since 2014's *Redeemer*, and he has worked in secondary parts in films in the United States, the United Kingdom, Indonesia, Colombia, and India, which do not necessarily require him to speak in English. Zaror's initially subaltern kick flicks in lead Chilean roles have led him to a niche stardom that has recently adapted itself to hegemonic global hierarchies, playing less prominent roles that feature counterhegemonic positions. In 2020, however, he is finalizing plans to play major villains with speaking roles in American productions.

Understanding Zaror's varied ethnic roles is key to understanding his ethnic hybridity and malleability as comparable to others working in the national film industry, even if an increasing number of his features are not Chilean productions per se. Furthermore, attempting to view Zaror's multinational casting as a reflection of Chilean cinema becoming more internationally collaborative is, in fact, the crux of a methodology of study that considers Chilean cinema beyond the nationalities of its funding, producers, and stars.[7] Zaror's roles in films that either are not set in Chile or disregard his cultural background in the plot allow him to cultivate a profile as an actor that is unlike most other Latin American actors.

A (FREUDIAN) BODY GENRE AND "GAY-SEEING" MASCULINITY

The reasons for Zaror's rather unconventional stardom are manifold. First and foremost, Zaror is a star because of his body—which people are able to observe in detail—and what it is able to do. Linda Williams describes the "body genre" as a specific type of film that results in viewers' excess bodily reactions to the cinematic diegesis (1991, 5). She identifies melodrama, horror, and pornography as body genres. Aspects of timing are also specific to each body genre. In melodrama, tears flow because "it is too late" (e.g., the lover is gone already). In horror, the body jumps or jolts because "it is too soon" (e.g., the monster appears unpredictably). In pornography, the body reacts with pleasure in "perfect timing" (e.g., orgasm is reached for viewer and subject at the same time). Martial arts films could be considered a body genre as well, as most of their plots fall into these three sorts of timing. First off, the not-yet-hero protagonist loses a beloved member of his social circle (a lover, a family member, a master) too soon and often unexpectedly. The lead confronts the villain too late, since his lover or family member is already punished or deceased. Later, after being initially defeated by the villain, the hero's journey must include training, discipline, and an epiphany, building up to the final fight. Most martial arts films conclude with a triumph over the villain with one last perfect kick or punch, usually in vivid fashion or in slow motion, with repeated sequences from different angles, resembling the perfect timing of pornographic pleasure. Additionally, violent triumph can be followed by a romantic final kiss or at least gratitude from the damsel-in-distress archetype, timing the ending with cathartic satisfaction. This overarching pattern not only is clear in all of the films where Zaror is the lead (all of his Chilean features and *Chinango*, made in Mexico) but also demonstrates that the genre of martial arts utilizes timing patterns, with a delayed and reformulated bodily response reminiscent of the three body genres Williams identifies.

Although the female body has commonly been objectified in film and other forms of media, in early cinema we find various examples of the male body being at the center of attention. For instance, the forty-two-second film "Sandow, the Bodybuilder" (1894), starring German bodybuilder Eugen Sandow, focuses solely on the muscular actor. Thus, it could be argued that Sandow is not only a pioneer of modern bodybuilding competitions but also possibly the first film actor in history. Furthermore, boxing was the first "sport film" recorded, and live sports have since evolved into a mainstream mass-media phenomenon. One common thread in these early films is their androcentric nature; the male performer—not only his body but also his distinctive movements—is the camera's, and by extension the viewer's, main focus.

The spectacle of Lee's chiseled body prompts the emulation of the *kiai*, and perhaps the serious discipline of bodybuilding and practice in the martial arts. Cinematic masculinity, as represented by Lee and Zaror, is mimicked by the viewers. It is not surprising, for instance, to find Lee's topless image from film stills and photo shoots in martial arts dojos, combat sport facilities, and gyms. In Freudian terms, the star's image becomes the viewer's Ideal Ego. Male bodybuilding in martial arts films has a delayed physical response from viewers. The body responds with disciplined mimicry, to re-create the spectacle of bodybuilding and acrobatics. After all, at some point, Zaror was, like many viewers today, also an ordinary person watching extraordinary actors on-screen. In fact, several interviews confirm that his desire to be on film came from watching other films that featured fighting and action scenes, and he has highlighted Robert Rodriguez as one of his main influences and inspirations.

Undoubtedly, the martial arts genre objectifies the female body as well (e.g., Lee's *Way of the Dragon* and Díaz's *Kiltro* and *Mirageman*). In many features, the female body is punished or abused, and the plot drives the hero to seek vengeance. But at the same time, the modern martial arts genre also favors the presentation of the male martial artist's body, inheriting the sexualizing gaze from the male's point of view and adding the male body as an idealized objectified element. In Freudian and Jungian terms, the star's entire body becomes the phallic object, the symbol of power and envy. The martial arts hero needs nothing but the body to fight.

In the 1980s and 1990s, much of Chilean manhood was constructed in the media through the heteronormative lenses of soap operas that featured Euro-Chilean, Euro-Mexican, Euro-Brazilian, or Euro-Venezuelan actors, and Hollywood films with white males who seduced women from all ethnic backgrounds. Chilean popular media featuring men without hegemonic, white racial features was hard to come by. Masculine beauty was not merely in the eye of the beholder but in the "blue eyes" of the creators of that objectifying subjective beauty. Scholars such as Peter Chua, Dune C. Fujino, and Darrell Hamamoto have pointed out that there is an "internalized white masculinity" that dominates the entire world, a hegemonic masculinity that is being challenged. Fascination with European male beauty in Chile is evident, whether in history or mass Chilean culture. For instance, many are quick to point out that Chilean independence leader Bernardo O'Higgins had Irish heritage or that Augusto Pinochet's eyes were "ice-blue."[8]

When Edward Said published his seminal *Orientalism* (1978), little had been written about Asian-American media representation and even less about Asian-American masculinity. Generally speaking, martial arts movies do not fall into the criticism that Said's *Orientalism* analyzes. In fact, Zaror's feature films do the reverse of Said's argument: that is, they promote an imagined "Orient" that is presented as superior to the creator's culture (in this case, Chileans), although it does fall into the exoticism and otherness with which any representation copes.[9] For instance, the Palestine/Korea duality presented in *Kiltro* demonstrates a second-order or secondhand Orientalism, in which the East is not merely showcased as exotic or erotic, promoting a paternalistic point of view toward it, but, rather, the "Oriental" world is viewed through cinematic metareferences, which include Hong Kong martial arts films, B movies, Westerns and other Hollywood movies, and television shows. The secondhand and even thirdhand Orientalisms in Zaror's early films have an innovative effect, as they reclaim masculinity for the "Oriental" male from the Westernized standard of masculinity. The new Latin American "macho" is transformed from the one portrayed in the hegemonic Hollywood cinema of past decades into a daring reformulation of the politics of gender (Park 2016, 12). Said did not explicitly write much about mass-media representation, but rightly asserted that postcolonial discourse subscribed to a masculine Europe dominating a "domesticated," feminized Orient. Thus, his visionary criticism of Orientalism can be reformulated to fit a more specific Asian American, African, and Latin American experience.

Nonhegemonic masculinity lacks or overemphasizes "proper" or "normal" masculinity. Among many other Asian American studies scholars, Peter Chua and Diane Fujino (1999) have pointed out that "U.S. institutional practices have rendered Asian-American men as simultaneously hypermasculine and emasculated" (391). In his seminal essay "The Western: Or the American Film Par Excellence," André Bazin insists that the western genre and American film are inseparable (1971, 140). I would argue that the martial arts genre is the masculine film par excellence. Kyle Green (2011), and more directly Mark Simpson (2008) and Magnus Stenius (2015), have stated that along with surfing culture and other martial arts culture, there is an underlying homoerotic experience in observing and desiring, in martial arts films, the male body in pain and pleasure. They have argued that not only is it a genre where hypermasculinity is exploited with discourses of presenting "a real man" but also that it is the most homoerotic masculine genre, second only to gay pornography. In "Visual Pleasure and Narrative Cinema," Laura Mulvey (1999) recognizes that, in film, the female body is displayed as a sexual object. In other words, the sexualized female body perpetuates a "*straight* male gaze" from viewers. The martial arts genre shifts the objectification of the voluptuous, naked female body to the chiseled lead role's body (e.g., films with Bruce Lee, Jackie Chan, Jet Li, Jean-Claude Van Damme, Sylvester Stallone, and Arnold Schwarzenegger), signaling "discursive change in the visual aesthetics of martial arts masculinity" (Bowman 2015, 67), while still perpetuating the female body as a sexual object.[10]

Since Lee's films, the male body has been exploited further, highlighting its musculature and combat abilities, although hegemonic hierarchies favor Western over Eastern representations (Middle East or Far East). This is arguably one of Lee's most evident legacies in representations of the male body and East Asian masculinity, although the objectification is not always linked to sexualization but, rather, morphs into the stereotypes of the "angry yellow man" or the "angry Asian man." In today's "Golden Age of Male Objectification" (Reid 2011), Zaror is capable of remasculinizing Arab-Chileans through the spectacle of his body, although he himself is not overtly reminding his viewers of his Arab heritage. Emasculation is a by-product of postcolonial hegemony, through which black, brown and yellow men are represented as either effeminate or dangerous; this idea is sometimes internalized by diasporic communities in the West. Zaror follows Lee's remasculinization through an overt display of musculature and combative stances, understanding the objectification of the male body as part of a market rhetoric that considers the chiseled male body a valuable commodity (Figure 8). In martial arts films, the Arab male is not as commonly represented as the East Asian male.[11]

In martial arts films, combat naturally evokes heterosexual male mating narratives. Dyer "points out that the symbolism of male sexuality is 'overwhelmingly centered on the genitals, especially the penis'" (1986, 90). Popular films and television often place women as objects of a "natural" male sex drive, therefore reinforcing a notion that women are what "male sexuality is ostensibly there for" (Yu 2012, 128). Commenting on Dyer's analysis from the eighties, Sabrina Yu insists that "the most common imagery of male sexuality at the time [was] equating male sexuality with the penis and its most popular media representation [was] having sex with a woman" (128). The representation of sex with a woman is often absent in martial arts films, or is found in the context of violence committed by the villain; the plot thus culminates with men combating rather than with sex. The hyperathleticism creates a homoerotic effect, as most martial arts films have historically targeted male viewers and fans, although many would consider the homoeroticism to be simply homosocial. Since *Enter the Dragon* (1973), many scenes have featured uncovered male bodies in box-office action movies, including the *Terminator* saga (featuring Schwarzenegger), Stallone's *Rocky*

Figure 8. Marko Zaror

and *Rambo* sagas, and Jean-Claude Van Damme's 1980s and 1990s flicks. Combat sports often feature the male body as the phallic object. The athlete's talent is intrinsically complemented by the exposed body, protecting the actual phallus (no blows below the belt),[12] and highlighting the pair of feet as the testicles and the movement of the body as the erection. The punches and kicks reformulate the ejaculating metaphor. The male star's body, whether static or in motion, becomes the spectacle, the focus of the plot, and the celebration of the narrative resolution, highlighting the homosocial nature of this body genre.

Zaror's acting career successfully began featuring his martial arts skills and physique. As he began a transnational career, his talents expanded to additional roles with acrobatic scenes in mixed-genre action films. Images of masculinity in *Chinango* (2005) and *Kiltro* (2006) reformulate the masculinity of the "Oriental" male. In *Kiltro* (2006), Zaror plays Zamir (pronounced "Sammy"), a biracial Arab-Chilean who falls in love with Kim, a biracial Korean-Chilean teenager. The movie showcases the actor's bare body in the entire second half of the film, beginning with his training in the desert, followed by occasional scenes in which he is completely naked. The bloody chest and abdominals in the final scenes pay homage to *Enter the Dragon* (1973), where Lee is mostly topless as he fights the vicious Han (Figure 9). In *Kiltro*, Zamir confronts Max, an Arab villain who captures Kim and her father. Orientalist emasculation is challenged as Zaror plays the hypermasculine dragon type with ease. Unsurprisingly, the film concludes with the final blow that annihilates Max and allows Zamir to romantically reconnect with Kim.

Chinango has a 1970s exploitation feel and plenty of sequences that feature the actor's bare body. The plot is a mash-up of stereotypical tropes about Mexican and Chinese culture (e.g., narco violence, drug lords, kung fu). *Chinango* opens with Zaror's character, Braulio Bo, walking through the fields and combating a gang who insults him as a *mariquita* (pejorative for gay); he responds with quick retribution. Braulio is sexually desired by his Euro-Mexican girlfriend Sofía (Susana González) and Liao Chen (Oyuki Ocman), an Asian-Mexican character. Liao and Braulio forsake their heritage and opt for a romantic relationship. Braulio is gentle with both women, even if he ends up confronting Liao at the end of the film. He does not embody the macho behavior that his Mexican enemies in the film explicitly manifest. In other words, Braulio is a "different kind" of masculine male compared to the aging Shaolin monk, who refrains from all sexual desires, and the Mexican drug lords, who exploit all of their sexual desires through prostitution and abusive sexual behavior. Braulio is a mix of gentleness and aggressiveness that is reserved to serve justice and punish evil. He woos Sofía and Liao with compliments, pretending to be weaker than he is when they playfully struggle to end up in bed; the camera focuses on the female body next to Zaror's musculature. He might not be aggressive with the two women, but he still follows Hollywood's formulaic schemes to perpetuate heteronormative masculinity through the spectacle of his body. What he lacks in Mexican macho hypermasculinity, he makes up for with shots of him posing, bench-pressing weights and flexing his muscles, or spinning kicks defying gravity, banking on the East Asian hypermasculinity inherited by Bruce Lee and the aftermath of martial arts film narratives.

In his second major Chilean installment, *Mirageman*, Zaror was featured as a vigilante, and the film was marketed as "the first Chilean superhero film." Díaz and Zaror's parody became a self-mocking film that combined tropes from Sam Raimi's *Spiderman* (2002) and other superhero films and television shows and Rodriguez and Tarantino's *Grindhouse* (2007). According to interviews, the production of the film faced obstacles

Figure 9. *Kiltro* (Ernesto Díaz Espinoza, 2006)

because its attempt to create a Chilean superhero film seemed overambitious to producers, but it beat two competing action flicks, *Rambo* (2008) and *Jumper* (2008), at the Chilean box office. Still, the film was not seen much outside Chile, ending up solely as a novelty with a cult following. Still, there were indications in 2009 that a Hollywood remake was in the works. The film is grounded in *niahísmo*[13] with regard to past political divisions in Chile. It is a reflection of Chilean cinematic bravado in a global market saturated with action flicks, particularly with the rise of the DC and Marvel Comics superhero genres, perhaps as a postcolonial strategy to present a superhero from a less developed country.

Mandrill (2009) has the over-the-top tagline "Cooler than Shaft, Hotter than Bond, Faster than Lee," paying homage to the Bond franchise and hitman exploitation films and combining martial arts with gunman action tropes. At this point, Zaror and Díaz Espinoza were expanding into the action genre that featured martial arts scenes, but these were not the only focus. *Mandrill* follows dubbing techniques similar to those of Robert Rodriguez's *El Mariachi* (which dubbed different voices over the diegetic actors' voices) in order to re-create a sound that evokes Hong Kong and Hollywood martial arts films dubbed into Spanish (Park 2016, 25–26). This double mimicry of dubbing lines into the actors' native Spanish reformulates Homi Bhabha's theory of mimicry, challenging the possibility of hierarchical representation by being aware of the mockery (1994, 85). Zaror's dubbing into Spanish acknowledges the reality of metacinematic pastiche, perhaps subverting the Bakhtinian polyphony of voices that re-create the subaltern discourse of martial arts. This constructs a cacophony of cinematic self-references that perpetuate the second and third degrees of Orientalist symbols.

In *Redeemer* (2014), Zaror plays Pardo, a suicidal former hitman who turns religious after his pregnant wife is murdered by a drug cartel. He becomes a vigilante who brutally punishes gang members in a rural coastal city in Chile, before asking them to repent and turn to God. The film contains four scenes where Pardo plays Russian roulette while praying to God. Those scenes are also an opportunity for him to flex his bulging biceps and show off his body covered with tattoos portraying religious imagery as he points a pistol at his head (Figure 10). The film follows the formulaic action story of a defeated leading man who, after an epiphany and inspiration from a romantic relationship, triumphs over the evil villain (a racist American who was behind the deaths of the protagonist's wife and unborn child). The

Figure 10. *Redeemer* (Ernesto Díaz Espinoza, 2014)

film fits into the general action genre, as it limits the martial arts tropes to fight scenes rather than letting them dictate the entire plot.

Zambo Dendé (2017), based on a Colombian comic book, features Zaror as Zambo Dendé, a "Zambo" and "cafuzo"[14] fighter who defends slaves and natives in a revisionist history of the Americas. This continues the trope of the hybrid identity of the Chilean martial artist. In this Colombian production, the objectification and homoeroticism of the body are subdued by the ideological commentary of resisting hegemonic oppression and re-creating historical revisionism through cinema. *Zambo Dendé* echoes cinematic historical revisionisms recently exemplified by Tarantino's *Inglourious Basterds* (2009) and *Django Unchained* (2012).

Perhaps, with these Latin American films, the Latin Dragon[15] has risen to martial arts stardom, following in the steps of the Eastern stars: Bruce Lee, Jackie Chan, Jet Li, and Donnie Yen. His casting in Marvel's *The Defenders*, produced by Netflix and coproduced in the United States, and his projects with Robert Rodriguez (*Alita: Battle Angel*), Daniel Zirlli (*Invincible* and *Affinity*), and up-and-coming Indonesian action filmmaker Kimo Stamboel (*One Good Thing*) could move Zaror away from cult subgenre fame and into mainstream global stardom.

ZAROR, THE VILLAIN, THE EXTRA: LATIN DRAGON OR *"CHUPACABRAS CHINO"*?

Zaror's sex appeal and athletic virtuosity have been mostly channeled into villains and supporting characters in non-Chilean films, with minimal diegetic importance, reinforcing his subalternity since "crossing over" to Hollywood. All of his roles in Chile have been starring ones. Hollywood villains, meanwhile, are either hypermasculine bullies (e.g., *Kickboxer*'s Tong Po) or emasculated flâneurs (e.g., *Enter the Dragon*'s Han and *Kiltro*'s Max Kalba). Some male villain roles have increased the cult aura of the constructed stardom and sex appeal, but the fact that these are supporting characters minimizes the sense of stardom.[16]

In *Undisputed 3* (2010), Zaror plays a Colombian fighter named Raúl "Dolor" Quiñones, opposite English martial artist Scott Adkins. While Zaror maintains some of the hypermasculine tropes of previous roles, this was his first as a villain in an exclusively martial arts film. In one of the scenes, the diegetic voice of Raúl recites the Spanish poet Federico García Lorca's "The poet asks his love to write" ["El poeta pide a su amor que le escriba"]. Lorca was ostracized, persecuted, and killed in 1936 during the Spanish Civil War, in part due to his homosexuality. Despite this literary citation of homoerotic innuendo,[17] even in the context of this (presumably heterosexual) masculinity, the villain is relegated to a one-dimensional character whose only goal is to defeat all fighters and satisfy a mafia that runs a prison.

In the Indian production *Sultan* (2016). Zaror plays a U.K. MMA fighter who is defeated by the lead Indian wrestler, played by Salman Khan. Zaror's character, Marcus, is an explicit colonial reference to imperial historical character Marcus Aurelius. In *Savage Dog* (2017), which features Scott Adkins in the lead, Zaror plays the main villain, the French henchman Rastignac. The story is set in Indochina in 1959, which several official summaries of the film describe as "a land beyond rule and a time without mercy and the birth of a legend." Zaror's one-dimensional character is an extension of merciless modern colonialism. He introduces himself with scripted lines before fighting, reminding us of Iñigo Montoya's line in 1987's *The Princess Bride*: "My name is Jean-Pierre Rastignac. I have been known by many names. But the one I'm most commonly associated with is the Exterminator. I face you as an equal. With the exception of this blade, we're quite fairly matched." The reference, however, might not be recognizable, as this film avoids comic relief, unlike Zaror's first two Chilean features, *Kiltro* and *Mirageman*.

Zaror's earlier stardom in his native country reformulated the remasculinization of the "Oriental" male in Latin America with some awareness of the actor's ethnic background in the media and his own recognition that he has Arab heritage. As he transitions to being cast in the United States and Southeast Asia in villainous and minor roles, Zaror seems to be less dragon-like and more *chupacabras*-like,[18] shape-shifting into characters with few lines. This is perhaps an effect of globalization and transnationalism. These roles in Hollywood have made Zaror into a versatile action star with no need for stuntmen. His character in Robert Rodriguez's *Machete Kills* (2013) is an adequate example of the constructed image that keeps changing in his transition to Hollywood. Zaror plays a character named "Zaror," a voiceless "genetically engineered super soldier clone" who is killed several times. The first time the clone dies, he is stabbed multiple times by Machete. He reappears as another clone but after being stabbed again by Machete's machete, he is entangled in ropes and chopped into pieces by a helicopter rotor blade in a gruesome and intentionally humorous way. Six or seven additional clones keep dying and reappearing: two are beheaded, several more are stabbed to death, mutilated, shot by a machine gun, and so on. Perhaps, just like Bruce Lee, Zaror needs to go through ethnicity-changing Kato-like television roles while abroad before outshining the titular lead characters with his own spark. Perhaps martial arts actors need to be *chupacabras* for some period of time before "entering the dragon."[19] Or perhaps his malleable ethnicity on-screen, and his move away from the martial arts genre, indicate Zaror's attempt to "be like water," as The Dragon famously declared.

THE STAR SO FAR: A DISTANT STAR IN THE GLOBAL "STAR-TOSPHERE"

The constellation of martial arts stars is saturated with celebrities who are recognized by a limited fan base. Perhaps Zaror is already a global star in the niche of martial arts fandom, given the compartmentalized consumption of genre films today. Bruce Lee, Jackie Chan, and Jet Li, and their "Western" counterparts Chuck Norris, Steven Seagal, and Jean-Claude Van Damme, are much better known than current figures like Thai martial arts star Tony Jaa (from the *Onk Bak* trilogy), Hong Kong's Donnie Yen (from the *Ip Man* trilogy and 2016's *Rogue One: A Star Wars Story*), and British actor Jason Statham (*Crank, War*) in the saturated martial arts "star-tosphere." Although mixed martial arts are becoming more profitable and mainstream today as a sport, the film genre itself is still consumed by a targeted and limited fan base that is miniscule compared to that of other genres, and even more miniscule in Chile.

Although Zaror's career has diversified into the superhero, drama, and action genres, none of his roles outside Latin America have featured him as the lead yet. He has successfully landed roles as the "last boss," which can often be considered a highly coveted role equal to, or above, the lead. Nonetheless, unlike with the horror, drama, or comedy genres, the role of the antagonist in action films is often one-dimensional, lacking the complexity of the lead. Another noticeable change in Zaror's acting in villain and supporting roles is the loss of a major quality of the traditional martial arts hero: he is no longer the romantic lead. As Zaror's career keeps evolving abroad, his hypermasculine and (homo)erotic undertones become less noticeable as they are overshadowed by secondary and villain roles. He is indeed a Latin Dragon, a Chilean martial arts star in Chile's constellation of a handful of Chilean fighters.[20] Zaror is distant from the global box office stars that cover Hollywood billboards with chiseled bodies that still inspire us to keep gazing and exercising to attain a "heavenly body," to use Dyer's term. A spectacular body like Zaror's, which defies gravity, confirms that Palestinian-Chilean men can jump. And kick. And be (distant) stars.[21]

NOTES

1   Historically, representation of "Oriental" males in cultural productions have been consistently demonized or emasculated. See Boone (2014), Hamamoto (1994), Hamamoto and Liu (2000), and for historical context, Michael Park (2013).

2   I refer here to award-winning documentaries (e.g., Maite Alberdi, Carmen Castillo, Patricio Guzmán), dramas (e.g., Pablo Larraín, Sebastián Lelio, Raúl Ruiz, Alicia Scherson, Andrés Wood), the rising horror/thriller genre (e.g., Jorge Olguín, Pablo Illanes, Patricio Valladares, and Lucio Rojas's filmography), experimental, and independent films (e.g., Matías Bize, Elisa Eliash, Alberto Fuguet, Alejandro Jodorowsky, Marialy Rivas, Marcela Said), and successful box-office comedies (e.g., Boris Quercia, Nicolás López). *Johnny 100 pesos* (1993) is considered one of the few commercially successful Chilean action films. However, the film is closer to a drama, with tropes from the hostage and thriller genres.

3   In the American film industry, nationalistic tendencies are evident: the *Undisputed* trilogy, the *Karate Kid* saga, the *Rocky* saga, the *Kickboxer* saga, and the *Under Siege* movies are several examples of this. Jean-Claude Van Damme is Belgian, but in U.S. productions he often plays nationalistic American

characters. For instance, he plays American soldiers, veterans, and members of law enforcement (e.g., as Colonel Guile in *Street Fighter* [1994], as Vietnam War soldier Luc Deveraux in *Universal Soldier* [1992], and as suicidal veteran Eddie Lomax in *Inferno* [1999]).

4   Matthew Polly's *Bruce Lee: A Life* (2018) has elaborate passages on Bruce Lee's racial and cultural background. Lee's Hong Kong–American hybrid identity is discussed in detail, with special attention to his lesser-known Dutch-Jewish maternal great-grandfather.

5   William Lyne (2000) argues that this 1970s and early 1980s subgenre highly influenced stereotypical African American characters, but at the same time represented African Americans in lead roles, rather than as secondary and neglected characters. Blaxploitation films are a major influence on Tarantino and Rodriguez films, which in turn became Zaror's main source of inspiration for *Kiltro, Chinango, Mirageman,* and *Redeemer*. Díaz Espinosa has suggested that his films attempted to create some sort of a "Latinoxploitation."

6   Zaror plays mythical characters that require little speaking, but that still highlight his physique and athleticism. In *Myths and Legends* he plays Marimoto, a fighter in a fantasy world, while in Robert Rodriguez's TV show *From Dusk Til Dawn: Season 3* he plays Zolo, an Aztec warrior trained in hell. In the action comedy *Green Ghost*, Zaror plays Drake, a half-human Mexican superhero, in a supporting role that pokes fun at DC and Marvel Comics superhero films that feature mainly white actors playing leads and their few minority sidekicks who offer comic relief (with the very few exceptions of *Black Panther* and *Black Lightning*). *Green Ghost* reverses the roles, as it features a secret group of Mexican superheroes, El Trío de la Luz (the trio of light), who are "forced by destiny to include their adopted [car salesman and local TV personality] gringo into their group to help fight to save humanity" (Clark 2018, n.p.).

7   After all, funding for Chilean films such as *Machuca* (2004) is not solely Chilean: Tornasol (Spain), Mamoun Hassan (UK), and Paraiso (France) also funded the project. The two leads of the "Chilean classic" *Johnny 100 pesos* (1993) were Mexican actors Armando Araiza and Patricia Rivera; the film was produced by Chilean and Mexican companies.

8   For more on attitudes toward non-European ancestry and interracial relationships, see Beckman (2009) and Lin Chou (2004).

9   In "South Reads Western and Eastern East" (Park 2010), I argue that in *Kiltro*, racial hierarchy is not clear, as many characters are racial, ethnic, and national hybrids. Chileans, in turn, are represented mockingly: a gesture of self-awareness about the ironies of a Chilean martial arts film made with Chilean lead actors. Characters that allegedly have Arab or East Asian roots are the leads, while the only seemingly Caucasian characters are two beer

drinkers in a desert, negligible in the diegesis. In *Redeemer*, meanwhile, the English-speaking American is an obnoxious enemy.

10   The link between martial arts films and erotic films is not merely theoretical but also historical, even in Chile. For example, in May of 2019, Cinemas Nilo and Mayo in Santiago were closed (Reyes 2019). These theaters used to specialize and feature martial arts films in the 1980s, but eventually became film theaters that exclusively showed adult films and became linked to sex trafficking.

11   An important comparison of male body objectification could include Bollywood and Turkish pop music that have gone through periods of popularity in Chile (i.e., the Turkish singer Tarkan in the 1990s, and the soap opera *Arabian Nights* [2006–9]).

12   In Oedipal terms, the martial artist becomes the castrating father-figure with the most desired phallic object—his own body. In the earlier stages of the martial arts film, formulaically speaking, the protagonist is also the inexperienced virgin-fighter who is defeated by the main villain. He then needs to train to acquire the right skills and body for victory, often experiencing a spiritual awakening and using his disciplined body to endure punishment and inflict punishment upon others, as a repayment for previous hardship and abuse. This is in accordance with Northrop Frye's modes of heroism or Joseph Campbell's idea of the "hero with a thousand faces."

13   I take this term from the common phrase "no estoy ni ahí" that expresses indifference in Chilean youth. Marketing attempted to foster a cult following with playful YouTube clips and commercials before the release. One clip shows Mirageman punishing a school bully and an obnoxious teacher with a one-punch knockout. A second clip re-creates a right-wing political campaign ad from the 1988 Chilean plebiscite, where Mirageman punches and knocks out Barney from *Barney & Friends*. These marketing plots dialogue with ideological discourse, but they themselves are not political.

14   These racial terms were used in the Spanish and Portuguese empires and are occasionally still employed today to identify individuals who have African and Amerindian ancestry.

15   Zaror markets himself on his own website, in web interviews, on social media, and in film magazines as "the Latin Dragon," a Chilean vigilante, gunman, and superhero.

16   In *Black Panther* (2018), the villain Erik Killmonger played by Michael B. Jordan—also the lead in Ryan Coogler's *Creed* (2015) from the Rocky saga—received far more attention for his muscular body transformation than did the body image of the lead role of Black Panther played by Chadwick Boseman. *Essence*, *Insider*, and *Entertainment Tonight* YouTube Channels,

Esquire Magazine, and *Men's Journal*, among many other mass media, featured Jordan's body transformation and muscular physique. We should also mention Heath Ledger's role as the Joker in Nolan's *The Dark Knight* (2008) and Loki, played by Tom Hiddleston in the Marvel Comics recent films. Female villains have traditionally been sexually objectified in cinema.

17 The verses recited by Zaror's character include the following passage: "I suffered you and my own veins I tore, / tiger and dove around your waist, / and fell in a hot duel of lilies and our bites." ["Pero yo te sufrí. Rasgué mis venas / Tigre y paloma sobre tu cintura / En duelo de mordiscos y azucenas"].

18 The *chupacabras* is a shape-shifting creature in popular and traditional urban myth in the Americas, that kills its victims in order to suck their blood (according to the definition of the Royal Spanish Academy, known by its Spanish-language acronym RAE). The adjective "*chino*" is literally "Chinese" but in some countries, it can also refer to someone of non-Chinese Asian parents, or even mixed-race parents (RAE).

19 Jackie Chan, for instance, was featured for a few seconds in Bruce Lee's *Fist of Fury* (1971) as an extra, and also as an extra in *All in the Family* (1975) before finding global success as the most recognized stunt performer in martial arts films.

20 On May 19, 2018, for the first time, UFC Fight Night was held in Santiago, with a sold-out attendance of eleven thousand. The main card included the Chilean MMA fighter Diego "Pitbull" Rivas and the victor, Argentinian Guido Cannetti. Rivas has gained some recognition as the only Chilean athlete to participate in the most competitive mixed martial arts league. The boxer Martín Vargas was Chile's first boxing world title contender, in the 1970s, and arguably the most recognized martial artist by local Chileans.

21 Roberto Bolaño's 1996 novel *Estrella distante*, translated as *Distant Star*, focuses in part on Chilean artists living abroad in artistic obscurity and misrecognition.

WORKS CITED

Bazin, André. 1971. *What Is Cinema: Volume II*. Berkeley: University of California Press.

Beckman, Ericka. 2009. "The Creolization of Imperial Reason: Chilean State Racism in the War of the Pacific." *Journal of Latin American Cultural Studies* 18 (1): 73–90.

Bhabha, Homi. 1994. *The Location of Culture*. New York: Routledge.

Bolaño, Roberto. 1996. *Estrella distante*. Barcelona: Anagrama.

Boone, Joseph Allen. 2014. *The Homoerotics of Orientalism*. New York: Columbia University Press.

Bowman, Paul. 2015. *Martial Arts Studies: Disrupting Disciplinary Boundaries*. London: Rowman & Littlefield International.

Breakfast at Tiffany's. 1961. Dir. Blake Edwards. Perf. Audrey Hepburn, George Peppard, Patricia Neal. Jurow-Shepherd.

Chan, Jachinson W. 2000. "Bruce Lee's Fictional Models of Masculinity." *Men and Masculinity*. 2 (4): 371–87.

Chinango. 2005. Dir. Peter Van Lengen. Perf. Marko Zaror, Hugo Stiglitz, Susana González. Full Moon Entertainment, Mandrill Films.

Chou, Diego L. 2004. *Chile y China: Inmigración y relaciones bilaterales, 1845–1970*. Santiago, Chile: Pontificia Universidad Católica de Chile, Instituto de Historia.

Chua, Peter, and Dune Fujino. 1999. "Negotiating New Asian-American Masculinities: Attitudes and Gender Expectations." *Journal of Men's Studies* 7 (3): 391–413.

Clark, Charlie. 2018. "Green Ghost: Storyline." *Internet Movie Database*. IMDb.com, Inc. June 1. https://www.imdb.com/title/tt4012916/?ref_=adv_li_tt.

"*Confident*." 2015. Dir. Robert Rodriguez. Perf. Jeff Fahey, Zane Holtz, Demi Lovato. Troublemaker Studios.

Dapena, Gerard. 2017. "Genre Films Then and Now." In *The Routledge Companion to Latin American Cinema*, 150–63. London: Routledge.

Django Unchained. 2012. Dir. Quentin Tarantino. Perf. Jamie Foxx, Christoph Waltz, Leonardo DiCaprio. The Weinstein Company, Columbia Pictures.

Dyer, Richard. 1979. *Stars*. London: British Film Institute.

———. 1986. *Heavenly Bodies: Film Stars and Society*. New York: St. Martin's Press.

Enter the Dragon. 1973. Dir. Robert Clouse. Perf. Bruce Lee, John Saxon, Jim Kelly. Warner Bros.

Green, Kyle. 2011. "It Hurts so It Is Real: Sensing the Seduction of Mixed Martial Arts." *Social & Cultural Geography* 12 (4): 377–96.

The Green Ghost. 2017. Dir. Michael Olmos. Perf. Danny Trejo, Michelle Lee, Marko Zaror. Mutt Productions, Zaror Entertainment.

Grindhouse. 2007. Dir. Robert Rodriguez, Eli Roth, Quentin Tarantino, Edgar Wright, and Rob Zombie. Perf. Kurt Russell, Zoë Bell, Rosario Dawson. Dimension Films.

Hamamoto, Darell. 1994. *Monitored Peril*. Minneapolis: University of Minnesota Press.

Hamamoto, Darell, and Sandra Liu. 2000. *Countervisions: Asian American Film Criticism*. Philadelphia: Temple University Press.

I Am Bruce Lee. 2012. Dir. Pete McCormack. Perf. Bruce Lee, Paul Bowman, Daniele Bolelli. LeeWay Media, Network Entertainment.

Inglourious Basterds. 2009. Dir. Quentin Tarantino. Perf. Brad Pitt, Diane Kruger, Eli Roth. Universal Pictures.

Jameson, Fredric. 1986. "Third-World Literature in the Era of Multinational Capitalism." *Social Text* 15: 65–88.

Jumper. 2008. Dir. Doug Liman. Perf. Hayden Christensen, Samuel L. Jackson, Jamie Bell. Twentieth-Century Fox.

Kiltro. 2006. Dir. Ernesto Díaz Espinoza. Perf. Marko Zaror, Miguel Ángel de Luca. Mandrill Films.

Lyne, William. 2000. "No Accident: From Black Power to Black Box Office." *African American Review* 34 (1): 39–59.

Machete Kills. 2013. Dir. Robert Rodriguez. Perf. Danny Trejo, Mel Gibson, Marko Zaror. AR Films, Aldamissa Entertainment.

Mandrill. 2009. Dir. Ernesto Díaz Espinoza. Perf. Marko Zaror, Celine Reymond, Alejandro Castillo. Mandrill Films.

Mirageman. 2007. Dir. Ernesto Díaz Espinoza. Perf. Marko Zaror, María Elena Swett, Ariel Mateluna. Mandrill Films.

Mulvey, Laura. 1999. "Visual Pleasure and Narrative Cinema." In *Film Theory and Criticism: Introductory Readings*, edited by Leo Braudy and Marshall Cohen, 833–44. New York: Oxford University Press.

Park, Michael. 2013. "Asian American Masculinity Eclipsed: A Legal and Historical Perspective of Emasculation Through U.S. Immigration Practices." *Modern American* 8 (1): 5–17.

Park, Moisés. 2010. "South Reads Western and Eastern East: Second-Hand Orientalism in *Kiltro*, a Chilean Martial Arts Film." In *One World Periphery Reads the Other: Knowing the "Oriental" in the Americas and the Iberian Peninsula*, 393–405. Newcastle upon Tyne: Cambridge Scholars Publishing.

———. 2016. "The Latin Dragon: The Remasculinization of the Oriental Male." In *Transnational Orientalisms in Contemporary Spanish in Latin American Cinema*, 9–32. Newcastle upon Tyne: Cambridge Scholars Press.

Polly, Matthew. 2018. *Bruce Lee: A Life*. New York: Simon & Schuster.

Rambo. 2008. Dir. Sylvester Stallone. Perf. Sylvester Stallone, Julie Benz, Matthew Marsden. Lionsgate.

Redeemer. 2014. Dir. Ernesto Díaz Espinoza. Perf. Marko Zaror, José Luís Mósca, Loreto Aravena. Moral Brothers Entertainment, XYZ Films.

Reid, Joe. 2011. "Are We Living in the Golden Age of Male Objectification?" *Vulture* September 12. https://www.vulture.com/2011/09/are_we_living_in_the_golden_ag.html.

Reyes, Patricia. 2019. "Dejan de funcionar cines triple X en el centro de Santiago: alcalde Alessandri terminó contratos." *Las últimas noticias*, June 7.

Said, Edward W. 1978. *Orientalism*. New York: Vintage.

Savage Dog. 2017. Dir. Jesse V. Johnson. Perf. Scott Adkins, Marko Zaror, Juju Chan. Cho Man Ro Enterprises, Compound B.

Simpson, Mark. 2008. "Fight Club: How Did the World's Straightest Sport Become So Gay? We Head to Montreal's Ultimate Fighting Championship to Find Out." *Out Magazine*, July 9.

Spider-Man. 2002. Dir. Sam Raimi. Perf. Tobey Maguire, Kirsten Dunst, Willem Dafoe. Columbia Pictures, Marvel Enterprises, and Laura Ziskin Productions.

Stenius, Magnus. 2015. "The Body in Pain and Pleasure: An Ethnography of Mixed Martial Arts." PhD diss., Umeå University.
Undisputed 3: Redemption. 2010. Dir. Isaac Florentine. Perf. Scott Adkins, Mykel Shannon Jenkins, Marko Zaror. Millennium Films.
The Way of the Dragon. 1972. Dir. Bruce Lee. Perf. Bruce Lee, Chuck Norris, Nora Miao. Golden Harvest Films.
Williams, Linda. 1991. "Film Bodies: Gender, Genre, and Excess." *Film Quarterly* 44 (4): 2–13.
Yu, Sabrina Q. 2012. *Jet Li: Chinese Masculinity and Transnational Film Stardom*. Edinburgh: Edinburgh University Press.
Zambo Dendé. 2017. Dir. Riccardo Gabrilli R. Darren Shahlavi, Carolina Guerra, Perf. Michelle Lee, Marko Zaror. 7Glab Entertainment.

OTHER TEXTS AND OTHER LANDS

Intermediality and Adaptation
Beyond Chile(an Cinema)

6

IL FUTURO BY ALICIA SCHERSON

Film and Cross-Cultural (Af)filiations

María Angélica Franken

TRANSNATIONAL AND TRANSMEDIAL STAKES: FROM LITERATURE TO FILMMAKING

The Chilean filmmaker Alicia Scherson premiered *Il Futuro*—a Chilean, German, Italian, and Spanish coproduction—in 2013.[1] This was her third solo production; the previous ones were *Play* (2004) and *Turistas / Tourists* (2009). More recently, she and Cristián Jiménez codirected *Vida de familia / Family Life* (2016). *Il Futuro*, meanwhile, is a film adaptation of *A Little Lumpen Novelita* (*Una novelita lumpen*) (2014) by the late Chilean writer Roberto Bolaño, who spent most of his years as a writer in Spain. This short novel, originally published in 2002, was commissioned by Random House Mondadori, a publishing house from Barcelona, as part of the Year Zero Collection, in which several Latin American writers were invited to choose a world capital in which to narrate a story addressing the global context of the turn of the twenty-first century. Bolaño chose Rome.

As can be seen from its title sequence onward, as well as the aforementioned context of its production, there is no doubt that *Il Futuro* is meant for an international audience. At the same time, it aligns itself with the formal and aesthetic explorations in contemporary Chilean filmmaking that emerged at the Valdivia Film Festival in 2005.[2] Scherson's movie, which contains dialogue in Italian and English, is also part of a trend whereby the topics, production, and cast in national filmmaking have developed a transnational signature. The main characters are played by the Dutch actor Rutger Hauer and Manuela Martelli, a Chilean actress trained abroad. Scherson filmed on location in Rome, to develop the story of two young orphans; the film suggests their parents were Chilean exiles.

In what follows, I analyze *Il Futuro*'s intermedial transfer from literature to film, focusing on the relationship between Chilean national film and literary imaginaries and the global themes and aesthetics that the movie adopts. The film goes beyond the traditional, local perspective held not only by many previous Chilean films but also by previous adaptations of Chilean literature to film. I therefore argue that *Il Futuro*'s discursive and aesthetic dialogue with Roberto Bolaño's novella reveals affiliations to certain cultural and cinephilic imaginaries previously unexplored in Chilean cinema. First, I examine the narrative of formation of the protagonist, Bianca, which revolves around her decisions about whom she decides to associate herself with: an intimate, feminist story line that follows the traditional literary and film genre of the melodrama. Then, I turn to Scherson's personal aesthetic, whereby affective objects and bodies raise questions about time and space. In doing so, I analyze her transcultural reinterpretation of certain aspects of the Italian cinematic tradition. Taken together, these sections address Bianca's family or community (dis)affiliations at the level of content, and Scherson's genre and cinema (af)filiations (to melodrama and Peplum cinema, specifically) at the level of form.

My analysis assumes that the systems and languages of literature and cinema are different. *Il Futuro* falls under the category of the aesthetic regime of art, defined by Jacques Rancière (2004) as a system of norms that question the representative system, and which are unique to modern cinema. Disconnected from literary models of analysis, and based on the difference between showing and telling, Rancière's ultimate goal is to discover the specificity of the language of images. In this sense, when I refer to cinema, I am reflecting upon the specificity of its own language and modes of expression as a medium; however, it is also in dialogue, through intermedial interferences, with other languages, including literature.

My discussion also focuses on the concept of transmediality, understood by Alfonso de Toro as "a transcultural phenomenon as opposed to a national phenomenon, given that medial processes have always had transnational and transcultural effects, since the beginning of modernity" ["el caso de la transmedialidad (como el de la transtextualidad) se trata de un fenómeno transcultural y no nacional, ya que los procesos mediales tienen siempre efectos transnacionales y transculturales desde el inicio de la Modernidad"] (2008, 104). In other words, transmediality obviates borders and implies the transgression of limits in the broadest sense—hence the prefix "trans." Consequently, "transmedial elements imply a transcultural, transtextual, and transdisciplinary origin, because they draw from various systems and subsystems" ["[l]os elementos transmediales implican un proceder transcultural, transtextual y transdisciplinario porque se alimentan de diversos sistemas y subsistemas"] (104). The transmedial establishes itself as an epistemological resource that, for the purposes of this study, permits an equal dialogue between two kinds of media—literature and cinema—and allows for the interaction between national and heterogeneous global imaginaries: "a dialogue without hierarchy, open and nomadic, that brings together diverse identities and cultures in a dynamic interaction" ["un diálogo desjerarquizado, abierto y nómada que hace confluir diversas identidades y culturas en una interacción dinámica"] (103). A transmedial concept that goes hand in hand with a transcultural performance allows for an analysis of *Il Futuro* based on connections and hybridizations that Scherson updates and redefines, from global cultural imaginaries,[3] to linkages of genre and text, to intermedial dialogues between cinema and literature.

A FEMALE COMING-OF-AGE STORY: FAMILIAL AND MELODRAMATIC (AF)FILIATIONS

The voice and perspective—the "occularization," in André Gaudreault and François Jost's (2008) terms—of Bianca, the protagonist, offer a particularly female story of (self) formation, in dialogue with melodramatic motifs. The first images of the film, which uses a vintage aesthetic, show the parents' car accident: the original, disruptive action that propels the plot forward. The images are narrated by Bianca in voice-over, quoting, in Italian, the first lines of *A Little Lumpen Novelita*: "Now I'm a mother and a married woman, but not long ago I led a life of crime. My brother and I had become orphaned. Somehow, that justified everything. We didn't have anyone. And it all happened overnight" ["Ora sono una madre e una donna sposata, però non molto tempo fa ero una delinquente. Io e mio fratello siamo rimasti orfani. Questo, in qualche modo, giustificava tutto. Non avevamo nessuno. E tutto accadde da un momento all'altro"]. Most of the time, the subjective camera takes on Bianca's point of view. The female narrator speaks about the action we see in the film from an indefinite present time—she has since married and become a mother. The fictional memoir is the guiding theme of the story that hints at melodrama and its imaginary; it also constitutes a coming-of-age narrative, or *Bildungsroman*,[4] given that Bianca, who starts out the film in a fairly precarious situation, is now fully integrated into Roman society as an adult.

Following the death of her biological parents, the seventeen-year-old Bianca drops out of school in Rome to work in a hair salon, and agrees to participate in the plan of her younger brother and his two friends—bodybuilders and foreigners known as *Libio* ("The Libyan") and *Boloñés* ("The Bolognese")—to rob an old blind man named Maciste. Bianca meets the wealthy Maciste, a famous actor of Peplum Italian cinema and a bodybuilding champion during the 1970s, by offering him her sexual services. In this way, she gains entry into the mansion where Maciste lives by himself. The imaginaries that supplement Bianca's path from adolescence to adulthood offer a (de)formative role internalized by the narrator herself when she attempts to seduce Maciste, who is blind. Her goal is to find a safe with money in his house: "Now I will be a criminal, I thought without fear. From here on my story gets even fuzzier" ["Adesso sarò una delinquente, pensai senza paura. A partir da quel momento la mia storia diventa ancora piu torbida"].

In *Il Futuro*, the conflict between Bianca's outside world and inner life—which her coming-of-age process must address—is materialized in her sensitivity to light. This is the immediate effect of her parents' car accident, as the novel points out: "After that, the days were different. Or the passing of the days. Or the thing that joins one day and the next but at the same time marks the boundary between them. Suddenly the night stopped existing and everything was constant sun and light" (Bolaño 2014, 4). The strong light does not hinder the process of change—Bianca constantly states that she is changing—and her movements through the city of Rome illustrate her notion of the passing of time. Indeed, the name Bianca (the color white in Italian) highlights her youth, sexuality, and virginity at the beginning of the story; her lack of experience makes her something of a blank slate. In terms of the cinematographic image, the luminosity with which she perceives the outside world is visually reinforced by the ways in which the actress who plays her is illuminated (Figure 11).[5] Bianca's photosensitivity allows her to move easily through Maciste's dark old mansion, searching for the money; however, her visual disorder does not translate into an ethical or spiritual orientation, nor an ability to envision her future. The glow only lights up the external bodies of the present, as a tangible or sensory experience, not an intellectual one.

Figure 11. Bianca (the color white in Italian) develops photosensitivity after the death of her biological parents, in *Il Futuro / The Future* (Alicia Scherson, 2013). Photo courtesy of Ricardo de Angelis.

Endings vary in the traditional female *Bildungsroman*, but they often relate to the protagonist's willingness to accept a destiny and social order imposed upon her; *Il Futuro*, however, offers a more heterogeneous approach. Some stories end with a physical or symbolic death; in others, the heroines give up on internal struggles in return for a stable and conventional future involving marriage and family; in others, they abandon their homes and find, in a university or other institution, a space of apprenticeship that allows them to achieve self-fulfillment (Gómez Viu 2009, 116). Bianca's story follows the patriarchal pattern of integration with the family and a particular social structure, but this conventional ending contrasts with the film's formal experimentation. Indeed, many female-focused coming-of-age stories involve variety in their use of the point of view, and tend to be less linear and chronological in comparison to those where men are the protagonists (Lagos 1996, 56).

Representations of Bianca's dreams lend density to the narrator's process of development, and they alter the linear and chronological order of the story. For example, one of Bianca's key dreams occurs just after an extreme close-up on her face, with a voice-over in which she affirms that she is becoming a criminal and that her story is becoming more and more blurry (see the previous quote from the film). Bianca dreams that her parents appear for a few seconds in the middle of a desert highway, before turning into dogs. These surreal narrative discontinuities are constructed as shots that "don't articulate the story; they are simply optical and auditory sensations" ["no articulan el relato, simplemente son sensaciones ópticas y sonoras"] (Urrutia Neno 2010, 53). As in Scherson's other films, dreams are interruptions that reveal the protagonist's feelings more clearly than the plot does; in the terms of Ismail Xavier, they exceed the narrative (2008, 240). Because of this, inserting this dream sequence intensifies the protagonist's personal conflict about becoming a criminal. Parents and adults—with the exception of Maciste—are absent in the orphans' lives; Bianca's parents quickly turn into animals. Dreams become virtual images—or crystal images, in Deleuzian terms—and they are a gateway not only to alternative universes (de los Ríos 2015, 106) but also to new ways of understanding the character's inner conflicts.

The presence of a love affair is a central topic in coming-of-age stories; it is related to the affective and sexual learning process of the young hero. In the case of young women, this experience has yet another component: the fantasy or imaginary around female sexuality (Lagos 1996, 81). This is another dimension of the transmedial dialogue between the female *Bildungsroman* and melodrama (Brooks 1976): both discursive genres share daydreams, sexual fantasies, themes of marriage and maternity, the clash between desires and society, and secrets (Monterde 1994). In *Il Futuro*, Bianca's first experience of love is central to her development. Although Bianca approaches Maciste in order to deceive him and steal his money, in the novel she ends up falling in love: "I'm ashamed of this now, but one night I told him that I was in love with him and I asked him what his feelings were for me. He didn't answer" (Bolaño 2014, 92). Although the film has a more subtle approach to her feelings, the end of the relationship is the end of Bianca's process of (de)formation: her reentry into society, no longer as an offender or a *lumpen*, but rather as a mother and a married woman. The heroine manages to fit within a logic of tradition and melodrama: she finds a certain happy ending, even though her apparent conformity to convention is the result of transgression.

Mentors who contribute to the heroine's coming-of-age—friends, tutors, teachers, counselors—are also crucial to any developmental story focused on a female character. In *Il Futuro*, Maciste has a major influence on Bianca.

He teaches her the art of lovemaking, and he represents the wisdom that Bianca lacks, even as he longs for her youth. In Bianca's telling, Maciste is a good man, but he feels that he is rotting from the inside: the past is slowly eating away at him. His past is thus projected as wisdom, but also in terms of putrefaction, because it has no sense of progression toward a future. On the other hand, the *Libio* and the *Boloñés* are two characters of a negative or de-formative nature. They are pimps who use Bianca as a sexual object for their own pleasure, but they get her to start thinking about the future, even if it appears only in crudely economic terms. Unlike Maciste, they represent the idea of a future tied to ignorance, youth (no progress), and delinquency (negative learning).

Edward Said (1983) argues for nuancing ideas about biological filiation, in favor of other forms of affiliations and relationships among human beings that might cause particular symbolic orders to cohere. He proposes that institutions, relationships, and communities without a biological link can still guarantee the concept of affiliation (17), if not filiation. This transition from filiation to affiliation is part of the modern cultural process (18–19), and a lack of biological filiation still provides a "compensatory order . . . whether it is a party, an institution, a culture, a set of beliefs, or even a world-vision" (19). Bianca and her brother articulate new communities, albeit clearly atypical and dysfunctional, with the *Libio*, the *Boloñés*, and Maciste. In this sense, their relationships operate not under a familial logic (birth, nationality, profession) but rather under an affiliative one (social and political conviction, economic circumstances, voluntary effort, deliberate reflection), in Said's terms (25). The relationship with the foreign bodybuilders stems from economic uncertainty, emotionless sex, and the overwhelming hope for a better economic future. Bianca's relationship with Maciste is justified in a sexual contract, too, but it is sustained in chosen affections and shared shortcomings: loneliness and blindness (due to a lack, or excess, of light).

These new affiliative experiences notwithstanding, Bianca's narration and the film anticipate the end from the very beginning: the reestablishment of an altered affiliative order. The project of robbing Maciste is abandoned, the bodybuilders are expelled from the home, and the original family unit is restored. Ultimately, the visual representation of these transitions and affiliative changes allows us to reflect on the film at another level: the (af)filiations and cinematographic legacies that Scherson questions and redefines in *Il Futuro* and in her particular reading of the work of Roberto Bolaño.

The ways in which these dis/af/filiations at the level of content find their counterparts at the level of form, in *Il Futuro*, will be the topic of the next section of this chapter. Bianca's new affiliations—her decision to eventually marry and live a conventional life—relate to Alicia Scherson's own ways of interacting with the Chilean and European film traditions of the twentieth century. For Bianca and her brother, meanwhile, the importance of bodies and bodywork relates to the visual treatment of material elements in recent Chilean cinema.

AFFILIATIONS AND RESIGNIFICATIONS OF A CINEPHILE IMAGINARY: CROSS-CULTURAL STAKES

This section moves from content-based to form-based affiliations, to examine the traditions that Scherson plays with throughout the film. However, these formal elements characterize not only the work of Alicia Scherson but also much of the *Novísimo* Chilean cinema movement (Cavallo and Maza 2011; Urrutia Neno 2013). In this sense, Scherson dialogues not only with the transcultural and transnational components of her film—lending affects and meanings to objects, bodies, and spaces, such as Maciste, his house, and the city of Rome—but also with the well-recognized tendency toward aesthetic experimentation in recent Chilean cinema. Scherson elaborates upon the novel's reflection on time and its material expression in space, in the terms of Bakhtin's (1986) concept of the chronotope: "The ability to *see time*, to *read time* in the spatial whole of the world and, on the other hand, to perceive the filling of space not as an immobile background, a given that is completed once and for all, but as an emerging whole, an event" (Bakhtin 25, emphasis in original). The leitmotif of the future—which gives the film its title and permeates the entire story—both mobilizes and immobilizes Bianca's discourses and formative processes. The future also materializes in the image: in the aesthetic work of light that illuminates spaces and bodies, in the microscopic and estranged view of objects on-screen, in a panoramic sequence of the Roman ruins, and at Cinecittà, the movie studio where Maciste once worked. Hence, time and space acquire a special status that is consistent with the concrete events that initiate and mobilize them: the car accident and the light that permeates and disturbs Bianca's sight. In these ways, Scherson selectively affiliates herself with both global and domestic cinematic trends.

The first sequence of the film projects the parents' car in motion, the mother's handkerchief blowing in the wind; later the car takes the form of unrecognizable scraps.[6] The parents function as an absence, but their energy is materialized in objects such as a cigarette butt, a cup of coffee with lipstick on it, or dishwashing gloves. Spaces can be recognized from what they contain, and by the gaze that is exerted upon them. The extreme close-up shots on such objects render them signifiers of other things. For example, while Bolaño reveals Bianca's sense of orphanhood through her first-person narration in the novella, Scherson focuses her camera on the inert objects that attest to Bianca's loneliness: the dirty dishes, the parents' unoccupied bedroom, and the television that always stays on. The objects come to mediate the reminders to Bianca of the absence of her parents. This representation of objects offers a new assessment of their forms and content (Estévez 2010, 28). It establishes a complex relationship with the past when brought to the present, since these objects have lost their original notion of usefulness and have become strange and unfamiliar (29). This estranging view that materializes a particular time in the past is linked, following Peller's reading of Benjamin, with the childhood view that is alienated from the objects' utility, opening these objects up to a sense of otherness (Peller 2010, 4). Hence, Bianca's and the camera's microscopic gazes upon certain objects—deliberately reinforced with extradiegetic music and expanded intradiegetic sounds made by the same objects—play with references of closeness and alienation. This gaze reveals the deep meaning of those objects, heretofore apparently meaningless. For Bianca and the spectator, they evoke again and again, as happens in childhood with the act of repetition (Peller 2010, 2), the traumatizing experience of the loss of the primary filiation; that is, the loss of the parents.

Scherson represents bodies on-screen in two visually and materially opposed ways: as lack or as excess. Maciste's blindness contrasts with Bianca's photosensitivity, exposing light as excess, which contrasts with the penumbra of Maciste's house. This house—another helpless and ruined body—is the site of sexual games in which the characters are connected to one another as opposites. Bianca's slimness, highlighted with lighting that frames her naked body covered in body lotion, emphasizes the huge size of Maciste, who continues lifting weights in order to keep his aging body in shape. When Maciste's and Bianca's oiled bodies appear illuminated together in bed (Figure 12), Scherson is reinforcing—on film—a series of oppositions that Bolaño already imagines in the novel.[7] Meanwhile, the parents' bodies are replaced by the materiality of the objects they have left behind, as we have seen. Other characters' bodies also acquire prominence and excess, whether as products held in exchange (as with Bianca's prostitution), or by the excessive work done to them (as when the *Libio* and the *Boloñés* exercise to win a bodybuilding competition), and in the transferral to the film image this motif is strengthened.

Meanwhile, we can establish a link between the city of Rome, the home of Maciste, and his body as a ruin. *Il Futuro* is thus a chronotope of ruin, since it allegorizes superimposed past times and spaces. This is consistent with the material notion of the future represented in the movie. In the film, Bianca states:

> [Maciste] was wrong. Deep down I was always thinking about the future. I thought about it so much that the present had become part of the future, the strangest part. For me, the future resembled a room in Maciste's house, but with sharper focus, the furniture covered in old sheets and blankets, as if the owners of the house . . . had gone away on a trip and didn't want dust to collect on their things. And that was my future and how I thought about it, if you could call it thinking, and if that is what you could call it a future. [[Maciste] Era lì che si sbagliava. Io pensavo sempre al futuro. Pensavo così tanto al

Figure 12. Maciste's and Bianca's oiled bodies appear illuminated together in bed, in *Il Futuro / The Future* (Alicia Scherson, 2013). Photo courtesy of Ricardo de Angelis.

> futuro che il presente era arrivato a diventare parte del futuro, la parte più strana del futuro. Per me il futuro assomigliava a una stanza qualsiasi della casa di Maciste, ma con più chiarezza e con i mobili coperti da vecchie lenzuola, come se i padroni di casa fossero partiti per un viaggio e non volessero che la polvere si accumulasse sopra i mobili. Questo era il mio futuro e così pensavo a lui, se questo si può definire pensare, e se questo si può chiamare futuro.]

The tragedy of the parents causes Bianca to gain some degree of foresight, making her future both spatial and corporeal. The future thus appears to her not as an ethereal promise but rather as the material reflection of the present: "the future that was opening up like a mirror of the present or a mirror of the past, but opening up" (Bolaño 2014, 93). Indeed, according to Álvaro Bisama (2013), time and ideology "threatened the narrator's collapse, the characters, the language" ["amenaza [con] el colapso de la narradora, de los personajes, del lenguaje"] ("Bianca contra Bianca"). However, the movie seems to indicate a way out. The future is threatening—the catastrophes of European authoritarianism and xenophobia are omnipresent[8]—but at least there is a future for a marginal character like Bianca. Toward the end of the story, when the criminal plan falls apart—Bianca decides to sabotage the plan to rob Maciste—the *Libio* and the *Boloñés* are expelled from the house, and order is restored. Bianca is once again able to see darkness: "That night, for the first time in a long time, night was really night, dark and fragile, and edged with fears" (Bolaño 2014, 108).

This restoration of order would seem to explain Scherson's decision to change the title of the film: it is a reflection on time that permeates both the novel and the movie. Indeed, Scherson reappropriates twentieth-century Italy's complex and heterogeneous film tradition, affiliating it with Chilean cinema in a number of ways. For *A Little Lumpen Novelita*, Bolaño chose the city of Rome at the turn of the twenty-first century, but Scherson emphasizes the reflections on time that have prevailed in discussions of contemporary cinema both in Chile and at the global level. Casting Dutch actor Rutger Hauer to play Maciste is the film's first major cultural and cinephilic reference point. Hauer, who starred in Ridley Scott's classic science fiction film *Blade Runner* (1982), among other major films, personifies a decrepit actor who was once a famous Peplum film artist, and in this way Scherson offers a nod to the star system imaginary in both the U.S. and European film industries. Here, fiction and reality coexist and mutually reinforce one another; Scherson's "play" with both of them prompts a self-reflexivity typical of current Chilean cinema (Urrutia Neno 2013).

Il Futuro also revisits Rome's past as a cultural imaginary for Western cinema, where current generations revisit old film genres and anachronistic movie stars. Scherson takes up that fantasy world and translates it into a reflection on time, introducing images from the Cinecittà film studios and sequences of movies shot on the very same sets where Maciste once starred as Hercules.[9] During their sexual encounters, Maciste tells Bianca that in the 1960s, when he was in his prime, he played mythological figures in Peplum films and was surrounded by well-known actors and movie stars.[10] In a further self-reflective turn, the young protagonists of *Il Futuro* discuss the characteristics of the Peplum genre after watching a video on TV: "'They have no rhythm, the characters are superficial, and the plot takes arbitrary turns.' 'What do you know about art?' 'Is this art?'" ["'Non hanno ritmo, i personaggi sono superficiali, e la trama faccia arbitrari.' 'Que ni sai tu di arte?' 'È questa arte?'"]. The critical stance that *Il Futuro* takes toward this film tradition is another element of Scherson's disaffiliations vis-à-vis global cinema.

The melodrama that permeated Maciste's films, in which he saved damsels in distress and fought evil rulers, intensifies Bianca's identification with her lover. Bianca defines herself in the novel as "omnivorous: I liked romance" (Bolaño 2014, 13); her *Bildungsroman* is peppered with the sexual fantasies that accompany many female coming-of-age stories (Monterde 1994, 64). In certain sequences showing Bianca watching Maciste's old films, the camera moves from Bianca's perspective, watching the hero fighting wild animals and rescuing Dolly Plimpton from being burned alive, to show her watching the screen: the TV frame becomes the frame of an old theater. Scherson's use of this frame within a frame emphasizes Bianca's formation as both a cinematic and a sexual connoisseur.

Bianca's amorous connection with Maciste is mediated by Italian television, B cinema, pornography, and Peplum cinema rented in video stores that she watches with her brother and his friends. According to Valeria de los Ríos (2015), "unlike modern cinephile constructions, in which the characters replace literature for cinema, high culture for popular culture, these *lumpen* characters of Bolaño barely aspire to watch television" ["A diferencia de las construcciones cinéfilo-modernas, en las que los personajes reemplazan la literatura por el cine, la alta cultura por la cultura popular, estos personajes lumperizados de Bolaño a duras penas aspiran a ver televisión"] (105). This sequence reflects the passage from the big screen to the small screen; an apt metaphor for television eclipsing auteur and popular cinema in Italy in the 1970s, bringing about the decline of the country's cinema at a local and global level (León and Bedoya 2017, 52).

Scherson also delves deeply into the cinephilic imaginary that Bolaño establishes in the novel. The importance of TV as a new format and the video store as the only media space of sociability in the literary version are complemented in *Il Futuro* with the Cinecittà studio sequences (Figure 13). Cinecittà, the first film studio in Europe, inaugurated in 1937 under Mussolini, sought to compete with the Hollywood studios and the Nazi propaganda films of the UFA studios in Germany. The productions of this Italian studio, governed by the ideological parameters of fascist propaganda, were meant to attract a massive popular audience. Cinecittà's temporary closure, due to bombings and Nazi occupation during the Second World War, allowed for the emergence of one of the major European film trends of the twentieth century: Italian neorealism. This movement, unlike studio cinema, opted for authentic locations, nonprofessional actors, and scripts based on real events

Figure 13. Cinecittà studio as a space of sociability in *Il Futuro* / *The Future* (Alicia Scherson, 2013). Photo courtesy of Massimiliano Cilli.

to represent postwar Europe's social reality; it was also extremely influential for Latin American cinema (Traverso 2007, 166). After the war and thanks to government grants, some of the very same neorealist filmmakers trained at the Centro Sperimentale di Cinematografia, including Vittorio De Sica, Luchino Visconti, and Roberto Rosellini, shot at Cinecittà. Meanwhile, Peplum superproductions such as *Quo Vadis* (1951) by Mervyn LeRoy and *La Dolce Vita* (1960) by Federico Fellini, were released in the 1950s and 1960s. According to Patricia Espinosa (2009), Bolaño recycles the character of Maciste that appeared for the first time in the foundational silent film *Cabiria* (Giovanni Pastrone, 1914), as well as the character of the helpless and idealistic prostitute of Fellini's film *Nights of Cabiria* (1957). Meanwhile, the relationships between Latin American cinema and the Centro Sperimentale di Cinematografia are countless: in addition to a number of Latin American directors, various authors of the Latin American "Boom," including Manuel Puig, Gabriel García Márquez, and José Donoso, were all trained in that school, which was the major center of neorealism.[11] In this sense, Rome is a key site for understanding not only Latin American cinephilia but also transmedial movement between Latin American film and literature.

CONCLUSION

Through this complex web of influences, Scherson identifies herself in *Il Futuro* less with a traditional cinematographic style than with a more global, popular style focusing on the decay and ruin of a complex and contradictory film tradition. Thus, Fellini and the Peplum cinema coexist, mimicking the contradictions inherent in Italian cinematography, whose Cinecittà studios are probably the country's most important contribution to the history of cinema. In this way, Scherson adopts a heterogeneous strategy similar to that of Bolaño, whose Spanish-language title for *A Little Lumpen Novelita* is an ironic reference to Donoso's 1973 work *Tres novelitas burguesas* (*Three Bourgeois Novellas*). Scherson repeats Bolaño's gesture of appropriating minor, marginal, and hybrid artistic genres. It is striking that she would choose to adapt *A Little Lumpen Novelita*—one of Bolaño's minor works, in the opinion of many literary critics. By distancing herself from issues and problems local to Chile, and focusing instead on universal dilemmas in global and historical settings such as Rome at the turn of the century, she moves away from canonical readings of Bolaño, Chilean cinema, and world cinema as a whole. In this sense, Scherson connects Bianca's development process, at the narrative level, to her own development as a filmmaker at the level of form, meditating upon time and space and their expression in the context of a more experimental, open cinema.

Moving intermedially between *Bildungsroman* cinematic and literary forms, between material manifestations of time and space, and between European and Latin American global and local imaginaries, *Il Futuro* revisits and redefines Scherson's (af)filiations with different cinematographic traditions around the world. Scherson's (trans)national, (trans)medial, and (trans)cultural leaps confirm that she is more connected than ever with recent Chilean cinema that thoughtfully interrogates its past and present affiliations. In this sense, she is a key part of a community of Chilean filmmakers and writers, including Cristián Jiménez, Marialy Rivas, Álvaro Bisama, and Alejandro Zambra, among others, who were born in the 1970s and grew up under the dictatorial imaginary. In their work, they address their biological filiations, their traumatic cultural affiliations (to the dictatorship), and their new disciplinary and transcultural affiliations to the film and literature of the globalized twenty-first century.

NOTES

1   *Il Futuro* was awarded Best Director and Best Actress at the Huelva Latin American Film Festival and received the KNF Award at the Rotterdam Film Festival.

2   Thanks to Alicia Scherson for access to the images from *Il Futuro*, photographed by Ricardo de Angelis and Massimiliano Cilli.

3   For more information about this "movement," see the introduction to this volume, as well as *El Novísimo cine chileno* (Cavallo and Maza 2011) or *Un cine centrífugo* (Urrutia Neno 2013).

4   This chapter follows the ideas of Bronislaw Baczko, who defines the social imaginary as societies' "permanent work of invention of their own global representations as image-ideas through which they provide themselves with an identity, perceive their divisions, legitimize their power, develop patterns for their members" ["trabajo permanente de invención de sus propias representaciones globales como ideas-imágenes por medio de las cuales se dan una identidad, perciben sus divisiones, legitiman su poder, elaboran modelos formativos para sus miembros"] (Baczko 1991, 27).

5   The *Bildungsroman* is the name given to novels "whose main topic is the literary representation of the experiences of a young protagonist, from

childhood or adolescence to adulthood, in a learning process whose final goal is to establish the personality of the individual and his/her integration into society" ["cuyo tema principal es la representación literaria de las experiencias de un joven protagonista, desde su niñez o adolescencia hasta su madurez, en un proceso de aprendizaje cuya finalidad es lograr la consolidación de la personalidad del individuo y su integración en la sociedad"] (Gómez Viu 2009, 108). In parallel to these experiences of formation, there is ongoing reflection about them. The concept of *Bildung* has an active and reflective sense, since the character is both actor and recipient vis-à-vis his or her experience: "the hero becomes him/herself by confronting external reality" ["el héroe se hace a sí mismo en el combate con la realidad externa"] (Rodríguez Fontela 1996, 33). In this sense, the *Bildungsroman* involves open-ended novels or tales "whose true ending resides in the hero's indefinite formation, and not in overcoming the conflict between the hero and the world" ["cuyo verdadero final reside en la autoformación indefinida del héroe y no en la superación positiva del conflicto entre el héroe y el mundo"] (Gómez Viu 2009, 108–9). The conflict between the desires of the hero and those of society never resolves itself fully or harmoniously; for this reason, the central topic of the genre is the process and the consolidation of the personality of the individual and his or her integration–more or less successful—into society. While neither *Il Futuro* nor *A Little Lumpen Novelita* are necessarily *Bildungsromane* in themselves, we can identify the ways in which they have appropriated certain imaginaries from that genre, each resignifying them in their own way, in their renderings of the process of Bianca's formation so she can have her own family.

6   The poetic image of the machine is part of Scherson's entire cinematographic oeuvre.

7   "Then, as I walked over to his chair, I noticed that a ray of moonlight, fat as a wave, rolled into the gym. Maciste undressed me. He felt my face and my hips and my legs. Then he got up and went to get the bottles of lotion and liniment" (Bolaño 2014, 68).

8   It is possible to read the novel and the film in political terms. Although this topic is beyond the scope of this essay, the film could be related to the reflections on fascism that Bolaño insinuates in the novel, reflections that have been developed more fully in his other novels and essays.

9   See Jacqueline Reich's discussion of the Maciste figure in *The Maciste Films of Italian Silent Cinema* (2015).

10 In the novel, Maciste states that his artistic name is Franco Bruno, and people used to call him Mister Universe. His real name was Giovanni Dellacroce (Bolaño 2014, 72).

11   In those years, the aesthetic and political influence of Italian neorealism on the New Chilean Cinema of filmmakers such as Raúl Ruiz, Aldo Francia, and Miguel Littin was notable. They were influenced by their new language for approaching Latin American social reality. José Donoso would also have a positive experience with European cinema that would influence his own writing: at the request of Michelangelo Antonioni, he wrote an original script that would later result in his celebrated novel *Casa de Campo* (Cabezón-Doty 1998, 46–47). Meanwhile, the Argentine Manuel Puig had a much more negative experience at the Centro Sperimentale, later calling it orthodox and dogmatic (Cabezón-Doty 1998, 43). Puig would clearly distance himself from the experimentation formally defined as the New Latin American Cinema at the Viña del Mar International Film Festival in 1967.

WORKS CITED

Baczko, Bronislaw. 1991. *Los imaginarios sociales. Memorias y esperanzas colectivas*. Buenos Aires: Nueva Visión.

Bakhtin, M. M. 1986. *Speech Genres & Other Late Essays*. Translated by Vern W. McGee. Edited by Caryl Emerson and Michael Holquist. Austin: University of Texas Press.

Bisama, Álvaro. 2013. "Bianca contra Bianca." *Revista Qué pasa*, last modified June 5, 2013.

Bolaño, Roberto. 2014. *A Little Lumpen Novelita*. Translated by Natasha Wimmer. New York: New Directions Publishing.

Brooks, Peter. 1976. *The Melodramatic Imagination*. New Haven, CT: Yale University Press.

Cabezón-Doty, Claudia. 1998. "Literatura y cine latinoamericanos en diálogo intermedial." *Taller de Letras* 26: 29–54.

Cavallo, Ascanio, and Gonzalo Maza, eds. 2011. *El novísimo cine chileno*. Santiago: Uqbar Ediciones.

de los Ríos, Valeria. 2015. "Visualidad, política y animalidad en *Una novelita lumpen* de Roberto Bolaño y en *Il Futuro* de Alicia Scherson." *Confluencia: Revista Hispánica de Cultura y Literatura* 31: 101–9.

de Toro, Alfonso. 2008. "Frida Kahlo y las vanguardias europeas: Transpictoralidad—Transmedialidad." *Aisthesis* 43: 101–31.

Espinosa, Patricia. 2009. "Tormenta sin ruido (sobre *Una novelita lumpen*)." *Archivo Bolaño*, last modified November 1, 2009. https://garciamadero.blogspot.com/2009/11/tormenta-sin-ruido-sobre-una-novelita.html.

Estévez, Antonella. 2010. "Dolores políticos. Reacciones cinematográficas. Resistencias melancólicas en el cine chileno contemporáneo." *Aisthesis* 47: 15–32.

Gaudreault, André, and François Jost. 2008. *El relato cinematográfico*. Barcelona: Paidós.

Gómez Viu, Carmen. 2009. "El Bildungsroman y la novela de formación femenina hispanoamericana contemporánea." *EPOS* 25: 107–17.

Il Futuro. 2013. Directed by Alicia Scherson. Jirafa Films, Pandora Film Produktion, Movimento Film, Astronauta Films, Jaleo Films.

Lagos, María Inés. 1996. *En tono mayor: Novelas de formación de protagonista femenina en Hispanoamérica*. Santiago: Cuarto Propio.

León Frías, Isaac, and Ricardo Bedoya. 2017. "Hablando de cine italiano: Revisión de un panorama difícil." *Ventana indiscreta* 18: 50–55.

Monterde, José Enrique. 1994. "Dossier: Melodrama." *Dirigido por* 223: 50–67.

Peller, Mariela. 2010. "Un recuerdo de infancia. Juego, experiencia y memoria en los escritos de Walter Benjamin." *Nómadas. Revista Crítica de Ciencias Sociales y Jurídicas* 27: 1–11.

Rancière, Jacques. 2004. *The Politics of Aesthetics: The Distribution of the Sensible*. New York: Continuum International Publishing Group.

Reich, Jacqueline. 2015. *The Maciste Films of Italian Silent Cinema*. Bloomington: Indiana University Press.

Rodríguez Fontela, María de los Ángeles. 1996. *La novela de autoformación. Una aproximación teórica e histórica al Bildungsroman desde la narrativa hispánica*. Kassel: Editorial Reichenberger.

Said, Edward W. 1983. *The World, the Text, and the Critic*. Cambridge: Harvard University Press.

Traverso, Antonio. 2007. "Migrations of Cinema: Italian Neorealism and Brazilian Cinema." In *Italian Neorealism and Global Cinema*, edited by Laura Ruperto and Kristi Wilson, 165–86. Detroit: Wayne State University Press.

Urrutia Neno, Carolina. 2010. "Alicia Scherson." In *El novísimo Cine Chileno*, edited by Ascanio Cavallo and Gonzalo Maza, 49–58. Santiago: Uqbar Ediciones.

———. 2013. *Un cine centrífugo: Ficciones chilenas 2005–2010*. Santiago: Cuarto Propio.

Xavier, Ismael. 2008. *El discurso cinematográfico. La opacidad y la transparencia*. Buenos Aires: Manantial.

7

VIDEO BUILT THE CINEMA STAR

Alex Anwandter's *Nunca vas a estar solo*

Arturo Márquez-Gómez

FROM AUDIOVISUAL REPERTOIRES TO THE "ZAMUDIO ARCHIVE"

In the title of this chapter I evoke The Buggles' hit "Video Killed the Radio Star" (1979) to analyze part of Alex Anwandter's audiovisual oeuvre. My aim is to show that far from being "killed," or at least overshadowed, by the music video format, Anwandter has developed from a musician to a film director by directing his own music videos for his four studio albums, *Odisea / Odyssey* (2010), *Rebeldes / Rebels* (2011) *Amiga / Friend* (2016a), and more recently, *Latinoamericana / Latin American* (2018a). It is through the dynamic and ductile genre of the music video that Anwandter has conveyed a rich and lyrical universe, providing a new language and unseen images of the LGBTQ+ community in Chile.

Anwandter's growing artistic awareness of LGBTQ+ themes and his engagement with directing music videos is at the heart of his first film, *Nunca vas a estar solo / You'll Never Be Alone* (2016), in which he fictionalizes the incidents surrounding the death of Daniel Zamudio, a twenty-four-year-old gay man brutally assaulted in the San Borja Park in downtown Santiago on March 2, 2012. This violent episode has generated a considerable number of audiovisual productions besides Anwandter's, such as the television miniseries *Zamudio: Perdidos en la noche / Zamudio: Lost in the Night*[1] (2015), directed by Juan Ignacio Sabatini, the film *Jesús* (2016) by Fernando Guzzoni, and the play *¿Qué mató a Daniel? / What Killed Daniel?* (2017) by the Menjunje theater company.[2]

These fictional works, along with a substantial collection of paratexts (press, laws, books, films), constitute what I call the "Zamudio archive." This notion of an archive in relationship to LGBTQ+ issues stems from Jack Halberstam's lucid reflections on Brandon Teena's transphobic murder in Nebraska in 1993.[3] Although archives offer artists a "productive narrative, a set of representations, a history, a memorial, and a time capsule" (Halberstam 2005, 23), they can also lead to "comforting fictions" that risk erasing the social contexts in which these incidents occurred. In the case of the Zamudio archive, more than comforting fictions, we could speak about the initial versions of the crime that focused primarily on homophobia as the motive without considering the socioeconomic profile of the victim and his aggressors, later revealed through Rodrigo Fluxá's journalistic investigation *Solos en la noche: Zamudio y sus asesinos / Alone in the Night: Zamudio and his Killers* (2014).

My argument in this chapter is twofold. First, I will examine several music videos by Anwandter, which are a vital element of his audiovisual project because they allow him to test out different themes and artistic personae that later inform *Nunca vas a estar solo*. Second, I will show how the music video's global aesthetic and representational power in the current mediascape shapes certain sequences in the film, in order to make the Zamudio archive intelligible to international audiences. As one would expect from a musician like Anwandter, music infuses the film with extra texture, an elusive language with which to revisit the Zamudio archive, creating alternative visions of it without falling into the comforting fictions that Halberstam warned against.

In the film, Anwandter creates a hybrid soundtrack made of instrumental scoring he arranged and preexisting music such as *boleros*, pop songs from the Chilean New Wave, and a classical piece by Gustav Mahler. These varied genres fulfill music's traditional role in forging the audience's emotional responses, but in their interactions with the visual, they broaden the audience's comprehension of the characters' subjective and social positions in contemporary Chile's culture of violence.[4] Anwandter's previous work in music video,[5] which has also continued since the film, informs the ways in which music intertwines with the images in the film to such a degree that some of the film's sequences work like music videos. This use of music in contemporary filmmaking is common, according to Carol Vernallis (2013), who states that music and visuals "can be so tightly interwoven in some segments of the contemporary film that we might see them as music video sequences" (209).

There are several "music video sequences" in *Nunca vas a estar solo* in which the author expresses his own musical sensibility. These sequences are also a crucial tool for forging engagement between the audience and the film's characters, connecting spectators with a story told from the perspectives of Pablo, an avid dance student passionate about drag, and his workaholic father, Juan, who for years has worked supervising a small mannequin factory. Pablo's perspective is replaced by the father's after the young man is brutally beaten by his homophobic neighbor, Martín, and Pablo's closeted boyfriend Félix, who is also the nephew of a nosy neighbor, Lucy. Pablo frequents the disco, either with his friend Mari or alone, to hang out and see the performances of drag queens; in fact, Pablo wants to audition for a drag show. However, one night on his way back from the disco, he is intercepted and attacked by Martín. The next day, Pablo does not go to the drag tryout, and decides to dye his hair blond. While walking around the neighborhood with Mari, he is chased by Martín, another man, and Félix, who knocks him down. In daylight and in the middle of a public square, Pablo is brutally beaten and left alone and unconscious for hours. Viewers thus have a limited amount of time to get to know Pablo and understand the story from his point of view. The ensuing shift to Juan's perspective reflects a sudden change in Juan's previously idealistic notions about Chile: he has a painful realization of the proximity of violence in his daily interactions with friends, neighbors, and bureaucratic institutions.

To better understand how music and moving images interact in *Nunca vas a estar solo*, I will use the notion of the "musical moment" coined by Amy Herzog (2009) to refer to sequences in the film "when music, typically a popular song, inverts the image-sound hierarchy to occupy a dominant position in a filmic work" (7). Diegetic music in the film, particularity the "amorous discourse"[6] of the *boleros*, allows audiences to connect with Pablo's desires by syncing the rhythms of the *boleros* to the editing of different shots, directing us to listen to how the lyrics express multiple layers of affect. The early sequence in which Pablo rehearses his drag number in his room offers a good way to illustrate Herzog's concept. We see Pablo dressed in women's clothes and makeup, sensually dancing in his room while the old-fashioned cassette player plays the *bolero* "Sufrir / Suffering" by the iconic Chilean singer Lucho Gatica. The slow tempo of the *bolero* determines the editing of several shots that capture Pablo dancing and gesturing in front of a mirror. Simultaneously, the dramatic lyrics, evoking longing for a lost lover, help us gain a better understanding of Pablo's affective world. According to Claudia Gorbman (2007), the lyrics of a song produce "a more active reading than orchestral underscoring: they define action, setting, and character, they engage references, parallelism, and metaphors, and sometimes, they elaborate complex structures of point of view" (65). In the case of Pablo's performance, the title "Sufrir" may lead us to consider his silenced relationship with the closeted Félix, his cold relationship with a father who barely understands what it is to have a gay son, and ultimately, his place in a normative society that will eventually punish him for being different. In this musical moment, the slow tempo of the *bolero* molds the editing of different and multiple shots resulting in the sensation of an expansion of the time that we spend with Pablo and his affective world.

Musical moments, as Herzog proposes, change the temporal logic of the film, "lingering in a suspended present rather than advancing the action directly. Movements within the frame are not oriented toward action but toward visualizing the trajectory of the song" (7). In the aforementioned sequence of *Nunca vas a estar solo*, the diegetic *bolero* marks a sharp digression from the action; its performativity contrasts with the background noises of the punishing city in which Pablo lives, and momentarily takes us away from his dull reality to a moment where the character fantasizes about himself as someone else. Through these intense musicalized moments in the film, we perceive what the action of the film itself does not convey about Pablo.

Finally, two other aspects of the use of music in the film are worth mentioning here. The first relates the prevalent use of the *bolero* in Anwandter's film to its use by other queer global filmmakers like Pedro Almódovar, Arturo Ripstein, and Wong Kar-Wai, who have adopted the *bolero* to portray the often-violent dramas of their gender nonconforming characters. This intertextuality emphasizes the representation of the LGBTQ+ audiences and their empathetic connection with Anwandter's film. Secondly, in conveying a critical message that deals with issues of violence and discrimination, Anwandter's most recent albums, *Amiga* (2016a) and *Latinoamericana* (2018a), draw from previous political and sexual archives in music and literature, such as those of Víctor Jara and Pedro Lemebel, whose artistic projects provide both a critical and a lyrical path to approach the social marginality and violence evidenced in the Zamudio case.[7] These concerns with violence and marginality ironically feed into what Carolina Urrutia calls the "turn to reality" in contemporary Chilean film and television, characterized by its exploration of "real and current events that have marked our times and have shaped the political agenda, but most sharply, the mediatic and journalistic agendas." ["acontecimientos reales y coyunturales, que son particulares de nuestra época y que, desde diferentes lugares, han marcado la agenda política, pero sobre todo la agenda periodística, mediática"] (Urrutia 2017, 111). More than delving into official versions of an archive, these films[8] actively transform it, reshape it, and challenge accounts that Chilean society keeps reproducing in order to forget.

BUILDING THE CINEMA STAR: THE GLOBAL AESTHETICS OF THE MUSIC VIDEO

Here, I will reflect on the repertoire of lyrics, songs, and iconography that Anwandter developed in the music videos prior to the film. I will analyze how they have actively built a cinema star by representing the artist in various stages of physical and ideological transformation; in short, the music videos foreshadow many of the film's themes. Music videos have historically been a suitable audiovisual genre for artists to actively "bolster their personas, comment upon celebrity culture, and air their political views" (Arnold and Cookney 2017, 7). They have also represented (or misrepresented) issues of sexual and gender identity, race, and class. Thus, they have been greatly criticized for reproducing stereotypes and misconceptions, but also studied because of their openness to representing marginalized groups. The Anglophone academy has been actively reconsidering the impact of music videos on popular culture and the contemporary mediascape, focusing on their aesthetics and representational practices. For example, in the context of MTV and other music TV channels, Goodwin (1992) and Vernallis (2004) have focused on how music videos edit moving images, music—its rhythm, pace, and timbre—and lyrics. Goodwin notes that another important feature of the music video is its use of close-ups of the artist to promote their image in the music industry. However, in the fast changing mediascape that Vernallis (2013) characterizes as one of "accelerated aesthetics," Internet-based platforms like YouTube, Vevo, and Pitchfork have reshaped the conceptualization and production of music videos. Railton and Watson (2011) state that new ways of archiving and circulating video have resulted in more autonomous practices, less dependent on television's programing and regulations, and therefore more open to changing stereotypes, questioning monolithic notions of the national body and subjectivity and displaying previously unseen bodies and affective relationships on screens around the world. It is therefore necessary to reconsider the music video's powerful representational capacity in what is today a contested mediascape, defined by digital television, apps, social media, and multiple screen technologies.

All of these elements are crucial to understanding Anwandter's engagement with directing music videos, especially because he has progressively and actively integrated representations of LGBTQ+ people in them. Because of the new ways of distributing music videos on the web to global audiences, such representational practices broadly circulate without the restrictions present in television programming, which is always subject to editorial imperatives. The fact that Daniel Zamudio contacted Anwandter through social media to express his admiration for the latter's work speaks to new forms of fandom, but also to the ability of these cultural products to more easily reach wider sectors of the population and niche audiences. Anwandter is not alone in creating a more positive and intimate depiction of the LGBTQ+ community in Chile through music and music videos. In fact, during the last decade, a national musical scene of bands and soloists have represented their non-heterosexual identity visually in public interviews and social media and have lyrically explored sexual diversity in their songs and music videos.[9] This poses various questions regarding the commercial nature of their projects, particularly in terms of how these musicians perceive themselves modifying perceptions and intervening in Chilean culture.

As "vehicles to create images,"[10] music videos allow Anwandter to position himself in the aforementioned local scene and regional mediascape as a queer Latinx artist, fusing and reshaping national, regional, and global queer references. This has been particularly relevant in *Amiga* (2016a), an album in which the artist invited several foreign artists to perform, including Ale Sergi and Juliana Gattas from the Argentinian pop music band Miranda!, and the Mexican soloist Julieta Venegas. Also, in Anwandter's latest music video, "Locura / Madness" (2018b), he connects the uncertainties of the Chilean political scenario, marked by right-wing political parties, with a more troublesome global political landscape, personified by the current president of the United States, Donald Trump. Anwandter's persona has also been forged on social media, where the artist—like his contemporaries—actively promotes his new albums and concerts and publicly engages in current local and global issues. We must also consider live performances and other types of promotional media as expanding, explaining, and deepening the audience's understanding of the artist's project. However, due to YouTube's ubiquity in current media, I propose that it is in music videos where Anwandter has consolidated his audiovisual project as a queer Latinx artist most powerfully.

The music videos from the album *Rebeldes / Rebels* (2012b) are the most eloquent in exemplifying this process of representation. The music video for "Tatuaje / Tattoo" (2012c), a song that Anwandter dedicated to Zamudio at the Lollapalooza festival in April 2012, is shot in black and white, except in a short close-up on a male hand applying red nail polish. The lyrics of the song reflect on the durability of relationships over time, and the permanent marks they leave on each partner. The video shows different close-ups of male and female bodies in contact, their faces obscured but exposing the skin as a site of inscription of tattoos. These shots are intertwined with close-ups of Anwandter lip-synching and showing off his own tattoos (which are also exhibited on the album cover). Black-and-white images, and the elusive use of light, create shadows and chiaroscuros that accentuate skin textures and the edges of interacting bodies. As the video continues, these kinetic bodies are contrasted with shots of static male and female mannequins, and pieces of them spread on the floor. In their motionlessness, these idealistic and perfectly measured bodies that codify aesthetic standards for consumers come to represent the phantasmagoric, still, and permanent presences of those who are no longer there (Figure 14). "Tattoo" is a good example of Anwandter's cinematic gaze; mannequins later become a crucial element of the *mise-en-scène* of *Nunca vas a estar solo*, in the representation of Juan's job as a supervisor of a mannequin factory, an allegorical site for the manufacture of normative bodies and subjectivities in contemporary Chile. After Pablo is brutally beaten and left alone in the park at night, a close-up shows us his wounded head and face before we abruptly cut to a worker inside the factory sculpting the head of a dummy with a sanding machine.[11]

Figure 14. The artist portrays himself surrounded by mannequins in "Tatuaje/Tattoo" (Alex Anwandter, 2012).

On the other hand, Anwandter's vision of a multiracial and a sexually diverse Chile is most expressively shown in the music video "¿Cómo puedes vivir contigo mismo? / How Can You Live with Yourself?" (2012a). The music video refashions Jennie Livingston's iconic documentary *Paris Is Burning* (1991)[12] in 2012 Chile. Anwandter translates the foreign ball scene of the eighties in New York City into an imagined contemporary subculture. The song is a daring reflection on identities and the ways in which media and sociocultural context mediate them. The festive music video emphasizes through costume, makeup, and *voguing* that identity is a performative, unfinished, and collective process, marked by members of a nurturing community. Unlike Livingston—who never appears in front of the camera, as bell hooks once criticized—Anwandter participates in the action, inscribing himself as part of this diverse community. By revisiting this globally known documentary, Anwandter places himself within a global scene of queer artists, expanding his references and creating new symbolic spaces for a local LGBTQ+ community.

In *Amiga* (2016a), his third album, Anwandter directed the music video for the song "Siempre es viernes en mi corazón / It's Always Friday in My Heart" (2016b), a bold meditation on the ideologically oppressive regimes of labor, religion, and the state in Chile. The lyrics of the song explicitly confront the church and state as repressive institutions, saying, "The church sends me to hell / And the congress thinks I'm sick" ["La iglesia me manda al infierno / Y el congreso piensa que estoy enfermo"]. In the video, these institutions are represented by an illuminated crucifix placed next to a pop art portrait of far-right politician Jaime Guzmán,[13] and when Anwandter sings "If I want to set something on fire / Let it be the church and the congress" ["Si quiero prenderle fuego a algo / Que sea a la iglesia y el congreso"], the visuals show an inverted crucifix and a hand setting Guzmán's image on fire. Sexual diversity in *Amiga* (2016a), which was made after *Nunca vas a estar solo*, is inscribed in a wider critique of systematic and daily oppression, such as machismo and police violence. For this album, Anwandter was nominated for Latin Grammy Awards in two categories: Best New Artist and Best Short Form Music Video for "It is Always Friday in my Heart." During the awards ceremony, he played "Manifiesto," a piano ballad that imagines the experience of a transgender woman in a hostile sociocultural context: "Today I am a woman / The 'fag' of the town / Even if they set me on fire" ["Hoy soy mujer, hoy soy mujer / El maricón del pueblo / Aunque me prendan fuego"]. The vocals in "Manifiesto" disregard explicit ideologies and religions, establishing the body as a space of resistance: "I want to be a manifesto / embodied / yes, a body that will shoot" ["Yo quiero ser un manifiesto / Hecho cuerpo / Sí, un cuerpo que va a disparar"]. Singing about transgender people and enunciating the word *maricón* in such a formal event was an intervention aimed at defying a musical field that traditionally has sung to the heterosexual world. The song also conveyed a message to a wider Spanish-speaking audience in the Americas.

As I have shown, music videos are vital elements in Anwandter's oeuvre. They provide a virtual space in which to display a thematic project related to the LGBTQ+ community. Music videos also visualize these thematic changes in conjunction with his artistic persona. Anwandter confronts oppressive systems of exclusion, and his project emerges from personal experiences that have made him "exposed to, and aware of, very concrete forms of violence represented by the hyper-*machista*, hyper-homophobic, and hyper-sexist cultures in Latin America. . . . I have never felt part of a fight for gay rights; I see myself closer to an effort to dismantle a system of violence."[14] There is no doubt that this notion of his project branches from his own experience with the Zamudio archive: "the death of Daniel Zamudio affected me a lot. . . . It was a sort of engine that pushed me to continue challenging the world."[15]

In his most recent album, *Latinoamericana*, Anwandter aims for a wider regional audience by referencing, in the music video "Locura / Madness" (2018), several regional musical performers such as a mariachi, a samba dancer, and what seems to be a housewife playing a cowbell. Anwandter appears as the director of a show for which these characters audition, but also as a loner with a rifle driving an old car. The song reflects upon political and personal uncertainty in the current global scenario, marked by the reemergence of extreme conservatism and the advancement of far-right governments. Toward the bridge of the song, images of a room lit in red cut to a shot of a television transmitting fragments from Trump's presidential campaign in 2016. Toward the end, aligning with Trump, there are three other figures: Argentina's former president Mauricio Macri, Chile's current president Sebastián Piñera, and the Catholic bishop Ricardo Ezzati, accused of complicity with pedophilia cases at the heart of the Catholic Church. As in "Siempre es viernes en mi corazón" (2016b), church and state—this time in connection with foreign politics—are at the epicenter of Anwandter's critique. What is crucial for us to note is how Anwandter's perspective has widened to progressively incorporate and elaborate foreign cinematic works such as *Paris Is Burning*, and to musically absorb divergent musical traditions, to elaborate a complex critique of conservative neoliberalism in the Americas.

MUSIC MOMENTS AND GLOBAL MESSAGES IN *NUNCA VAS A ESTAR SOLO*

Anwandter's music videos comprise incipient explorations of a cinematic gaze that is developed in *Nunca vas a estar solo*, where we can observe the aesthetic influence of music videos in its re-creation of the Zamudio archive. Here, I will analyze the "musical moments" that elaborate and project the Zamudio archive for international viewers. Like many spectators who have followed Anwandter's music career, I was struck by the fact that none of his catchy and danceable songs were included in the film. Instead, he uses music from another era, such as the *boleros* sung by Lucho Gatica, the pop songs of the Chilean New Wave (*Nueva Ola*) from the seventies, and the classical piece by Gustav Mahler. This hybridized music score is the result of Anwandter's sensibility toward the rhythm and pace of the music and his awareness of how important they can be in engaging the audience. Before analyzing the use of this preexisting music in certain sequences of the film, let me briefly note that Anwandter did compose the instrumental score that opens the film, a somber melody that portrays Santiago's smoggy dawn and orangey sunsets. This melody is repeated throughout the film, first to open it and present the protagonists (Pablo running with Félix in the streets and Juan standing still in the subway station) and later to accompany transitional long shots of the city.

Amalgamating music and the moving image, the two sequences I will analyze in this section resemble the structure of music videos. I will analyze these sequences using Herzog's notion of the "musical moment," to examine how they emotionally disrupt the course of the narration and therefore connect the fictional reconstruction of the "Zamudio archive" with local and foreign audiences. Musical moments occur in a film when music takes over the moving image and occupies a predominant position. In *Nunca vas a estar solo* there are several musical moments, but I will focus my analysis on two specific ones. The first, briefly mentioned before, follows Pablo rehearsing a drag number in his room and is scored with the *bolero* "Sufrir" by Lucho Gatica and the band Los Cuatro Soles. The second musical moment is a longer sequence almost completely scored by Gustav Mahler's[16] *Kindertotenlieder* that stages Juan's visit to Pablo's school, his roaming around the city, and his time at the mannequin factory after the attack. In both musical moments, the rhythm, pace, and timbre of the songs sculpt the editing of the images, prescribing "the cinematography and the pacing and timing of edits. The temporal logic of the film shifts, lingering in a suspended present rather than advancing the action directly" (Herzog 2004, 7). More than advancing the story or following a particular action, the camera movements are governed by the song's trajectory, and for a few minutes we are impacted by these sudden realms of sound and moving images that provoke sensory and affective responses in us: "what the musical moment does, then, is registered within the affective responses of the audience" (Herzog 2004, 9). This is particularly important for Anwandter's approach to the Zamudio archive, because music provides these criminalized figures with a wider emotional dimension that we do not otherwise get as an audience, given that this dimension is often overlooked by official press discourses. Whether by the *bolero* or the classical piece, we as spectators are transported by the music and immersed in the character's intricate emotional states.

Musical moments in cinema can be seen as part of a larger historical process of "remediation," in which film language influences music video aesthetics, and vice versa. Using that framework, Mathias Bonde Korsgaard (2017) notes how some characteristic traits of the music video are replicated in films: closer framing and close-ups, a freer camera that engages with the body's movement, faster and rhythmic editing, the use of color and showy appearances, and finally, an emphasis on visual spectacle.

These traits are vital elements for considering the first musical moment of the film, which focuses on the early scene of Pablo alone, rehearsing his drag number at home in full makeup, and almost dressed up, when he is interrupted by the nosy neighbor Lucy. Pablo does not open the door and instead squats down and hides while Lucy, with the excuse of returning some knives, starts interrogating him about whether he has a girlfriend. These questions reveal Lucy's assumptions about, and encroachment upon, Pablo's sex life; her intention is probably to expose him as a gay man. In her constant questioning of Pablo and her nephew Félix, Lucy shadily suggests that she knows more about the two of them than she is saying.[17]

Once Pablo is liberated from this intrusion, he returns to his room, a constricted private space of freedom. We begin the musical moment with a straight-on close-up of the control panel of a silver cassette player, colored by an intense red light that contrasts with the previous sequence, which had been dully illuminated. Pablo's hand enters the frame and presses play, and the *bolero* "Sufrir" starts with a soft masculine voice. We then cut to a black screen with the title of the film, written in Spanish in red capital letters: NUNCA VAS A ESTAR SOLO.[18] In the next shot, the camera abandons its static straight-on position to follow Pablo's kinetic body as he performs in front of the mirror. Multiple shots in different scales show Pablo and parts of his body, lip-synching "Sufrir" and dramatically gesturing in front of the mirror (Figure 15). The camera pans around the room, stops in front of Pablo, and closely surrounds him in different shots of his face and body. We see Pablo wearing makeup and a sequined dress held by a strap around the neck.[19] As a microphone, Pablo holds a phallic blue light stick, a prop that suggests a humorous and playful drag performance. The dress exposes his shoulders, arms, and part of his back, which are haptically accentuated by the red light that floods the room. Likewise, the red light suggests the sensual, transgressive nature of his act, intensifying the embodiment of the performance and, therefore, our audiovisual experience. The red light also tints the white curtains to pink, while the conventionally masculine blue of the walls is transformed into a purplish color. This is the room where, in a later sequence, Pablo and Félix have sex, smoke marihuana, and barely exchange a word. The sensuous composition of this musical moment marks a divergence from the secret, silent, and cold sexual intercourse between Pablo and Félix.[20] The red light in the musical moment signals Pablo's temporary but intense *jouissance*.

The lyrics of the *bolero* speak about the experiences of longing for a lost love, and hopelessly ask where the lover may be: "Living, hoping for a maybe / Is better than knowing that s/he will never come back" ["Vivir,

Figure 15. Pablo rehearsing the *bolero* "Sufrir" in *Nunca vas a estar solo / You'll Never be Alone* (Alex Anwandter, 2016).

esperando un quizá / Es mejor que saber que nunca volverá"]. The suffering that the lyrics evoke does not align completely with the pleasure that Pablo is displaying on this imaginary stage. The referential nature of the lyrics creates an intimate universe that otherwise would not be available to the spectator, linking Pablo's transforming body to a discourse of loss and pain. Also important to note is that the suffering intoned by the masculine voice of Lucho Gatica is performed by this aspiring drag queen, which creates an elusive discordance that expresses a queer appropriation of the *bolero* musical tradition, like the one that Anwandter himself enacts in his albums. The idea of suffering is not limited to the terrain marked by the hidden relationship with Félix; it could potentially inform the audience of Pablo's longings and the conflicts with his more immediate social environment of hostile and gossipy neighbors. In the Spanish-language lyrics of the song, the verb "sufrir / to suffer" rhymes with the verb "vivir / to live," suggesting a semantic similarity between the two words. As a short music video, this musical moment combines noncontinuous shots of Pablo and a sensuous *mise-en-scène*, scored by the slow pace of the *bolero*. These cinematic elements are manipulated by Anwandter to enrich the quality of time that we spend with Pablo, a character who continually suffers the violence of discrimination. This brief sequence—lasting no more than a minute and half—allows us to break away from the continuous narrative and see Pablo wholly absorbed in his performance. Through its inclusion early in the film, this musical moment not only tells us about Pablo's inner world but also emphasizes the contrast between the subjectivity of the protagonist and the gloomy environment where he dwells.

The second musical moment is defined by Gustav Mahler's *Kindertotenlieder*, "Songs of the Dead Children" (1901), particularly the song "Now I See Well, Why Such Dark Flames."[21] It stages Juan dealing with Pablo being in a coma, in a sequence that starts with Juan entering the dance school that his son attended. A low-angled shot shows him going upstairs as he follows the diegetic music coming from one of the rehearsal rooms. As he enters, some students are practicing a choreography to Mahler's piece, and the instructor invites Juan to enter and watch the performance in which his son could have participated. The sun streams through barred windows, while around the floor other students watch their classmates performing. The editing alternates between wide shots of the whole space and the dancers performing, and close-ups of Juan's reactions to the nimble dancers approaching and embracing one another's bodies. In synchronized steps, three dancers turn from one side to another, until one of them falls and remains on the floor while the other two cling to his body. Eye-line matching between Juan's static stance and this bodily representation of death indicate to us a growing consciousness in Juan about his son's health status. The choreography's dramatic progression forces Juan to realize the dimension of his loss; the dancing bodies on display are performing death, but affectively connect their bodies by touching and embracing each other in this send-off dance. Along with Juan we can imagine Pablo performing, and we are brought back to the other musical moment where Pablo freely rehearsed the *bolero* in his room. We feel his phantasmagoric presence, his yearnings as a dancer, and this whole artistic dimension that was unknown to his own father.

In contrast to the previous musical moment, the music here bridges toward a completely new sequence, becoming nondiegetic. Mahler's piece now scores a crestfallen Juan going home alone on the subway, at his office fixated on the computer screen, and at the warehouse where the motionless mannequins are stored and subjected to his scrutinizing quality control (Figure 16). In the darkness of the storage room, Juan carefully walks around these representations of bodies that, as a silent choir, seem to interrogate him about how to go on with his life. The musical moment ends with a straight-on shot of Juan seated at his son's bedside at the hospital, where the latter lies unconscious.

The connections in this musical piece are illustrative, representing the dark and painful experience of a father losing a child and the aching sense of regret and helplessness that goes along with it. This musical moment

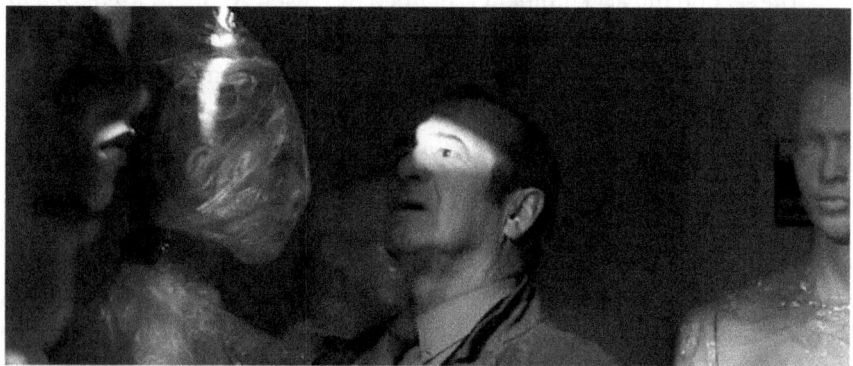

Figure 16. Juan scrutinizes the quality of the mannequins at the warehouse in *Nunca vas a estar solo / You'll Never Be Alone* (Alex Anwandter, 2016).

dramatizes Juan's painful transition from seeing the kinetic bodies of the dancers, to observing the static dummies, to watching his son lying unconscious in the hospital. The mannequins in the film remind us of Anwandter's music video "Tattoo," where they evoke the presence of lost friends or lovers. In the film, they retain this meaning but also serve to create a heteronormative allegory where fixed sexual and gender categories are clearly delimited from one another. In that sense, Pablo's yearning for dance goes beyond the frenzied nights at the disco and the rehearsals and signals to us young queer bodies in constant movement, transformation, and defiance.

The operatic German voice in this sequence does not offer the clarity of the *bolero*'s lyrics. However, without knowing the meaning of the German lyrics we can still rely on the solemnity and desolate tone of the song, which connects us to Juan's loss. Including Mahler's piece in a soundtrack populated by popular music speaks to Anwandter's own perspective on music. In an interview while discussing the variety of genres present in the album *Amiga* (2016a), the artist pointed out that current listening practices are diverse: "We all listen to different types of music, going from one type to another in YouTube, iTunes, whatever. So, my question is, how am I supposed to have a coherent style when the world out there does not work in that way?"[22] The variety of genres also speaks to the diversity that the artist has aimed to create in his music and now in his film.

As Claudia Gorbman (2003) notes, the use of music in films bonds "shot to shot, narrative event to meaning, spectator to narrative, spectator to audience" (39). In the two aforementioned musical moments, the use of the music intensely links the audience to the two main characters in the film. The musical moment, resembling the production of music videos in Anwandter's career, is a crucial element for providing an alternative affective dimension to the Zamudio archive. Politically, *Nunca vas a estar solo*, like other Chilean films that have "turned to reality" (in Urrutia's terms), provides the audience with an insight not only into how homophobic aggression significantly affects victims and their families but also into how it is representative of legitimized, structural cultures of violence in Chile. Aesthetically, these musical moments and their rich audiovisuality contrast with the impersonal and dismal realities that these characters are facing.

CONCLUSIONS: REFASHIONING LGBTQ+ LEGACIES

While watching *Nunca vas a estar solo*, the memory of what happened to Daniel Zamudio in March of 2012 is always present. The violence that lurks within and emerges from Chile's contemporary history has been and still is a concern to many artists and film directors, including Anwandter. He has systematically explored these issues in his work, and *Nunca vas a estar solo* is an eloquent fusion of his musical sensibility, his politics, and his imaginative power to create new images. Analyzing the musical moments in *Nunca vas a estar solo* pushes us to think about Zamudio. We know he loved the song "Tattoo," and, like Pablo, he probably danced to this or other songs by Anwandter in the disco or in a more intimate space. It is uncanny that the artist that Zamudio admired ended up making a film fictionalizing the young man's final days.

In the current open and contested Internet-based mediascape, music videos are a crucial virtual space for challenging homogeneous representations and visualizing sexual diversity. By imagining and daringly representing the historically overlooked LGBTQ+ community in Chile, Anwandter and other artists[23] have spoken up about nonheterosexual affects and lives. Moreover, songs widely played by the local radio, and music videos on YouTube, seem to be filling an important institutional gap in Chile in relation to the defense and protection of sexual diversity. Although there have been advances for the LGBTQ+ community,[24] there is still a need to reconsider the cultural contexts in which the rights of LGBTQ+ people are made vulnerable. Watching and listening to Anwandter's audiovisual and cinematic oeuvre, one can easily trace the artist's active efforts to address those issues, and more importantly, propose alternative images of movement, change, and transformation. Music videos are a representational antidote to institutional passivity and social indifference. In both of the musical moments discussed in this chapter, in which the intertwining of music and moving images stages Pablo and Juan in conflicting passages between bodily movements and mannequin stasis, we see their desire to express themselves in the face of the fear that pushes them to hide, and their willingness to challenge the cultural imperatives of conformity, apathy, and passivity.

NOTES

1. This and all other translations into English, unless otherwise noted, are my own.

2. *Zamudio: Lost in the Night* was transmitted in four episodes between March and April of 2015 by Televisión Nacional de Chile (Available on the channel's website: https://www.tvn.cl/programas/zamudio/capitulos/). In *Jesús*, Guzzoni imagines his protagonist as an apathetic, bisexual young man passionate about K-pop (contemporary Korean popular music and culture) and dance competitions. During a night out "partying," he becomes involved in a ferocious, deadly attack on another young person. In addition to adopting the perspective of an aggressor, the director highlights the figure of the absent and vindictive father who is also capable of betrayal.

3. Brandon Teena's case inspired Kimberly Peirce's film *Boys Don't Cry* (1999) which Halberstam analyzed and criticized in *In a Queer Time and Place: Transgender Bodies, Subcultural Lives* (2005).

4. See Johan Galtung's (1990) notion of "culture of violence," defined as "aspects of the culture, the symbolic sphere of our existence . . . that can be used to justify or legitimize direct or structural violence" (291). Aligning with this concept are Anwandter's own reflections on violence against women and LGBTQ+ people that he expressed in a personal interview in August 2016. I see this "culture of violence" in close connection with the sense of impunity installed and legitimized in Chile during and after the dictatorship.

5. Several "novísimo" filmmakers like Sebastián Lelio, Alberto Fuguet, and Pablo Larraín have also explored the music video as an audiovisual genre either before or after starting their careers as filmmakers.

6. This is what Iris Zavala calls it in her groundbreaking study *El Bolero: Historia de un amor* (2000).

7. Both authors' works are "repackaged" in Anwandter's songs, albeit not in *Nunca vas a estar solo*; rather, references to their work can be found in the album *Amiga* (2016a) and the song "Manifiesto." Lemebel's unmistakable "queer eye"—"ojo de loca no se equivoca"—can be appreciated, obliquely, in the *bolero* sequences of *Nunca vas a estar solo*, as a paratext: his chronicle "Lucho Gatica (El terciopelo ajado del bolero) /Lucho Gatica (Bolero's Worn Velvet)" could be seen as shaping Anwandter's reconsideration of the musical genre in his approach to the "Zamudio archive."

8. Urrutia includes the films *Aquí no ha pasado nada / Much Ado About Nothing* (2016) by Alejandro Fernández Almendras, *Rara* (2016) by Pepa San Martín, and Anwandter's.

9 Among these artists we can mention Javiera Mena (*Esquemas juveniles / Juvenile Schemes*, 2006; *Mena*, 2010; *Otra Era / Another Era*, 2014; *Espejo / Mirror*, 2018), (Me llamo) Sebastián (*Salvador*, 2010; *Adiós, vesícula mía / Farewell, my Gallbladder*, 2011; *El hambre / The Craving*, 2013; *La belleza / The Beauty*, 2015; *La sombra / The Shadow*, 2017), the female duo Marineros (*O Marineros / The Sailors*, 2015), and the band Planeta No (*Odio / Hatred*, 2015).

10 Alex Anwandter, interview with Arturo Márquez-Gómez, August 12, 2016.

11 In *Nunca vas a estar solo*, mannequins retain a wide array of meanings. Their uncanny presence in the film reminds us of those images created by Luis Buñuel's *Ensayo de un crimen / The Criminal Life of Archibaldo de la Cruz* (1955), Mario Brava's *Sei Donne per L'Assassino* (1964), Rainer Werner Fassbinder's *The Bitter Tears of Petra Von Kant* (1972), and François Truffaut's *La Chambre Verte* (1978).

12 This 1991 documentary was categorized by Ruby Rich under the rubric of the New Queer Cinema. For a critical view on the documentary, see bell hooks' essay "Is Paris Burning?" in her collection of essays *Black Looks: Race and Representation* (1992), and Judith Butler's chapter "Gender is Burning: Questions on Appropriation and Subversion" in *Bodies that Matter* (1993).

13 Guzmán, a closeted gay man, was one of the authors of the conservative Chilean Constitution installed by the Pinochet dictatorship in 1980.

14 Alex Anwandter, interview with Arturo Márquez-Gómez, August 12, 2016.

15 Alex Anwandter, interview with Arturo Márquez-Gómez, August 12, 2016.

16 Anwandter also uses Mahler's piece Symphony No. 4, Ruhevoll (Poco adagio) to open his music video "Siempre es viernes en mi corazón" (2016b). Violently, through the sound of the alarm clock, the classical music stops, and the sound of machinery leads us to the electronic music of the song.

17 Later in the film, in a conversation with Lucy, Juan realizes that Pablo's attack was probably motivated by the gossip Lucy had spread. Juan has been drinking and reacts violently against his neighbor. An interesting element here is how some of the interactions among Lucy, the father, and the son occur with the doors closed. We don't see Lucy, but we do hear her, likely suggesting her potential involvement in the *copucha* (gossip).

18 The same font design is used by Anwandter in the opening of the music video "Siempre es viernes en mi corazón" (2016b), suggesting a fluid continuity between his music videos and film.

19 This drag number evokes the figure of la Manuela from José Donoso's novel *El lugar sin límites / Hell Has no Limits* (1966), adapted into a 1978 film by the Mexican director Arturo Ripstein. The *paso doble* "El relicario" is a melody

20   that is repeatedly referenced in the novel and accompanies Manuela's flashbacks and her brutal beating by Pancho Vega and Octavio.

20   Is not clear to the spectator how close the relationship between Pablo and Félix is, especially because the latter is also actively involved in the attack on Pablo and later in violently confronting and insulting Juan. Félix comes to represent the repressed closeted gay man, who privately performs one identity and publicly performs another.

21   The "Kindertotenlieder" was a series of 428 poems written by the German poet Friedrich Rückert, who lost two of his children in less than a month in 1833. Between 1901 and 1904, the Austro-Bohemian composer and musician Gustav Mahler (1860–1911) selected five of them and turned them into a "lieder," a short musical arrangement for a poem.

22   Alex Anwandter, interview with Arturo Márquez-Gómez, August 12, 2016.

23   The band *Planeta No*, in their music video "Maricón Zara," also evokes the crime of Daniel Zamudio as a structuring and defining event of a community. Likewise, the soloist (Me llamo) Sebastián also imagines the violence against LGBTQ+ people in his music video "Hijos del peligro / Sons of Danger," where a mass shooting happens inside a club. The video was released months after the 2016 shooting in the Pulse discotheque in Orlando, Florida, connecting art with current events of a local and global scale.

24   These include the promulgation of the Anti-Discrimination Law (20.609)—the so-called Zamudio Law—in June of 2012, only a few months after Daniel's death. Chile's Gender Identity Law (21.120) was passed in November of 2018, allowing transgender people to legally change their sex through a less bureaucratic proceeding.

WORKS CITED

Anwandter, Alex. 2011. *Rebeldes*. National Records. MP3.

———. 2012a. "¿Cómo puedes vivir contigo mismo?" Filmed May 2012. YouTube video, 4:41 min. Posted May 22, 2012. https://www.youtube.com/watch?v=OWaf8Ndcr18.

———. 2012b. "Tatuaje." YouTube video, 3:49 min. Posted June 13, 2012. https://www.youtube.com/watch?v=XhPHhJ5tOYY.

———. 2016a. *Amiga*. National Records, April, CD.

———. 2016b. "Siempre es viernes en mi corazón." YouTube video, 5:47 min. Posted May 20. https://www.youtube.com/watch?v=uPzfHg2LAu8.

———. 2018a. *Latinoamericana*. National Records. MP3.

———. 2018b. "Locura." YouTube video, 3:57 min. Posted September 28, 2018. https://www.youtube.com/watch?v=-WY4zcUYYzo.

Arnold, Gina, Daniel Cookney, Kirsty Fairclough, and Michael Goddard. 2017. *Music/Video Histories, Aesthetics, Media*. London: Bloomsbury Academic.
Butler, Judith. 1993. *Bodies That Matter: On the Discursive Limits of Sex*. New York: Routledge.
Donoso, José. 1966. *El lugar sin límites*. Mexico City: Joaquín Mortiz.
El lugar sin límites. 1978. Directed by Arturo Ripstein, written by José Donoso. México: Conacite dos.
Fluxá, Rodrigo. 2014. *Solos en la noche: Zamudio y sus asesinos*. Santiago: Catalonia. Kindle.
Gatica, Lucho. 1993. "Sufrir." In *The Originals. Lucho Gatica in Concert*, YOYO USA. CD.
Galtung, Johan. 1990. "Cultural Violence." *Journal of Peace Research* 27 (3): 291–305.
Goodwin, Andrew. 1992. *Dancing in the Distraction Factory: Music Television and Popular Culture*. Minneapolis: University of Minnesota Press.
Gorbman, Claudia. 2003. "Why Music? The Sound Film and Its Spectator." In *Movie Music the Film Reader*, edited by Kay Dickinson, 37–47, London: Routledge.
———. 2007. "Hearing *Thelma & Louise*. Active Reading of the Hybrid Pop Score." In *Thelma & Louise Live! The Cultural Afterlife of an American Film*, edited by Bernie Cook, 65–89. Austin: University of Texas Press.
Halberstam, Judith (Jack). 2005. *In a Queer Time and Place: Transgender Bodies, Subcultural Lives*. New York: New York University Press.
Herzog, Amy. 2009. *Dreams of Difference and Songs of the Same: The Image of Time in Musical Film*. Minneapolis: University of Minnesota Press.
hooks, bell. 1992. *Black Looks: Race and Representation*. Boston: South End Press.
Jesús. 2016. Directed by Fernando Guzzoni. Santiago, Chile: Burning Blue, JBA Production, Quijote Films, UNA Films.
Korsgaard, Mathias Bonde. 2017. *Music Video After MTV: Audiovisual Studies, New Media, and Popular Music*. London: Routledge.
Malher, Gustav, and Friedrich Rückert. 1959. "Nun Seh' Ich Wohl, Warum So Dunkle Flammen" in *Mahler: Lieder eines fahrenden Gesellen & Kindertotenlieder—Wolf: Lieder*. Interpreted by Dietrich Fischer-Dieskau and Berlin Philharmonic Orchestra. France: Diapason D'Or.
Nunca vas a estar solo. 2016. Directed by Alex Anwandter. Chile: 5AM Producciones, Araucaria Cine.
Railton, Diane, and Paul Watson. 2011. *Music Video and the Politics of Representation*. Edinburgh: Edinburgh University Press.
Urrutia, Carolina. 2017. "El giro narrativo: Nuevas tendencias en los géneros de representación en el cine y televisión contemporáneos." In *V Panorama del Audiovisual Chileno*, edited by Johanna Wittle and Enrique Núñez, 109–18. Santiago: Universidad Católica de Chile.

Vernallis, Carol. 2004. *Experiencing Music Video: Aesthetics and Cultural Context*. Chichester and New York: Columbia University Press.
———. 2013. *Unruly Media: YouTube, Music Video, and the New Digital Cinema*. New York: Oxford University Press.
Zavala, Iris. 2000. *El bolero: Historia de un amor*. Madrid: Editorial Celeste.

8

INTIMACIES AND GLOBAL AESTHETICS IN *VIDA DE FAMILIA* BY ALICIA SCHERSON AND CRISTIÁN JIMÉNEZ

Vania Barraza

In the introduction to the literary anthology *McOndo* (1996), Alberto Fuguet recalls how an editor once declined to include Fuguet's work in the American literary magazine *The Iowa Review*. The editor alleged that the text submitted for publication lacked magical realism. It was not "Latin American" enough because the story could have been written "in any First World country" ["en cualquier país del Primer Mundo"] (Fuguet 1996, 10). In response to the rejection, Fuguet and Sergio Gómez edited a collection of seventeen short stories launching what is today the well-known McOndo literary movement.

The introduction quickly came to be regarded as a manifesto. Fuguet and Gómez rejected the rural exoticism and folklore that were considered traditional means of representing Latin American cultures in the "Boom" novels—Gabriel García Márquez's work took place in the fictional rural town of *Macondo*—to focus instead on urban lifestyles, mass media, and, specifically, the influence of U.S. pop culture in the region. They identified themselves as heirs to a mestizo and impure culture, pledging allegiance to the global village, the Internet, and the erasure of nations and geographical identities. Shifting away from narratives dealing with politicized, collective experiences, they moved their attention to subjective anecdotes in a (neoliberal) changing world.[1]

Both the *McOndo* declaration and the ensuing literary movement can be viewed as part of the history of Latin American literature,[2] but they also can be perceived as an anticipation of the Chilean film renaissance that emerged a decade later. Around 2005, a young group of filmmakers introduced new, intimate narratives, aesthetics, and means of production and distribution. Concurrently, they revisited the representation of local space, the Chilean people, and Chile's national imaginary. The conflicts and settings of this cinema appeared to be situated in any country of the world (see Jacobesen 2013, 12), and did not necessarily display *Chilenidad* ("Chileanness"). Interestingly, Fuguet became a key figure in this contemporary cinema movement after entering his film *Se arrienda / For Rent* for competition in the 2005 Valdivia International Film Festival (FICValdivia). There, four other young directors also premiered works that, in essence, marked a turning point in recent Chilean cinematography.[3] Alicia Scherson—a biologist by training who continued her education in film studies—debuted with *Play*, a visually stimulating and colorful production about an indigenous woman fascinated with the urban life of Santiago de Chile. Her film received international recognition when she was named Best Director at the Tribeca Film Festival in 2005.

In the years following, Scherson became a well-known member of the newest generation of filmmakers, and more recently she codirected, along with Cristián Jiménez, *Vida de familia / Family Life* (2017), a low-key comedy based on a short story of the same title by Alejandro Zambra (2015), that premiered in the Sundance Film Festival competition. Scherson and Jiménez have a long-standing history of collaboration, and both have directed movies based on literary works.[4] They cowrote the script for *Ilusiones ópticas / Optical Illusions* (2009), Jiménez's directorial debut. In turn, he appeared briefly in Scherson's *Il futuro* (2013).

As representatives of the same generation of filmmakers, the individual and collaborative works of Scherson and Jiménez (born in 1974 and 1975, respectively) reveal a common interest in exploring, within a contained, detached, and estranged aesthetic, relationships, affections and identity crises. Their filmmaking aligns with contemporary trends in Chilean cinema that revolve around individual challenges, quests, and conflicts, rendering decontextualized, stylish narratives accessible to global viewers. Still, although aesthetics appear to take priority over social issues in their films—a common trend within twenty-first-century Chilean feature cinema—themes such as local spatial tensions, gender, and allegorical narratives of memory and national identity have subtly emerged in their filmmaking.

Vida de familia focuses on Martín, a melancholic single man in his forties, housesitting for Bruno, a distant relative. Because most of the mise-en-scène of Zambra's tale is set in the private sphere, the city seems relegated to a minor role. Indeed, this lack of clear geographical references recalls McOndo's uprooting, since the story could be taking place in the trendy house of an intellectual in any metropolis. Only a few shots depict the actual filming location: the Barrio Yungay neighborhood in Santiago, Chile.

However, these scarce exterior scenes offer a discreet commentary on Chilean history that may be overlooked by international audiences. *Vida de familia* addresses mourning and memory as individual experiences, but these themes—personal yet universal—have deep relevance within the local context. Accordingly, in line with the work of a new generation of filmmakers, this intimate, nationally untethered movie indirectly addresses sensitive topics related to collective and national interests, developing a film project that appeals to local and international audiences equally, but in different ways.

This chapter discusses how *Vida de familia* interweaves individual and social themes using a global aesthetic, revitalizing within this (dis)engaged narrative questions about social filmmaking within an international circuit in the twenty-first century. First, I briefly discuss how Chilean directors have dissociated their filmmaking from the politically committed productions of previous generations (from the late 1960s to the early 1990s). Next, I examine an aesthetic that has become a trademark for a new generation of filmmakers, and, finally, I study how *Vida de familia* connects to global spectators, while addressing—in the background of the story—local issues too. Although a(n apparent) lack of interest in social issues prevails in the cinema of Scherson and Jiménez, I explore how *Vida de familia* allows for sensitive political topics to appeal to both global and local audiences.

THE GENERATION OF 2005: A BRIEF HISTORICAL BACKGROUND

The generation of filmmakers who emerged around 2005 is known as the *Novísimos* (Cavallo and Maza 2011), the young cinema (Estévez 2011, 78), Generation 2000 (Parada Poblete 2012), the Generation of 2005 (Kemp 2010), or the Chilean Independent Cinema (Larraín 2010; Jara 2017). Directors of this active and emergent movement—including Fuguet, Scherson, and Jiménez—distanced their narratives from the politically entrenched New Chilean Cinema and the cinema filmed in exile, the latter of which mainly focused on expatriate experiences, government repression, national identity, and the representation of the working classes or Chilean history.

Unlike the *McOndo* manifesto, the new generation did not express interest in sharing a group identity or a common discourse, nor did it evidently have a leader or spokesperson. A disconnection from overt political discourse pervaded its films. Thus, while McOndo's writers reacted against the Boom and magical realism (a movement associated with the Cuban Revolution of 1959, the main political event of its time), these young filmmakers appeared to show indifference to the militant project of New Latin American Cinema. Given that recent Chilean film production does not contain open social criticism in line with the discourse of previous generations, some critics propose that this cinema of "wireless puppets" manipulated by the market (Salinas Muñoz and Stange Marcus 2015, 231–32) is just a reflection of the neoliberal system (see also Póo, Salinas, and Stange 2012, Trejo 2009, 2011, and Saavedra 2013).

Contrary to this, scholars such as Antonella Estévez (2010, 2011, 2017), Catalina Donoso Pinto (2007), and Carolina Urrutia Neno (2010, 2013) suggest that although these new fiction films cannot be related to an explicit ideological discourse—due to their primary focus on intimacy and everyday life—their alienated representation of life, estrangement, and melancholic tone reflect a political feeling of unease. Indeed, Mario Jara (2017) perceives a certain continuity between the New Chilean Cinema and the new generation; although themes diverge, the personal narrative seeks to address "social flaws, in the new problems piercing Chilean society" ["las fisuras sociales, en las nuevas problemáticas que taladran a la sociedad chilena"] (Jara 2017, 104).

In *El cine en Chile* (Barraza 2018), meanwhile, I have studied how some filmmakers have been creating coded strategies for criticizing or expressing apprehension regarding sociopolitical conditions in contemporary Chile. Consequently, although Chilean film production does not always contain a political statement or an open social criticism in line with the New Cinema, it is no less true that its social reality appears to reflect, albeit indirectly, the effects of neoliberalism in contemporary Chilean society (Barraza 2018, 17).

While I have previously discussed the political detachment of this cinematic production (see Barraza 2012a, 2012b, 2013, 2015, 2018), here I study recent Chilean filmmaking as an intersection between global and domestic values, to posit that national issues make themselves evident in these narratives, revealing tensions and negotiations not only within a local context but also between domestic and transnational circuits. The political perspective of recent cinema is perhaps subtler and more diluted, as it is found in the background of intimate stories, because the sense of community in Chile was weakened under the military dictatorship.

VIDA DE FAMILIA: A(N INTER)NATIONAL DRAMA

Martín, the house sitter, and Bruno, the homeowner, find themselves on opposite sides of adult life and its ensuing responsibilities in *Vida de familia*. While the inexpressive Martín is informal, unemployed, and solitary, Bruno is a respected family man and a college professor, an expert in Chilean poetry who has been invited to teach at a French university for a semester. He explains to his friend (played by Zambra himself) that Martín, a distant cousin, will stay at the property. Bruno was unable to find a temporary renter, but after Bruno ran into Martín at the funeral of the latter's father, Martín agreed to take care of the house. The beautiful Consuelo (Blanca Lewin) and their seven-year-old daughter Sofi (Adara Casassus) complete Bruno's modern yet traditional family.[5]

Consuelo seems to have some doubts regarding her relationship with Bruno. During a phone conversation early in the film, she states apathetically, "I feel good. I'm happy" ["Me siento bien. Soy feliz"] in front of a bathroom mirror, trying to sound convincing (Figure 17). Immediately, she adds, "I feel sure enough to rule out the other hypothesis" ["segura como para descartar la otra hipótesis"], referring to another possibility that is never fully articulated. Next, she turns her body toward a full-length mirror on her left, on the other side of the room, and concludes that she and Bruno reached an understanding, and that they "just had to look at it differently. Something that was blocking us just finally burst" ["Como que había que hablarlo todo desde otro lugar. No sé, como que estalló una wevá que estaba puro taponeándolo todo"]. Based on this intimate and self-reflexive scene, in which Consuelo is viewed solely from behind while the camera pans across the room, reflecting her image from two different angles, *Vida de familia* posits a conflict between what characters say about themselves, and their real identities and feelings. The tension that emerges by opposing voice and image is a cue that is further developed by the plot when Martín arrives at the house.

Consuelo's scene aligns with the concept of "centrifugal cinema" coined by Carolina Urrutia Neno to classify Chilean film productions released during

Figure 17. Consuelo in the bathroom in *Vida de Familia / Family Life* (Alicia Scherson and Cristián Jiménez, 2017)

the first decade of the new century (Urrutia Neno 2013, 13). Based on Gilles Deleuze's concept of the Time-Image, discussed in his seminal work, *Cinema* (1986, 1989), and Jacques Rancière's study on the "The Pensive Image" (2011), Urrutia Neno notes that the new generation of Chilean filmmakers renounces linear stories inspired by (re)action, cause and effect, and clearly motivated characters, to focus on the significance of particular, and occasionally decontextualized, spaces, contexts, and scenarios (Urrutia Neno 2013, 18–22). Following Deleuze's theory, this cinema results in an essayistic and experimental tone, a hybridization of fiction and documentary, and self-reflexiveness. Indeed, in *Vida de familia*, Consuelo's marital conflict is not developed any further by the script. The plot does not reveal any further contrast between what she affirms about her marriage and her (secret) emotions. Soon, she leaves for France with her family.

However, the disconnection between saying and seeing introduced by Consuelo in the privacy of the bathroom continues as a motif when Martín moves into the house. Mississippi, the family cat, gets lost, and when posting a missing flyer on the street, Martín meets Paz, or "Pachi," the single mother of little Sebas. Martín pretends to be Bruno and tells Pachi that he teaches Chilean literature at the university. Hence, in *Vida de familia* the tension between what is said and what is known is not based on negation—a sound and sight opposition, as elements denying each other—but on exploring the narrative effects of that disconnect. Viewers know Martín is lying; the character creates a fantasy for both Pachi and the audience (although the latter is aware of the deception). While spectators have more information than Martín's costar regarding his identity, though, they do not have access to his motives.

Ultimately, Scherson and Jiménez do not examine fakery (i.e., art, performance, metafiction) as a contradiction that divides mimesis and reality according to traditional conceptions (following Artaud's or Brecht's theoretical models). The story is clearly not driven to unmask the farce or to distrust Martín; rather, the movie reveals how filmmaking provides, in Rancière's terms, an individual, but shared experience:

> The collective power shared by spectators does not stem from the fact that they are members of a collective body or from some specific form of interactivity. It is the power each of them has to translate what she perceives in her own way, to link it to the unique intellectual adventure that makes her similar to all the rest in as much as this adventure is not like any other. This shared power of the equality of intelligence links individuals, makes them exchange their intellectual adventures, in so far as it keeps them separate from one another, equally capable of using the power everyone has to plot her own [interpretation]. (Rancière 2011, 16–17)

Vida de familia is an invitation to local and international spectators to enjoy an unconstrained and intellectually engaged experience.

Scherson and Jiménez skillfully articulate an intimate narrative addressing separate topics that are relevant within the national and global context. The movie refers to local issues that might be unnoticed in a transnational reading: while the house-sitting story withholds geographical indicators (making the film more approachable for international audiences), certain place indicators do offer interesting interpretations of recent Chilean history. An oblique, nonverbal treatment of mourning and memory touches on sensitive topics pertaining to the postdictatorship.

Pachi sees Consuelo's photograph in the living room (originally, the picture frame had a photo of the poet Jorge Teillier, but Martín replaces it with an image of Bruno's wife) in her first visit to the house. He tells her that he got divorced a year ago. Indeed, Martín explains to Pachi that he was abandoned by his wife, who took his daughter with her and rarely lets him see her, thereby manipulating him emotionally.

The mutual attraction between Martín and Pachi is immediate, and eventually Pachi, Martín, and Sebas become an ideal family that is completed when the cat returns home. They go to the playground, go to the park, and enjoy playing together in the house. Martín leaves behind his black leather jacket and starts to wear Bruno's blazer, while Pachi adopts Consuelo's cardigan.

Vida de familia's plot about the process of building a(n artificial) family is a universally applicable story that will particularly appeal to upper-middle-class spectators in their forties who might be interested in reflecting on the choices they made when becoming adults (i.e., committing to a long-term relationship, having children, obtaining a mortgage, pursuing a career, and so on). Once alone in the house, Martín curiously explores Bruno's property: the books, the stylish paintings, the piano, the furniture, all of which are material expressions of professional success. In contrast to this comfortable life, Martín's single possession is a suitcase filled with old photo albums and an old cigar box. Bruno stands for what Martín has not become, a choice that can be made by those with favored social and economic conditions.

Although indifferent to the prospect of having a family when he originally arrives at the house, Martín eventually starts fantasizing about Bruno's life. Interestingly, he firmly stated to Bruno that he didn't like to read; by extension, he is not interested in fiction. However, upon meeting Pachi, he begins starring in a fictitious life, pretending he is dedicated to the study of literature. Alternatively, some viewers might fantasize about the freewheeling (albeit melancholic) life of Martín.[6] Many audiences from countries in the "global north" can also identify with Martín's character, interpreted by Jorge Becker, because his physical appearance is clearly defined by European traits.

AN UPROOTED STORY FOR A GLOBAL AUDIENCE

Due to its primary focus on private and emotional relationships, *Vida de familia* does not center on public spaces. Most scenes are located in the family house (Alicia Scherson's, in real life) with its exquisite decorations, luminous kitchen, and rooftop terrace. Exterior sequences reveal little about the city, so audiences from diverse geographical backgrounds can relate to this charming middle-class dwelling. David Martin-Jones and María Soledad Montañez note that this cinema of "auto-erasure," made by filmmakers seeking to reach diverse audiences with stories that may appeal internationally, is the result of complex negotiations among producers, distributors, and filmmakers to access global markets (2013, 27). In this visual strategy, the nation effectively "disappears" from the image (27), decontextualizing or deterritorializing a local geography. Studying the Uruguayan Control Z film production company, the authors outline common narrative choices in this "Festival Film" cinema:

> a lack of establishing shots (thereby avoiding potential audience perplexity over foregrounded locations which are not internationally recognizable); tight framing of characters against mundane backgrounds, such that interiors are rendered anonymous (e.g., houses, shops, buses, hotel rooms, cafés, bars, supermarkets), as are exteriors (e.g., a street, a bus stop, a rooftop, a shopping district, a football match, a seaside resort, a beach); episodic narratives which provide psychological explorations of characters seen through quotidian routines or even repetitious activities rather than extensive dialogue; an at-times intrusive use of music to accompany the image; and extensive use of long takes and static camera positions, which further focus viewer attention on the mundane existence of the characters. (34)

This local rootlessness, which can be seen as the result of filmmakers' attempts to gain acceptance within specific distribution contexts (i.e., international film festivals, European theaters) has become a common trend throughout Latin America. Amanda Rueda identifies a generalized refusal to define a place of enunciation or identity (2008, 27). Interestingly enough, the real identity and feelings of Martín remain an unsolved mystery in *Vida de familia*, transforming this lack of information into a relevant topic in the film.

Scholars including Miriam Ross (2011), Tamara Falicov (2007a, 2007b, 2010, 2016), and Libia Villazana (2008) have examined the effects of film festivals and international funds as a neocolonial relationship between affluent nations and the Global South (formerly known as Third World countries) in which several interests interact (producers, distribution channels, exhibitors, buyers, festival programmers, private corporations, and so on). Falicov observes various degrees of influence and dependency between the European/Asian/North American funders and those from the Global South seeking funds to begin or complete a project (a "Festival Film" production) (Falicov 2016, 218). She concludes that "Though this opportunity might present itself as welcome for some, it also might have some larger implications, such as reinforcing a power dynamic between northern gatekeepers and cultural arbiters and Global South filmmakers in terms of what films might be selected for these specific funds" (221). According to this, "Indie" films would not be as independent as they claim to be.

In spite of having the stylistic features of a "film festival" production, *Vida de familia* is a domestic, low-budget film that received support only from CORFO, a Chilean governmental organization,[7] and a postproduction grant from the Universidad de Chile, where Scherson is a faculty member.[8] This makes it all the more significant that the film was selected for the Sundance Film Festival, and nominated at the Rotterdam International Film Festival, on top of winning the Miami Film Festival, in 2017. This shows that "Global South" productions can be successful within the Global Art Cinema circuit even when they do not follow the usual steps to receive funding that Falicov outlines.

After directing larger productions (*Il futuro*, *La voz en off / Voice Over*), both directors were looking to develop smaller projects. Indeed, this non-festival-funded production originated as a more informal project among friends, shortly after Scherson moved to the house and had her first child.

ON INTIMACIES, (LOCAL) MEMORY, AND SEARCHES FOR IDENTITY

The aesthetics of detachment found in *Vida de familia* are common in recent Latin American filmmaking. Nadia Lie observes that numerous films use "the feeling of disaffection as a 'transnational affect,' which activates the cinephile background of the international audience targeted" (2018, 22). In Chile, melancholy became a trademark of the newest generation of filmmakers; this feature has been studied by Antonella Estévez as a combination of the senselessness of the subject in contemporary society and the dissatisfaction resulting from the incomplete task of mourning that took place in the country after the authoritarian regime (2010, 18; 2017, 28).⁹ Consequently, Martín's melancholy can be perceived as a stylistic feature used to connect the film with international audiences, but also as a recurring theme pertaining to local aesthetics, history, and spectators. Martín is clearly grieving his father's death, but, following Estévez, this poetics of melancholy is related to Chile's struggle to address its traumatic past. In *Vida de familia*, Martín's unresolved task of mourning is reflected by his rejection of grief as a collective experience, in order to instead isolate himself in the house. In turn, his melancholy is complemented by a sense of nostalgia, as seen in his fixation on contemplating and editing pictures from his youth. The Greek root of nostalgia—*nostos*—means "return home," and the movie captures images of Martín's childhood without providing many details about his personal history as an adult. For example, once the family has left, Martín opens his luggage, seeking the photo albums. Next, he digitizes pictures of himself as a child, both on his own and in groups, using Bruno's desktop computer (Figure 18). Evoking Michelangelo Antonioni's 1966 film *Blow-up* (based on Julio Cortázar's celebrated short story "Las babas del diablo"), he zooms in on the photographs until his pixelated face fills the computer screen entirely. Martín's nostalgic search for the warmth of his childhood appears unattainable: it is literally—and visually—out of focus.

In another scene, Martín scratches his own face out of a picture, leaving evident traces of the erasure. The plot does not explain his reasons for copying and manipulating these images. His personal thoughts are inaccessible to viewers, but evidently he is experiencing an identity crisis that goes beyond the charade of pretending to be a family man. Symbolically, Martín embodies Jorge Teillier's poem "A Man Alone in a Lonely House" ("Un hombre solo en una casa sola"), which focuses on images of defeat, abandonment, and broken memories.¹⁰ The main image of the poem, relevant in Zambra's narrative, is the metaphor of the individual longing for his birth house: this synthesizes the idea of the impossible return to a primal locus inhabited with remembrances.¹¹

Mourning and identity, which have indefinite historical and spatial references in this movie, take on national implications in the few exterior sequences. The night Martín and Pachi meet, they stand in front of a wall covered with graffiti, posters, and flyers containing political slogans. In addition to allusions to the conflict between the Chilean State and the

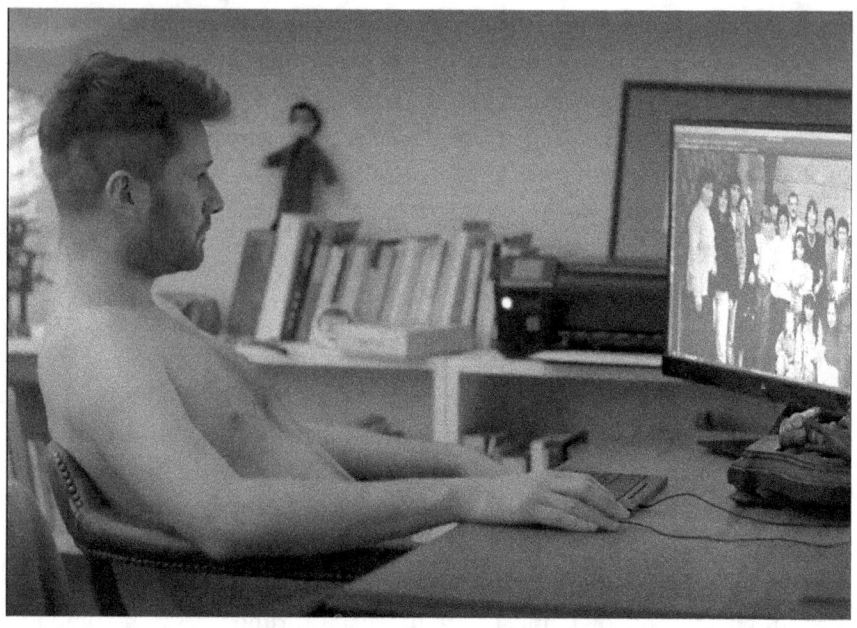

Figure 18. Martín digitizing pictures of himself as a child, in *Vida de Familia / Family Life* (Alicia Scherson and Cristián Jiménez, 2017).

Mapuche people (i.e., "Viva la lucha mapuche," or "Long live the Mapuche struggle," and a mention of M. Catrileo[12]), viewers see in the corner of the wall the slogan "A 30 años nada ni nadie está olvidado" ("30 years later, nothing and no one is forgotten"). The message recalls the assassination of Communist Party members José Manuel Parada, Manuel Guerrero, and Santiago Nattino under Pinochet's dictatorship in 1985. The triple murder provoked outrage and led to the dissolution of the Directorate of Police Communications (Dirección de Comunicaciones de Carabineros, DICOMCAR), an intelligence unit developed by the national police during the dictatorship.

These indirect political references also appear in a previous sequence, when Martín posts lost pet flyers. He walks around the Barrio Yungay, passes by the Quinta Normal Metro Station, and finally stands in an esplanade next to the Museum of Memory and Human Rights (Museo de la Memoria y los Derechos Humanos) in a wide shot (Figure 19).[13] The museum was established to commemorate the victims of human rights violations during Pinochet's military regime.

Figure 19. Martín in front of the Museum of Memory and Human Rights, in *Vida de familia / Family Life* (Alicia Scherson and Cristián Jiménez, 2017).

Theoretical discussions of Chile's postdictatorship concur that the dominant politics of the democratic transition intended to publicly deny or ignore the horror, violence, and human rights violations carried out by Augusto Pinochet's regime (1973–90) (Wilde 1999; Richard 2004, 2007; Stern 2000; Hite 2005; Winn 2007), reducing discussion of such traumatic topics to the private sphere. After the democratic restoration, the topic of the dictatorship's military repression was excluded from public debate. The goal of the Concertación governments (1990–2010) was to look ahead, to insert the country within the global economy, legitimizing the market model imposed by totalitarianism, and to avoid addressing a delicate traumatic past.[14] Except for limited symbolic acts of memory restitution—for example the investigations held by the National Commissions on Human Rights Violations (Rettig Report [1991], Valech Report [2004 and 2010]) and the Museum of Memory and Human Rights (MMDH) (2010)—Chile's violent authoritarian repression of its own citizens is a collective experience barely addressed by the Concertación governments.[15]

While the Museum of Memory and Human Rights is the main site, in the post-Pinochet era, for remembering the dreadful past, Martín, in contrast, is a character whose past is never told. Hence, the visual composition overlaps the individual with his relationship to the collective trauma; he is a person whose memory is not openly discussed, in front of a museum full of memories. Under this interpretation, obvious to Chilean viewers but not to global audiences, *Vida de familia* addresses an unrooted personal and psychological identity crisis, and also suggests that Martín is a synecdoche of Chile's own tense confrontation with its history. Consequently, in this film by Scherson and Jiménez, the character's psychology subtly intermingles with national issues.

CONCLUSION

The aesthetic of emotional containment, detachment, and (dis)location prevalent in *Vida de familia* revolves around identity issues and appeals to transnational audiences and to an international market niche. The local uprooting and the character's disaffection may facilitate the film's access to international circuits, reinforcing an erasure of local identity. However, beyond classifying this cinematography merely as a film festival production, it is important to explore the global and local negotiations converging in this type of filmmaking. Scherson and Jiménez have skillfully entered into the international circuit with their previous work, but in *Vida de familia*, both cineastes return to a nonindustrial production, indirectly addressing topics of local collective interest (mourning, melancholia, nostalgia). Hence, this type of cinematography reexamines the opposition between individual and collective identity, public and private sphere, local and global dimensions, and makes intimacy a locus to reflect upon the relationship between cinema and politics.

NOTES

1   "The great theme of Latin American identity (who are we?) seemed to move towards the issue of personal identity (who am I?). McOndo's stories center on individual and private realities. We assume that this is one of the inheritances of the global privatization fever" ["El gran tema de la identidad latinoamericana (¿quiénes somos?) pareció dejar paso al tema de la identidad personal (¿quién soy?). Los cuentos de *McOndo* se centran en realidades

individuales y privadas. Suponemos que ésta es una de las herencias de la fiebre privatizadora mundial."] (Fuguet, 1996: 13, emphasis added). This and all other translations from Spanish here, unless otherwise specified, are my own.

2   In Chile, Fuguet and Gómez's narrative is identified as part of the literary movement known as the New Chilean Narrative of the 1990s. Other writers in this group include Gonzalo Contreras, Arturo Fontaine Talavera, Carlos Franz, Ana María del Río, Carlos Cerda, Marco Antonio de la Parra, and José Leandro Urbina.

3   These films were *En la cama / In Bed* by Matías Bize; *La sagrada familia / The Sacred Family* by Sebastián Lelio (as Sebastián Campos at that time), *Mi mejor enemigo / My Best Enemy* by Álex Bowen, and *Play*, by Alicia Scherson.

4   After filming *Turistas / Tourists* (2009), Scherson directed her largest coproduction, *Il Futuro / The Future* (2013), based on Roberto Bolaño's novella *A Little Lumpen Novelita / Una novelita lumpen*. Jiménez, meanwhile, directed a film version of Alejandro Zambra's celebrated novella *Bonsai* (2011), followed by *La voz en off / Voice Over* (2014).

5   Zambra's tale emphasizes that "they never married, although they act like a married couple, perhaps worse than a married couple" (2015, 194).

6   However, the few shots shown in *Vida de familia* of the Cuban director Jorge Molina's exploitation movie *Ferozz: The Wild Red Riding Hood* (2010), given by Pachi to Martín, and later found by Consuelo, subtly indicate an acid commentary on the family as a decadent institution corrupted by violence, incest, and bestiality.

7   Specifically, the Audiovisual Industry Support Program (Programa de Apoyo a la Industria Audiovisual) of Chile's Production Development Corporation (Corporación de Fomento de la Producción de Chile, or CORFO).

8   Support Program for Research, Innovation, and Artistic Creation (Concurso Apoyo a Eventos de Investigación, Innovación y Creación Artística), funded by the Vicerrectoría de Investigación y Desarrollo (VID) at the Universidad de Chile.

9   Nelly Richard characterizes the postdictatorship period as a time in which there prevailed a "consensual model of a 'democracy of agreements' formulated by the Chilean government of the Transition (1989) that marked a passage from politics as antagonism . . . to a politics of transaction" (Richard 2004, 15). This 'politics of transaction' develops into a number of negotiations of traumatic memories reflected in contemporary historical cinema, which made the military regime into a critical topic for the reclaimed democracy and the intended national "reconciliation." Further discussion on memory and melancholia is addressed below.

10   Un hombre solo en una casa sola
     No tiene deseos de encender el fuego
     No tiene deseos de dormir o estar despierto
     Un hombre solo en una casa enferma.
     . . .
     [A man alone in a lonely house
     He has no desire to light the fire
     He has no desire to sleep or be awake
     A man alone in a sick house.]

     (Teillier 1993, 14).

11   The house, describing a physical location or a mental state, symbolizes a place of identity and belonging, two critical elements the protagonist of *Vida de familia* lacks. Teillier's poetry of the *lar*, or home, which Zambra recalls in his book *Tema libre* (2019), describes the main character's nostalgic desire to recuperate a sense of place, a lost paradise, a homecoming. It is not a coincidence then that early in the movie, in an attempt to counterbalance his own rootlessness, Martín replaces the portrait of the Chilean poet with the picture of Consuelo, the wife and mother of the house. In *Ways of Going Home*, a novel in which Zambra develops a journey to the memory switching between past and present, the family embodies the house.

12   M. Catrileo refers to Matías Catrileo, a Mapuche student killed by the police during an occupation by indigenous people of a hacienda in 2008, in a protest to recover their ancestral lands.

13   According to two truth commissions, Pinochet's government assassinated or forcefully made disappear approximately three thousand Chileans and tortured another thirty thousand. The significance of the museum can be interpreted using the Jewish concept of Zakhor, which means "remember," a call for remembrance in the book of Deuteronomy referring to Amalek's attack against the children of Israel after their departure from Egypt. The Torah here issues a somewhat contradictory message regarding Amalek: to remember, not to forget, and also to erase the memory of Amalek. Zakhor then integrates the idea of remembering and forgetting simultaneously. The Museum has become a place to commemorate the past, but also a place to overcome this dreadful past.

14   For further arguments regarding Chile's postdictatorhisp discussed according to the allegory of mourning and melancholy see Moreiras (1993), Avelar (1999), Richard (1994), and Lazzara (2008).

15   For this reason, the post-Pinochet democratic governments have been perceived as a continuation of the authoritarian regime. In this context, the Museum of Memory and Human Rights inaugurated by President Michelle Bachelet in 2010 was considered a belated yet still controversial public memorial.

WORKS CITED

Avelar, Idelber. 1999. *The Untimely Present: Postdictatorial Latin American Fiction and the Task of Mourning.* Durham, NC: Duke University Press.

Barraza Toledo, Vania. 2012a. "Chilenos en Barcelona: entre el deseo, lo (a)político y el olvido en *199 recetas para ser feliz*." In *Capital Inscriptions: Essays on Literature, Film and Urban Space in Honor of Malcolm Alan Compitello*, edited by Benjamin Fraser, 195–211. Newark: Juan de la Cuesta.

———. 2012b. "*Play*, de Alicia Scherson: La flâneuse, la ciudad y los otros." In *Fronteras de la memoria: Cartografías de género en artes visuales, cine y literatura en las Américas y España*, edited by Bernardita Llanos and Ana María Goetschel, 117–37. Santiago: Editorial Cuarto Propio.

———. 2013. "Historia y simulacros de la memoria en *31 de abril* de Víctor Cubillos." In *Enfoques al cine chileno en dos siglos*, edited by Mónica Villarroel, 151–60. Santiago: LOM Ediciones.

———. 2015. "From *Sanhattan* to *Nashvegas*: The Aesthetics of Detachment in Alberto Fuguet's Filmmaking." *Hispania* 98 (3): 442–51.

———. 2018. *El cine en Chile (2005–2015): Políticas y poéticas del nuevo siglo*. Santiago: Editorial Cuarto Propio.

Cavallo, Ascanio, and Gonzalo Maza, eds. 2011. *El novísimo cine chileno.* Santiago: Uqbar Editores.

Deleuze, Gilles. *Cinema 1: The Movement-Image*. 1986. Translated by H. Tomlinson and B. Habberjam. Minneapolis: University of Minnesota Press.

———. *Cinema 2: The Time-Image*. 1989. Translated by H. Tomlinson and R. Galeta. Minneapolis: University of Minnesota Press.

Donoso Pinto, Catalina. 2007. *Películas que escuchan: Reconstrucción de la identidad en once filmes chilenos y argentinos*. Buenos Aires: Corregidor.

Estévez, Antonella. 2010. "Dolores políticos: Reacciones cinematográficas. Resistencias melancólicas en el cine chileno contemporáneo." *Aisthesis* 47 (July): 15–32.

———. 2011. "Joven cine chileno: En la movilización de los márgenes." In *El cine que fue: 100 años de cine chileno*, edited by Claudia Barril and José M. Santa Cruz, 75–83. Santiago: Arcis.

———. 2017. *Una Gramática de la Melancolía Cinematográfica: La modernidad y el no duelo en cierto cine chileno contemporáneo*. Santiago: Ediciones Radio Universidad de Chile.

Falicov, Tamara L. 2007a. *The Cinematic Tango: Contemporary Argentine Film*. New York: Wallflower Press.

———. 2007b. "Programa Ibermedia: Co-Production and the Cultural Politics of Constructing an Ibero-American Audiovisual Space." *Spectator* 27 (2): 21–30.

———. 2010. "Migrating South to North: The Role of Film Festivals in Shaping and Funding Global South Video." In *Locating, Migrating, Media*, edited by G. Elmer, C. H. Davis, J. Marchessault, and J. McCullough, 3–22. Lanham, MD: Lexington.

———. 2016. "The 'Festival Film': Film Festival Funds as Cultural Intermediaries." In *Film Festivals: History, Theory, Method, Practice*, edited by Marijke de Valck, Brendan Kredell, and Skadi Loist, 209–29. New York: Routledge.
Fuguet, Alberto, and Sergio Gómez, eds. 1996. "Prólogo." In *McOndo*, 11–20. Barcelona: Grijalbo.
Hite, Katherine. 2005. "Breaking the Silence in Post-Authoritarian Chile." In *Partisan Histories: The Past in Contemporary Global Politics*, edited by Padraic Kenney and Max Paul Friedman, 55–73. New York: Palgrave Macmillan.
Jacobsen, Udo. 2013. "Presentación. Como un espejo." Foreword to *Intimidades desencantadas: La poética cinematográfica del dos mil*, by Carlos Saavedra, 11–13. Santiago: Editorial Cuarto Propio.
Jara, Mario. 2017. "Historia de un largo viaje: Cine chileno contemporáneo." *Fuera de Campo* 1 (3): 98–107.
Kemp, Leah Harmon. 2010. *Citizenship in Chilean Post-Dictatorship Film, 1900–2005*. Los Angeles: Department of Spanish and Portuguese, University of California. Ann Arbor: ProQuest/UMI.
Larraín, Carolina. 2010. "Nuevas tendencias del cine chileno tras la llegada del cine digital." *Aisthesis* 47 (July): 156–71.
Lazzara, Michael. 2008. *Prismas de la memoria: Narración y trauma en la transición chilena*. Santiago: Cuarto Propio.
Lie, Nadia. 2018. "The Aesthetics of Disaffection in the Latin American Festival Film." *L'Atalante* 26: 13–25.
Martin-Jones, David, and María Soledad Montañez. 2013. "Uruguay Disappears: Small Cinemas, Control Z Films, and the Aesthetics and Politics of Auto-Erasure." *Cinema Journal* 53 (1): 26–51.
Moreiras, Alberto. 1993. "Postdictadura y reforma del pensamiento." *Revista de Crítica Cultural* 7 (November): 26–35.
Parada Poblete, María Marcela. 2012. "Cine chileno en dos tiempos: La operación visual sobre el cuadro-encuadre teatral-cinematográfico." Paper presented at the LASA Conference, San Francisco, CA, May 23–26.
Póo, Ximena, Claudio Salinas, and Hans Stange. 2012. "Políticas de la subjetividad en el 'novísimo' cine chileno." *Comunicación y Medios* 26: 5–11.
Rancière, Jacques. 2011. *The Emancipated Spectator*. Translated by Gregory Elliott. London: Verso.
Richard, Nelly. 1994. *La insubordinación de los signos (cambio político, transformaciones culturales y poéticas de la crisis)*. Santiago: Cuarto Propio.
———. 2004. *Cultural Residues: Chile in Transition*. Minneapolis: University of Minnesota Press.
———. 2007. "Márgenes e instituciones, la escena de Avanzada." In *Fracturas de la memoria: Arte y pensamiento crítico*, 13–28. Buenos Aires: Siglo XXI.
Ross, Miriam. 2011. "The Film Festival as Producer: Latin American Films and Rotterdam's Hubert Bals Fund." *Screen* 52 no. 2 (Summer): 261–67.
Rueda, Amanda. 2008. "1989–2008. 20 años de cine latinoamericano: tendencias y evoluciones." *Cinémas d'Amérique Latine* 16: 18–31.

Saavedra, Carlos. 2013. *Intimidades desencantadas: La poética cinematográfica del dos mil*. Santiago: Editorial Cuarto Propio.

Salinas Muñoz, Claudio, and Hans Stange Marcus. 2015. "Títeres sin hilos. Sobre el discurso político en el novísimo cine chileno." *Aisthesis* 57 (July): 219–33.

Stern, Steve J. 2000. "De la memoria suelta a la memoria emblemática: Hacia el recordar y el olvidar como proceso histórico (Chile, 1973–1998)." In *Memoria para un nuevo siglo: Chile, miradas a la segunda mitad del siglo XX.*, edited by Myriam Olguín Tenorio et al., 11–33. Santiago: Ediciones Lom.

Teillier, Jorge. 1993. "Un hombre solo en una casa sola." In *El molino y la higuera*, 14. Santiago: Ediciones del Azafrán.

Trejo, Roberto. 2009. *Cine, neoliberalismo y cultura: Crítica de la economía política del cine chileno contemporáneo*. Santiago: Arcis.

———. 2011. "El cine chileno en la primera década del siglo XXI: El agotamiento ideológico de una estrategia de desarrollo material." In *El cine que fue: 100 años de cine chileno*, edited by Claudia Barril and José M. Santa Cruz, 84–101. Santiago: Arcis.

Urrutia Neno, Carolina. 2010. "Hacia una política en tránsito: Ficción en el cine chileno (2008–2010)." *Aisthesis* 47 (July): 33–44.

———. *Un cine centrífugo: Ficciones chilenas 2005–2010*. 2013. Santiago: Editorial Cuarto Propio.

Vida de familia / Family Life. 2017. Directed by Cristián Jiménez and Alicia Scherson. Santiago, Chile: Peso Pluma.

Villazana, Libia. 2008. "Hegemony Conditions in the Coproduction Cinema of Latin America: The Role of Spain." *Framework* 49, no. 2: 65–85.

Wilde, Alexander. 1999. "Irruptions of Memory: Expressive Politics in Chile's Transition to Democracy." *Journal of Latin American Studies* 31, no. 2 (May): 473–500.

Winn, Peter. 2007. "El pasado está presente Historia y memoria en el Chile contemporáneo." *Historizar el pasado vivo en América latina*, edited by Anne Pérotin-Dumon. http://www.historizarelpasadovivo.cl/es_resultado_textos.php?categoria=Chile%3A+los+caminos+de+la+historia+y+la+memoria&titulo=El+pasado+est%E1+presente.+Historia+y+memoria+en+el+Chile+contempor%E1neo.

Zambra, Alejandro. 2014. *Ways of Going Home*. Translated by Megan McDowell. New York: Farrar, Straus and Giroux.

———. 2015. "Family Life." In *My Documents*, translated by Megan McDowell, 193–220. San Francisco: McSweeney's Publishing.

———. 2019. *Tema libre*. Barcelona: Anagrama.

MIGRATIONS OF GENDER AND GENRE

9

A HOUSE WITHOUT LIMITS

Framing Camila José Donoso's *Casa Roshell* through Disidentification and Disappropriation

Mónica Ramón Ríos

GENEALOGIES

In 1966, the Chilean novelist José Donoso published *El lugar sin límites / Hell Has No Limits* (1966), written while he was in Mexico. The novel focuses on Manuela, a transgender character who works in a brothel and nightclub run by the daughter she fathered in a small, forgotten town in Chile. Manuela wakes up one day, toothless and hungover, to the rumors of the return of an old lover who has publicly promised to kill her. At the end of the day, the lover appears, with equal parts desire and self-loathing, only to complete the tragedy that has been announced from the beginning of the novel: out in the open, dry fields owned by the wealthy don Alejo, the readers are left with her lifeless body.[1] Fifty-one years later, Chilean filmmaker Camila José Donoso presented her second feature film, *Casa Roshell*, about another club featuring transgender characters. The nightspot run by Roshell Terranova in Mexico City is a home where people–many of whom live as men on the outside–can dress up and become women. As in *El lugar sin límites*, the club is also a house, but here, situated in a big city, the inside becomes a safe haven and an activist center where people undergoing the transition from male to female can experience the free flow of desire, sexual identities, and affective transmissions without the dangers of the outside world.

The similarities between José Donoso's novel and Camila José Donoso's film are notable: both are part of transnational creative processes that link Chile with Mexico, both investigate the lives of transgender characters, and both envision the space of a house to represent safety and freedom. But in terms of the ethical projects that they announce, the novel and the film diverge: whereas *El lugar sin límites* emphasizes tragedy, violence, and the repression of desire,[2] *Casa Roshell* celebrates all kinds of affective bonds. Although there seems to be a clear genealogy linking these two stories, reinforced by the names of both creators, in *Casa Roshell* Camila José Donoso did not explicitly use, quote, or enter into dialogue with the novel *El lugar sin límites* or any of José Donoso's literary oeuvre.[3] By distancing herself from the references to *El lugar sin límites* and its hellish scenery,[4] Camila José Donoso uses the limits of a house to celebrate nonviolent affective bonds and erotic fantasies honed in gender-fluid communities.

The year 2017 was a milestone for Chilean and Latin American transgender communities on film. While *Casa Roshell* premiered in the Berlinale and was shown in many countries in the festival circuit, another film with a transgender character performed by a transgender actress, Daniela Vega, took over the awards season, including winning the Oscar for Best Foreign Film.[5] In many ways, however, Sebastián Lelio's *Una mujer fantástica / A Fantastic Woman* stands in opposition to the aesthetic and ethical project of *Casa Roshell*. In *Una mujer fantástica* there is a comfortable "fiction of identity" that can easily be made visible by the commercial film circuit and by Chilean conservatives, validated by Daniela Vega's young, white beauty, the silence with which her character confronts the hatred shown by Chilean upper-class society represented in the film, and the frame of melodrama that aligns Lelio's film with works by other recognized male filmmakers invested in portraying women.[6]

While *Una mujer fantástica* follows a melodramatic model, *Casa Roshell* is constructed upon what Camila José Donoso has called *transficción*: an always-localized politics of creative experimentation that highlights the continuum between the lives of trans people and the characters they play, and between representation, presentation, and activism. Biologist and theorist Jorge Díaz (2015) came up with this definition in relation to the play *Cuerpos para odiar (Bodies to Hate)*. Naomi Orellana argued that Donoso introduced a formal "disobedience" into her film by incorporating documentary methodologies, combining different formats, and creating continuity between "people and characters" ["personas y personajes"]. Orellana (2017) also points out that *transficción* is the product of a creative alliance between the filmmaker (Donoso) and the owner of the club (Roshell), which the writer defines as a "complicit gaze" ["mirada cómplice"].[7]

In comparison to Lelio's melodrama, Donoso's depiction of a grassroots transgender organization using *transficción* or transgenre techniques of documentary and fiction film is a more complex critique of the fictions of identity. "The fiction of identity," writes José Muñoz, "is one that is accessed with relative ease by most majoritarian subjects" (1999, 5); in other words, it has a comfortable place within the dominant public sphere. On the contrary, Muñoz continues, "minoritarian subjects need to interface with different subcultural fields to activate their own senses of self" (5). These identities-in-difference, unable to relate unproblematically with the cultural logics of heteronormativity, white supremacy, and misogyny, incorporate a multiplicity of interlocking identity components, and contribute to the function of a counterpublic sphere (5–7). Club Roshell, as portrayed by Donoso's cinematographic language, houses this very multiplicity: instead of providing answers or a suitable identitarian fiction for each character, Donoso provides kaleidoscopic approaches to the self in order to refuse the easy classification into categories that nonbinary subjects usually perform. As such, the prefix *trans* becomes a key word of sorts in Donoso's work and provides an environment within which to create gender, sexual, and territorial transitions. The transnational aspect of this production model also resonates in the project *Transfrontera*, a film school created by Donoso that moves every couple of years to different locations near the border between Perú, Bolivia, and Chile (a border still disputed today). In *Casa Roshell*, Donoso uses an aesthetic language that speaks to the transitional state of the characters' gender identity, but also to the transitional stages between documentary and fiction film, as well as to her transnational production model.

In opposition to the spotlight cast on *Una mujer fantástica*, *Casa Roshell* remains partially in the shadows because it interpellates a persistent fluidity vis-à-vis every dominant identity. With its alternative circulation and its lack of melodrama, Donoso's film offers a cinematic language that we could define as minoritarian. *Casa Roshell* uses documentary and other collective methodologies to create a fiction film about non-elite transgender characters and the men who visit the club to engage in love and sex with them. Donoso emphasizes the connections among radical feminism, cinematic language that pays homage to the New Latin American Cinema of the 1960s, the affect-driven political engagement of the transgender community, and the aesthetic representations of the *travesti*, the *loca*, and the various sexual identities existing between the male and the female.[8] These specific marks of Latin American gender identity stand in clear opposition to what Cristeva Cabello (2015) calls *identidades rosa*—that is, marketable images of the trans community—but also to the uncomplicated political nomenclatures of queer community forged in the Global North. In short, Donoso's aesthetic influences in *Casa Roshell* constitute a critique of conservative definitions of gender, but also social class, colonialism, and racial divisions.[9]

In the following pages, I will argue that the film *Casa Roshell* investigates identity-based fluidity in terms of the framing of the film. Following Gilles Deleuze and Anne Friedberg, I understand the frame aesthetically as the intersection of the film's architecture and the meanings mobilized by the limits of the visible. But in *Casa Roshell* the frames are multiple; they work in such a way that the architecture of the house becomes integrated with the architecture of the film. Inside *Casa Roshell*'s master frame, we see many other frames: windows, doors, security camera feeds, and especially mirrors that, together with an overpopulation of medium shots and close-ups, construct a space impossible to map out. If we consider that the narrative space of the house can be read as the image of the construction of the self,[10] Donoso is also pointing to the lack of fixed identities and the changing subjectivities that dwell at Roshell's club. In *Casa Roshell*, the real—understood as the capacity of an image to document a presence—is remediated through several procedures, redirecting our spectatorial gaze to a diverse set of meanings. So, while the film seeks to localize the radical politics of a Mexican trans community, the cinematographic language erases the frontiers between what is true and what is virtual, between fixed and fake identities, between the local and the transnational. It is in that fluidity that Donoso creates what I call a politics of the interior, which is both spatial and affective.

A HOME FOR FICTION

Camila José Donoso was born in 1988 and studied film in Chile. She directed several shorts before she presented her first feature film, titled *Naomi Campbel* and codirected with Nicolás Videla, in 2013.[11] This film is also centered on a transgender woman, Yermén, who plays herself in scenes that are both improvised and scripted, shot sometimes with nonactors and other times with professional performers, but always in situations and locations taken from the actress/character's real life. In the middle section of the film, while she is in the process of auditioning for a reality show, Yermén asks another participant, Naomi: "And would you like to be in television and in a reality show? So people can know everything about your life and know how you behave in everyday life?" ["¿A usted le gustaría ir a la televisión y estar en un reality? ¿Que todo el mundo supiera su vida?"]. Not only is Paula Yermén Dinamarca a trans woman well known in Chilean activist circles, highlighting the exposure of her intimacy in the film; she is also making explicit what is at stake in this project—namely, there are lives outside of what is being constructed inside the frames of the film.

In 2016, while Donoso was living in Mexico City, she met Roshell Terranova at the latter's club and activist center. Donoso spent six months doing research, which consisted of creating affective bonds with the individuals that congregated at Club Roshell and recording conversations that later became the basis for scripted scenes played either by the same people who were involved in the "original" scenes, or by actors. The film was shot in six days, and it is structured as one night at Club Roshell. Despite the fact that the film is named after Roshell Terranova and bears the name of the director, the narrative does not favor continuity in relation to a main character, but rather focuses on the juxtaposition and simultaneity of situations involving the women and men who gather at the club. The result is a choir of voices that incorporates the collective as an authorial force, pluralizing the space of the author.

In a personal interview in Santiago de Chile in 2017, Donoso told me that the main issue her crew faced while shooting the film was the lack of depth of field. Club Roshell functions in a medium-sized building with many small rooms. Incapable of establishing long shots, of which there are only a few during the film, the crew was forced to find new ways to open up the depth of field by placing the camera to film fixed shots outside rooms and incorporating door frames and mirrors into static master frames. The result was a highly suggestive use of multiple frames or frames-within-frames created by elements within the diegetic world.

To understand how the limits of the visible function in *Casa Roshell*, I want to outline how the frame has been discussed in aesthetic theory. As Gilles Deleuze (1986) states, the frame of a screen is not only visible but also legible, which means that it has certain physical attributes, and that it can also be charged with meaning. For Deleuze, framing is limitation, both architecturally and in terms of signification. He maintains that framing determines the closed system of the shot: "The screen, as the frame of frames, gives a common standard to things which don't have one" (1986, 14), providing a "closed visual system" (15). That closed visual system is related to "the point of view" of the narration, and also to what Pascal Bonitzer calls *le décadrage*, or the spaces outside the frame (Deleuze 1986, 17). But as Anne Friedberg argues (2006), the immobile film screen is part of a longer history of technologies of the look. She traces the frame and its point of view back to Leon Battista Alberti and his description of a painting as an "open window" with its corresponding perspectival vanishing point. Describing further how she understands the "ontological cut" performed by a screen, Friedberg writes: "The frame [of the screen] becomes the threshold–the liminal site–of tensions between the immobility of a spectator/viewer/user and the mobility of images seen through the mediated 'windows' of film, television, and computer screens" (2006, 6). In Friedberg's argument, the window becomes a metaphor for the screen. At the same time, "The mirror's opacity, reflected light, and inverse image suggest a visual system quite different to the window's . . . [transparency or] unmediated image" (15). The mirror mediates, reflects, and reverses. Thus, screens, windows, and mirrors all become metaphors of the frame that modify, each in their own way, the comprehension of the bodies we see in action.

Casa Roshell incorporates all of these literal and metaphorical aspects in its framing. In one of the first sequences of the film, we see a series of men skillfully transforming themselves into women. A fixed shot introduces us to the process of putting on makeup: the person is framed at the right half of the screen; on the left, we see the surroundings of a dressing room. As the scene progresses, we suddenly see her hand appear on the opposite side of the frame, forcing us to understand that what we see is not a direct document of the character but a refracted image (Figure 20). This superimposition of surfaces forces us to reevaluate what we see on the screen: we are seeing the character in reverse at the same time we are seeing the character leaving behind his identity as a male and becoming a woman. We are being pushed to see what is outside the limits of the frame, to incorporate *le décadrage* into our scopic field.

However, Jacques Derrida (1987) had already described the frame as a "context marked by performative fiction" (3) that centers the criteria by which a viewer or critic distinguishes between the inside and the outside (*ergon/parergon*) of an aesthetic object. When analyzing this distinction (Kant's, originally), Derrida points out that the frame is at the limit between work and absence of work, and thus constitutive of the work; without this performative fiction, the aesthetic object would be incomplete. Derrida writes: "Kant replies to our question 'What is a frame?' by saying: it's a *parergon*, a hybrid of outside and inside, but a hybrid which is not a mixture

Figure 20. What we see is not a direct document of the character but a refracted image in *Casa Roshell* (Camila José Donoso, 2017).

or half-measure, but an outside which is called to the inside of the inside in order to constitute it as an inside" (63).

Casa Roshell complicates this affirmation by installing an image of the outside as seen from the inside. In several moments in the film, we get close-ups of security cameras surveying the streets outside the club, establishing a limit that is at the same time visual, spatial, and ontological. The first time we are exposed to this footage (Figure 21), we see a shot divided into four smaller frames, showing us various angles of the streets and the club's reception area. The frame in the upper left corner takes over most of the shot: between the parked cars and the quiet streets, we distinguish a man in a suit. In the next shot, also divided into four smaller frames, we see a trans woman in the reception area letting him into the house. In one of the previous scenes, we heard someone explaining the services provided by Club Roshell and telling the caller: "Te esperamos. Es tu casa" ["See you soon. This is your home too."]. The subtitles, which translate this as "You're welcome," fail to convey the nuance of the reply: the inside is, more than a space, an invitation to come home, again drawing a relationship between this closed space and the expressions of potential selfhood. The images of the security cameras–a street, parked cars, passersby–are placed in the film to establish a threshold between the outside and the inside; the former, a place to be monitored, the latter, a place of freedom behind closed doors.

A House Without Limits • 227

Figure 21. The outside as seen from the inside of Club Roshell, in *Casa Roshell* (Camila José Donoso, 2017).

We could further say, with Derrida's description, that the house becomes an inside because the outside is presented to us with this particular visual texture, thus establishing the first piece of a fragmented map.

As Elizabeth Grosz (2002) reminds us, this economy of space is not new for queer groups. In her writings on architecture and difference, she states that the uses that the gay community has made of spaces modify the social structures attached to them, allowing us to think of buildings not in terms of sedimentation (of meanings and of forms of occupation, to use her terms) but as open spaces. She writes: "the closet is *both* a prison and a safe space. . . . The closet allows people to not be seen as gay but to feel safe as gay" (8). She then expands this idea to others: "women, or gays, or other minorities, aren't 'imprisoned' in or by space, because space (unless we are talking about a literal prison) is never fixed or contained, and thus always open to various uses in the future" (8). The nightlife and bar scenes developed by these communities are also spaces inhabited and defined by sexual pleasure. Néstor Perlongher names the scene similarly as *el mundo de la noche*, which he describes as a closed universe, the negative contrast of the heterosexual diurnal world.[12] When Grosz writes that "space is the ongoing possibility of a different inhabitation" (8), she could easily have been referring to Roshell's club (9). Donoso's film does not incorporate any establishing shot of the outside of the house that could place us as objective viewers or critics. On the contrary, as spectators we get lost in the many spaces of the house, unable to understand its architecture. Expanding upon Deleuze's description referred to above, the master frame does not provide clear limits to the visible; we are invited to become insiders.

An element of the soundtrack, designed by Camila José Donoso and Mauricio Flores, also outlines this fluctuation of meanings by incorporating awkwardly strident reverberations of airplanes taking off in several moments in the film. Beyond the obvious indication that we are at a location near the airport, the sounds of the airplanes are not always used diegetically; sometimes they are situated as bridges between dissimilar sequences, or they are used in transitions. However, these flights do not take us outside to the streets we are watching through the security footage but to places far away, which are embodied in the wigs, eye shadow, heels, and dreams of the women we see.

While *Casa Roshell* populates the master frame with various other windows into the fiction, the ontological cut performed by the limits of the visible seems to escape the viewer. Not only are we unable to map out the house; the juxtaposition of scenes, more by thematic contiguity than by narrative continuity, contributes to a sense of indetermination. But such indetermination–which we could formulate as a lack of the ontological cut performed by the master frame, an incorporation of the *décadrage* into the visible, as an outside that becomes visible inside, or as a reconfiguration of the limits of the visible–is also an invitation for the spectator to come home, revealing the sites of fluidity within our own position as subject of the look. By using multiple frames to complicate the architecture of the house—another house without limits—the film seems to interpellate us: Where would we rather be?

A POLITICS OF THE INTERIOR: DISIDENTIFICATION AND THE SCOPIC FIELDS

In the first shots when we are introduced to Roshell Terranova, the pivotal character in the film, we can see her face only through mirrors, making her only obliquely accessible (Figure 22). The multiple frames, superimposing different points of view together, reinforce the idea that we are in the presence of a multitude of potential onlookers, the spectator of the film being one of many. As a matter of fact, many minutes of the film are devoted to showing close-ups of men just looking at the women, emphasized by low-key lighting. What is framed there is not really the men but the sensual communication happening through their eyes, as if they are simultaneously dazzled, confused, and seduced by the oblique presence of the women.

Figure 22. The first time we see Roshell Terranova, in *Casa Roshell* (Camila José Donoso, 2017).

In several other shots, the women are presented as images refracted into mirrors. While we hear Roshell engaged in a conversation with a client offscreen, a static medium shot shows us Lili lighting a cigarette at the bar behind a window, which holds three open mirror panels instead of translucent glass. While the space where the woman moves around is illuminated with high-key lighting, the camera is placed on the side of the window with no light, situating us as voyeurs. At one point, after she has arranged bottles and glasses, Lili leans over near the window. Her face lights up with a white, colder light–probably because she is looking at a computer screen–showing us the left portion of her face on the right side of the frame, while in the mirror at the center of the frame we see a close-up of her two delineated eyes and her full red lips (Figure 23). But in neither of those images can we clearly see her face in full. This fragmentation keeps our gazes hanging on to what we cannot clearly make out.

The multiple frames in the film are necessarily tied to the various gazes, as they transmit and instigate pleasures and desires. In other words, if we understand the gaze as Laura Mulvey (1990) does–as the unidirectional scopic pleasure that is already inscribed in the narrative of the film, forcing the viewer to occupy the position of the male spectator–the various forms of looking in *Casa Roshell* destroy that monologic, normative gaze.[13] I would suggest the film investigates other forms of scopic pleasures, including the

Figure 23. We never see Lili's face in full, in *Casa Roshell* (Camila José Donoso, 2017).

male gaze, the oppositional gaze,[14] or the forensic gaze,[15] among others that have been theorized in film studies. When the camera in *Casa Roshell* frames the men looking, we scrutinize their fascination with these women, revealing affects that flow not in one direction but from everywhere to everywhere else. In many senses, we also become those men, fascinated by the women but also fascinated by the others' fascination.

To better understand how the film works through the multiplicity of those scopic pleasures, I would like to propose two other concepts to help us read the film: the glide and allurement. In an interview with Marguerite Duras about her novel and script *Destroy She Said*, which first appeared in *Cahiers du Cinéma*, Jean Narboni describes Duras's work as follows: "*Destroy* is made up structurally of people watching each other at different levels. . . . There is a sort of perpetual *gliding* that goes beyond the narrator–or the absence of a narrator" (Narboni and Rivette 1986, 94). Later, he continues: "[it is] not at all like something tying the whole thing together. Not a 'gaze,' not something static, but *a watching function*, so to speak" (94–95, emphasis added). Duras answers: "There is no primacy of one character over another in *Destroy She Said*. There is a *gliding* from one character to another" (Narboni and Rivette 1986, 96). According to this dialogue, "the glide," as a watching function, happens in the uncertainty of what one sees, in the uncertainty of who is looking at whom. In other

A House Without Limits • 231

words, the glide refuses the closure that the gaze transposes, because gliding requires not only having someone look back at the onlooker but also not being sure of what one is looking at.

We can see these mobile gazes in several moments in the film, when a group of women are sitting at a table. Through the use of mirrors, the shot manages to include the visual field of the shot and the countershot simultaneously. In one of them (Figure 24), two women are sitting at a table talking about surgical sex change operations, while in the mirror that hangs behind them we see Roshell's reflection. With the use of mirrors placed in the foreground of the shot, we see on both sides of the screen another woman sitting and the man that in other parts of the film will be identified as Alberto. He is looking at the woman inquisitively from behind. Because of the lightning, we can barely make out the actual distribution of the characters in the room. This puzzling shot is emphasized by a discontinuous dialogue that jumps from the two women at the center of the frame to the man and women in the corner, our eyes unable to discern exactly where an utterance is coming from or whom it is directed to.

This puzzling feature of some scenes resonates with several spaces that are barely insinuated by the film's frames. In one of the rare long shots, we catch a glimpse of a taped striptease, giving us a visual sense of the sex that, we hear, also takes place on the club's premises. Later, we learn through the dialogues

Figure 24. The shot simultaneously includes the visual field of the shot and the countershot, in *Casa Roshell* (Camila José Donoso, 2017).

about "the dark room," which is separated from the rest of the scene by a curtain. Through those thick, velvety drapes, very similar to the ones we will later see on the stage, the characters disappear from our visual frame to enter into a space of full intimate encounter. As a technology of the *décadrage*, and as an element that blocks our view while hailing our scopic desires, the curtain divides the space between the visible, where bodies are fully dressed but ready to be looked at, and another, forbidden space where bodies are totally exposed. The curtain stresses the idea that the spectacular natures of the people gathered in *Casa Roshell* are not just a representation but an invitation that happens in the convergence of performative selves with affectivity. This idea is activated in the transition from the first sequences—when the men are transforming into women—to the scenes in the nightclub. After we have seen her put on her makeup, dress, and wig, Lili crosses from the backstage of the house to the club through a stage curtain, thus announcing the beginning of the spectacle.

These bodies, as surfaces on which identity and desire are displayed, become alluring images that overcome any onlooker. As Steven Shaviro has described in his *Post-Cinematic Affect*, allurement describes an ontological condition experienced when what we look at displays certain qualities, but also insinuates the presence of a hidden, deeper level of existence. Allurement takes place when one is forced to acknowledge a hidden depth that is, at the same time, inaccessible. "The alluring object," he writes, "insistently displays the fact that it is separate from, and more than, its qualities–which means that it exceeds everything that I feel and know about it" (2010, 9). The dark room, the outside, the *décadrage*, the fragmented space, and the fragmented ways in which the women are presented are all manifestations of the inaccessible nature of these identities, of alluring images that exist for and through the presentation of their constructed identities. At the same time, they are also a promise of something that escapes us; those alluring images reveal the fallible capacities of our eyes to apprehend what we see, a lack that also invites us to experience a pleasure that can only happen in the space of a club or in the space of a film, both houses for these identitarian fluidities.

In the refraction of their image, in the remediation of their identities, the women of *Casa Roshell* become those alluring objects. One of the recurrent images in Donoso's film is of the women posing. As Sylvia Molloy reminds us, the pose incarnates an accentuated visibility in which the person posing uses exaggeration to force the look of the other upon him- or herself, to force a reading and a discourse (2012, 44). On a smartphone that is being shown to us on screen, we see a woman posing with several short dresses; before, we had seen another phone with a woman posing as a siren; the camera fixes on Roshell and other women moving their eyes intently, and on a fixed shot of a woman dressed in traditional Oaxacan attire with flowers on her head and a drink in her hand, enjoying the fact that she appears before the camera. What do the men who attend the club—and what do we as spectators—see when we look at these women, women who mere hours ago entered the club dressed as men themselves? The camera (al)lures us into watching different kinds of bodies, celebrating the disparity between sizes, ages, and colors, between personalities and poses, discarding singular readings of trans women as white, young, and fit. The pleasure in posing as a woman stands in opposition to their hard-working, conventionally male lives on the outside.

The sequence of the "Personality Workshop" led by Roshell offers some insight into the alluring dynamic between the virtual and the real. In one shot, we see a group of women sitting down in full drag; in the countershot, we see Roshell in a close-up addressing them. She stands in front of a curtain explaining how to train their male bodies to look like [*parecer*] women. A cut takes us to an extreme close-up of Roshell's mouth delineated in red lipstick and surrounded by golden curls, explaining what to do to achieve this "optical illusion." Such illusions are fulfilled not only with the help of the correct clothes and wig but also when each woman consciously brings in the image they want to project. Roshell wants everybody to ask themselves: "What kind of girl do I want to be?" ["¿Qué tipo de chica quiero ser?"] Intellectual, naïve, aggressive, a mermaid, or a Marilyn Monroe? In that question, the reality of the brown male body intersects with the virtuality of the female image as a site of freedom and potentiality, not limited by national or racial boundaries.

This "look like" or *parecer* is the expression of an interior that becomes real even as it embodies a consciously constructed fiction. This expression of intimate desires through the intersection of performance and biography is a dynamic we have already recognized in *transficción*. As Muñoz would put it–and here I transpose his analysis of James Baldwin's literature–these are disidentificatory selves, "whose relation to the social [are] not overdetermined by universalizing rhetorics of selfhood. The real self who comes into being through fiction is not the self who produces fictions but is instead produced by fiction" (1999, 20). Like the images in Donoso's film, for Muñoz, "fiction then becomes a contested field of self production" (20) in disidentificatory performances, by incorporating and reworking the dominant ideology, including the harmful, shameful, or contradictory components of any identity (12). Muñoz elaborates the term "disidentification" as the psychoanalytic expression of a subject that is formed by simultaneously working within and opposing a dominant cultural form:

> Disidentification is [a] mode of dealing with dominant ideology, one that neither opts to assimilate within such a structure nor strictly opposes it; rather, disidentification is a strategy that works *on and against* dominant ideology ... a strategy that tries to transform a cultural logic from within, always laboring to enact permanent structures of change while at the same time valuing the importance of local everyday struggles of resistance. (1999, 11–12)

Disidentification stands on ambivalent ground in relation to the psychoanalytic models of desire and identification that traditionally define models of heterosexuality; subjects that disidentify inhabit both models, creating identificatory bonds with the object they desire.

Casa Roshell not only integrates disidentificatory strategies but also shows how its subjects act them out. At one point in the film, a static medium shot frames a man with gray hair wearing a gray suit and smoking in a masculine manner. As he walks behind the curtain that leads to "the dark room," he seems to be one of the men who go to the club to look at and interact with the women. Later, we see Roshell in the bar hearing a story told by someone offscreen about how he is going on a trip with his wife, who recently walked in on him while he was trying on a dress. In the countershot, we see the same man we had seen smoking, now gleefully telling the story to Roshell. We had seen him before in full drag; he wore short skirts, a black bob, and played the shy girl. At a later point in the film, she will sit on a table with another woman who also wears short skirts and uses a short bob; when framed by a two-shot, the two look oddly similar. They recognize each other, and although they never mention the word family, we understand that they grew up as brothers. The stories they exchange of how they started to cross-dress are so similar that again it seems that they are talking to a mirror. But that intimate confession of pleasures, shame, and pain happens as the film erases the brothers' previous relationship–they introduce themselves to one another, as if it were the first time they met–and replaces it with the anagnorisis of this other common experience.

It is this idea of the common that surfaces in Roshell's club. At one point in the film, a woman explains to Alberto, one of the clients at the club, that he also transitioned in a way: not from hetero- to homosexuality but to the realization that there are other kinds of women, and that he liked them. This takes us to another scene: in a fixed medium two-shot, a young man is standing next to an older man sitting on a chair, both looking to the center of the club. The old man gets a call, which identifies him as a doctor. When he hangs up, the young man identifies himself as a lawyer and, he continues, as bisexual. Without looking at him, his eyes persistently fixed on the dance floor, the doctor answers, saying he is heterosexual. The young man, a bit startled, asks him why he is at Roshell's club when he could be at any strip club. "What I see here," says the doctor, "are women." This "What I see" seems to be the point of the entire film: through her camera, Donoso acknowledges the existence of identities in constant transformation through the superimposition of visual mediations. But the doctor also says, "What I see *here*." "*Estamos dentro*," he remarks; "we are inside." That flux, that lack of limits, is paradoxically possible only within the confines of the house–and, I speculate, of the film. *Casa Roshell* becomes "a house without limits" insofar as its interior is clearly separated from an outside. The outside is the place where the women live as men, while the interior is free from those particular fictions of identity to allow them to imagine and consciously perform other such fictions. Mirroring what the novelist Donoso described at the end of his novel, when the transgender character Manuela is most likely murdered in the open fields surrounding the town, the filmmaker Donoso disidentifies with that tragic representation of the hardships of trans women. Instead, her film celebrates "the powerful and seductive sites of self creation" (Muñoz 1999, 4) in which the house becomes the home for the fluctuating designs and shapes of interiority, where pain is converted into contestation.

A FILMMAKER WHO DISAPPROPRIATES TRANS CULTURE

As I commented at the beginning of this chapter, melodrama, with its legible moral order and hyperbolic codes, is a common way to understand the hardships of the trans community on film. However, the hyperlegibility of a melodramatic frame for trans characters, as with *Una mujer fantástica*, erases from local politics the effects of colonialism and the unequal distribution of global capital. Cutting herself loose from those genealogies, Camila José Donoso invokes the cinematic language of New Latin American Cinema, a tradition that, with all its hunger, imperfections, and Third-World aesthetics, takes up the relationship between the film creator, the social sphere, and the minorities presented on the screen. I am interested in how Donoso's production model follows a methodology similar to Jorge Sanjinés's *Yawar Mallku / The Blood of the Condor* (1969) and *El coraje del pueblo / The Courage of the People* (1971): like him, she appears in the credits as a cowriter alongside the communities she portrays. In such projects, the script blossoms from a conversation between the bearers of a local experience and the bearer of the transnational language of film, impregnating the language of fiction with that of documentary. The actors play themselves in scripted scenes taken from situations that either they or somebody else in that group have already experienced.

Donoso uses both professional and nonprofessional actors to present localized experiences remediated through fiction. But while Sanjinés's objective was to represent and denounce abuses by foreign and state-run companies in Bolivia, Donoso follows a logic that deprioritizes certain aspects of the trans community favored by mainstream media–mainly white, young, thin, fit bodies–in order to explore the spectacular nature of multiple identities fantasized about and lived within the confines of the club. The camera and those consciously constructed identities complement each other perfectly: the ways in which these interiorities are carved out and performed seem to call for a camera to document their presence. And although the characters in the film do not evade the problems and struggles of living as transgender women, they present that way of life as a personal, social, and political opportunity.[16]

In many ways, Donoso, who defines herself as a feminist, is not appropriating the culture of these activist trans women but, following Cristina Rivera Garza's conceptualization, she is *disappropriating* it. For Rivera Garza, disappropriation defines a language that "[opens] itself up to include the voices of others in evident and creative ways, taking care to avoid the obvious risks: subsuming them into the author's own reach or reifying them in unequal exchanges characterized by profit or prestige for a select few" (2018, 34). By showing how literature (in the case of Rivera Garza) or film (in the case of Donoso) uses nonartistic material, the disappropriating writer and, I add, filmmaker, "return all writing [and image creation] to its plural origin, and thus construct future horizons in which writing [and film] joins the assembly in order to participate and contribute to the common good" (34, with my additions in brackets). Rivera Garza theorizes further:

> disappropriation exposes the plurality that precedes individuality in the creative process, opening a window onto the material layering often concealed by appropriative texts. In other words, disappropriation reveals the communal work of a language's practitioners and marks it as a source of creative work itself. In turn, it shows us the forms of self-production and the stories shared by collective subjects of enunciation. More than denouncing appropriation by means of an opposite discourse (often based on the same appropriative logic), disappropriation announces it; that is, it cracks it open, manifesting it in aesthetically relevant ways. (44)

Like disidentification, disappropriation is also a call to action with a utopian component, a survival strategy of minority subject practices: by reinterpreting the past, by using the memory of a community that is in a constant state of waiting, disappropriative creations "blaze into the future" (Rivera Garza 2018, 34). Such a dynamic of hope emerges from a dissensus with how the wealth (in material terms but also the representation within the dominant public sphere) of the present has been distributed. As such, disappropriative language investigates "internal horizons": how the intimate, localized experiences of bodies in context–and in contact with each other–inform the proposals undertaken by those who struggle (Rivera Garza 2018, 54).

Casa Roshell not only represents reality but also presents it in relation to the cinematic traditions of the Global South, thus localizing "a politics of the interior" in the one of the largest cities in Latin America. The director shifts the film's social function from a figure cohered by a body of work to a figure where communal forces converge. The understanding between Donoso's aesthetic language and the performance of purposefully fluid identities, between her camera and the visibility of interiorities at Roshell's club, brings together the constant transition of the *I*'s and that which is captured by the *eyes*. At the same time, the authorial becomes a space for the collective and the film becomes a space of encounter; it produces a tradition that will be reproduced in each viewing, and the utopian desires that are awaiting disidentification and disappropriation are actualized to bring the future and hope to this, our present.

NOTES

1. The end of Donoso's novel is actually quite ambiguous, with several possible endings. In Arturo Ripstein's 1978 adaptation of the novel to the silver screen, the director chooses this tragic ending. For details about the ending, see Levine (2000, 287) and Grant (2002, 254–55).

2. Rubí Carreño reminds us how in Japonesita's house violence is one of the marks of femininity, whether cisgendered or trans, and that violence, fear, and submission are some of the affects that construct Manuela's erotic fantasies in *El lugar sin límites* (2007, 134).

3. Camila José has no family relation to José. According to the filmmaker, the only time the story by José Donoso came up was when Roshell Terranova mentioned *El lugar sin límites* in reference to Ripstein's film adaptation when they were discussing *Casa Roshell* (email communication with the director). The two films portray trans characters in very different ways, starting with the production models and the authorial figures delineated by each director: such models are hierarchical in Arturo Ripstein's film, but much more collaborative in Camila José Donoso's project. In the former, the tragic ending becomes a destiny for queer people, while in the latter, as we will see below, queerness becomes a potentiality (in terms of José Esteban Muñoz's argument in his book *Cruising Utopia*).

4. Established by the novel's epigraph, taken from Marlowe's *Faust*, Rodrigo Cánovas places "the literary brothel" as a grotesque heterotopia of peripheral modernity, and as a marginal and transgressive space capable of pointing to an intellectual deconstruction of our culture (2003, 6). José Donoso's literary brothel becomes, for Cánovas, an index of something else (an allegory of culture) and not a place where sexualities are re/presented.

5. After *Una mujer fantástica* won the golden statuette for Best Foreign Language Film, the newly elected conservative and historically misogynistic and homophobic Chilean government declared it would pass a law prohibiting discrimination against transgender people, which caused an uproar in more radicalized trans and feminist circles, which felt that the government was appropriating their political agenda.

6. Such filmmakers include Pedro Almodóvar—whose production company was involved in Lelio's film—as well as King Vidor and Douglas Sirk. In 2015, Cristeva Cabello referred to such connections between melodrama and the trans community as "an ever-proliferating romance literature that softens the classic script of pain that ensues when non-heterosexual lives are suffocated by family institutions" ["una proliferante literatura rosa que dulcifica las relaciones no heterosexuales escritas en el clásico guion del dolor sofocado por las

instituciones familiares"] (2015, 9), which could be easily be applied to the comparison I am pointing out here. See also Ríos 2018.

7   Donoso's use of *transficción* is inspired by the methodologies of Jean Rouch, but she sees it everywhere in contemporary films. She explains this in a forthcoming volume dedicated to the term.

8   In this article, I use the word "trans" as a term that incorporates all of those identities, inspired by Jack Halberstam's (2018) term "trans*" (with an asterisk), which refuses any easy classification of sexualities and genders. It is necessary, nonetheless, to point to the specific ways in which that term is embodied in Latin America. For example, Néstor Perlongher writes, while observing a corner of São Paulo in his *La prostitución masculina*: "Many of those who are part of that crowd are readily identifiable for the *entendidos* of the night: *putas*, *travestis*, and all sorts of feminine homosexuality: *locas* (effeminate), *maricones* or *tías* (mature effeminate people over 35), gays (a modern synonym of homosexual which groups those who are not openly effeminate), and *chongos*–young men who do not necessarily consider themselves homosexual or even brag about not being homosexual but who consent in negotiating (sexually) with locas" ["Muchos de los que componen esa muchedumbre son, con todo, identificables a primera vista para los *entendidos* de la noche: putas, travestis y todos los géneros de las homosexualidades femeninas: *locas* (afeminados), *maricones* o *tías* (afeminados maduros, de más de 35 años), *gays* (sinónimo moderno de homosexual que agrupa a los no abiertamente feminoides), *chongos*– muchachos que sin necesariamente considerarse homosexuales o incluso, jactándose de no serlo, consienten en 'transar' (relacionarse sexualmente) con las *locas*"] (1993, 25, emphasis in original). In that same book, Perlongher defines the *travesti* as a "radical femininity" ["feminidad radical"], identified by her "performative representation of femininity, including the disturbing turgidity of fetish" ["artificiosa representación de la femeneidad, a la que no le son ajenas las turbadoras turgencias del fetiche"] (10).

9   For more on the links between the *loca*, the *travesti*, class, and forms of colonialism, see Pedro Lemebel's chronicles "La loca del carrito" (2015), "Solos en la madrugada" (2015), and "La historia de Margarito" (2015), or "La esquina es mi corazón" (2018), among others.

10 The use of the house in *Casa Roshell* also establishes a dialogue with Chilean literary tradition, which either links the house with domesticity and femininity (Carreño 2009, 56–60) or with the brothel (Cánovas 2003, 13–37). Roshell's club represents something else: walls that give safety, spaces that are not mappable, and a shelter that seems to multiply, deconstructing the several fictions of identity related to the image of the house.

11 Nicolás Videla also presented a film in 2017 about a transgender character, titled *El diablo es magnifico / The Devil is Magnificent*.

12 This discussion appears in Perlongher's text about what he calls "the homosexual ghetto." The interesting part of his observations is that this ghetto is in a contiguous relation to other marginal codes or territories. And the consequence is that it modifies not only the landscape [paisaje], but also the relational passages [pasajes]: "A fluid hyperterritorialization, in constant movement, where the diverse inhabitants distribute and negotiate their schedules and zones of influences" ["Especie de hiperterritorialización fluyente, en permanente movimiento, donde las diversas poblaciones distribuyen y negocian sus itinerarios y sus zonas de influencia"] (1993, 14).

13 This monologic gaze is exactly what we see in Ripstein's *El lugar sin límites*. On the one hand, in the scene where Japonesa has sex (and makes a deal) with Manuela to win a bet she has made with don Alejo, the sexual intercourse subtly reminds us of matrimony: in the end, not only do they get a house with the blessing of don Alejo but also a daughter is born from their "performed" lovemaking. This is the same gaze that later frames Manuela's cadaver.

14 bell hooks theorizes the gaze of the dominated, a looking back that is a site of resistance. She writes: "subordinates in relations of power learn experientially that there is a critical gaze, one that 'looks' to document, one that is oppositional. In resistance struggles, the power of the dominated to assert agency by claiming and cultivating 'awareness' politicizes 'looking' relations—one learns to look a certain way to resist" (2009, 255).

15 The forensic gaze has been investigated in relation to the surge of crime fiction and TV shows that use forensics to solve a crime, with its origins in Edgar Allan Poe's stories and the scientific practice of dissecting and classifying bodies. Implying that there is a readability to the cadavers, the dissected and exhibited bodies acquire an iconic immobility that may be linked with fetishistic scopophilia. These ideas have been useful for studying accounts of femicides in Latin American literature. See, for example, Close (2018), Pierson (2010), and Peláez (2014).

16 I take these words from a description made in Carlos Motta's *Gender Talents (2015)*, a multimedia work described as follows: "portraits of trans and intersex activists who thoughtfully perform gender as a personal, social, and political opportunity rather than as a social condemnation."

WORKS CITED

Cabello, Cristeva. 2015. *Patrimonio sexual: Crónica de un circo transformista para una arqueología de la disidencia sexual*. Santiago: Trío Editorial.

Cánovas, Rodrigo. 2003. *Sexualidad y cultura en la novela hispanoamericana: La alegoría del prostíbulo*. Santiago: Lom.

Carreño, Rubí. 2007. *Leche amarga: Violencia y erotismo en la narrativa chilena del siglo XX (Bombal, Brunet, Donoso, Eltit)*. Santiago: Cuarto Propio.
Casa Roshell. 2017. Directed by Camila José Donoso. Ciudad de México, México: Tonalá Lab.
Close, Glen. 2018. *Female Corpses in Fiction: A Transatlantic Perspective*. New York: Palgrave McMillan.
Deleuze, Gilles. 1986. *Cinema 1. The Movement-Imagen*. Translated by Hugh Tomlison and Barbara Habberjam. London: Continuum.
Derrida, Jacques. 1987. *The Truth in Painting*. Chicago: University of Chicago Press.
Díaz, Jorge. 2015. "Cuerpos para odiar: deseos disidentes para una trans-escena." *El desconcierto*, August 1. http://www.eldesconcierto.cl/2015/08/01/cuerpos-para-odiar-deseos-disidentes-para-una-trans-escena/.
Donoso, José. 1966. *El lugar sin límites*. México: Joaquín Mortiz.
El coraje del pueblo. 1971. Directed by Jorge Sanjinés. La Paz, Bolivia: Grupo Ukamau.
El lugar sin límites. 1978. Directed by Arturo Ripstein, written by José Donoso. México: Conacite dos.
Friedberg, Anne. 2006. *The Virtual Window: From Alberti to Microsoft*. Cambridge: MIT Press.
Grant, Catherine. 2002. "La función de 'los autores': La adaptación cinematográfica transnacional de *El lugar sin límites*." *Revista Iberoamericana*, 68, no. 199 (April–June): 253–68.
Grosz, Elizabeth. 2002. *Architecture from the Outside*. Cambridge: MIT Press.
Halberstam, Jack. 2018. *Trans*: A Quick and Quirky Guide of Gender Variability*. Berkeley: University of California Press.
hooks, bell. (1996) 2009. "The Oppositional Gaze: Black Female Spectators." In *Reel to Real: Sex and Class in the Movies*, 253–74. New York: Routledge.
Lemebel, Pedro. (1998) 2015. *De perlas y cicatrices*. Santiago: Seix Barral.
———. (1995) 2018. *La esquina es mi corazón*. Santiago: Seix Barral.
Levine, Susan Jill. 2000. *Manuel Puig and The Spider Woman: His Life and Fictions*. London: Faber and Faber.
Molloy, Sylvia. 2012. "Las políticas de la pose." In *Poses de fin de siglo: Desbordes del género en la modernidad*, 41–45. Buenos Aires: Eterna Cadencia.
Motta, Carlos. 2015. "Gender Talents." *Carlos Motta, Artist*. https://carlosmotta.com/project/gender-talents-2013-in-progress/.
Mulvey, Laura. 1990. "Visual Pleasure and Narrative Cinema." In *Issues in Feminist Film Criticism*, edited by Patricia Erens, 28–40. Bloomington: Indiana University Press.
Muñoz, José Esteban. 1999. *Disidentifications: Queers of Color and the Performance of Politics*. Minneapolis: University of Minnesota Press.
———. 2009. *Cruising Utopia: The Then and There of Queer Futurity*. New York: NYU Press.

Naomi Campbel. 2013. Directed by Camila José Donoso and Nicolás Videla. Santiago: Cusicanqui Films.

Narboni, Jean, and Jacques Rivette. 1986. "An interview with Marguerite Duras by Jacques Rivette and Jean Narboni." In *Destroy She Said*, by Marguerite Duras, translated by Helen Lane Cumberford, 91–132. New York: Grove Press.

Orellana, Naomi. 2017. "Casa Roshell: Transficción filmada en club travesti mexicano." *El Mostrador*, November 10. https://www.elmostrador.cl/cultura/2017/11/10/casa-roshell-transficcion-filmada-en-club-travesti-mexicano/.

Peláez, Sol. 2014. "Counting Violence: Roberto Bolaño and *2666*." *Chasqui* 43 (2): 30–47.

Perlongher. Néstor. 1993. *La prostitución masculina*. Buenos Aires: Ediciones de La Urraca.

Pierson, David. 2010. "Evidential Bodies: The Forensic and Abject Gazes in C.S.I.: Crime Scene Investigation." *Journal of Communication Inquiry* 34 (2): 184–203.

Ríos, Mónica Ramón. 2018. "Una mujer con adjetivo." *La Tempestad*, March 2 https://www.latempestad.mx/mujer-fantastica-lelio/.

Rivera Garza, Cristina. 2018. "Disappropriation for Beginners." In *Literaturas y Feminismo*, edited by Mónica Ríos. Santiago: Sangría Editora.

Shaviro. Steven. 2010. *Post-Cinematic Affect*. Ropley: O-Books.

Una mujer fantástica. 2017. Directed by Sebastián Lelio. Santiago: Fábula.

Yawar Mallku. 1969. Directed by Jorge Sanjinés. Bolivia: Grupo Ukamau.

10

THE INTERNATIONAL (UN)INTELLIGIBILITY OF CHILEAN TRANS* FILM

Carl Fischer

CHILEAN SEXUAL DISSIDENCE AS GLOBAL DISTINCTION?

Over the past fifty years, being a "model" country in the world—whether for the rigors of its neoliberal system or its status as the first-ever Marxist democracy—has been key to Chile's political and economic conception of itself. Moreover, its "model" economy has been personified in such a way that heterosexual men are often figured as the ideal protagonists of that economy. This was key to the dictatorship's entire rhetoric, as Robert Neustadt (1995) has pointed out: "Nuclear families were to support the great 'national family,' *la patria*, as directed by Pinochet, the father figure purportedly serving the will of God. The *discurso pinochetista* deployed the image of the ideal woman within the symbolism of the Catholic church, the Madonna, in order to (re)produce *la patria*" (220).[1] This "national family," and the men at the head of it, have been key elements of the discourse used by official Chile to position itself in the world.[2]

At the same time, however, Chile has a long tradition of queer and trans*[3] cultural production. This canon of sorts stretches from José Donoso's memorable character La Manuela in the 1966 novella (and 1978 film, by Arturo Ripstein) *El lugar sin límites / Hell Has No Limits*, to Carlos Leppe's performance art in the 1970s and '80s, to the *travestis* photographed by Paz Errázuriz in her series *La manzana de Adán / Adam's Apple* (1984). It would also have to include the performance art/choreography of Francisco Coppello, the "art actions" of Las Yeguas del Apocalipsis and Pedro Lemebel in the late 1980s, and the Chilean-German performance artist Lorenza Böttner, who—having no arms—painted and sculpted with her feet and mouth;[4] Juan Domingo Dávila's 1994 painting of Simón Bolívar in drag is also an important political intervention that made use of trans* aesthetics. A remarkable number of trans* films have come out of Chile very recently, too, in a very short span of time, including Sebastián Lelio's 2017 film *Una mujer fantástica / A Fantastic Woman*, which won an Oscar in 2018 for Best Foreign Film. The country's reputation in the world for sexually transgressive art, then, from the "boom" in Latin American literature during the sixties to the international film festival circuit of today, is another one of the primary ways in which Chilean culture has become internationally visible. The fact that Chile is *also* known around the world for its conservative, neoliberal economic structures often serves to heighten the comparative transgressiveness of its queer art and film, whose ability to "break away" from the history of authoritarianism that has sought to contain them becomes a key part of their cachet abroad.[5] Although, as Jack Halberstam (2018) points out, trans* bodies on film have "represented a condition of radical instability against which other gendered identities appeared legible, knowable, and natural" (96), they can also serve as clear signifiers that make trans* struggles intelligible across borders, cultures, and languages.

In what follows, I will explore Chilean films about trans* people in relation to how Chilean culture has been officially and unofficially promoted on the global stage. To do so, I will investigate the aesthetics and the circumstances of production and distribution of two recent Chilean trans* films: *Una mujer fantástica*, which made major incursions in the international art house circuit, arguably because it was made in explicit dialogue with liberal ideas around the world about what it means to be trans* and how trans* identities are telegraphed aesthetically; and Camila José Donoso and Nicolás Videla's *Naomi Campbel* (2013), whose more local (indeed, what Pedro Lemebel called "folkloric"[6]) representations of trans* life in Chile, tied to radical political movements, gained much less notoriety abroad. I will argue that internationally intelligible representations of trans* identities and political claims make for a more globally palatable, but also less pluralistic, international image of the trans* experience in Chile; by the same token, I will argue that a more pluralistic, historically grounded image of the trans* experience in Chile is unfortunately less globally palatable. These intersecting approaches to seeing and being seen—internationally and gender-wise—are at the heart of my analysis here.

CONTEXTUALIZING TRANS* POLITICS IN CHILEAN FILM

Since the end of the dictatorship, Chile has opened up considerably, with hard-won advances in civil liberties, gender equality, and political freedom. These advances have included the right to divorce (illegal until 2004), the abolition of the legal distinction between the rights of children born within and outside of marriage (in 1998), and the right to civil partnerships for same-sex couples (approved in 2015). They have also included a number of amendments that gradually abolished the "authoritarian enclaves" within the dictatorship-era constitution, that is, anti-democratic protections of Pinochet's interests built into the document when it was first promulgated in 1980. The election of a woman, Michelle Bachelet, to the presidency of the country for two terms, in 2006 and again in 2014, is yet another testament to Chile's opening, and indeed has become yet another facet of the argument that the country has made to figure itself as exceptional within Latin America and even the world.

Struggles for the rights of sexual minorities in Chile, particularly trans* people, are ongoing. Trans* identity became a major wedge issue in Chile's presidential elections in December 2017, given a bill under discussion in congress that would allow Chileans to legally change their sex. At a debate, then–presidential candidate Sebastián Piñera compared gender identity with clothing: "I don't agree with minors changing their sex with almost no bureaucratic hassle. Gender can't be like a shirt that you can change from one day to the next. Many cases of gender dysphoria get corrected with age" ["no estoy de acuerdo con que los menores puedan cambiar su sexo casi sin ningún trámite. El género no puede ser como una camisa que uno se cambia todos los días. Muchos casos de disforia de género se corrigen con la edad"] ("Debate" 2017).[7] Piñera's dismissal of the malleability of gender met with swift critique. Among others, Daniela Vega, the trans* star of *Una mujer fantástica*, publicly responded using the same terminology of "correction" employed by Piñera: "I want to tell you that I was a trans girl, and here I am, uncorrectable and happy. I invite the new president of the republic to correct the laws in order to protect the wealth of our people, namely, their diversity" ["Yo les quiero decir que fui una niña trans y aquí estoy, incorrectible y feliz. Yo invito al nuevo Presidente de la República a corregir leyes para resguardar la riqueza de nuestro pueblo que es su diversidad"] ("Daniela Vega" 2017). The fact that one of the responses to Piñera that achieved the greatest resonance came from a trans* film actress, who later on garnered international prominence as an Oscar presenter and actress in several multinational film and television projects, serves to highlight the importance of film for how domestic issues related to trans* people intersect with Chile's economic, political, and cultural projection of itself in the world.

Although the so-called Gender Identity Law was finally passed in late 2018, making it possible for Chileans to change their sex with a minimum of bureaucratic hassle, the long debate about trans* identity that preceded the law's passing is reflected in the large quantity of trans* films that have recently come out in Chile. These have included Francisco Aguilar's *Claudia tocada por la luna / Claudia Touched by the Moon* (2018); Constanza Gallardo's *En tránsito / In Transit*, Nicolás Videla's *El diablo es magnífico / The Devil is Magnificent*, and Camila José Donoso's *Casa Roshell*, all from 2017; Lorena Giachino's 2013 documentary *El gran circo pobre de Timoteo / Timoteo's Fabulous Ragged Circus*, about a relatively well-known circus with trans* characters; and 2008's *Empaná de pino / Meat Empanada*, directed by Wincy Oyarce and starring the late, great trans* personality Hija de Perra.

Chilean film industry insiders have ably talked up the transgressive aspects of how the country's queer and trans* cultural production coexists alongside an often-stifling conservatism, in order to promote the groundbreaking aspects of the country's filmmakers' work. One place in which this promotion has explicitly taken place is through CinemaChile, a public-private agency responsible for the promotion of Chilean audiovisual production (film, virtual reality, and television series) around the world. Created in 2009 by the Chilean Film and Television Producer's Union (APCT) and ProChile, a division of the country's foreign ministry devoted to promoting tourism, exports, and foreign investment opportunities, CinemaChile has aggressively worked to connect Chilean filmmakers to the international film festival circuit and other aspects of the industry at large. They have done this by attending international festivals, particularly those deemed to be "Class A"; conducting studies on international audiences; interfacing with the press; and providing opportunities for Chilean filmmakers to network with buyers, producers, programmers, and distributors.[8]

In a 2018 interview apropos of Chile's presence at Spain's prestigious San Sebastián International Film Festival, Elisa Leiva, CinemaChile's head of international relations, spoke specifically about the appeal of queer Chilean cinema as a form of political resistance to the heteronormativity of its national context: "The extensive production of LGBT film in recent years is a reaction to a homophobic, sexist, Catholic society. So these films and the issues they explore have to do with resisting a society that has ostracized and harmed LGBT people for a long time" ["En torno al cine LGBT la amplia producción de estos últimos años surge como reacción a una sociedad homofóbica, machista, católica. Entonces este cine y la exploración en esta tematica está en la resistencia de una sociedad que ha invisibilizado por mucho tiempo y ha violentado a personas LGBT"] ("CinemaChile" 2018).[9] This indicates that the extent to which Chilean films are said to transgress the hetero- and cis-normative boundaries of their society can be used as a marketing strategy for those films. Similarly, CinemaChile's executive director, Constanza Aravena, comments in the same interview that "We are a small country but with a lot of productions. The domestic market is miniscule, [and] no film could sustain itself only by showing in Chile. All independent *auteur* cinema thus turns to the global circuit. So our market is worldwide" ["Somos un país pequeño pero con una producción muy grande. El mercado doméstico es enano, no hay una producción que pueda subsistir sólo [*sic*] estrenándose en Chile. Todo el cine independiente autoral se vuelca en el circuito mundial. Así que nuestro mercado es global"] ("CinemaChile" 2018). This marketing strategy is thus necessarily a global one.

Is it possible, though, for Chilean trans* films to position themselves in the global film market while also making meaningful gestures to the radical archive of leftist, feminist, queer, and trans* cultural production that has emerged in the country over the years? As Antoine Damiens (2018) shows in the North American and European context, this is a struggle that many queer and trans* films have had, particularly when seeking out international distribution. Such films often have to choose between positioning themselves as "LGBTQ" and positioning themselves for general audiences; it is difficult to achieve both. In this sense, Damiens talks about the concept of "queer relay," that is, using "ambivalent communication [that] alternately borrowed from . . . and rejected . . . the criteria of legitimacy associated with the queer field" (35). Damiens leans on the theories of Pierre Bourdieu to examine the marketing strategies for LGBTQ films that seek to appeal to queer- and trans*-friendly audiences while also using language broad and "ambivalent" enough to not limit the films' "value" to wider, straight audiences.[10]

In Chilean trans* films, similar choices get made, at the levels of both production and distribution. Although the tradition of trans* and queer aesthetics in Chilean art and literature—one that often includes a democratizing bent, given that it has come about amidst a long tradition of antiauthoritarian struggle[11]—is a lens through which foreigners can understand the country's national culture, the deep history behind this is often too complex to telegraph in detail within one feature film. Moreover, to do so might further limit the appeal of the film to broader audiences—a formidable challenge for any film taking sexual dissidence as a central theme. Therefore, the fact that struggles in Chile for trans* liberation are deeply and historically rooted in communities of activists and dissidents sometimes falls by the wayside, leading to a much more moderate, and even oversimplified, political representation of these struggles. Given that film festivals "'have a vested interest in sustaining the discourse of autonomous art, because their position of power depends on it' (2014: 78), yet they are deeply invested in fostering economic growth (81)" (Damiens 2018, 30–31, quoting Marijke de Valck), films' success on the global art house cinema circuit, which functions symbiotically with film festivals, depends on rendering political issues that are local to Chile easily intelligible to foreigners. For Chilean trans* films, this sometimes means moderating and simplifying certain political stances.

While it is generally true, as Macarena Gómez-Barris (2018) argues, that queer and trans* "struggles for recognition can be articulated against the histories of state disappearance" (66) in Chile and elsewhere, and that that articulation can be done globally, some of those struggles are more intelligible to foreign audiences than others. When films like *Una mujer fantástica* take more moderate political stances regarding trans* people—less grounded in the Chilean tradition of trans* cultural production and more oriented toward broader, liberal discourses of human rights—are these necessary tactics for making trans* representation more accessible to broader audiences? Or do they simply water down attempts at political resistance? Why have Chilean films like *Naomi Campbel*, which offers a more historically rigorous, politically radical, and community-based approach to trans* representation, had relatively less international success and visibility?

FANTASTIC WOMEN, INTELLIGIBLE STRUGGLES?

In this section, I will offer close readings of several moments in these two films, in order to examine the relationships between their respective political stances and the aesthetics of their representations of trans* people. I argue that the different ways in which the trans* subjects on-screen take stances vis-à-vis Chilean politics and their own identities directly correlate with how palatable the films' subject matter can be rendered for international art house audiences.

Una mujer fantástica tells the story of Marina, a trans* woman played by Vega, whose partner Orlando dies suddenly toward the beginning of the film. The ensuing narrative arc follows Marina's attempts to mourn Orlando, despite the objections of his conservative, upper-class family to her presence. Because Marina is with Orlando when he dies, she becomes subject to unwanted scrutiny from the police as they investigate his death; this gives the film an opening to critique the various (and often clumsy) biopolitical attempts by the Chilean state to surveil, classify, and silence her. The film thus centers on a liberal discourse of human rights: the right to mourn a loved one, and the right to receive humane treatment, or at least due process, from the police.

Marina seems like a character conscientiously constructed to maximize her relatability to liberal, compassionate art house audiences around the world. Indeed, *Una mujer fantástica* fits within many of the criteria of what Tamara Falicov (2016) has categorized as "film festival films," particularly its "aesthetic and narrative conventions [intended] for an educated audience and . . . a higher socioeconomic class stratum" (213). These conventions have two implications for this film. They maximize the relatability of otherwise "foreign" characters and settings, and they minimize the ideological or ethical estrangement that straight audiences might feel toward trans* or queer characters or themes, following Damiens's idea of "queer relay." This leads to a depoliticization of what it means to be trans* in the film—a level of political "detachment" reminiscent of the earlier films of the *Novísimo* Generation of Chilean filmmakers, including Lelio himself.[12] Marina exhibits no radical political beliefs, and has no visible attachment to a community of other trans* people. She has had access to the means to physically present herself as less ambiguously female, she is white, and she has a reliable, albeit small, network of social and familial support. In this sense, Marina's movements through upper-middle-class Chile are meant to downplay her difference, or marginality, and accentuate her similarities to the upper-middle-class audiences around the world that tend to see films like Lelio's. Like several other critics,[13] Ivana Peric (2018) has written about this flattening of particularity and "annulment" of difference in *Una mujer fantástica*, stating that "Lelio constructs an atemporal drama, potentially situated anywhere in the world, whose only variation is the supposed marginal condition of the protagonist—who, in any case, finds herself diluted in a story whose structure is like any other" ["Lelio construye un drama atemporal y potencialmente situado en cualquier parte del mundo cuya única variación es la supuesta condición marginal que padece la protagonista que sin embargo se diluye en una historia cuya estructura es la de cualquier otra"].

Peric's emphasis on the film's "atemporal" nature is key here, in that she implies that a more "temporally" oriented film might politicize the trans* experience more radically than *Una mujer fantástica* does. It is precisely on time that Halberstam has concentrated in his extensive writing about the political possibilities of queer and trans* films and other forms of representation. Given that such films can potentially call into question what he calls "predictable life narratives," that is, "governmental logics of rule [that] make possible everything from inheritance claims to insurance algorithms" (2018, 86), an examination of how temporality works in *Una mujer fantástica* is perhaps the best way to get at how it does its best to maximize—not question—the predictability and accessibility to broad audiences of Marina's "life narrative."

Peric's take on the film's (a)temporality seems to suggest that if it were situated more clearly in time—making more explicit references to the current situation of Chilean trans* people—it would have more political value. In this case, however, the temporalities of *Una mujer fantástica* are extremely predictable: the film shapes Marina's trajectory throughout the film into a classical, melodramatic narrative arc. The main narrative of the film is about Marina's stoicism in the face of the adversities and indignities that she has to face. For example, when Marina is subjected to a forensic police technician who has to photograph her naked body, for reasons that boil down to the fact that one particular investigator wants to humiliate her, she silently submits (Figure 25). This tactic of passive acquiescence cements her position as victim, and establishes a simple, Manichean conflict between her and an uncomprehending state. In this way, when Marina triumphantly exhibits her talent as an opera singer in the film's final, uplifting scene—here she does express herself, as Mónica Ríos (2018) points out—the audience is left with the idea that she has found some kind of transcendent redemption. Here, the historical and political nuances of how struggles for trans* rights in Chile have taken place are occluded by the more straight/forward temporalities of melodrama.

Figure 25. Marina silently submits to a forensic police technician who photographs her naked body, in *Una mujer fantástica / A Fantastic Woman* (Sebastián Lelio, 2017).

The "dilution" of trans* politics in *Una mujer fantástica*, to use Peric's (2018) term, is coupled with a dilution of Chilean politics as well; the obvious gestures made in the film to the legacy of the dictatorship also work to make it easily digestible for "educated" foreign audiences, whose primary knowledge of Chile might be related to Pinochet. For example, as Gómez-Barris discusses, when Marina is barred from attending Orlando's funeral by his "legitimate" family, it "repeats the histories of female relatives of the disappeared who by being in relation to political dissidents were themselves cast as abject" (Gómez-Barris 2018, 63). But this and other gestures to Chilean political history in the film[14] are rather superficial, limiting themselves to easily recognizable references to the dictatorship; as Ríos points out, Marina's antagonists are "mostly schematic characters, and pretty stupid ones at that" ["personajes más bien esquemáticos y, la verdad, bastante estúpidos"]. Possible alliances between Marina and other independent women in the film—such as her boss, who treats her primarily with suspicion, or even her sister—are left unexplored, despite the possibilities currently signaled by affective and activist coalitions between feminists and trans* people in Chile (and around the world). No connections are drawn on-screen between Marina's struggles and the struggles for recognition of other trans* people in Chile. For that matter, no connections are drawn between denials by the state of Marina's bodily autonomy and the systematic denials of Chilean women's control over their own bodies—particularly in the form of the right to abortion, which was outlawed by the dictatorship and finally legalized under narrow circumstances in 2017, the year *Una mujer fantástica* premiered. Rather than exploring more nuanced connections between politics today and the dictatorial past, thereby challenging the preconceived notions of viewers—whether by estranging straight audiences' notions of temporality or by exploring more subtle connections between the dictatorship and trans* oppression—the film seems to confirm them. Viewers come away from the film patting themselves on the back, safe in their convictions that trans* people *are* just like them, and feeling compassion for Marina's struggles against a nebulous, unproblematic concept of dictatorship-era patriarchy.

The film's redemptive treatment of Marina and her trajectory is thus nothing short of (self-) righteous. This is to the film's detriment, in the opinion of Anthony Lane (2018): "In ethical terms, *A Fantastic Woman* is impeccable, corralling us in outrage at an intolerant society. . . . Lelio's own stance, in short, could not be clearer; dramatically, though, it has a flattening effect" (60). Whether this flatness was in fact the cause of the film's success is not clear, but it certainly correlates with it: *Una mujer fantástica* had commercial releases in at least thirty-five countries. In addition to its Oscar, it won a number of film festival awards, including the Berlin International Film Festival's Special Jury Prize and the Film Independent Spirit Awards' Best International Film Award. Having garnered mainstream acclaim around the world, the film has emphasized the long-standing importance of trans* people for internationally circulating Chilean cultural production. However, it has done so despite, or perhaps because of, its refusal to pose too much of a political challenge to its viewers.

Donoso and Videla's *Naomi Campbel*, meanwhile, tells the story of Yermén, a trans* woman looking for a way to pay for gender confirmation surgery. Narrated in loosely autobiographical, partially interchangeable episodes, the film is much more challenging to the conventionally linear life narratives that straight and cisgender viewers might be more familiar with. Unlike *Una mujer fantástica*, in which the camera maintains its admiring gaze on Marina at all times, *Naomi Campbel* is structured around the ways in which viewers see *alongside* Yermén. These multiple viewpoints give viewers access to a multitude of gazes that they otherwise might not have and divert their gaze away from trans* people as objects. For Halberstam, this is another key aspect of trans* representation, closely related to how trans* people complicate temporality: "different life narratives" of queer and trans* temporality mean alternative ways of being in relation to others, and new practices of occupying space. For example . . . we might privilege friendship networks over extended families when assessing the structures of intimacy that sustain queer lives, and we might also think about transgenderism in particular as not simply a contrapuntal relationship between bodily form and content but as an altered relation to seeing and being seen. (2018, 87)

In this sense, what Yermén sees, and what viewers see, is tied to the ways in which the time line of her life diverges from the predictable timetables of cisgender life. For example, in scenes related to Yermén's job as a tarot card reader for a pay-per-minute phone service, the viewer sees the esoteric reach of her vision into the future. Yermén, instead of being the object of others' gaze (particularly since she works over the phone and not in person), becomes an arbiter, and indeed an authority, for her callers. Her eye becomes a lens that disorders and reinterprets her interlocutors' expectations. Indeed, Yermén's eye literally interrupts viewers' gaze at four points throughout the film, when she takes up the camera herself, documenting and commenting upon the men of her peripheral Santiago neighborhood

Figure 26. Yermén controlling the camera herself, commenting upon the men of her peripheral Santiago neighborhood through voice-over, in *Naomi Campbel* (Camila José Donoso and Nicolás Videla, 2013).

through voice-over (Figure 26). By removing herself as the object of the gaze, Yermén disrupts the order of a narrative time line otherwise structured around her story.

In one pivotal scene, in which Yermén auditions for a reality show that might pay for her gender confirmation surgery, we see how she is able to disrupt preconceived notions about her. This disruption primarily takes place in terms of temporality: she corrects the preconceived notions of the producer who interviews her about her plans for the future. Yermén looks straight into the camera in the office of the show's producers, and comes to control the terms of the conversation, deciding what to reveal and resisting the clichés and narrative arcs that reality TV often tries to impose on its subjects:

> **Interviewer:** Yermén, I imagine that this operation will be very important in your life, *going forward*. How do you imagine your life as a woman?
> **Yermén:** The thing is, I'm already a woman.
>
> **Interviewer:** Ok, so why do you want to get an operation, then?
> **Yermén:** To reinvent myself, to give myself a gift, to look more beautiful.
>
> **Interviewer:** Do you have problems in your intimate life, your love life?
> **Yermén:** Eh, no.
>
> **Interviewer:** No?
> **Yermén:** No.
>
> **Interviewer:** So why do you want to get an operation?
> **Yermén:** Well, because of the issue of genitals, because of a discordance that I see. When I have an erection, it's very painful. After that, when there's an ejaculation, like what happens to men, I feel guilty, I get a feeling like I lost something, or dropped something.
>
> **Interviewer:** Is that related to the hormones that you take?
> **Yermén:** Yes, it could maybe be the hormonal process, the hormone therapy. But I'm pretty careful about that.

Interviewer: Eh, Yermén—

Yermén: —And, *after that* I have some disorders, not psychological ones but more biological. Like, with an ejaculation, which I don't like, my breasts get smaller, and afterwards I have to spend an entire week fixing them by taking estrogen.

Interviewer: Ok, so without a doubt, the operation can help you quite a bit, then. What would you do *after* the operation? How do you think the operation would help you?

Yermén: I'd stop being a tarot reader, I'd leave the neighborhood, I'd quit reading cards, I'd start to enjoy the post-op process, because I wouldn't think about it from the perspective of pain or guilt; I'd think about it as a time where I reinvented myself, where I gave myself a present, where I feel more beautiful. And I'd leave the neighborhood, so that—excuse the expression—the people that live there won't yell at me, saying things like "look, the faggot got himself a pussy," and I wouldn't stay in the same circle. I'd completely reinvent myself.

[**Entrevistador:** Yermén, me imagino que esta operación puede ser muy importante en tu vida, *en el futuro*. ¿Cómo te imaginas tu vida, siendo mujer?

Yermén: Es que yo ya soy mujer.

Entrevistador: Entonces ¿para qué te quieres operar?

Yermén: Para darme un regalo, para reinventarme, verme más bonita.

Entrevistador: ¿Tú tienes problemas en tu vida íntima, tu vida afectiva?

Yermén: Eh, no.

Entrevistador: ¿No?

Yermén: No.

Entrevistador: Entonces ¿por qué te quieres operar?

Yermén: Ah, por un tema genital, por las discordancias que yo veo, porque cuando tengo una erección, me genera mucho dolor. Posterior a eso, cuando hay una eyaculación, como les pasa a los hombres, eso a mí me provoca un sentimiento de culpa, un sentimiento como que perdí algo, como que se me cayó algo.

Entrevistador: ¿Eso tiene que ver con las hormonas que tú tomas?
Yermén: Sí, puede ser a lo mejor el proceso hormonal, la terapia hormonal. Pero en eso yo voy con bastante cuidado.

Entrevistador: Eh, Yermén—
Yermén:—Además, *posterior a eso* yo igual tengo ciertos trastornos, que no son psíquicos, son biológicos, por ejemplo, con una eyaculación, cosa que no me gusta, se me achican los pechos, y tengo que estar como una semana entera después renovándolos con el consumo de estrógeno.

Entrevistador: Ya, bueno, sin duda la operación te puede ayudar bastante, entonces. Tú ¿qué harías *después* de la operación? ¿Cómo crees que te ayudaría la operación?
Yermén: Dejaría de ser tarotista, me iría de la población, no usaría más las cartas, empezaría a disfrutar el proceso pos-operatorio, porque no lo asumiría de repente tanto desde el dolor o desde la culpa, lo asumiría desde la visión de que me reinventé, de que me di un regalo, de que me siento más bonita, y me iría de la población para que—perdóname la expresión—la gente que vive ahí no me grite después, "mira, el maricón se hizo un choro," y siga siendo todo parte del mismo círculo. Me reinventaría completamente.] (*Naomi Campbel*, emphases added).

Yermén challenges the assumptions about temporality made by her cisgender male interviewer. Not only is she *already* a woman (rather than trying to become one); she insists on the gender confirmation surgery not as a clear "before-and-after"–type break in her identity but rather as plastic surgery similar to any other aesthetic procedure, such as a breast enlargement. The operation is not a way for the show to "help her"; it becomes a way for her to reinvent *herself*: she is hardly a helpless victim in the process. By disrupting the chronological terms that her interlocutor seeks to impose on her—with all the assumptions about her sex life they entail—Yermén takes control of the terms of her own representation. The operation may not necessarily be a happy ending for her, in the narrative terms that her interlocutor might be imagining, but it would have positive consequences.

Meanwhile, by taking a more radical stance vis-à-vis Chilean politics—albeit one less immediately intelligible to non-Chileans—*Naomi Campbel* draws connections between Yermén's story and those of other trans* people in Chile, but also those of other marginalized populations in the country. First of all, Yermén is marked as a political activist: Paula Yermén Dinamarca, the trans* actress who plays her, is a well-known activist in Chile.[15] In the film, Yermén is a resident of La Victoria, a peripheral Santiago neighborhood known for its historical opposition to the Pinochet dictatorship. La Victoria is home to a network of activists who appear in the film as themselves and explicitly link their past struggles against the dictatorship to their friendship with Yermén. When Yermén attends a birthday party for Lucha, one of these activists, Lucha gives a speech to this effect: "I love you all very much, I've known you all for a long time, we all went through the same things, and so, we have to . . ." When she trails off, another man picks up the thread: "we have to live healthily, calmly, without hurting each other, with happiness and friendship." "Yes," Lucha continues, "because we're in a country that's a bit freer now." ["Yo los quiero mucho, los conozco hace muchos años, todos vivimos lo mismo, y bueno, hay que . . ." "Hay que vivir la vida de manera sana, tranquilos, sin agredimientos, con pura alegría y amistad." "Ahora sí, porque estamos en un país que es un poquito más libre."] However, the context behind the activism of these people would be lost on viewers unfamiliar with the details of Chile's transition to democracy.[16] *Naomi Campbel* also draws a parallel between Yermén's militant politics and those of its directors: Camila José Donoso is a militant of CUDS, an organization of activists focused on sexual dissidence.[17] In this sense, the film points to a rich tapestry of advocacy and activism on behalf of sexual minorities in Chile—a network with deep ties to pro-democracy activism. Most of this would be lost to general audiences, even art house audiences casually familiar with Chilean politics.

The title of the film comes from the assumed name of an Afro-Colombian woman that Yermén meets at the reality show audition. Naomi Campbel is hoping the show will pay for plastic surgery to look more like the supermodel of the same name. The friendship that the film portrays between these two marginalized women in Chile (Figure 27) is a way of drawing

Figure 27. The friendship between Naomi Campbel and Yermén Dinamarca is a way of drawing parallels between Yermén's story and those of other vulnerable people in the country, in *Naomi Campbel* (Camila José Donoso and Nicolás Videla, 2013).

parallels between Yermén's story and those of other vulnerable people in the country, thereby radically broadening the kinds of subjects portrayed in Chilean popular culture. Moreover, it asks complex questions about the status of Chile's growing immigrant population—many of whom, particularly those who are more dark skinned, experience forms of discrimination similar to those experienced by trans* people. Viewers from abroad, possibly unfamiliar with the most recent influx of Haitian, Venezuelan, and Colombian immigrants to Chile, might not be able to properly contextualize the implications of the interactions between Yermén and Naomi.

Despite a limited commercial domestic release in 2015 and appearances in a few international film festivals, *Naomi Campbel* received much less international attention than *Una mujer fantástica* did. Although its much more nuanced approach to trans* politics and their place in the complex tapestry of Chile's postdictatorial present is not necessarily the reason it was much less seen by foreign audiences, this may have played a role. Moreover, several other factors of its distribution complicated its viewership abroad. It was produced by a Chilean university (the Universidad Mayor) rather than a formal production company. Also, the question remains as to whether its appearance in film festivals less oriented toward LGBTQ issues[18] may have affected its viewership. Hope remains that Donoso and Videla's future film endeavors, particularly those structured around queer and trans* topics, will be more successful in their attempts at "queer relay," so as to reach the audiences that might be most interested in, and engaged with, the subject matter of their films.

CONCLUSION

Is it possible, then, for a film to challenge certain narratives inherent to Chilean national(ist) thinking—and to cisgender, straight life—while also being central to the recognition and success of Chilean cultural production abroad? Based on these two case studies, the answer would appear to be no. The success of *Una mujer fantástica* correlates with the fact that its approach to trans* life confirms, rather than challenges, its viewers' preconceived notions about Chile and its trans* people. Meanwhile, the critical challenges to these notions that *Naomi Campbel* forces its viewers to face render many aspects of its politics largely unintelligible to broad audiences, and the details of its distribution bear out a smaller viewership. In this sense, it remains an unanswered question whether Chile's imagined status as a "model" abroad is due to, or despite, its extensive archive of trans* and queer cultural production, particularly film. The same goes for whether the international fame of that trans* and queer cultural production is due to, or despite, the heterosexist and cisgenderist underpinnings of Chile's claims to exceptionalism.

NOTES

1 For a broader discussion of the linkage between politics and reproductive heterosexuality, see Edelman (2004).

2 See Fischer (2016) for more information about this point.

3 The idea of inserting an asterisk (*) after the word "trans" is meant to convey the capaciousness of the term, to include transgender, transsexual, transitioning people, and other constituencies who may have different approaches to the meaning of trans*. See, on this point, Halberstam (2018): "the asterisk modifies the meaning of transitivity by refusing to situate transition in relation to a destination, a final form, a specific shape, or an established configuration of desire and identity. . . . it makes trans* people the authors of their own categorizations" (4).

4 Bolaño and Lemebel wrote about Lorenza Böttner, in *Estrella distante* (1996) and *Loco afán* (1996), respectively, and Böttner was the subject of a solo exhibition, curated by Paul B. Preciado, at the Virreina Centro de la Imagen in Barcelona and the Württembergischer Kunstverein in Stuttgart, in 2018 and 2019.

5   Although neoliberalism and authoritarianism are no longer explicitly connected in Chile, given that the country's economy currently functions in a democratic context, it is important to point out that the roots of Chile's current economic system lie in the Pinochet dictatorship. Tomás Moulián (2002) has explored many of the neoliberal continuities in Chile that connect its dictatorial past and its democratic present.

6   This term comes from Lemebel's chronicle "La noche de los visones" (roughly, "The Night of the Mink Coats"), which talks about a photo of a group of queer people right at the end of the Salvador Allende years who, for Lemebel, remain untouched by global gay culture, which he considers Eurocentric: "the *locas* [are] still twisted, still folkloric in their illegal mannerisms. It looks like an archaic frieze where the interference of the gay master narrative hadn't yet left its mark" ["las locas [están] aún torcidas, aún folclóricas en sus ademanes ilegales. Pareciera un friso arcaico donde la intromisión del patrón gay todavía no había puesto su marca"] (26, my translation). For a wonderful discussion of the challenges, and promise, of translating Lemebel's complex wordplay from Spanish into English, see Concilio (2016).

7   All translations from Spanish here are my own, unless otherwise noted.

8   For more information about how these networks are formed around the world, see the work of María Paz Peirano, both in this volume and also in texts such as "Film Mobilities and Circulation Practices in the Construction of Recent Chilean Cinema" (2018).

9   Many thanks to Elizabeth Ramírez Soto for bringing this interview to my attention.

10 One example Damiens uses to make his point is Céline Sciamma's 2011 film *Tomboy*, which was marketed to broad audiences in its native France—with critics "insisting on the cruelty of childhood and passage to adulthood and puberty"—whereas in the United States, marketers "highlighted its trans* undertones" (2018, 36).

11 The feminist writer Julieta Kirkwood was a pioneer in making this connection between struggles for gender equality and struggles for democracy. See her treatise *Ser política en Chile* (1986) for more information.

12 See the introduction to this volume for a more detailed account of the supposedly apolitical generation of Chilean filmmakers known as the *Novísimos*, a term originally coined by Ascanio Cavallo and Gonzalo Maza (2011). Many critics have focused on how the apolitical, inward-looking themes of many Chilean films are reflective of the rise of neoliberal individualism and of a turn away from the more militant, collective aesthetics of the past. A further indication of the detachment of the film from the communities it depicts is Lelio's insensitive (to say the least, considering the fact that he mentioned his

13. wife and children in many of the promotional interviews he did for *Una mujer fantástica*) comment that he himself is trans*, since he also changed his last name when he was younger—a right that trans* people are fighting for ("Sebastián Lelio" 2018).

14. Mónica Ríos, Pablo Solari, and Anthony Lane take similar positions about the "flatness" of *Una mujer fantástica*, critiquing its excessive attempts to be relatable to broad audiences.

15. Another example of a political bent in the film, as described by Gómez-Barris, is when members of Marina's partner's family grab her off the street and drive her around, harassing her: this "repeats the motif of the DINA, the secret police that throughout the 1970s snatched those believed to be political dissidents from the public sphere, taking them to torture and concentration camps" (2018, 64).

16. Indeed, Dinamarca has worked for the passage of the gender identity law and makes an argument for it on the website of MOVILH, one of Chile's LGBT organizations. For more information, see http://movilh.cl/trans/.

17. For more information about La Victoria's history, see, among other texts, Claudio di Girólamo's 1984 film *Andrés de La Victoria*. Meanwhile, in 1985, Augusto Góngora directed an episode of the TV show *Teleanálisis* about the military occupation of La Victoria during the dictatorship.

18. CUDS, the Coordinadora Universitaria por la Disidencia Sexual (University Organization for Sexual Dissidence), is a loosely affiliated group of activists focused on the theory and praxis of queerness in Chile. A 2011 edited volume of writings by a number of its members, titled *Por un feminismo sin mujeres*, offers a useful overview of their ideas.

19. In 2014, *Naomi Campbel* was shown in Sweden (at the Göteborg International Film Festival), in Poland (at the Planete+ Doc Film Festival), in Germany (at the Hamburg Film Festival), and in Spain; in 2015, it was shown in New York City at the Art of the Real Film Festival.

WORKS CITED

Bolaño, Roberto. 1996. *Estrella distante*. Barcelona: Anagrama.
Cavallo, Ascanio, and Gonzalo Maza, eds. 2011. *El novísimo cine chileno*. Santiago de Chile: Uqbar Editores.
"CinemaChile: ¿por qué el éxito del cine chileno LGBTI?" 2018. *Premios Sebastiane*, September 24. https://premiosebastiane.com/2018/09/24/cinema-chile-por-que-el-exito-del-cine-chileno-lgbti/.
Concilio, Arielle A. 2016. "Pedro Lemebel and the Translatxrsation: On a Genderqueer Translation Praxis," *TSQ* 3 (3–4): 462–84.

Coordinadora Universitaria por la Disidencia Sexual (CUDS). 2011. *Por un feminismo sin mujeres*. Santiago de Chile: Coordinadora Universitaria por la Disidencia Sexual.

Damiens, Antoine. 2018. "The Queer Film Ecosystem: Symbolic Economy, Festivals, and Queer Cinema's Legs." *Studies in European Cinema* 15 (1): 25–40.

"Daniela Vega manda recado a Piñera: 'Yo fui una niña trans y aquí estoy, incorrectible y feliz'" 2017. *El Mostrador*, December 19. http://www.elmostrador.cl/braga/2017/12/19/daniela-vega-manda-recado-a-pinera-yo-fui-una-nina-trans-y-aqui-estoy-incorrectible-y-feliz/.

"Debate presidencial sin riesgos: Piñera compara la identidad de género con una camisa y Guillier mantiene ambigüedad sobre las AFP," 2017. *El Mostrador* online, December 7. http://www.elmostrador.cl/noticias/pais/2017/12/07/debate-presidencial-sin-riesgos-pinera-compara-la-identidad-de-genero-con-una-camisa-y-guillier-mantiene-ambiguedad-sobre-las-afp/.

Edelman, Lee. 2004. *No Future: Queer Theory and the Death Drive*. Durham, NC: Duke University Press.

Falicov, Tamara. 2016. "The 'Festival Film': Film Festival Funds as Cultural Intermediaries." In *Film Festivals: History, Theory, Method, Practice*, edited by Marijke de Valck, Brendan Kredell, and Skadi Loist, 209–29. New York: Routledge.

Fischer, Carl. 2016. *Queering the Chilean Way: Cultures of Exceptionalism and Sexual Dissidence, 1965–2015*. New York: Palgrave MacMillan.

Gómez-Barris, Macarena. 2018. *Beyond the Pink Tide: Art and Political Undercurrents in the Americas*. Oakland: University of California Press.

Halberstam, Jack. 2018. *Trans*: A Quick and Quirky Account of Gender Variability*. Oakland: University of California Press.

Kirkwood, Julieta. 1986. *Ser política en Chile: Las feministas y los partidos*. Santiago de Chile: FLACSO.

Lane, Anthony. 2018. "Fighting to Be Heard: *The Final Year* and *A Fantastic Woman*." *New Yorker* 93, no. 46 (January 29): 58–60.

Lemebel, Pedro. 2000. *Loco afán*. Barcelona: Anagrama.

Moulián, Tomás. 2002. *Chile actual: Anatomía de un mito*. Santiago de Chile: LOM Ediciones.

Naomi Campbel. 2013. Dir. Camila José Donoso and Nicolás Videla. Universidad Mayor.

Neustadt, Robert. 1995. "Diamela Eltit: Clearing Space for Critical Performance." *Women & Performance: A Journal of Feminist Theory* 7, no. 2: 219–39.

Peirano, María Paz. 2018. "Film Mobilities and Circulation Practices in the Construction of Recent Chilean Cinema." In *Envisioning Networked Urban Mobilities: Art, Performances, Impacts*, edited by Aslak Aamot, Sven Kesserling, Peter Peters, and Kevin Hannam, 35–47. New York: Routledge.

Peric, Ivana. 2018. "*Una mujer fantástica* y la anulación de las diferencias." *El Desconcierto* online, January 29. http://www.eldesconcierto.cl/2018/01/29/una-mujer-fantastica-y-la-anulacion-de-las-diferencias/.

Ríos, Mónica. 2018. "Una mujer con adjetivo." *La tempestad* online, March 2. https://www.latempestad.mx/mujer-fantastica-lelio/.

"Sebastián Lelio: 'También soy trans, cuando era niño cambié el apellido de Lelio a Campos y más tarde recuperé el primero.'" 2018. *El Desconcierto* online, March 11. http://www.eldesconcierto.cl/2018/03/11/sebastian-lelio-tambien-soy-trans-cuando-era-nino-cambie-el-apellido-de-lelio-a-campos-y-mas-tarde-recupere-el-primero/.

Solari, Pablo. 2017. "*Una mujer fantástica*: Realismo quimérico." *El agente cine* online, April 18. https://elagentecine.cl/2017/04/18/una-mujer-fantastica-2-realismo-quimerico/.

Una mujer fantástica. 2017. Dir. Sebastián Lelio. Participant, Fábula, Komplizen Film, Muchas Gracias, Setembro Cine, Zweites Deutsches Fernsehen (ZDF), ARTE.

POLITICIZED INTIMACIES, TRANSNATIONAL AFFECTS: DEBATING (POST)MEMORY AND HISTORY

11

FILMMAKERS TO THE RESCUE OF CHILEAN MEMORY

Representations of Chile's Traumatic Past in Contemporary Documentary

Claudia Bossay

This chapter analyzes several Chilean documentaries from the past fifteen years that have offered different approaches to the country's transition to democracy. In light of the critical approaches that have emphasized affective aspects of documentary in Chile, I focus on communal forms of resistance and the internalization of trauma to argue that six films—*Actores secundarios / Secondary Actors* (Pachi Bustos and Jorge Leiva, 2004), *La ciudad de los fotógrafos / The City of Photographers* (Sebastián Moreno, 2006), *El edificio de los chilenos / The Chilean Building* (Macarena Aguiló and Susana Foxley, 2010), *Generation Exile* (Rodrigo Dorfman, 2009), *El pacto de Adriana / Adriana's Pact* (Lisette Orozco, 2017), and *El color del camaleón / The Color of the Chameleon* (Andrés Lübbert, 2017)—can be viewed as representations of the progression through the various stages of grief and trauma following the dictatorship. These films offer personal experiences that reflect on the horrors experienced by the directors, while simultaneously becoming exemplary forms of dealing with private traumatic experiences in the context of the global Cold War.

THE RETURN TO DEMOCRACY: MEMORY AND TRAUMA

During the Popular Unity years (1970–73), film and other art forms supported the government and aspired to help develop a "new man": empowered, decolonized, and socialist. Cinema was perceived as a political tool that could help pave the way for the revolutionary years to come, and was employed as one of the main distribution channels for the ideals and achievements of Allende's government. It should have been no surprise, then, that the dictatorship attacked cinema, managing to almost completely obliterate local production. Of the nearly four hundred screens that the country had in 1973, no more than seventy remained by 1989. Economically, the military regime did not allocate any funding to film production or distribution. Furthermore, it repealed two laws that subsidized film. In 1974, a new decree (no. 679) was added to the Cinematographic Censorship Council, stating that any film "expressing Marxist inspiration or contrary to public order, country or nationality" could be vetoed. Within a few years of the coup, almost all film schools had closed.[1]

During the first part of the transition to democracy, military authoritarianism was still legally supported through the Consejo de Seguridad del Estado, a national security council created through the 1980 constitution passed under Pinochet. It was made up of the president, the heads of the two chambers of Congress, the supreme court justices, the commanders-in-chief of the army, the navy, and the air force, and the director general of the police force (*Carabineros*). The fact that it comprised the three main bodies of government (executive, legislative, and judiciary) and representatives from all branches of the armed forces virtually turned it into a fourth power (De Ramón 2001, 256). Its biggest intervention was passing multiple amendments to the State Security Law (Ley de Seguridad Interior del Estado) that allowed the council to detain anyone participating in public disorder or acting against national sovereignty. These strategies of control made for a very tenuous form of democracy. Therefore, during the first years of the transition, political and social actors, including film directors, worked carefully not to directly exceed the limits imposed by the agreed-upon transition, in order to safeguard Chile's fragile stability. The lack of state support, the censorship of films and ideas, and the disappearance of infrastructure and people during the dictatorship created an atmosphere of censorship and self-censorship (Villarroel 2005, 28) that continued throughout the first decade of the return to democracy (Bossay 2015; Bossay and Peirano 2017).

Nonetheless, there was also a progressive professionalization of the field in this period. For example, the audiovisual sector was included in the economic treaty that Chile signed with the European Union in late 1990. In 2002, the censorship imposed by the dictatorship ended, and a new film rating system was created. In 2005, the Audiovisual Fund (Fondo Audiovisual) was created under the umbrella of the National Council of Audiovisual Art and Industry (CAIA, Consejo del Arte y la Industria Audiovisual). In 2006, the National Film Archive (Cineteca Nacional de Chile) was created (Bossay and Peirano 2017, 73–74). Hence, a structure began to operate that ensured better production, further distribution, and uncensored exhibition, as well as archival conservation; in other words, film came to be perceived as patrimony that needed to be cared for and studied. Increased public sponsorship of film production (Mouesca 2005); the strengthening of national and international professional networks among documentary filmmakers;[2] the emergence of the figure of the documentary film producer; and the reemergence of national film schools in the mid-1990s were all contributing factors to the rise in film production, despite its overall precariousness (Bossay and Peirano 2017, 72–74).

However, despite this expansion of the field, the idea that the dictatorship has already been represented too many times on film is floated in public debate following almost every release related to the subject (Morales 2017).[3] The notion that efforts to remember and memorialize the pain of the dictatorship could jeopardize Chile's democracy and neoliberalism has been referred to as "free market amnesia" (Klubock 2003, 277), which, in turn, has led to the argument that "Chilean cinema has remained conspicuously distanced from subjects and situations that directly address the traumas of the dictatorship and the concomitant experiences of exile and return" (Pino-Ojeda 2009, 134). Although this is numerically true, and reflections upon the trauma and its consequences did not grow in proportion to the increase in film productions in general, there is still a large and ever-growing corpus of films that do focus on the subject.

These films could be labeled as trauma films, a term originally coined by Janet Walker (2005) in regard to the corpus of films about the Holocaust and incest, which do not necessarily belong to a specific filmic movement or group, and which may be produced over an array of places and times. Like the films in her research, Chilean productions also "adopt catastrophe as their subject matter and formation of trauma as their aesthetic" (Walker 2005, xix). Furthermore, in contemporary trauma films, the memory of the past has been mediated by modernity and mass media, such as history films, television, museums, and the Internet. Therefore, memory is no longer transmitted from parents to children or from the individual to the collective, but rather by means of experimental installations, audiovisual representations, and other forms of memory technology, changing the traditional ways in which memory is shared (Landsberg 2004, 2–9).

For Alison Landsberg, these new memories are "prosthetic," because they are interchangeable, like artificial limbs, and are usually indicative of trauma. Prosthetic memories become essential when the organic memory of a period has been destroyed by the traumatic event, through the deaths of people who experienced it, through memory being suppressed, or because of communities that have not been able to fully articulate the trauma they experienced (Landsberg 2004, 113–20). These technologies allow people with no direct, embodied claim to the memories to incorporate this knowledge into their own archive of experience, particularly because they base their transmission of information on the affective realm. Therefore, these memories are not only collective but offer space for the individual processing of mass culture: "they are privately felt public memories" (Landsberg 2004, 19). Furthermore, they exist within the complexities of capital. The act of consuming different cultural forms of knowledge lies within the rules of producing these kinds of goods; prosthetic memories are capitalistic forms of dealing with trauma.

Chilean trauma films may be viewed as prosthetic memories because they are produced in a highly neoliberal market, and they negotiate the desire of the mass public watching them with a desire of political stance on heritage and memory. As such, many of these films are shown at universities and cultural institutions, such as the Museum of Memory and the National Film Archive. Furthermore, in a society were memory may be described as a battlefield (Jelin 2002) and conflicting memories share the narrations of the past (Stern 2009), these memories allow for a plethora of interpretations, which sometimes conflict. As prosthetic memories do not erase the differences among groups but rather rely on the empathic ability to understand a different reality from one's own, these films recognize the alterity of others and allow for those across all political spectrums to feel connected. They also allow non-Chileans to participate in this particular trauma, creating a global community of shared experiences. Just as the Holocaust must not only be the heritage of the survivors but rather belong to everyone, so should the memory of the Popular Unity and the dictatorship that followed.

The following sections will address different strategies used by these documentaries to rescue Chilean memory from oblivion and indifference. Propelled by the consolidation of a state that has subsidized film production, a "postmemory" generation (Hirsch 2008), formed by the daughters and sons of those who experienced the dictatorship in the flesh through exile, torture, or death, has taken a stand against oblivion with this corpus of trauma films. Here, traumatic events are analyzed and represented from new perspectives. Rather than representing direct traumatic experiences, this corpus reveals the inter- and transgenerational transmission of traumatic knowledge and experience. By examining these films in the context of the transnational theoretical framework of memory studies, this chapter will show how trauma and memory connect this corpus of films and filmmakers to others who are "working through" these issues in a variety of national settings.

A NEW MOVEMENT OF FILMMAKERS: *ACTORES SECUNDARIOS* AND *LA CIUDAD DE LOS FOTÓGRAFOS*

Coinciding with the growth of the film industry and audiences' return to cinema, and anticipating the 2005 boom of fiction films (Cavallo and Maza 2010; Urrutia Neno 2013), film critics in 2001 were already suggesting that documentary was changing in Chile. Even critics in the right-wing *El Mercurio*, Chile's main newspaper, acknowledged this growth in documentary filmmaking, despite the fact that many of the documentaries had political leanings that *El Mercurio*'s pages generally tended to dismiss: "Until now, documentary had kept a lower profile [here] than it has in developed countries. This year, however, there have been concrete advances towards bringing the documentary closer to mass audiences" ["Hasta ahora el documental había mantenido un perfil más bajo que en los países desarrollados. Este año, sin embargo, ha habido avances concretos para acercar el documental al público masivo"] ("El género" 2001). Following a documentary film festival in 2002, the same newspaper stated that "documentaries are the strongest and most interesting element in Chilean audiovisual production. . . . This year, documentaries have practiced politics like never before. They have brought a fresh perspective to the classic political documentary. The result is fascinating, ambiguous, and does not leave anyone indifferent" ["los documentales son lo más interesante y fuerte de la producción audiovisual chilena. . . . Este año, los documentales han hecho política como nunca antes, le han dado una vuelta de tuerca al clásico documental político. El resultado es fascinante, ambiguo y no deja indiferente"] (Sepúlveda 2002, 3).[4]

In 2004, the film collective led by Pachi Bustos and Jorge Leiva premiered *Actores secundarios*,[5] a documentary featuring members of the high school student movement who played an important role in protest marches and antidictatiorship organizations during the regime, but who are often ignored in traditional Chilean historiography. The film begins after the dictatorship, when students re-creating a 1985 school occupation[6] were expelled from their school. The administrators' exaggerated reaction is not explained, but it is suggested that they were scared of the idea of a new occupation movement. A spokesperson for the expelled students suggests that "it's curious how history repeats itself, and if a replica, a simulation of an occupation eighteen years ago, generates such a commotion, it proves that democracy itself is a simulation" ["Es curioso cómo la historia vuelve, como la historia cobra . . . da cuenta que un simulacro de toma, una réplica de una toma que ocurrió hace diez y ocho años . . . puede estabilizar o crear algo y que hoy muestra cómo la democracia que estamos viviendo es un simulacro"].

The documentary goes on to explore what it was like to be teenagers fighting for the country's democracy—"little soldiers," as one interviewee says—but it also shows how these highly politicized young people generated fear in the adult world. Above all, it shows the extreme power the teenagers acquired by taking to the streets and confronting the dictatorship. The former students recall how they wanted more from the schooling system and felt it was their right to have a high-quality, stimulating, and free education. One of them remembers realizing that when they came together in protests and occupations, they helped destabilize the regime and cause the fall of the dictatorship. Through their actions on the streets, the public space that had been used for militant politics in the 1970s overcame the sterility enforced upon it by the military regime. The documentary sheds light on the gestation of a new form of politics.[7]

The documentary goes even further, exploring how many of them felt like losers when democracy arrived, because the efforts they had put into destroying the regime did not translate into a return to socialism. Some discontinued their education and moved on to armed struggle instead. Of these, some felt disappointed by their decisions, and others even died because their superiors sent them to perform dangerous tasks; yet others were seen as criminals in the eyes of the new democratic government. This sense of defeat persisted because the ones who died for this cause were forgotten, and the parties sent those who survived to their lowest levels when democracy returned, despite their already-prominent political careers. In the words of an interviewee: "Our generation is still composed of second-class citizens, because none of us ended up in high-profile political positions, or as important technocrats" ["Nuestra generación sigue siendo secundarios ya que ninguno de nosotros accedió a grandes cargos políticos o grandes esferas de la tecnocracia"]. They were defeated, as another former student states, "because society didn't make space for me, and that was because I couldn't change society" ["porque la sociedad no me permite más, y eso es porque yo no logré cambiar la sociedad"]. *Actores secundarios* reminds us that the *Unidad Popular* and socialism were idealized by a generation of youngsters to such a degree that they had the courage to confront a violent and murderous dictatorship. Still, when democracy arrived, it did not fulfil their expectations.

The film therefore reveals a collective approach, similar to many films made during the Popular Unity period, but now as a form of resistance to the dictatorship and postdictatorship. In one segment, an insert of an official newspaper headline refers to the occupation of the Liceo Valentín Letelier by the student movement in October 1984. Under this slightly transparent insert, the public can see a brief manual tracking shot, advancing down the corridor of the school in present times. More than a simple pan, it moves in a semicircle, like a ship at sea. This unusual movement suggests the shaking of social structures caused by this first occupation, as well as the general sense of destabilization caused by the movement. The juxtaposition of material explored in these examples involves superimposing layers of information (newspapers, text-based documents, photographs) with images of the film's present, to create political palimpsests of the views that the protagonists had of themselves and their cause,[8] the views that the press had of them, and the massive divergence among them. Thus, the past is not something that belongs only to memory, to libraries or archives, but, like the former students, it has a real presence in the contemporary world, even if denied a leading role (Bossay 2014c). One of the directors was part of the student movement and the other was not, yet together with scriptwriters and researchers they manage to rescue this past from oblivion by combining the personal with the collective, marking the experience lived as a way of knowledge for the future. Perhaps traditional forms of memory break down, but then prosthetic memory comes to its aid in an attempt to remedy the sense of loss and defeat of the documentary subjects.

A similar strategy of narrating the power of community to help destabilize the dictatorship is shown in *La ciudad de los fotógrafos*[9] by Sebastián Moreno, about the Association of Independent Photographers (AFI, Asociación de Fotógrafos Independientes), an organization created to physically and legally protect local independent photojournalists from being arrested or beaten when they were out on the streets covering the different protests against the dictatorship. By interviewing the photographers who took a visual stand against impunity, and by revisiting their work and memories, this documentary reminds us of the inseparable bond between the dictatorship and the camera.[10] Photography helped destabilize the dictatorship: as the director's father suggests, "We started to realize the value that photography had as documentation. That was why they went after us so much" ["Nos fuimos dando cuenta de la importancia, el valor, que tenían la fotografía como documento. Por alguna razón nos perseguían tanto"]. On the other hand, photography served as a shield for the demonstrators, who invited the photographers so they could document the resistance and help in case they were detained. The visual element is linked to the fight for human rights, as the relatives of the disappeared hang photographs of their loved ones on their chests to prevent them from becoming a number, a statistic; so they can remain as people with faces and stories. Thus, we can see that "documentaries in general, and photography in particular, advocated for the demonstrators, the relatives, the fallen, and memory" ["los documentales en general, y la fotografía en particular fueron defensores de los manifestantes, de los deudos, de los caídos y de la memoria"] (Bossay 2014a).

Through photographs taken during the dictatorship, the documentary explores the power of the visual record, community, and resistance. For example, printed photographs are brought to the place where they were originally taken, and the creator of the images raises them until they end up covering the camera's view. This way, both images, separated by decades, are merged into a point of view that shares an interpretation of history, and in some cases, the lens, which is operated by Moreno, whose father was one of the photographers documenting the dictatorship. Thus, the frame we see not only binds the past and present of a place and a narration but also unites two generations who have experienced those same places differently.

In most documentaries, there is a certain distance between the camera and the action in the archival images, which provides security and anonymity while also capturing as much information as possible within one frame. This documentary, however, offers a symbolic and physical closeness to the action. International photographers or major agencies gave rolls of film to AFI photographers because the latter were the ones who dared to go into the protests, and this fearless attitude helped sell their photographs abroad and expose the dictatorship using visual evidence. The documentary recalls that the power of the photographers' movement was so great that for a couple of months the military regime forbade magazines and newspapers to publish photographs. The public is presented with inserts of the magazines of the time, with black or blank squares where the photographs should have been. It resignifies these records without photographs into images of the repression and the power of the photographers. In this way, through individual and collective interviews, the audience can imagine how these independent photographers became a community and therefore a force in the fight against the dictatorship.

The climax of the film narrates how the young photographer Rodrigo Rojas de Negri was burned to death at the hands of the military. Concluding the film, the photographers gather to pay homage to Rojas. In doing so, they also commemorate their own sacrifices and their powerful role in the fight against the dictatorship. They mourn for those who are gone, and mark the trauma they experienced. With a similar structure to that of *Actores secundarios*, *La ciudad de los fotógrafos* also presents a movement that fought against the dictatorship—not necessarily through party politics, as the students did, but through actions and records. *La ciudad de los fotógrafos* shows a greater confidence in the democratic future of Chile and a less nihilistic sense of dread about the past and the present. Still, concerns are expressed about how the violence experienced during the dictatorship changed everyone who recorded it, which extends the reflection to everyone who lived it.

In this way, two different documentaries reunite social groups that fought the dictatorship. The directors of these films were all children and teenagers during the dictatorship; they learned about the events that led to the dictatorship through their relatives and elders. *La ciudad de los fotógrafos* is more related to postmemory, but Leiva and Bustos experienced the violence of the student movement firsthand. *La ciudad de los fotógrafos* and *Actores secundarios* share a material and emotional presence of the past in the democratic present, where somehow the communities have lost their cohesiveness yet still remain connected though the presence of the past.

THE STORY WITHIN: THE PRIVATE SPHERE AS PART OF PUBLIC HISTORY

A slightly younger generation of postmemory filmmakers has explored more intimate aspects of their own experiences during the dictatorship and exile. Macarena Aguiló and Rodrigo Dorfman examine their own childhoods in their films, as well as their relationships with their parents and the convoluted period in which they lived. Aguiló and Susana Foxley's *El edificio de los chilenos*[11] focuses on Aguiló's experience in *Proyecto Hogares* [Project Homes], an institution in which foster parents took care of the children of militants from the MIR, a leftist group that clandestinely returned to Chile to fight Pinochet's dictatorship and left their children in the safety of exile. Rather than deciding which parent would return and which one would stay, they set up new families. A group of children became "social siblings" who, together with their foster parents, created a "social home." The film examines the experiences of Aguiló and her siblings and friends, and explores why their parents, particularly their mothers, made the decision to return to Chile and leave their children behind. To do so, the film begins with the abduction of Macarena by the DINA (National Intelligence Directorate), Pinochet's secret police and extermination squad, as a way of getting to her parents when she was just a child. This precipitated the family's decision to leave the country, live in exile, and eventually return to fight for Chile's freedom.

These itinerancies have led the documentary to be described as a "traveling memory" film (Ramírez Soto 2015), showcasing the direct impact of the horrors of the dictatorship on children.[12] The "travels" it takes are geographical and affective, representing the ways in which historical events affected generations of women in different ways (Bossay and Peirano 2017, 84–85), creating different relationships with these traumatic times. In this sense, it returns to issues that had been explored, albeit with another focus, in Carmen Castillo's *Calle Santa Fe / Santa Fe Street* (2007), where the director and Margarita Marchi (a fellow MIR militant and, incidentally, Aguiló's mother) reflect on the costs of their militant and feminist lifestyles.[13] In *Calle Santa Fe*, Aguiló is shown editing her documentary while Castillo watches, and together as affected parties, colleagues, and women, they reflect on Chile's history and the nature of memory and gender (as seen in Figure 28).

In the film, Aguiló interviews her foster ("social") father, her biological mother, and her social siblings. The film includes archival footage and animations to explore the more emotional aspects of Aguiló's memories and experiences of exile, and those of other children from *Proyecto Hogares*. Hence, the exercise of reliving childhood memories is mediated by the stories of the adults who experienced the trauma of the coup and exile, as well as by the trauma they unwittingly created in the children. This strengthens Janet Walker's suggestion that "probing the limits of the filmic—and

Figure 28. Castillo and Aguiló watching a version of edited footage, in *Calle Santa Fe / Santa Fe Street* (Carmen Castillo, 2007).

videographic—representation of traumatic past events has been for several decades a fully articulated project of feminist experimental autobiographical documentary theory and practice" (2005, 21). As a visual exercise in memory and its limits, it creatively fills in the silences and interprets firsthand experiences.

Similarly to Aguiló and Castillo's relationship, Rodrigo Dorfman shares a filmic practice with Ariel Dorfman, his father,[14] who was a cultural advisor in Allende's *Unidad Popular* and is now a renowned playwright, academic, and human rights activist. The younger Dorfman describes his family as "branded by exile," stating in his documentary *Generation Exile* that "exile is like a journey into death, where you lose everything that gives meaning to life." The documentary, filmed by Rodrigo both in Chile and the United States, narrates the story of his family to his daughter. "Dear Isabella," he begins, as the typing of an actual letter is seen on-screen. "Tomorrow is your seventh birthday, and I would like to be back in Durham to celebrate with you. This is the most important birthday in the history of our family . . . but now I need to be in Chile working on a documentary about the long exile of our family." This is followed by archival and family footage, juxtaposed with generic images of the historical horrors of the twentieth century.[15]

Generation Exile tells the story of post-traumatic spiritual explorations by Rodrigo and four women, including an Afro-Caribbean whirling dervish. Rodrigo weaves his personal story and the women's testimonies together to show many possible paths to recovery. He narrates how he heard a song from the Gnawa community in a dream and traveled to Morocco to find the Gnawa people, who told him that the nails he had been hammering onto Pinochet's image over the years—following the suggestion of a Chilean family exiled in Paris who hammered a nail into a picture of Pinochet for every day of exile—were causing him pain. He realizes that these nails are actually hurting him, and if they stay there, they will eventually start hurting his daughter. After undergoing a healing ritual with the Gnawa, he returns to the United States, where he joins the Center of Universal Light, led by a Turkish Sufi sheikh, to continue working through his experiences. There, he is told not to take the nails out of Pinochet's picture but to learn to love them.

Rodrigo's love for his daughter functions as the motor for his personal explorations. This leads him to consciously choose to continue traveling the world, thus coming to terms with his past and bringing new possibilities for the future generations of Dorfmans by undoing the power of the traumatic past. Like the mystic movements of the whirling dervishes, the documentary uses the turns to provide a visual interpretation of reality and explore the ever-changing world. The camera whirls and weaves stories together through editing-matches between two twirling scenes. These blurred, fast-paced images provide graphic proof of the instability that exile creates, and lend mystical power to how the interviewees work through their trauma (Figure 29). The expressionistic editing of the images manages to change the meaning of the Dorfman family's curse. Their nomadic identities offer new possibilities for self-definition, where both father and son understand identity as a constant construction, in which the static national borders of geography, gender, and religion combine in a transnational melting pot from which mutual support can and must arise. This film, like others by Dorfman, follows a logic of actively processing and healing pain, in both individual and collective experiences.

Hence, in both *El edificio de los chilenos* and *Generation Exile*, exile, family, children, and traumatic pasts come together to demonstrate that human rights violations, no matter where, when, or why, create pain that spans generations. Furthermore, the films record the experience of working through trauma, showing how family and communities, real and imagined, are essential in the healing processes. Chile's experience is undeniably tied to the fate of the world and the very varied consequences of the Cold War, which still hold power over daily life, whether in South America or elsewhere. Both of

Figure 29. The recurring trope of spinning dancers, in *Generation Exile* (Rodrigo Dorfman, 2009).

these films therefore situate Chilean trauma as part of a broader experience, sharing efforts to heal with the global community by representing an array of global cases together. Through international film festivals, these films act prosthetically for people in different times and places.

THE PERPETRATOR FILMS

The two documentaries that will be discussed in this final section, both released in 2017, are "perpetrator films," with filmmakers pointing their cameras at family members who held roles as victimizers during the dictatorship. Moving from those who were victims to those who perpetrated violence is another key aspect of postmemory cinema: by interrogating how the actions of those perpetrators have consequences for younger generations of people in their families, long-held silences and complacencies are disrupted. This issue has been present in the corpus of trauma film at least since Carmen Castillo's *La flaca Alejandra / Skinny Alejandra* (1994), a documentary account of a woman who collaborated with Pinochet's secret police; it has steadily grown in relevance since then. Perpetrator films depict the ways in which the silences maintained immediately following the dictatorship existed not only in the public sphere—to maintain Chile's then-fragile democracy—but also within families. The disruptions that occur in these families connect them with other families experiencing similar phenomena in post-traumatic contexts around the world.

Lissette Orozco's *El pacto de Adriana*[16] is one of the most recent examples of postmemory cinema in Chile. The film offers a no-holds-barred view of the director's aunt, Adriana Rivas, the personal secretary of Manuel Contreras[17] and an active member of the Lautaro Brigade, the extermination unit of Chile's dictatorship-era secret police, or DINA. This film is structured around a web of short scenes that spin together the stories of Adriana, Chile, the justice system, and Orozco's discovery of her favorite aunt's secret life and its pact of silence. Some of Adriana's testimonies come from interviews Orozco conducted with her as a loving relative rather than as a public figure. To portray Adriana's public persona and ground the documentary's claims, voices of experts are used. Accused of kidnapping and murder, Adriana fled the Chilean justice system for Australia, and she currently has a restriction order against her. Throughout the documentary, the audience witnesses how Adriana protects the members of the brigade. The director starts to perceive the violence of the dictatorship and its very real contemporary consequences for her family. Communication between niece and aunt goes from face-to-face conversations to intermittent video conferences, to unanswered letters from the aunt, to silence. Knowledge of the past eventually undoes their relationship.

About thirty minutes into the film, Orozco attends the commemoration of the fortieth anniversary of the coup d'état at the Memory and Human Rights Museum, where a previously unreleased radio recording of the 1973 bombing of the La Moneda Palace is revealed. The deafening noises of the Hawker Hunters can be heard in the background. The announcer screams over the whistling of the bombs, the fly-dives of the planes, and the thundering explosions. As we listen to this striking archival account, we see people embracing each other, sitting silently on the floor, solemn and weeping. The overpowering fusion of the audience's palpable pain with the vivid radio recording shocks and frustrates, due to the justice left unserved. For Orozco, the weight of the truth becomes overwhelming. The previous empathy she had felt toward her aunt starts to crack as she learns more about the country and Adriana's past. Finally, she reviews footage with a relative and realizes how her aunt has manipulated and humiliated her. The fragmented family, the end of Orozco's doubts, and the implications of Adriana's pact of silence are accompanied by the words of the director, who confesses to her impulse to look more toward the future than toward the past. She recognizes that there is nothing more for her to do, and hopes that the pain experienced by her family while she made the film is useful to those who do not yet know the truth about their relatives. The postmemory generation comes to terms with a horror story here, rather than an account of bravery and resistance.

This film gives viewers the chance to understand horror by perceiving it from the point of view of the perpetrator, although it does not try to make the audience feel empathy for Adriana. It becomes impossible to feel connected to her as she is revealed as an accomplice, torturer, and murderer, as well as an expert manipulator. However, it is possible to feel connected to the director and her wanderings through the traumatic past. Two important issues are raised in the documentary: it makes the audience wonder how Adriana could flee the country without any help, and, secondly, it portrays the tireless community of Chileans in Australia *funando*[18] Adriana. As they say in the documentary, "if there is no justice, there is *funa*" ["si no hay justicia, hay funa"]. As with *La ciudad de los fotógrafos*, the film shows a ritualistic form of commemorating past traumas that, at the same time, self-consciously indicates an awareness of its place in history.

Meanwhile, Andrés Lübbert's *El color del camaleón*[19] tells of how a group from the CNI (the name of a later iteration of Pinochet's secret police) forcibly trained civilians and members of the military to be murderers. Using both physical and psychological torture, they tried to convert certain people into soldiers and accomplices of the intelligence services. As the documentary states at the beginning, this commando training unit sought to make these "trainees" "lose all moral point of reference," and turn them into "savages" capable of committing violence without flinching. We obtain this shocking story from one of the survivors of this cruel process, who managed to escape from this situation and from Chile itself: Jorge Lübbert, the director's father. Andrés Lübbert has made at least four films about his father,[20] a renowned war cameraman, and in all of them, we can appreciate the difficult relationship between the two. Throughout the films, reflections that are almost a stream of consciousness fill in the gaps and silences left by the interviewees, especially Andrés's father, who in *El color del camaleón* stays silent for longer than he speaks.[21] Indeed, as Andrés tells his father, "If I didn't push you to talk, this would be a silent film [Si no te presionara para hablar, esta sería un película muda]." Here, Andrés's accented Spanish becomes a marker for experiences of alienation and resilience.[22] Meanwhile, Jorge's silence speaks of something he cannot reveal, a fear of what words summon.

Andrés Lübbert's tetralogy also uses archival material that sheds light on the lives of cameramen like his father. For example, we see the death of Leonardo Henricksen,[23] the arrival of exiled people in Belgium, and the video and war images filmed by Jorge Lübbert over the years invite us to think about how behind the protective shield of the lens there are people experiencing the very thing that overwhelms us as spectators. In this sense, *El color del camaleón* and *La ciudad de los fotógrafos* share a valorization of those who create the images we see, illuminating a historical period in which traditional forms of memory were broken and where access to archives was restricted. This reflection can even continue into the work of Andrés, when the camera appears with him in several shots; in the poignant final reflection of *El color del camaleón*, father and son film each other in a shot-reverse shot—an openhearted, earnest effort to break the silence. In this final scene, the cameras that accompany each man present them as creators on equal terms and establish a debate about the pain being passed down from generation to generation.

Lübbert's tetralogy is represented as a public working-through that spans from the therapy undergone by the father decades ago, through the father's work as a war cameraman, to the present work where the director deals with his father's torture and its still-evident consequences. The father's obvious fear of the military, the past, and the unspoken, makes him a victim. However, due to his work in the CNI, he was a victimizer in the past and was even investigated by the Stasi in Germany. As Andrés says in the film: "If you deny your past, your present is false. It doesn't exist. And you don't solve anything by doing it. How can it be that so many people in Chile still deny and justify what has happened?" ["Si niegas tu pasado, tu presente es falso. No existe. Y no solucionas nada haciéndolo. ¿Cómo puede ser que en Chile tanta gente aún niegue y justifique lo que ha pasado?"] Here, the director refers to how there are still Chileans who justify the death and torture of people and deny the human rights violations that took place. In a sense, he is arguing for a corpus of trauma films to continue growing and exploring the relationship between memory and history. Above all, *El color del camaleón* highlights what we still do not know about the past, and offers a chance to reflect on how to live out this new phase of our history, not from the private sphere but from the public one.

CONCLUSION

Although not all the films explored here are postmemory pieces per se, together they do show how new generations of filmmakers have evolved in their methods for representing trauma. More affective and emotional outcomes emerge from these documentaries, which portray the "long-term effect of living in close proximity to the pain, depression, and dissociation of persons who have witnessed and survived massive historical traumas" (Hirsch 2008, 112). They are invitations to keep working through trauma by giving voice to new agents of memory, to the groups that fought, to the grey areas, and even to the victimizers. This possibility of healing private wounds through the public practice of filming a documentary causes each case, each memory, and each testimony to go beyond the camera, screen, and projector, and invade our reality. It brings us face-to-face with the nature of the political actions that took place and invites us to exercise empathy and fight so this never happens to anyone again, in Chile or anywhere else in the world.

The reflections in *El Mercurio* of the early 2000s, quoted above, suggest that countries are perceived as developed to the extent that they deal with their past publicly through documentaries. Censorship laws changed at home, and international economic treaties and funding schemes boosted production and allowed for international participation in festivals, raising Chile's profile abroad. In parallel to this process, more and more of Chile's past was represented, reflected upon, and brought to the present though filmic interpretations. The films analyzed in this chapter ask how we want to face the past: are there possibilities for empathy with the victimizers? Are there ways to forgive? Is there still more yet to be known about this period? How will this alter the narratives and memoirs of the past that have yet to be written? For these same reasons, these works leave us with the bitter taste of justice unserved. Each of these films becomes a memory knot (Stern 2009) which allows us to rethink our past, evaluate the implications of the new information revealed, and (as most films do) put ourselves in the shoes of the protagonists, creating a prosthetic memory.

We also realize the power of communities, as well as their local and global connections. These films share a particularly generational approach; fathers, mothers, uncles and aunts—both biological and political—have marked the younger generation, just as Hirsch describes how the "role of the family [marks] a space of transmission" (103). As traditional forms of memory are broken after a trauma, new symbolic systems must narrate the horrors. It is not just history and its events, but also, and most importantly, the actions taken by those forced to live at the crossroads of political and social turmoil and loss of freedom and how they evolved over their life span that mark the next generation's lives, experiences, and professional careers.

The directors of these six documentaries were all small children at the start of the dictatorship, yet some of them organized as teenagers to fight the dictatorship. Bustos and Leiva share the values of community expressed in *La ciudad de los fotógrafos*, which in turn was directed by Moreno, who includes his father in his film. The next two films, made during the late 2000s and early 2010s, both explore transnational communities created through exile, and politics and religion are essential issues, as are filmmakers' relationships with their parents, and their own parenthood. The last two films are made by a slightly younger generation: Lübbert shares an upbringing in exile with the directors of the previous films, while Orozco was brought up in Chile. Both of them have complicated relationships with family members due to those family members' actions as perpetrators during the dictatorship. This transit, from Chile to exile and back to local communities, from children abused by the dictatorship to young directors taking charge of their own personal histories, is a transit permeated by prosthetic memories. Moreover, these films navigate the neoliberal nuances of film production and contemporary film festivals by representing trauma and reflecting upon its consequences through other elements of mass culture as well as personal archives. In this way, filmmakers have mixed their personal experiences with global and local history.

In some cases, these directors share a filmic responsibility with their relatives. In others, they express a yearning to share the communal experience of their own family with a broader, imagined community, thereby developing a filmic historiography, or, more accurately, a historiophoty of the private and public. These documentaries also share a deeply felt and experienced memory, and a history of generations of survivors. In this sense, these documentaries help to work though the relationships broken by the dictatorship, thus becoming revisionary acts that aim to heal broken bonds. These documentaries stand as examples of how filmmakers have come to the rescue of Chilean memory; they have become essential in the quest to free the memory of our traumatic past from oblivion, as well as to seek justice.

NOTES

1. For a more in-depth analysis of the different roles of cinema in each government, see Bossay 2014a.

2. Films about memory have been mostly promoted by female film directors and film producers who have championed the creation of stable professional networks (ChileDoc, which has played a pivotal role in promoting these films), active political organizations (ADOC, Asociación de Documentalistas de Chile), novel distribution platforms (Miradoc), and diverse exhibition initiatives throughout Chile and the global market. For a more in-depth analysis, see Bossay and Peirano (2017).

3. This could be supported by Tomás Moulian's analysis (1997) of the strategies for overcoming the dictatorship and building the political foundations to move forward. An almost compulsive oblivion was conceptualized by politicians as a compromise to obtain stability. Furthermore, stability went beyond democratic terms per se, and allowed neoliberalism to flourish.

4. *El Mercurio* is one of the oldest Spanish-language newspapers in the world, and the one with the largest circulation in the country. Its owner, Agustín Edwards, collaborated with the Nixon administration during the Popular Unity to undermine Allende; the newspaper defended the coup d'état and actively participated in the regime. Aiding in the cover-up of human rights crimes, this newspaper has been the voice of right-wing conservative, pro-dictatorship, anti-democratic Chile. It is thus worth noting the irony of *El Mercurio* covering documentaries committed to uncovering the abuses of the dictatorship, and even calling *Actores secundarios* "the film that consolidated the new [generation of] documentary filmmakers" ["El filme que consolidó a los nuevos documentalistas"] (Zavala 2005, C18). For further information on the role of this newspaper in Chilean politics, see the documentary *El diario de Agustín / Agustín's Newspaper* (Ignacio Agüero, 2008), which itself was subject to a certain degree of censorship when it premiered. However, *El Mercurio*'s cultural section has had plenty of non-right-wing collaborators, particularly in the film and music section from the 1990s and the 2000s.

5. In 2005, this film won Best Documentary at the Valdivia International Film Festival in Chile.

6. A *toma* or an occupation by force of a place (like a school or a factory) with the purpose of disrupting the normal pace of things and gaining visibility for a particular political issue is a common strategy in Chilean political struggles.

7. The young people called for the representation of all leftist parties, from those that promoted armed struggle to those in favor of nonviolence. This progressive and proactive form of politics helped mobilize thousands of

secondary students in each protest and occupation, and achieved real results. They sum up the responsibility they felt in their desire to "resolve history" ["resolver la historia"], a phrase that, the documentary shows, was far from naive: they took Chile's political future into their hands with great care and compromise.

8   See also Camilo Trumper's discussion of political palimpsests during the Popular Unity period (2016).

9   This film won Best Documentary in the African, Asian and Latin-American Festival in Milan, La Pintana Social Cinema Festival (PINTACANES), the Pedro Sienna Award, as well as Best Research from the Valparaiso Film Festival.

10 On this subject, see Ángeles Donoso Macaya's work on photography in Chile (2020).

11 This film won prizes at the Festival Internacional de Documentales de Santiago (FIDOCS), the Festival de Documentales de Chillán (CHILEREALITY) and PINTACANES, as well as DOK Leipzig, 2° Coral Documental, Festival Internacional de Cine de La Habana, and the New York Latino Film Festival, among others.

12 The 2004 National Commission on Political Prison and Torture, known as the Valech Commission, confirmed that during the dictatorship there were children who were subjected to political violence, detention, and torture. A second report in 2011 expanded the information, confirming that 2,200 people were under the age of eighteen at the time of their arrest. One of them was the three-year-old Aguiló.

13 Both Castillo and Marchi made sacrifices as mothers by sending their daughters to *Proyecto Hogares* so they could continue their militant work on behalf of Chile's freedom. While *Calle Santa Fe* deals with exile, the return to Chile, the history of the MIR, the tensions of combining motherhood with militant politics, and the connections with feminism, *El edificio de los chilenos* explores the perspectives of the children, who question their parents' decisions and speak out about the heretofore invisible emotional consequences of those decisions.

14 The films made by, or with scripts from, or about Ariel and Rodrigo Dorfman are narrated based on a leftist vision of the past, with a resistance to forgetting in spite of distance and time, and with astute cultural subversiveness based on mixing formats, languages, and experiences into cultural collages. For a more in-depth analysis of this documentary, see Bossay 2014b.

15 One side of Ariel's family had to emigrate due to economic problems in Odessa, as well as to flee the pogroms of Eastern Europe. Hence, theirs was an ethnic and religious exile as well. Ariel's father fled the fascist regime in Argentina in 1944 and was expelled due to McCarthyism in the United States,

before he finally arrived in Chile. Then Ariel joined the democratic revolution of Allende. Ariel, his father, and to a certain extent Rodrigo, all faced forced migration for political reasons.

16 This film won Best Film in the new directors' competition from the Mostra Internacional de Cinema in São Paulo, Brazil, the Peace Award in the International Film Festival in Berlin, and Best Documentary in Créteil Femmes Festival, in France.

17 Contreras was the head of the National Intelligence Directorate (DINA), Pinochet's secret police. He was sentenced to 529 years in prison for kidnapping, forced disappearance, and assassination.

18 An action or manifestation against individuals or groups, to denounce and disavow their actions, usually used to make visible torturers and human rights violators.

19 Winner of the Memory award at the Havana Film Festival, as well as Best Documentary from the Chilean Circle of Art Critics and SANFIC in Santiago.

20 The other three films were titled *Mi padre, mi historia* / "My Father, My History" (2004), *Búsqueda en el silencio* / "Search in Silence" (2007), and *La realidad* / "Reality" (2009). The English-language titles are personal translations, as these films were never released with official English titles.

21 Through an interview with Andrés, it became evident that there is a legal investigation underway, and that certain topics explored in the film actually go into the case against the military. *El pacto de Adriana* also explores the failure of the justice system.

22 Andrés grew up in Belgium; regarding language, he says: "voiceover [for this film] had to be in Spanish, because for me, this language is a link to my father and his story. . . . As part of his trauma [my father] didn't use this language with his children" (Lübbert 2017). Once Andrés learns enough Spanish, he breaks this cycle and starts communicating in Spanish with his father.

23 Henricksen was an Argentinian reporter who had worked for an Argentinian newsreel, and at the moment of his death was covering the Allende government for Swedish television. During an uprising before the coup, called the "Tanquetazo," Henricksen recorded the military movements, and eventually his own death. The camera and footage were recovered by Chile Films, and later become a newsreel of that day titled *Chile junio—1973 / June 1973* (1973). The footage was also included in *La batalla de Chile / The Battle of Chile* (1975, 1976, 1979), and more recently in the Argentinian documentary *Aunque me cueste la vida / Although It May Cost Me My Life* (Silvia Maturana, Pablo Navarro Espejo, 2009).

WORKS CITED

Actores secundarios. 2004. Directed by Pachi Bustos and Jorge Leiva. Santiago, Chile.

Aunque me cueste la vida. 2009. Silvia Maturana, Pablo Navarro Espejo. Buenos Aires, Argentina: Adoquín Video Digital.

Bossay, Claudia. 2014a "Dicotomías en las lecturas de lo visual en la Unidad Popular y la dictadura: El protagonismo de lo visual en el trauma histórico." *Comunicación y Medios.* Especial Bienal Cine Latinoamericano, 29: 106–18.

———. 2014b, "A Family History / A Country's History: The Films of Ariel and Rodrigo Dorfman." *Jewish Film & New Media: An International Journal* 2 (1): 64–88.

———. 2014c. "Documentando el pasado: Documentos históricos en documentales contemporáneos sobre la dictadura chilena." In *Travesía por el cine chileno y latinoamericano*, edited by Mónica Villarroel, 177–86. Santiago: LOM.

———. 2015. "Estética, memoria y política. Cortometrajes que recuerdan el trauma histórico chileno reciente." In *Memoria histórica y cine documental: Actas del IV congreso internacional de historia y cine*, edited by Josep María Caparrós Lera, Magí Crusells, and Francesc Sánchez Barba. Barcelona: Centre d'investigacions Film-Història, 2015.

Bossay, Claudia, and Peirano, María Paz. 2017. "Parando la olla documental: Women and Contemporary Chilean Documentary Film." In *Latin American Women Filmmakers Production, Politics, Poetics*, edited by Deborah Shaw and Debbie Martin, 70–95. London: I.B Tauris.

Calle Santa Fe. 2007. Directed by Carmen Castillo. Paris, France: Institut National de l'Audiovisuel (INA) and Les Films d'Ici.

Cavallo, Ascanio, and Gonzalo Maza, eds. 2010. *El novísimo cine chileno.* Santiago: Uqbar Editores.

Chile junio–1973. 1973. Directed by Eduardo Labarca. Santiago, Chile: Chilefilms.

De Ramón, Armando. 2001. *Historia de Chile: Desde la invasión incaica hasta nuestros días (1500–2000).* Buenos Aires: Biblos, Centro de Investigaciones Diego Barros.

Donoso Macaya, Ángeles. 2020. *The Insubordination of Photography: Documentary Practices Under Chile's Dictatorship.* Gainesville: University Press of Florida.

"El género documental gana terreno en las salas locales." 2001. In *Espectáculos (El Mercurio)*, July 21, C22.

El color del camaleón. 2017. Directed by Andrés Lübbert. Santiago, Chile, Belgium: Blume, Mollywood, Off World.

El diario de Agustín. 2008. Directed by Ignacio Agüero. Santiago, Chile: Amazonía Films.

El edificio de los chilenos. 2010. Directed by Macarena Aguiló and Susana Foxley. Belgium, Chile, Cuba, France: Aplaplac, Instituto Cubano del Arte e Industrias Cinematográficas (ICAIC), Les Films d'Ici.

El pacto de Adriana. 2017. Directed by Lizette Orozco. Santiago, Chile: Salmón Producciones, Storyboard Media.

Generation Exile. 2009. Directed by Rodrigo Dorfman. Santiago, Chile, United States: Melloweb.

Hirsch, Marianne. 2008. "The Generation of Postmemory." *Poetics Today* 29, no. 1 (Spring): 103–28.

Jelin, Elizabeth. 2002. *Los trabajos de la memoria*. Madrid: Siglo XXI.

Klubock, Thomas Miller. 2003. "History and Memory in Neoliberal Chile: Patricio Guzmán's *Obstinate Memory* and *The Battle of Chile*." *Radical History Review* 85: 272–81.

La batalla de Chile. 1975. 1976. 1979. Directed by Patricio Guzmán. La Habana, Cuba: Equipo Tercer Año, Instituto Cubano del Arte e Industrias Cinematográficas (ICAIC).

La ciudad de los fotógrafos. 2006. Directed by Sebastián Moreno. Santiago, Chile: Películas del pez.

La flaca Alejandra. 1994. Directed by Carmen Castillo and Guy Girard. Paris, France: Channel 4 Television Corporation, France 3, INA-France.

Landsberg, Alison. 2004. *Prosthetic Memory: The Transformation of American Remembrance in the Age of Mass Culture*. New York: Columbia University Press.

Morales, Marcelo. 2017. "¿Habla mucho el cine chileno del golpe y la dictadura?" *Cinechile.cl*, September 10. http://cinechile.cl/criticas-y-estudios/habla-mucho-el-cine-chileno-del-golpe-y-la-dictadura/.

Mouesca, Jacqueline. *2005. El documental, la otra cara del cine*. Santiago: LOM.

Moulian, Tomás. 1997, *Chile actual: Anatomía de un mito*. Santiago: LOM.

Pino-Ojeda, Walescka. 2009. "Latent Image, Chilean Cinema and the Abject." *Latin American Perspectives* 36 (5): 133–46.

Ramírez Soto, Elizabeth. 2015. "Traveling Memories: Women's Reminiscences of Displaced Childhood in Chilean Postdictatorship Documentary." In *Doing Women's Films: History Reframing Cinemas, Past and Future*, edited by Christine Gledhill and Julia Knight, 139–50. Champaign: University of Illinois Press.

Sepúlveda, Alfredo. 2002. "Cigarros sin filtro." *Wiken* (*El Mercurio*), December 12, 3.

Stern, Steve. 2009. *Recordando el Chile de Pinochet: En vísperas de Londres 1998*. Santiago: UDP ediciones.

Trumper, Camilo. 2016. *Ephemeral Histories: Public Art, Politics, and the Struggle for the Streets in Chile*. Oakland: University of California Press.

Urrutia Neno, Carolina. 2013. *Un cine centrífugo: Ficciones chilenas 2005–2010*. Santiago: Uqbar Editores.

Villarroel, Mónica. 2005. *La voz de los cineastas: Cine e identidad chilena en el umbral del milenio*. Santiago: Editorial Cuarto Propio.

Walker, Janet. 2005. *Trauma Cinema: Documenting Incest and the Holocaust*. Berkeley: University of California Press.

Zavala, Fernando. 2005. "*Actores secundarios*, el film que consolidó los nuevos documentalistas." *Espectáculos* (*El Mercurio*), August 22, C18.

12

THE LIFE OF THINGS

Materiality and Affectivity in *Atrapados en Japón* by Vivienne Barry

María Constanza Vergara Reyes
Translated by Elsa Maxwell

This chapter was made possible thanks to a grant from Chile's National Fund for Scientific and Technological Development, abbreviated FONDECYT. The grant is no. 1170129, adjudicated to a project titled "Perspectivas ampliadas: Formas de vida, comunidad y poética en las narrativas contemporáneas en Chile, México y Argentina" [Broadened Perspectives: Ways of Life, Community, and Poetics in Contemporary Chilean, Mexican, and Argentine Narrative].

Born in 1953, Vivienne Barry is a Chilean journalist who has dedicated her career to animation film. Barry, like many other Chilean nationals, went into exile during Augusto Pinochet's civilian-military dictatorship, which led her to study animation in Dresden, Germany. Since returning to Chile, she has been recognized for her work creating children's television programs using the stop-motion technique. After directing and writing various short animated films, in 2015 she released a full-length documentary in which she combines the stop-motion aesthetic with real scenes and events. In this article, I analyze the film *Atrapados en Japón / Trapped in Japan* and the diverse materials it includes: family photos, mid-twentieth-century news footage, old objects, travel souvenirs, and different animation techniques.[1]

In this documentary, Barry imagines her father, Carlos Barry Silva, and his trip with five Chilean colleagues to Japan and Manchuria in 1941. Carlos Barry worked for the newspaper *El chileno* and was invited on an official visit to multiple cities in the Japanese Empire along with Mario Planet from the newspaper *La Hora*; Jorge Vial Jones from *La Nación*; Augusto Iglesias from *La Opinión*; Roberto Aburto from *El Diario Ilustrado*; and Gustavo Labarca Garat from *El Imparcial*. The tour, which initially was slated to last three months, went on for more than a year because just when the party planned to return to Chile, Japanese ships were blockaded in response to the bombing of Pearl Harbor and the United States' declaration of war on Japan. For this reason, the Chilean journalists were forced to return to Tokyo and suddenly became war correspondents.[2]

Even though the documentary title makes reference to the travelers' forced voyage in the context of the Second World War, the film adds other layers of meaning in which the director becomes the protagonist. In this way, the film is linked to a broader tradition of first-person documentaries sparked by the experience of displacement.[3] The Argentine critic Pablo Piedras makes references to Hamid Naficy and Michael Renov's contributions when he states: "In the analyzed documentaries, the shared aspects that connect the emergence of the first-person is the filmmakers' displacement and exile; the former widens their experience and viewpoint, whereas the latter emerges as an emergency situation that propels an explicit manifestation of their subjectivity" ["Los aspectos compartidos que conectan la irrupción de la primera persona en los documentales examinados son los desplazamientos de los cineastas como apertura de la experiencia y de la mirada, y el destierro como situación de emergencia que impulsa la manifestación explícita de la subjetividad"] (2014, 58).[4] By reconstructing and imagining the history of her father, Barry's documentary not only engages with a global tendency to relate different types of exile to personal reflections on identity and memory but also employs a narrative structure present in recent Chilean cultural production. As noted by other critics, the dialogue between the director's autobiography and an ancestor's biography is a recurring device in postdictatorial Chilean literature and documentary film. For example, films like *En algún lugar del cielo / Some Place in the Sky* by Alejandra Carmona (2003), *Mi vida con Carlos / My Life with Carlos* by Germán Berger-Hertz (2010), and *La quemadura / The Burn* by René Ballesteros (2010) dramatize family searches through first-person accounts in which their own histories are intertwined with reconstructions of the lives of their ancestors.[5] It is important to note that in these documentaries, exile also plays an important role, either because the director was exiled at a young age, as in the case of Carmona and Berger-Hertz, or, as in the case of some of the directors, because they were living abroad at the moment of the film's recording.

In the case of Barry, the director lost her father at an early age, but not for reasons related to the politics of the dictatorship; thus, the film addresses events that occurred between 1941 and 1942 and that are global in nature: the Second World War. In a similar vein, and in contrast to the aforementioned postdictatorship documentaries, Barry's film does not include conversations with family members or talking heads who discuss the past. Here, I am interested in *Atrapados en Japón* because filiation is constructed from a very different material repertoire and by using methods that accentuate a highly affective perspective. As we shall see later on, this experimental style is typical of contemporary films that focus on personal themes related to interculturality. It is also a material way of representing the experience of subjects who have inhabited different spaces. Specifically, I would like to propose that the way the documentary represents the process of searching is related more to touch than to sight; it is an exercise of producing closeness more than an intellectual understanding or historical research. In the same way, I aim to establish that the presence and centrality of objects, both in the narrative and in the scenes, invite us to experience the story relationally, and therefore affectively.

THE SPECTER OF THE FATHER

One of the original elements of this production is the way in which the film is narrated: it alternates two voices and two time frames in the present tense. The first time frame corresponds to the voice-over of the director, who positions herself in the role of the daughter and performatively constructs her point of enunciation (via a letter to her father); the second time frame is a masculine voice-over identified with her father (it is actually the voice of Juan Diego Spoerer, also a filmmaker) and is based on a compilation of notes, chronicles, and travel journals from different members of his travel group, as explained in the final credits.[6]

I am particularly interested in the (re)construction of the father figure because it situates the director in a Frankenstein-like role. Like the protagonist of Mary Shelley's novel, Vivienne Barry is capable of giving life to inert material by assembling fragments that configure a new subject in the present; but in this case, the result is not a monster but a father figure. In this operation, Carlos Barry's subjectivity ceases to be unique and complete and is rather presented as heterogeneous, performative, and accessible only through materiality. As the director states in a 2012 interview: "My father wrote a travelogue, but it was only a few pages long. . . . So I read books by others on the trip and met with others who shared their journals. But even so, I do not know everything that happened" ["Mi padre tenía un diario de viaje, pero a las pocas páginas se terminaba. . . . Entonces, leí libros de gente que hizo el viaje, y me encontré con personas que aportaron otros diarios. Pero aún hoy no sé todo lo que pasó"] (Olave 2012). The father figure, then, is constructed from a collective story, and his discourse is, in reality, a combination of voices articulated in a new narration. Consider Jo Labanyi's statement apropos of affect theory:

> I do not propose that we abandon the study of subjectivity, but would like to argue for a concept of subjectivity that is based on relationality with others and with things. That means paying attention to feelings as well as ideas, and viewing feelings, not as properties of the self, but as produced through the interaction between self and world. And it means seeing that interaction, not as the coming together of two separate entities, but as a process of entanglement in which boundaries do not hold. (2010, 223)

Nothing in *Atrapados en Japón* is contemplated in an isolated or limited sense: even the trips are presented as fluid processes in which the camera moves across the landscape. The film's setting accentuates the viewer's sensation of this, as the world is experienced as a continuum between Chile, Japan, Korea, and China. Movement by train and across oceans contributes to this sensation as the subjects interact with the landscape and their surroundings. Additionally, by using an articulated voice-over and two first-person voices, the documentary explores new forms of occupying a site of enunciation without circumscribing the story to a closed, intimate, and unique subjectivity. Despite Vivienne's admiration for her father, the particular simulation of his viewpoint denies all possible exceptionalisms of his character; just as the journal entries reflect a common experience, what he lived was also experienced by others.

The film's two protagonists live in different time periods, but they come together because of the documentary's staging. The use of fading is a common device in this film. Just as a voice-over is added to the images, the staging also creates a sense of continuity by overlapping a past photo with a scene that takes place in the present. The voices are alternated like private correspondence: the staging proposes a prerecorded dialogue that simulates closeness, but that also dramatizes distance. As Patrizia Violi (1987) explains, the epistolary exchange assumes that the interlocutors do not share time nor space, so they must imagine each other. In private correspondence, Violi suggests, the subjects simulate a conversation and devise strategies to re-create closeness, thus navigating the spatial and temporal distance that separates them. Seventy-four years have passed between Carlos Barry's trip and the moment when his daughter reads his notes, inquires about his writings, shares her opinions, and wonders about what he saw and felt.

The (re)construction of the father introduces two fundamental methods in the film: on the one hand, the dialogue of voices between father and daughter, and on the other, diverse scenes of reenactment of what is thought to have happened on the trip. Even though there are newspaper chronicles, archival news footage, abundant black-and-white photographs, and copious documents about the journey, the object of the film is not to establish what happened with absolute certainty but rather to explore her father's youth with curiosity. When Vivienne is able to identify the woman who repeatedly appears in her father's postcards and photos as the Chinese-Japanese singer and actress Yoshiko Yamaguchi, she asks: "Did you fall in love? Did you perhaps make love for the first time? . . . Did you sing with her as you did with me? . . . Perhaps you imagined that she died in Hiroshima" ["¿Te enamoraste? ¿Te iniciaste quizás allá en el amor? . . . ¿Cantabas con ella como lo hacías conmigo? . . . Quizás imaginaste que murió en Hiroshima"] (Figure 30). Questions, hypotheses, assumptions. To fall in love, to imagine. The first-person voice is not that of a traditional biography because it does not aim to investigate her father's actions, but rather to explore his sensations and what he experienced as he faced new contexts and situations.

As Bill Nichols argues, reenactment scenes underscore a type of narration that is based on a hypothesis and the collective construction of stories: "Reenactments are clearly *a* view rather than *the* view from which the past yields its truth" (2008, 80, emphasis in original). In *Atrapados en Japón*, we observe different types of reenactments: some are highly stylized and created with varying animation techniques (for example, boats that move across a sketched map), whereas others are more traditional, or what Nichols calls "realist dramatization" (2008, 84).[7] One that is very relevant, repeated at the

Figure 30. Old photos of Chinese-Japanese singer and actress Yoshiko Yamaguchi, in *Atrapados en Japón / Trapped in Japan* (Vivienne Barry, 2015).

beginning and the end of the story, is that which narrates the death and burial of her father when the director was eleven years old: in a black-and-white sequence, we watch a small girl play near the gates of the mausoleum and in the passageways of the cemetery where Carlos Barry Silva is buried. This type of reenactment, associated with the docudrama and frequently used in television shows to illustrate flashbacks, is used only in this sequence, which is also the only one in which Vivienne takes a leading role. Animation is generally used when the film re-creates an event that occurred before the director was born—for example, a part of the father's trip, or a situation that occurred in an exotic place. The images are much more stylized and therefore less realistic, which creates a greater sense of distance and underscores the phantasmatic aspects of the scene. In this respect, Nichols states:

> Unlike the contemporaneous representation of an event—the classic documentary image, where an indexical link between the image and historical occurrence exists—the reenactment forfeits its indexical bond to the original event. It draws its fantasmatic power from this very fact. The shift of levels engenders an impossible task for the reenactment: to retrieve a lost object

in its original form even as the very act of retrieval generates a
new object and a new pleasure. (2008, 74)

The fantasmatic power of the reenactments is especially visible in the scenes that narrate the trip to Yokohama. The masculine voice-over reads different journal entries while aboard, while we watch black-and-white images of the journalists during the journey: sunbathing on the deck; leaning on the rails, spending time as a group. The sequences continue with an account of life on board the *Rakuyo Maru*, the Japanese luxury boat that transported them. But this time we listen to the ambient sound (music from the time period, laughter, indistinguishable voices, and glasses clinking) surrounding the passengers as they enjoy themselves, while the camera slides across a solitary ship, apparently abandoned. In the images we see, there are no subjects, just hallways and rooms in a type of labyrinth of memory. Elizabeth Ramírez Soto has already noted the material relationship between reenactment and travel in other Chilean documentaries by women who explore the experience of exile during early childhood. Ramírez Soto uses the term "traveling memories" to reference an itinerant memory both in time and space, which is materially expressed through frequent traveling shots (2015, 143). In this way, travel is both material and metaphorical, and in this case, it refers to the experience of attempting to grasp an unknown and distant country.

Although Nichols argues that reenactment loses the indexical link with the past event, the way in which Barry uses her father's inherited objects by animating them in stop-motion problematizes this affirmation. For example, in the sequence that narrates the 1942 bombing of Tokyo, the director transforms a doll into a witness of historical events. The sound of bullets and bombs brings continuity to a series of alternating scenes between the doll's face and the besieged city. In this case, the animation not only gives movement to the object but also transforms it into a protagonist of the event. This sequence reaffirms a device observed throughout the film: the doll is employed as a creative sign. She is a protagonist because she was there; she emerges from the past and is transformed into an opportunity to connect with an earlier moment. However, that direct link with the past does not diminish the fantasmatic power of the sequence; on the contrary, it underlines the impossibility of total comprehension solely through the index: neither the archival footage nor the past objects can fully account for an earlier experience.

Luz Horne identifies "documentary fiction" as a method that combines reenactments and animated sequences with other material and archival scenes, and suggests that it is a tendency in current Latin American narrative. Concretely, Horne studies the ways in which fiction surfaces in Andrés di Tella's 2007 documentary *Fotografías / Photographs*. Although Horne does not specifically mention the reenactments, her description of the sequences suggests that she is referring to them:

> In contrast to the type of art that values the document—because it produces the anticipation of meaning—or memorial or confessional art, which seeks to express a deep and authentic interior, this type of documentary narrative (whether film or textual), *recovers that which interrupts the ambition of objectivity; it highlights the value of what is lost or forgotten*: a type of dysfunctionality or unproductive, idle, and undisciplined remainder. The affective excess reveals the failure of the archival effort and reminds us that even though these works are sustained by the search for proof and documentation, they are also simultaneously about fiction. [Frente a un tipo de arte basado en el valor del documento—en donde se produce una anticipación del sentido—o frente a un arte memorialístico o confesional, que busca la expresión de un interior profundo y auténtico, en este tipo de narrativa documental (ya sea fílmica o textual), *se rescata aquello que interrumpe la ambición objetiva; se subraya el valor de lo que se pierde o se olvida*: una cierta disfuncionalidad, un resto improductivo, ocioso e indisciplinado. Es este exceso afectivo que se cuela como falla en el esfuerzo archivístico el que nos recuerda que, aunque estas obras parecen basar su actividad en la búsqueda de pruebas y documentos, se trata, simultáneamente, de ficciones.] (Horne 2016, 840–41, emphasis added)

Fotografías is also a first-person documentary in which the director explores the relationship to his heritage, in this case, his mother's, who is of Indian origin. Even though di Tella reflects directly on his own cultural identity, both documentaries highlight the theme of a relationship with an unknown and highly exoticized country. In this sense, the emergence of fictional elements also acts as a way to deactivate clichés about India and Japan. In the case of Barry, the use of this resource and others I have already mentioned highlights her own position as a director. These resources propose a new agreement with her viewers, underscoring the value of what is lost or forgotten, eluding the main character, and problematizing the protagonist's role as the sole agent of action by intersecting their subjectivity with the experience of others.

SOUVENIRS THAT COME TO LIFE

In the beginning, there is a doll: the first sequence of the documentary is in stop-motion animation and consists of multiple dolls in traditional dress who move across the screen. Just as the film begins with this image, we are later told that the doll was the very genesis of the project: she was always on display in the family home. When the director went into exile, the doll was left, together with other cherished objects, in the hands of Armandina, the family's nanny.[8] After many years, Armandina contacted Vivienne in order to return her inheritance. It is interesting how the narrative about the doll implies thinking about different positions and types of global circulation: her father's trip to the East, the daughter's exile in Germany, the exotic souvenir that becomes a sign of home and paternal legacy. As the Argentine filmmaker Andrés di Tella affirms:

> The personal archive does not need to be original. It is not a collection of unobtainable rarities. The most valuable piece of an archive is what you overlooked, forgot or thought was lost. When one starts to rummage through archives, the prize is to find what you weren't looking for. What we have forgotten is what has conserved the most life: Proust's Magdalene. [El archivo personal no tiene por qué ser algo demasiado original. No se trata de ser coleccionista de rarezas inconseguibles. La pieza más valiosa del archivo es la que pasaste por alto o habías descartado o no recordabas o la que estaba perdida. Cuando uno se pone a hurgar en los archivos, el premio es encontrar lo que no estabas buscando. Lo que mejor hemos olvidado es lo

que más vida conserva: la magdalena de Proust.] (Firbas and Meira Monteiro 2006, 85)

In this case, the doll acts as a detonator of memory, of curiosity, and of the documentary project in itself precisely because it had intrigued Vivienne since early childhood. At the beginning of documentary, she says: "It seemed as if [the doll's] eyes were watching me" ["Parecía que sus ojos [de la muñeca] me estaban mirando"] (Figure 31). This particular way of referring to and giving life to the doll blurs the limits between subject and object: if Barry directs the animation, we also know that the doll affects and interpellates her. From a young age, she wanted to hold and be close to her; she has a lasting impact on the director.

In the beginning, Barry's voice-over narrates the child's desire to claim and play with her father's souvenirs from his trip East: she numbers the jugs, Buddhas, little ivory elephants, books with silk covers and embroidered dragons, and, of course, the doll in the glass case. This image projects a Chilean home full of Eastern objects on display as a sign of refinement and cosmopolitanism. At that time, her father warned her: "Look, but don't touch" ["Se mira, pero no se toca"]. This initial statement is connected to another at the end, when Barry states, "I studied journalism in order to write

Figure 31. A stop-motion sequence with the Japanese doll, in *Atrapados en Japón / Trapped in Japan* (Vivienne Barry, 2015).

like you but in the end I focused on film animation, an art which consists of giving a character a soul, of giving life to inanimate objects. Perhaps because of your death and the dolls" ["Estudié periodismo queriendo escribir como tú, pero finalmente me dediqué al cine de animación, ese arte que consiste en dar alma a personajes, en dar vida a objetos inanimados. Quizás debido a tu muerte y a las muñecas"].[9] This statement resonates with Jane Bennett's ideas in her book *Vibrant Matter*, in which she connects the experience of growing up in a world plagued by animated objects with the possible origin of contemporary ideas about material vitality and the power of things (Bennett 2001, vii).

The things belong to another time and place; Vivienne recovers them, and in doing so, she realizes what is really irrecoverable: her father, and a detailed account of his trip to the East. Susan Stewart (2013) affirms that souvenirs are metonymic, and dependent on narration to overcome their incomplete status. In this case, the souvenirs exist in the absence of the story of the trip. As such, the documentary is developed with the certainty of incompleteness. The director's reconstruction of the trip carefully follows her father's path as a way to trace his steps, but without pretending to finish or close his story.

Even though the voice-over statements coincide in space (the visit to Japan), the film clearly shows the differences between the two travel experiences: her father's journey as a reporter of the East turned war correspondent, and hers, which is marked by a nostalgic tone that frequently refers to exile and loss. Toward the end she states: "departures have left a mark on us: abandonments, absences, farewells, separations, distances, exiles and changes" ["las partidas nos han marcado: abandonos, ausencias, despedidas, separaciones, distancias, exilios y cambios"]. Vivienne's voice-over narrates her own journey to Japan, but unlike a personal diary or chronicle, it does not focus on daily experience. On the contrary, it is more reflexive and retrospective, in an autobiographical style. More than the day-to-day of a tourist's route, Barry's journey triggers a series of vital reflections that connect the mourning for her father with other losses; likewise, she links culture shock with different sensations of otherness. *Atrapados en Japón* is crisscrossed with experiences of displacement, and its narrative is chronologically organized around her father's round-trip: from the ship's departure from Valparaíso in 1941 to its turbulent return in 1942, when it first had to pass by Africa so passengers could transfer from the Red Cross vessel to one bearing a Swedish flag, in the context of an international prisoner exchange.

The displacement theme is further evident in the continual use of traveling images: train windows, scenes of the sea filmed aboard a boat, and the already-mentioned use of epistolary correspondence as a plot device.

The journey is narrated by different subjectivities and in different styles. We observe, for example, a close-up of a newspaper column signed by Mario Planet: "I say it because I saw it: Japan, myth of the East" ["Lo afirmo porque lo vi: Japón, mito del Oriente"]. Likewise, the masculine voice-over affirms that the imperial servants requested the journalists be "objective and to create an exact concept of reality" ["objetivos y formarse un concepto exacto de la realidad"]. Although Vivienne replicates the trip of her father and his friends, the product of her journey does not attempt to be objective or exact; neither does it establish its veracity from a witness position. In fact, in her reconstruction of the journalists' trip, Barry questions the aspiration of objectivity, as all the records suggest that the Empire's official invitation was more interested in propaganda than impartiality. The meetings with the Japanese servants, military authorities, and ministers highlight the Japanese efforts to establish an official version of the Empire's activities, one that would justify and praise its actions, especially those related to the Manchurian occupation. The act of closing the train curtains while traveling through occupied territories in Korea and China so the visitors would not see the poverty and exploitation reveals a biased and imposed vision of reality. After the bombing of Pearl Harbor, when the journalists found themselves in the middle of an international conflict, the situation became even more sinister, as the violence heretofore hidden under the guise of a tourist trip became more evident.[10]

Among the inherited souvenirs, Barry finds a small figurine of four monkeys carved out of wood, which serves as an enigma to be resolved over the course of the documentary. At the beginning, the director's voice-over asks with which monkey she should identify: with the one who does not see; with the one who cannot hear; with the one who does not speak; or with the one who goes out to explore the world. Later she affirms: "On the contrary, the wise monkeys serve as an omen of you and your companions, controlled, silenced, and censured in all of your movements" ["Más bien, los monos sabios representaban un presagio: tú y tus compañeros, controlados, acallados, y censurados en todos sus movimientos"]. It important to note the way in which the question of the monkeys' significance pivots from the personal to the political on an international scale; and from a father-daughter relationship to the relationship of a war correspondent and the authorities of one of the countries involved in the conflict. There is no one solution to the question raised by Vivienne; what is relevant is how these different layers coexist with the potential responses: one is strictly personal and the other is situated within a global context.

Instead of attempting to establish an objective account and an official version of events, Barry, as we have seen, presents a first-person narrative that is ostensibly incomplete. From the journalistic archives, she searches for the most emotional aspects of the journey (the masculine voice-over states: "All the charm I initially felt for these lands has turned into terror" ["Todo el encanto que sentía en un principio por estas tierras comienza a convertirse en pavor"]). She wishes to have been there, where her father was, in order to feel (more than to know) some part of that experience.

Even though we have argued that Barry's documentary does not act as a traditional biography, there is one element that is closely related to this genre. As Leonor Arfuch states while reflecting on the exercise of biographical writing:

> In the biographical genres, there is, as Bakhtin already noted . . . an unfolding of the self that is in a certain sense related to the biographer and the autobiographer: the former must immerse herself in the life of the other in order to construct the character; the latter must escape herself in order to see the self *from the eyes of the other* in order to objectify the story. [Hay en los géneros biográficos, como ya advertía Bajtín . . . un desdoblamiento de sí que equipara en cierto modo al biógrafo y al autobiógrafo: el primero, para construir su personaje, debe realizar una inmersión en la vida de otro; el segundo, al objetivar su relato, realiza un extrañamiento de sí para verse *con los ojos de otro*.] (2013, 49, emphasis in original)

Arfuch refers to the experience of the English biographer Michael Holroyd, who employs a research process that includes not only going to the archives and revising manuscripts, letters, and drafts but also visiting places such as their subject's home, garden, and library in order to *look* at their things (Arfuch 2013, 48).[11] This act of positioning or imagining oneself in the place of the other and observing from their perspective introduces an emotional element to the staging and dialogue that directly relates to Barry's statements. For example, when she recounts her father's stay at the Imperial Hotel of Tokyo, followed by a scene in which she looks through a window, she reflects:

> Nothing was left of the original building, but that part of the city was still intact. It is as if I were transported in time. Through the windows I see the Hibiya Park and the Imperial Palace, with its stone walls and enormous pine trees. These beautiful images that accompanied you day after day, so long ago. Today they are in front of me. [Del edificio original no queda nada, pero esta parte de la ciudad sigue intacta. Es como haberme transportado en el tiempo. Por las ventanas estoy mirando el Parque de Hibiya y el Palacio Imperial, con sus muros de piedra y pinos enormes. Estas bellas imágenes que te acompañaron día tras día, hace tanto tiempo. Hoy las tengo frente a mí.]

Vivienne Barry re-creates the trip to Japan by following her father's footsteps; she stays in the same hotel, goes to the same parks, and visits the same temples. What we see are the details: close-ups of textures, shadows, and hands and fingers handling old photos and papers. Viewed affectively, these scenes suggest that knowledge should be an embodied experience and not merely an intellectual one.

While watching a close-up sequence of elderly faces, we hear the following: "On the streets of China and Japan I searched for elderly people, closely looking at them. I imagined a cruel past lodged in their wrinkles, experiences that you knew and that I wish to know. Their presence comforted me" ["Por las calles de China y Japón fui buscando personas ancianas, mirándolas con detención. En sus arrugas imaginé experiencias de un pasado cruel, ese que tú conociste y que yo quisiera tocar. Sus presencias me reconfortaron"]. She longs to touch their past experience; if she visits the same temple, it is only to walk along the same paved streets and to move across the same surface. Throughout the documentary, we observe this tactile desire in multiple close-up shots that transform items into tangible objects for the audience: the rust on the ship, the print on a fabric, carved furniture, the moss on trees, a temple's ornaments, and the geisha's face makeup. The family archive is also a part of these tangible objects. These shots suggest that the act of reading letters and books is not as important as handling them: the director appears only a few times during the film, but on multiple occasions her hands are shown holding faded papers, selecting black-and-white photos, and turning the pages of books (Figure 32).

Certainly, I am interpreting this from the perspective of Laura Marks, whose book, *The Skin of the Film*, distinguishes between haptic and optic visuality. The latter "depends on a separation between the viewing subject and the object. Haptic looking tends to move over the surface of its object rather than to plunge into illusionistic depth, not to distinguish form so much as to discern texture. It is more inclined to move than to focus, more inclined to graze than to gaze" (2000, 162). The author argues that the difference between these types of visuality is a matter of scale: from up-close to afar, it is a process of combining them. Marks reflects on the forms of film that can appeal to other senses not represented technically. In other words, how to go beyond the audiovisual (129). In this vein, she affirms that "[t]actile epistemologies conceive of knowledge gained not on the model of vision but through physical contact" (138). According to the author, memory is codified by the contact senses (smell, touch, taste). Marks offers these ideas based on the analysis of different films belonging to what she identifies as "intercultural film":[12] movies with a distinct experimental style that evoke individual and collective memories and that represent a diasporic

Figure 32. Going through the family archive in *Atrapados en Japón / Trapped in Japan* (Vivienne Barry, 2015).

life experience. In this way, cultural difference is rendered representable for the filmmakers and accessible to audiences.

These statements are particularly meaningful when we think about their relationship with *Atrapados en Japón*. It is not only about touching the past and an earlier experience but also acquiring a type of knowledge that implies a bodily experience: to be there; to see the same things; to smell the same parks, the same sea, the same temples; to touch the texture of the past. Once again, the extreme close-ups transform the objects into materials or things ("the thing-power" to which Bennett refers [2001, 2]). The camera does not describe them from a distance but rather confronts us with their remnants and history. Like photographs and old books, the doll and other travel souvenirs do not represent the father; they do not serve as his replacement. On the contrary, they have their own history, leave their own tracks, and are composed of temporal layers that connect us to the past corporally and imaginatively.

ABSENCES AND PRESENCES

In *Atrapados en Japón*, we observe the way in which photographs from the 1940s not only possess an important creative charge but also are the protagonists: they were held, carried, and used by her father and thus hold an invisible trace of contact and closeness to him. Instead of taking on the role of biographer or detective, Vivienne Barry does not aim to solve an enigma or fix a paternal image of her father. On the contrary, her attitude is playful: she touches, jumbles, mixes, and simulates. In the absence of interviewees, experts, or conversations, the souvenirs are the witnesses of past experience: "none of you are here, but the objects are" ["todos ustedes ya no están, pero los objetos quedaron"], the director states in voice-over.

Even though the documentary engages with the first-person film tradition that narrates displacement and travel experiences, *Atrapados en Japón* also subverts various assumptions of autobiographical film. The use of self as a site of enunciation is shared by two voices and two trajectories: by the father in the context of war, and by the daughter in a contemporary context. Furthermore, the masculine voice is constructed from collective stories in different genres and formats. As we have seen, this relational way of constructing subjectivity links it to methods that employ an affective approach to staging. By underscoring the relationship between the subjects, and between them and the objects, the documentary highlights the common elements of experience and the importance of always thinking of subjects in relation to others and their context. In this way, it problematizes the usual divide between the intimate and the collective, and the subject and the object.

Moreover, the film poses various questions about how to connect ourselves with the past. The copious archival material, both familial and journalistic, is not sufficient to fully immerse oneself in the experience of a group of Chileans trapped in an international conflict. Nor is it enough for a daughter still mourning the premature loss of her father. As such, the documentary proposes the incorporation of fictional elements, such as reenactments, in order to imagine possible situations and to provide a concrete image of something forgotten or invisible. In this materialization, the old souvenirs and materials become special protagonists, presented not from an optic vision but rather from a haptic one.

In contrast to other first-person films narrated by daughters or sons, *Atrapados en Japón* produces a sense of emotional closeness by using multiple strategies: the fading of the scenes; a dialogue with an absent voice; the combination of diverse types of images; the use of close-ups; and the prominent role of the photos' and objects' materiality. As we have seen, it is not so much what they represent but rather the path they have traveled: where they were, to whom they belonged, what their wrinkles and marks say, to what they connect us, and what they invite us to imagine.

NOTES

1. The documentary, financed by state institutions such as CORFO and the Audio-Visual Fund of the National Council for Culture and Arts (*Fondo Audiovisual del Consejo Nacional de la Cultura y las Artes*), was released at multiple international festivals and received awards at the Valdivia Film Festival, the Women's Film Festival, and the BioBío Film Festival.

2. This invitation came about in the context of Japan's increasing interest in establishing tighter relationships with countries in the Americas. During the 1930s, the Japanese government implemented a strategy of commercial and cultural exchange with many Latin American nations, in parallel with their expansionist strategy in Asia. In 1937, the U.S. President Franklin D. Roosevelt, concerned by this growing contact, requested a detailed report of Japan's activities in the Americas from multiple agencies. "The intelligence reports included reports on the activities of Japanese Embassies and Japanese businessmen that were increasingly involved in commercial activities" (Hernández 2014, 120). In the particular case of Chile, it is believed that the interest was not only business-oriented but also strategic in nature: "Mount

suggests a link between politicians sympathetic to the Association of Friends of Japan, presided by the conservative Senator Maximiano Errázuriz Valdés, and the specific interests of the Japanese diplomatic corps led by the Minister Yamagata Keyoshi" (Iacobelli 2016, 102). It is thought that this early contact was crucial for establishing the neutral position held by countries like Chile and Argentina during the Second World War.

3   Furthermore, critics like Giuliana Bruno (2002) argue that the relationship between film and travel goes back to the beginning of filmmaking. See *Atlas of Emotion: Journeys in Art, Architecture, and Film*.

4   This and other translations of secondary sources only published in Spanish were rendered by the translator.

5   See, among others, Sarah Roos (2013), Lorena Amaro (2014), and María Teresa Johansson and Constanza Vergara (2014). This corpus of personal documentaries narrated from the enunciation site of children, grandchildren, and nieces or nephews also includes: *El edificio de los chilenos / The Chilean Building* (Macarena Aguiló, 2010), *Genoveva* (Paola Castillo, 2014), *Allende mi abuelo Allende / Beyond My Grandfather Allende* (Marcia Tambutti, 2015), *El color del camaleón / The Color of the Chameleon* (Andrés Lübbert, 2017), and *El pacto de Adriana / Adriana's Pact* (Lissette Orozco, 2017).

6   The lines in the final credits are the following: "[this] story is based on Jorge Vial Jones' journal; Carlos Barry Silva's and Augusto Iglesias' notes; Mario Planet's chronicles, and the books *Evacuation Ships* by Max Hill and *Barcos de evacuación y diez crónicas de Oriente* by Rodrigo Aburto. All of them participated in this story" ["relato basado en el diario de Jorge Vial Jones, anotaciones de Carlos Barry Silva y Augusto Iglesias, crónicas de Mario Planet, libros *Evacuation Ships* de Max Hill y *Barcos de evacuación y diez crónicas de Oriente* de Rodrigo Aburto. Todos ellos participaron en esta historia"].

7   For a discussion of the use of reenactments in documentaries by Chilean women, see Elizabeth Ramírez Soto (2015).

8   In a 2015 interview, the director states: "It is a very personal movie. It has to do with a Japanese doll that was in my house when I was young. I looked at it and it scared me a little; it was strange. She had a white face with golden lines. When I left Chile to go into exile, the doll was stored by my nanny, who raised me. And I never thought about it again. Until one day, about eight years ago, my former nanny called me and said 'Hey, why don't you come and pick up these things I have saved for you?' So I went and when I took the doll out of a glass box, it was like holding a saint, something sacred. I took it home and thought: 'I must do something with this,' because I knew there was a powerful story behind that doll, even though it was unknown to me. Thus the film was born" ["Esta es una película muy personal, tiene mucho que ver con una muñeca japonesa que había en mi casa cuando yo era chica. La miraba y me

daba un poco de miedo, era rara: tenía la cara blanca, unas líneas doradas. Esa muñeca quedó guardada cuando yo me fui de Chile al exilio, me la guardó mi nana, quien me crió. Y nunca más la tomé en cuenta después. Un día, hace aproximadamente ocho años, quien era mi nana me llamó y me dijo: 'Oye ¿Por qué no vienes a buscar estas cosas que te tengo guardadas?' Fui entonces, y cuando tomé la muñeca que estaba en una caja de vidrio, era como llevar un santo, algo sagrado. La llevé mi casa y pensé; 'tengo que hacer algo con esto,' porque detrás de esa muñeca yo sabía que había una historia potente, que yo no sabía. Desde ahí nace la película."] (Puga 2015).

9 One of the aspects criticized in the film is the occasionally infantile position adopted by the director in the exchange with her father. There are sequences that put more weight on the nostalgia for childhood than on the narration of the present moment of adulthood. See, for example, Marisol Águila (2016).

10 From the beginning, the imminent outbreak of a major war was insinuated: the ship that took them to Tokyo could not follow its habitual course along Mexico and California, as the United States had placed an embargo on Japanese petroleum. Consequently, they had to sail directly from Callao to Yokohama, which meant an unusual number of days without docking at any port.

11 Arfuch cites a Spanish translation of essays by Holroyd titled *Cómo se escribe una vida*, compiled by Matías Serra Bradford and translated by Laura Wittner, published in Buenos Aires in 2011 by La Bestia Equilátera.

12 At the beginning of her book, the author writes: "Intercultural cinema is characterized by experimental styles that attempt to represent the experience of living between two or more cultural regimes of knowledge, or living as a minority in the still majority white, Euro-American West. The violent disjunctions in space and time that characterize diasporan experience—the physical effects of exile, immigration, and displacement—also, I will argue, cause a disjunction in notions of truth. Intercultural films and videos offer a variety of ways of knowing and representing the world" (Marks 2000, 1).

WORKS CITED

Atrapados en Japón. 2015. Directed by Vivienne Barry. Santiago, Chile: Vivienne Barry Producciones Audiovisuales.

Águila, Marisol. 2016. "Atrapados en Japón: El complejo de Electra." *El agente cine*, August 25. http://elagentecine.cl/criticas-2/atrapados-en-japon-el-complejo-de-electra/.

Amaro, Lorena. 2014. "Formas de salir de casa, o cómo escapar del Ogro: Relatos de filiación en la literatura chilena reciente." *Literatura y Lingüística* 29: 109–29.

Arfuch, Leonor. 2013. *Memoria y autobiografía: Exploraciones en los límites*. Buenos Aires: Fondo de Cultura Económica.

Bennett, Jane. 2001. *Vibrant Matter. A Political Ecology of Things*. Durham: Duke University Press.

Bruno, Giuliana. 2002. *Atlas of Emotion: Journeys in Art, Architecture, and Film*. New York: Verso.

Firbas, Paul, and Pedro Meira Monteiro. 2006. *Andrés di Tella: Cine documental y archivo personal. Conversación en Princeton*. Buenos Aires: Siglo XXI.

Hernández, Sergio. 2014. "Migración, comercio y guerra: Las relaciones entre Japón, México y Estados Unidos antes de Pearl Harbor." *México y la Cuenca del Pacífico* 6: 103–38.

Horne, Luz. 2016. "Ficciones documentales: Exceso afectivo y surgimiento de la ficción en *Fotografías* de Andrés di Tella." *Revista Iberoamericana* 257 (October-December): 837–53.

Iacobelli, Pedro. 2016. "La 'neutralidad' chilena en la Segunda Guerra Mundial (1939–1943): Un análisis historiográfico con énfasis en la literatura sobre las relaciones Chile-Japón." *Revista de Historia y Geografía* 34: 95–108.

Johansson, María Teresa, and Constanza Vergara. 2014. "Filman los hijos: Nuevo testimonio en los documentales *En algún lugar del cielo* de Alejandra Carmona y *Mi vida con Carlos* de Germán Berger-Hertz." *Meridional: Revista Chilena de Estudios Latinoamericanos* 2: 89–105.

Labanyi, Jo. 2010. "Doing Things: Emotion, Affect, and Materiality." *Journal of Spanish Cultural Studies* 11 (3–4): 223–33.

Marks, Laura. 2000. *The Skin of the Film: Intercultural Cinema, Embodiment, and the Senses*. Durham, NC: Duke University Press.

Nichols, Bill. 2008. "Documentary Reenactment and the Fantasmatic Subject." *Critical Inquiry* 35 (1): 72–89.

Olave, Daniel. 2012. "Documental rescata odisea de periodistas chilenos en Japón," *El Mercurio*, April 9.

Piedras, Pablo. 2014. *El cine documental en primera persona*. Buenos Aires: Paidós.

Puga, Amanda. 2015. "FICValdivia. Vivienne Barry, directora de *Atrapados en Japón*: 'la verdadera historia es que yo busco a mi padre.'" October 20. http://web.archive.org/web/20160417032249/http://galaxiaup.com/ficvaldivia-vivienne-barry-directora-de-atrapados-en-japon-la-verdadera-historia-es-que-yo-busco-a-mi-padre/.

Ramírez Soto, Elizabeth. 2015. "Traveling Memories: Women's Reminiscences of Displaced Childhood in Chilean Postdictatorship Documentary." In *Doing Women's Film History: Reframing Cinemas, Past and Future*, edited by Christine Gledhill and Julia Knight, 139–50. Chicago: University of Illinois Press.

Roos, Sarah. 2013. "Micro y macrohistoria en los *relatos de filiación* chilenos." *Aisthesis* 54: 335–51.

Stewart, Susan. 2013. *El ansia: Narrativas de la miniatura, lo gigantesco, el souvenir y la colección*. Rosario: Beatriz Viterbo.

Violi, Patricia. 1987. "La intimidad de la ausencia: Formas de la estructura epistolar." *Revista de Occidente* 68: 87–99.

13

DISPLACEMENT, EMPLACEMENT, AND THE POLITICS OF EXILIC CHILDHOOD IN SERGIO CASTILLA'S *GRINGUITO*

Camilo Trumper

My grandmother passed away while I was writing this chapter. Her passing was not unexpected—she lived past her 104th birthday—but it was jarring. My first memories of my grandmother are those of a young child, almost nine years old, having recently moved to Chile alongside parents who had "returned" from dictatorship abroad. As we grew closer later in life, she lovingly confirmed something I had suspected since childhood—my grandmother had found me odd. When we first met, she did not quite understand my reticence around an extended family I did not know, as a child of Chilean exiles in Canada, where warm greetings and good-byes, and familial hugs, were not part of my everyday. She noticed that, in Chile, I did not fully, easily inhabit the language and culture, even if I was perfectly fluent in Spanish. In my earliest memories of her, we navigated this distance best around a table, coming together over french fries she chopped rustically and salted generously, a ritual we would continue into her ninth decade and my third. She would speak to this inescapable otherness when she later lovingly confessed that I had been "a difficult child" ["un niño mañoso"].[1] Her admission referred to the complicated knot of shyness, unfamiliarity, deflection, and critical distance that marked me as a child of exile "returning" to a place I knew only through the home culture my exiled parents had created abroad, a home culture that reflected their own longing for a Chile that no longer existed. For a young child who had grown up nostalgic for a "home" I "never experienced except as narrative," the place was for me inescapably foreign, yet one for which I had an overwhelming curiosity (Thomas 2017: 154–55). My grandmother's Chile was eerily familiar yet also irrevocably foreign; it was a place in which I was a stranger, but to which I wanted to belong.

My grandmother's death brought to the fore the irresistible, unavoidable weight of history. I learned of it half a world away, too far to return to Chile in time to participate in any ritual of mourning I knew she would appreciate. Her passing made me face how a history of state-sponsored violence that was a step removed for me, born almost half a decade after the September 1973 military coup that had sent my parents into exile, would nevertheless determine how I would know my grandmother and she would know me. This history manifested itself between my grandmother and me in paradoxical ways. It defined ours as a relationship informed both by inevitable distance and by deep synesthetic care.

Of course, I had known the weight of this history as long as I had known anything. But it was a fact that was almost too hard, too weighty to articulate; speaking it, or having to speak it, was often heartbreaking. I had recently left Chile after almost a year's stay when my youngest aunt, her youngest daughter, passed away suddenly, at the age I am now. I saw my grandmother six months later. Sitting in her apartment, she held my hand, and told me quietly, matter-of-factly, "I needed you" ["me hiciste falta"] and (she implied) you weren't here. The fact of being and not being, of constant displacement, shaped our connection.

Alongside her loss itself, my grandmother's passing was jarring because it illuminated the seemingly paradoxical, dialectical connection between presence and absence, exile and return, memory and identity, politics and the everyday—precisely the issues that I analyze in this piece through a close reading of Sergio Castilla's *Gringuito* (1998), a film that, I argue, explores the intimate, mundane politics of childhood in the context of exile and return to Chile. In what follows, I will argue that Castilla's *Gringuito* is a story of childhood as a political category. This category is at once defined by both violence and exile, as an exilic identity and practice, and as a creative subjectivity weighted with Chile's history of state violence and the legacies of dictatorship. It is also a vantage point or locus of analytics and enunciation, through which to tear down and rebuild radical new worlds of intimate connection and possibility in the interstices of state control. Finally, it is a field in which the main characters' political subjectivities are imagined and (re)negotiated.[2]

Gringuito, an early postdictatorship film, is the story of a Chilean family that returns to Santiago, Chile, with their eight-year-old son. Castilla's film follows two central stories of return ["retorno"]. The first is that of Jorge, the father of a young boy, who returns from exile only to grapple with the effects of trauma and the history of dictatorship. The second is that of Jorge's son, Iván, who arrives in a city and country he does not know, armed with only an amorphous fear of dictatorship, disappearance, and violence that he does not yet fully comprehend.[3] Uncertain of his new surroundings and jealous of the sibling about to be born into the family, Iván runs away from home. He quickly befriends an itinerant fruit vendor, Flaco, whom he had previously spied from the safety of his parents' apartment window, and who introduces him to a Santiago marked by vibrant street life and deep poverty. Castilla's young protagonist explores the city, searching for community among an eclectic group of characters—vendors, prostitutes, and street kids.

The exact time period remains unclear—this film could be set at the end of the Pinochet dictatorship or early in the years after the fall of Pinochet and the return to democracy. This ambiguity alludes to the persistence and legacy of violence, a crucial aspect of the cinema of exile, which often charts the effects of terror and trauma upon exiled subjects, and how these legacies shape the experience of return. Inhabiting this uncertainty, Castilla's feature engages in a broader conversation about the insidious, lasting effects of political violence on the very construction, nature, and experience of childhood.

"I AM NOT A *GRINGUITO*": THE POLITICS OF EXILIC CHILDHOOD

"I am not a little gringo." The young child protagonist of Castilla's film's repeated negative assertion of identity defines the film's narrative arc. Iván suffers a double displacement—a child of Chilean refugees in New York, he is forced to leave the United States when his parents are finally able to return to Chile. On the eve of their departure, Iván marks his place and asserts his belonging in what is a space of exile for his parents. "This is Ivan's room," he writes on the wall of his empty space; then, happily reading his own written assertion out loud, he underscores the possessive, and tellingly pronounces (and writes) his name without the Spanish inflection or *tilde*—Ivan rather than Iván.

But we quickly learn that Iván's location and identity are inherently unstable, shaped by a history that is not fully his own. Still in New York, Iván's father Jorge tells a friend, in voice-over, "I have horrible memories [of Chile]. I remember visiting the morgue, thinking my father was dead. But at the same time, I have the best memories. . . . I remember yelling 'Gringos, gringos, gringos . . . go home! Gringos go home. Now I have my own little *gringuito*." His father's affective connection to Chile is complex, informed by familial roots, childhood memories, and past political commitments, and ruptured only by state-sponsored terror. Iván has no such connection, yet his own identity, and his distance or difference from his parents, is indelibly linked to, and defined by, this selfsame history of political exile. In other words, Iván is a *gringuito* in relationship to a place and a history he understands only secondhand, through his parents' own longing and fear; yet this identity is written onto him, a condition he cannot escape no matter how often he denies it.

Iván's complex relationship to exile, language, and identity is reinforced in what Hamid Naficy (2001) describes as a recurrent trope of accented or exilic cinema: the homecoming journey, represented here, metonymically, in the airplane ride "home."[4] Halfway between the United States and Chile, a flight attendant approaches Iván, to ask, in Spanish, if he needs anything. Iván responds tersely, in English—"I don't speak Spanish"—before replacing his headphones and shutting himself off from his immediate surroundings. His refusal to speak is another creative negation—"I am not a *gringuito*" gives way here to the seemingly contradictory "I don't speak Spanish," and vice-versa. These negative rehearsals act as separate but related claims to an inchoate identity at once rooted in nationality, place, and language, now unsettled by a *retorno* that immediately marks him as "other" in the eyes of strangers and family alike, but does not define the terms and limits of his otherness in easily legible ways.

Focusing on a child "returning" to a Chile he has never known, Castilla is able to explore how exilic identities are rebuilt in new contexts, and against expectations rooted in the past. Iván's exilic journey suggests how displacement transforms subjects whose identities are shaped, but not defined, by the latent history of state terror. If *retorno* is what drives the film, the core of the narrative is the journey of discovery and self-fashioning that Iván undertakes once in Chile, in which he attempts to answer the question implied in his negation of exilic identity imposed—if he is not a *gringuito*, then who is he? Who can he be in this new place?

The unsettling effects that this journey will have on Iván's identity are immediately clear upon his landing in Chile, as the joy of reunion is muted by evident social and political tensions among the families. Castilla presents Iván's maternal grandmother, Teté, as a key foil to the nuclear family at the center of the story. Teté quickly establishes crucial distance from Jorge and his parents. Jorge's own father, we know, was apprehended and possibly disappeared after the coup. Jorge wears his fear and distrust of the authorities openly, suspiciously eyeing each policeman he encounters. In contrast, we later learn that Iván's mother, Camila, traveled to the United States to study, rather than for political reasons. Jorge's exile, then, is the unavoidable mark of political difference that extends to his son, a stain indelibly linked to Iván's outsider status. Jorge *is* a *retornado*, and Iván *is* a *gringuito*. These conditions are unavoidably, if uncomfortably, connected.

Castilla indicates this distance formally and symbolically at the very moment of *retorno*, when Jorge, Camila, and Iván emerge from the plane and appear before Camila's parents, Teté and Mario, at the airport. Camila approaches her parents, who wait behind clear glass. She remains visible to but separate from her family and her past, with whom connection is possible but muffled, mediated. The symbolic point here is powerful: exile remains an irreconcilable divide, a prism that, while invisible, filters the relationship and possibility for understanding between family members, a condition that becomes inextricably linked to the act of seeing, and to the making of subjectivity.

Iván's grandmother, Teté, makes this identification clear when she happily suggests that the expected second child will, finally, be her first Chilean grandchild, before turning to Iván only to refer to him by his hated nickname. Upon his protests, she avers: "Well, he might not look like a *gringuito* but he is a *gringuito*. Don't you see that he speaks to me in English?" ["Bueno, es que no parecerá un gringuito, pero es un gringuito. ¿No ves que me habla en inglés?"]. Iván's negation is rendered invalid by the very act of speaking it. In his grandmother's eyes, language proves Iván's otherness. Yet, his is also a racialized difference. For Teté, Iván's otherness is an ontological condition, paradoxically strengthened rather than belied by his brown skin. She quickly tempers her husband's enthusiasm at seeing their grandson so grown up: "Look, the boy is so grown up," ["Mira, está grande ese niño,"] the grandfather, Mario, coos. She responds, "Ooh. But he's darker and darker every day. He takes after Jorge's mother . . . [A] vulgar morena" ["Uy, pero cada día más negrito. Salió a la mamá de Jorge . . . [Una morena] vulgar."].[5] In short, Teté filters multiple forms of difference through the prism of race: her remarks suggest that the family's political and spatial transgressions, which led to the father's exile, are also written on the body, expressed there as *negrito* and vulgar.

Scholars have stressed that, far from natural or static, childhood remains a powerful, malleable, and creative social construct. The sociologist Chris Jenks (1996), for instance, traces the "erratic evolution of the image of childhood and its changing modes of recognition and reception," and shows how childhood develops as a malleable construction whose defining social characteristic is its ability to represent and hold together seemingly disparate or opposing categories (3).[6] Building on Jenks, José Miguel Palacios and Catalina Donoso Pinto (2017) argue that, in reconciling apparent paradoxes, the discourse of childhood "often feeds contradictory or opposing ideas" to powerful effect, and is often generative of different "imaginaries" or "sociopolitical projects" (49). Childhood is not "natural." It both has a history and is part of a broader process by which complex historical and political projects and, indeed, identities, are built.

Iván's childhood is a wonderful example of this complexity, as it focalizes a number of complex, seemingly contradictory constructions. It is particularly significant for Teté, who makes explicit connections between exile, foreignness, and politics in relation to a very particular invention of childhood. Iván's grandparents debate the terms of childhood after their grandson escapes into the city:

> **Teté:** Iván is strolling through [Santa Lucía Hill] park. And, in the meantime, Camila is waiting to give birth to my grandchild.
>
> **Mario:** Iván is also your grandchild.
>
> **T:** Look, I've given up on him. He's the worst of both worlds: *gringo* and leftist.
>
> **M:** Iván is a child. That's it!
>
> **T:** But he acts like a leftist, doing whatever he wants.
>
> **M:** All children do what they want. That doesn't make him a communist, or a leftist, or a hippie, or a liberal, or anything. Children like to be free and, if anything, that makes him right-wing!

[**Teté:** Iván [está] paseando con la empleada por el cerro. Y mientras tanto, Camila está esperando para parir a mi nieto.

Mario: Iván también es tu nieto.

T: Mira, a ese lo doy por perdido. Es la peor mezcla: gringo con izquierdista.

M: Iván es un niño. ¡Y punto!

T: Pero se comporta como izquierdista. Haciendo lo que le da la gana.

M: Todos los niños tratan de hacer lo que les gusta. Eso no lo hace ni comunista, ni izquierdista, ni hippie ni liberal ni nada. A los niños les gusta la libertad, y eso los hace más bien de derecha.]

Though Mario partially rejects his wife's politicizing of children and childhood, this conversation is a debate about politics. Childhood emerges here as a potent, if flexible, construct, an invention that refracts and recombines these various social and political strands and themes, a form upon which can be layered intersecting categories of otherness. Iván's grandmother's formulation holds together an apparent paradox—*gringuito* and *negrito*—to project a potent, if uncomfortable, identity upon her grandson, one that doubles his otherness in a nation shaped by over a decade and a half of military rule.[7]

DISPLACEMENT, *RETORNO*, AND THE MAKING OF AN IMPOSSIBLE EXILIC SUBJECT

The film's most dynamic sequence begins when Iván escapes the home, first to the Cerro Santa Lucía, and from there, across the Alameda, Santiago's main thoroughfare, and then back across the Alameda and up to the Mapocho River. With each crossing, Iván transgresses the symbolic, social divide that separates middle- and working-class Santiago. Initially fascinated by this newfound freedom to explore, unmoored from his family's past, Iván navigates the margins of the city's complex social world. In his curious wanderings, Iván befriends a mobile fruit vendor, Flaco, who sells his goods from a cart he carries through the city. Flaco's itinerancy provides Iván the opportunity to transgress the social and physical map that bounds his parent's world. With Flaco, Iván finds those urban spaces beyond his parents' social map, interstitial spaces where he can meander without the threat of being caught, willingly adrift in a part of the city for which he and his parents have no referent—the market, the shantytown, the brothel. Iván is not only out of place here but also outside of the logic of place that defines his parents' past and present city. In fact, *Gringuito*'s key conceit—that Iván can be lost, even though he is mere blocks from his parents' apartment—is legible only in this context: Jorge cannot even bring himself to look for his son, because, on the one hand, Jorge cannot imagine, let alone navigate, the urban landscape that lies beyond his own social world, bounded as it is by class, and, on the other hand, because of the lingering effects of violence and exile, he is triggered by his interactions with police. Iván's wanderings highlight the social distance that separates his family from what they would see as "the other Santiago," which appears, through Iván's gaze, as a complex, and sometimes inscrutable and threatening, social world.

The boy's itinerancy offers him the space in which to explore and fashion a wholly new relationship to the site of his *retorno*—to create a new identity or subjectivity, navigate surprising, sometimes baffling social mores, and explore new forms of social bonds. His relationship to Flaco is the initial catalyst for this exploration. Initially circumspect, Iván soon initiates a conversation in Spanish with Flaco. Almost halfway through the film, this is the first time that Iván reveals that he can not only understand but also speak Spanish, albeit with an erratic accent.[8]

With Flaco, Iván moves immediately from observation to narration, weaving an imagined reality out of these experiences, spinning a tale of his own imagined orphanhood that incorporates many of the details of daily life that he has observed in his first moments in Chile, that reflects and reshapes what he has recently seen and experienced. Iván implores Flaco to care for him, but his story is only partially legible, as Iván cannot quite understand or navigate the social and cultural codes of this new exilic space. Iván tells Flaco that he was recently orphaned when his mother died giving birth to his little brother, and that his father, out jogging, was killed by the shot of the cannon that marks the stroke of noon from the height of the Cerro Santa Lucía. Flaco, alerted by Iván's "accented" speech, his odd mispronunciations, and his partial knowledge of social norms, listens to Iván's tale skeptically, knowing that it is manufactured. The sound of the cannon, fantastical to

Iván, is an ordinary fact of daily life for Flaco; his father's runs through city streets, normal for Iván, who has seen him jog through New York City, is an unusual affectation in the late dictatorship or early postdictatorship Chilean context. This partial understanding is repeated throughout the film. Flaco meets it with sarcasm—"Man, you sure do look like a gringo" ["La media pinta de gringo que tenís"], he sneers, inverting Teté's interpellation of Iván by suggesting that his dark skin and scuffed clothes are incommensurable with foreignness and the status that proximity to the United States confers. Iván, who slips in and out of different accents in Spanish, is not fully believable as an inhabitant of either world—neither fully *gringuito* nor *chileno*.

Yet it is his partial mastery of language, and his ability to slip between cultural registers, that makes Iván a creative subject, a hybrid character who can navigate, and eventually fashion, a unique, open-ended exilic subjectivity. Iván's and Flaco's budding relationship is shaped not by any already existing shared social bond but instead by the space they open up in which to construct the creative fiction of a new identity. Iván's rehearsal of an origin story in which he is an orphan, unmoored from his parents' past and position, is significant not because it is or is not believable but rather because it is his attempt to engage his new world from the context of his own past experience "at home" and now "abroad." It is a creative engagement with a Chile he has known only as nostalgia, transformed here through a curious narration, "with its hallucinatory quality and creative mix of fact and fiction" (Lury 2005, 308, 311). It is here that Iván begins to fashion a new, hybrid, and creative "exilic subjectivity" that is located or rooted truly "in-between" multiple worlds.[9]

While I have addressed Iván's exilic creativity through language, and the practice of translation, interpretation, or mixing, his experience of urban itinerancy is also embodied and synesthetic, and Castilla represents this experience through a particular attention to materiality and mise-en-scène. As we have seen, Jorge's return to Chile is marked by a claustrophobic interiority. His world is marked by recurrence—by a compulsive return to the same places, the same routes. Iván's is more complex. The Chile in which Iván is first immersed by his parents is defined initially by distance, and a removed curiosity. We see the first glimpses of Santiago focalized through Iván's perspective, as he looks curiously out the window of his grandparents' car, taking in the streets and walls of the surrounding shantytowns, the car window mediating the relationship, offering a safe remove from which Iván learns to practice or exert the gaze from a privileged class position. Castilla represents Iván's increasingly complex social position, making repeated visual reference to distance. Iván remains, at first, ensconced in the family's apartment, familiarizing himself with his new social world extending from his grandparents, parents, and the nanny, María. He engages the city from his bedroom window, safely above the movement of the street, a vantage point that affords him a partial authority and limited view of his exilic surroundings. It is from his window that he catches a first, limited view of Flaco pulling his cart through the neighborhood, a glimpse of his mother suffering labor pains, and an early sense of his nanny's sexuality as she engages with her boyfriend in his taxi under the apartment. Iván rehearses this disquieting partial mastery when first escaping from home, climbing to the apex of Santa Lucía Hill, a position from which he surveys the city and begins to claim his space in it.

This marks a turning point in the film's formal strategy, the moment where Iván renounces his position of authoritative distance and interiority and immerses himself in the street. The focus of the film's mise-en-scène shifts here, moving from relatively detached and austere surroundings to a more complex aesthetic. Iván's journey through Santiago city streets traces a sort of baroque excess as a defining characteristic of the child's journey. Iván is first fascinated by the sights and sounds of urban mobility, escaping through crowds and speeding cars into the city's teeming marketplace, fascinated by the size, texture, variety, and novelty of the fruits and vegetables, navigating a strange sensory world. The camera here follows Iván, intermittently positioned at the height of the child, and often shooting him through crowds of people; aurally, the film suggests a synesthetic immersion, overwhelming the scene with the shouts of street vendors or of traffic, fading out intermittently to provide a sense, in voice-over, of the child's thoughts and memories. Flaco's cart provides the clearest example of the transformative potential of mobility and of Iván's curious, creative itinerancy. Iván's movement through the city perched atop Flaco's cart appears to be truly exhilarating, and his immersion into Flaco's home equally exilic. Iván jumps carelessly on the rusted remains of automobiles, and is fascinated by the frenzied footwork and movement of the handkerchief Flaco spins in an improvised folkloric dance. They douse each other with water, and enjoy a freedom Iván has not yet known in Chile. But these are not the only examples of Iván's itinerant freedom, as his journey is marked by sensory excess. When Flaco takes him into a neighborhood brothel, Iván is immersed in an overwrought sensual—aural, visual, and material—world, a truly transgressive moment in which Iván is at first a wide-eyed spectator and then, briefly, an active participant, made first to drink a pisco sour and then to perform an impromptu piece from Madame Butterfly on stage. Later, Iván finds a group of young men running up and sliding down a statue in a central park, involving his entire body in a transgressive engagement with his new urban surroundings. He follows this group into the cemetery, dancing amidst the gravestones, before being chased away by the police in an aural and embodied journey through restricted spaces. Even as he is progressively stripped of material possessions—his clothes tattered, his shoes stolen—the material world he inhabits becomes ever more excessive. Castilla, like many exiled or accented filmmakers before him, immerses his protagonist "within a more complex system of visual signs to which he looks for his emerging identity" (Solomon, 2017, 153). It is within this material world that Iván begins to build a new sense of his world in exile, and a new presentation of self.

In fact, the "routes" that Iván traces through Santiago are creative, a means of fashioning a new subjectivity that unsettles the political and social relations that are a legacy of dictatorship and displacement. In fact, as cultural geographers like Esther Peeren remind us, "time and space are not something we find before us, but something we do by enacting its cultural laws . . . time and time again." There is, in other words, a performative aspect at work in these spatial-temporal sites. Similarly, Peeren continues, "not only is all performativity necessarily embedded in time-space, but time-space is itself a performative structure in the sense that it is not simply there but established and maintained by means of repeated social practices" (2006, 71–72). Particular formations of time-space ground the interpolation of complex, even contradictory exilic identities; these "exilic subjectivities" are in "a continuous [state of] becoming that is predicated on [and produced in] the various construction of time-space encountered and performatively enacted by the subject" (75). In Castilla's film, Iván's urban itinerancy is at once a performance of spatial and social transgression and a tactic by which to build a powerful, hybrid subjectivity, to transform the impossible or unthinkable subject into an exilic subject. In fact, Iván's exilic subjectivity is not so much *bound to* a singular place as it is *bound up with* the act of place-making, or what Naficy calls either "placement" or "emplacement" (2001, 152–53).[10] The routes Iván traces through the city, and the relationships he builds, loses, and rebuilds, enact and bring into being a complex exilic identity, a subjectivity born in the space between language, class, and generation. His wandering is therefore an "exilic," creative performance.[11]

My analysis of Castilla's film, and especially its emphasis on Iván's itinerancy and itinerant subjectivity as "exilic," builds on the work of Dennis O'Hearn and Andrej Grubačić (2016), for whom exilic spaces and subjectivities are marked by forced exclusion, exile, and imprisonment, *but also* by the possibility that historical actors can act *from* and *upon* these spaces and systems of exclusion. O'Hearn and Grubačić point out how different historical subjects carve out interstitial locations or positions in exile, and turn these spaces into incubators for different forms of sociability based not only on capitalistic exchange but also on mutual aid and solidarity.

These spaces and strategies are at once a product of power and a site of its contestation: exile defines a situation of exclusion, but also opens a space in which new forms of solidarity or struggle are possible. The study of these dialectically "exilic" spaces and strategies ultimately suggests a new, "transversal" approach to politics in which global and local processes intersect and define each other. As O'Hearn and Grubačić write:

> We propose to study exilic spaces because we have hope. We have hope that another society is possible, in which social relations of mutual aid predominate, and where the *work* of building community and producing joy is recognised. . . . We think that another approach to politics is both useful and necessary, in which the production and circulation of exilic spaces and practices are recognised as a central part of the *politics* of world economy. It is not just . . . the anti-systemic voice of resisting movements that produces dissonant notes in the world-system; the struggle is also expressed in silences and refusals that are sometimes less vocal, but no less confrontational. (163, emphasis in original)

Exile emerges here as a key example of this dialectic process: exile is the quintessential form of exclusion from the national body, a casting out, and stripping of citizenship; the exilic is also, however, a form of power or agency borne out of the margins, out of the peripheral or in-between places and positions engendered by exile itself. From this vantage point, exile and the exilic are mutually constitutive. I contend that the films of exile and *retorno* find or fashion such exilic space, strategies, and subjects in equally unexpected places—in dictatorship and democracy, at "home" and "abroad," in the home and on the street. They are themselves exilic—"accented" by the trauma of exile, they also experiment with a cinematic language that reimagines the terms and limits of exile and return, part of a larger project that Verónica Cortínez might call "a powerful example of memory and resistance in a truly democratic spirit" (2016, 195).

Iván's exilic position "outside" this social world yet fluent enough to at least partially navigate it forces him to search for, and ultimately build, unexpected forms of sociability and mutual aid. His relationship with Flaco is the catalyst here: Iván finds in Flaco an entry into a new local and national world, complete with new social forms—sexuality, humor, folkloric dance. But, above all, he asks for, and eventually receives, a form of familial care built on this itinerancy. Iván transforms Castilla's cinematic city—at least partially—into an exilic space, as per O'Hearn and Grubačić.

There are limits to the exilic potential of this performance. On one hand, there is real privilege behind Iván's itinerancy. Iván's *retorno* is marked by forced exclusion and displacement, but also facilitated by his parents' class and wealth, and because of it, he enjoys a freedom to explore and build an exilic identity that Flaco cannot access. While Iván has repeatedly denied his interpellated identity ("I am not a *gringuito*"), Flaco has no such opportunity. Iván reacts with surprise to Flaco's moniker ("But you're not slim" ["Pero tú no eres Flaco"]), Flaco acknowledges that his identity is fixed by forces over which he has no control ("I've always been Slim, and I'll always be Slim" ["Siempre he sido el Flaco, y siempre seré el Flaco"]).

On the other hand, Castilla suggests that there exist significant limits to the alternative forms of exilic sociability in the Santiago of the late dictatorship and early postdictatorship period, an era marked indelibly by fear that fragmented community and solidarity. Iván's relationship to Flaco is initially mediated directly by money, as Iván exchanges his "savings," U.S. dollars stored in a champagne bottle, for Flaco's care; and even then, Flaco abandons him in a brothel and then the street. Alone, Iván searches for aid, food, and companionship and is consistently rebuffed, threatened, or chased off. He finds his way to safety only upon reciting his parent's mantra, that, as an individual, he should exercise sovereignty over his own body. In this sense, Iván's transgression reveals to the viewer a Santiago city center shaped by the legacies of neoliberal dictatorship that have both reinscribed historic lines of gender, class, and race segregation and worked to fracture interpersonal solidarities through the mobilization of terror. In Naficy's terms, the exilic filmmaker might very well project upon the city a complex frame defined by the history of state violence, but in centering his study around a child protagonist, an unfinished subject, he fashions a contradictory, open-ended narrative, its own unfinished quality marked as much by the weight of dictatorship past and present as by the possibility of contestation and change (2001, 187).

The film's greatest achievement stems from its exploration of the child's creative itinerancy, the struggle for social and spatial "emplacement" that allows Iván to piece together a potentially radical, productive, exilic subjectivity. Iván is an exilic subject defined by a double displacement, caught in a double bind. To borrow from Mae Ngai, Castilla's protagonist is an "impossible" subject—a subject irredeemably "out of place" physically and politically, "a person who cannot be and a problem that cannot be solved" (2004, 3). Jorge, an adult *retornado*, is already an uncertain political subject whose place in the nation is simultaneously a social and historical reality and a political and legal impossibility—a subject robbed of full citizenship first by a military regime committed to "eradicating politics," and again limited during transition to the "post-dictatorship" period by the impunity that marked the *transición pactada*.[12] Iván, the child protagonist who experiences a "return" to Chile for the very first time, is caught in a further predicament: as a *child* of refugees born abroad, Iván is shaped by an exile he did not experience, forced to return to a place he never knew, to (re)visit a place for which he has no original reference (Ngai 2004, 3, 14). In other words, Castilla's protagonist occupies an unthinkable, interstitial position familiar to the "accented cinema" (Naficy 2001) of exile, yet redoubled again by childhood in Castilla's intergenerational narrative.

The construction of childhood is the crucial node around which this impossible, interstitial subject is built. Karen Lury builds on Paul Sutton's critique of Deleuze's influential conceptualization of the child witness, and instead suggests that "the child is no longer the helpless or 'passive' figure described by Deleuze" (Lury 2005, 307). Rather, their child subjects both "want" and "*act*," and "should therefore be understood as *agents* as well as subjects" (311). She suggests that

> the child whose agency we confront (even if we do not recognize it as agency) is frequently "impossible." Therefore—incoherently,

> unsystematically and frequently unavailingly—the child and childhood are resistant to becoming the "subject" of study. What interests me . . . is how this agency—the disruptive, impossible, unintelligible aspects of childhood and the child—is imagined, portrayed, and performed in film and television. (Lury 2005, 308)[13]

Gringuito is heir to this tradition of representing the child as a subject able to illuminate the intricacies of exile and return ("to help us see the world differently") and to suggest a different resolution or engagement with the legacies of violence (to "disrupt" and "recast" the afterlives of terror and trauma). Revisiting the child as an active subject, Castilla's "impossible" child protagonist emerges not as apolitical but rather as a subject able to "explore and engage with the political and social implications of a particularly traumatic period" of history.

Gringuito outlines a multifaceted "history of the impossible": it presents an unthinkable, paradoxical exilic subject "who cannot be," but it *also* suggests the solution to this problem "that cannot be solved." The part of the film told from Iván's perspective explores his uncertain political, social, and physical location, caught somewhere between home and abroad, exile and *retorno*. Castilla manifests Iván's unsettled location spatially. Iván escapes into the city while his mother appears to go into labor. Iván's flight turns into a metaphorical search for a place in which he may belong, a journey of self-discovery. I read this long sequence as an exploration of childhood marked by a dialectical relationship between displacement and (its apparent opposite) emplacement, an attempt to build a youthful, open-ended exilic subjectivity, tied to but distinct from his father's past and present (Naficy 2001, 152).

As borderlands thinkers have taught us, being "out of place" can be both the result and the product of exclusionary regimes and practices, and also a generative position, a "locus of enunciation" from which to build new forms of knowledge. José David Saldívar (2012) asks the provocative question, "How is the migratory subject, in an inter-American politics of location, to be conceptualized as revolutionary . . ." (Saldívar 2012, xxi–xxiii).[14] I read in Iván's character an answer to this question. Irredeemably "out of place," Iván unsettles these "'mutually inclusive'" chronotopes, both of which are marked, in different ways, by the entrenched and persistent influence of dictatorship, silence, and fear (Naficy 2001, 153). Iván is, in fact, marked by the ongoing engagement with his exilic position, ever striving to define an exilic subjectivity vis-à-vis his parents and their place. In other words, he is marginal to the very categories and chronotopes that organize the official story or narrative of exile and return, or dictatorship and democracy.

Naficy remarks on the accented film's particular ability to hold together these different constructions of place and time, and Castilla's Santiago city center emerges as an alternative chronotope, a place marked by very different, even contradictory, social and political constructions of space and time. If Jorge's childhood home functions to represent the effects that violence has upon the past, and upon memory, Castilla's treatment of Santiago's city center reveals the legacies of dictatorship on the social world of the streets, and suggests the continued afterlife of dictatorship in the present and future. This is a Santiago riven by twin legacies of dictatorship: it is a city segregated by class, in which a world of vendors, street gangs, and brothels lies beyond the edges of Iván's parents' world, and a world largely devoid of solidarities, where the only moments of mutual aid occur in response to the perceived threat of the police. In fact, Iván's early experience in the city is marked by exclusion rather than aid: he is abandoned, threatened, and robbed, and the adults he encounters recoil from his requests for help.

However, what sets this film apart is its recognition of other possible futures represented, or made possible, by Castilla's treatment of childhood, and of Iván's impossible exilic subject-position. Iván's childhood has no place in Pinochet's Chile—he is not only out of place but outside of it, and because of this, his experience, his exilic wandering, unsettles and restructures these relationships, proposing the possibility of a sort of "in between" position that prompts us to rethink the relationship between past and present, nostalgia and creativity, exile and return; an "in between" position that offers a "third space," an alternative position and possibility that lies beyond, and promises to reconfigure, the original dialectic.[15] In other words, Iván's position—the exilic place he builds and then speaks from—is shaped by, but also has the potential to reshape, the legacies of dictatorship in new and surprising ways. Through Iván, Castilla's accented cinema is not content to simply hold together or reconcile "mutually inclusive chronotopes, which may reinforce, coexist with, or contradict one another" (Naficy 2001, 153) but instead offers a means of exploring the limits of these constructions, and a prism through which to imagine alternative experiences, identities, and subjectivities rooted in exile *and* return.

In fact, the film's narrative structure depends, until its final sequence, on the central assumption that Iván, our exilic subject, is able to transgress the myriad social and physical boundaries that structure the city as chronotope; yet, once again, the limits of this subjectivity are built into Iván's performance of his exilic childhood. Castilla presents Iván as a unique subject able to move through, and reconcile, different social worlds, producing a sort of borderlands, or border-crossing epistemology; a new, transgressive cognitive and social map of the city.[16] By the film's dénouement, his escape and then his return to the family home have set in motion the processes that resolve many of the film's central tensions and "reconcile" many of the film's antagonisms. Most concretely, Teté and Jorge tearfully recognize that the distance between them has been structured by dictatorship and exile, and, after Jorge apologizes to her, they share in their fear for Iván and walk home, arm in arm, to find the new baby born; Iván recants his stories, and Flaco agrees to help him find his family. More symbolically, when Iván returns home, he finally speaks to his nanny in Spanish, and greets his little sister, hybridizing English and Spanish, to welcome her to a family and a nation that had seemed irreconcilably fractured by political, generational, and linguistic difference: "*Linda*," he coos, in Spanish. Then, mixing Spanish and English, "Welcome to Chile, *hermanita*."[17] The film here concludes on a paradoxical note: as Iván's transgressions transform an impossible subject into an exilic one, his displaced or fractured identity successfully reconciles an otherwise unthinkable position—a subject who is at once "other" or "outside" the logic of the nation yet also provides the template for a new national subject or citizen. On one hand, Iván's return to his family rehearses the official language of the state in the "transition to democracy," the logic and language of reconciliation, where reconciliation of perpetrator and victim of state violence takes precedence over justice as the way "forward." On the other hand, Iván's own hybrid identity unsettles this simple narrative of reconciliation, and instead introduces a transgressive subjectivity into, and as part of, the national imaginary, suggesting that (the history and afterlife of) dictatorship, displacement, and exile are an integral, unavoidable part of postdictatorship Chile.[18]

If Castilla's dénouement seems, at first, to buttress the language of reconciliation, he soon introduces a heartrending reminder of the limits of such a project in a Chile marked by a long history of political and social violence that has never been addressed. Castilla's Santiago is fractured not only by state-sponsored violence and its afterlives but also by class and status. We see this, again, in the film's final scenes, and in the unraveling of Iván and Flaco's relationship. Here, the class divide that separates Iván's and Flaco's worlds is reified rather than challenged. Iván and Flaco establish a relationship of mutual support and caring only toward the very end of the film, and then Iván immediately, if unknowingly, fractures those bonds. The pair returns to the Cerro Santa Lucía, where Iván recovers the original position he had occupied at the beginning of the film: above, and distant from, the city and the street. It is a position of alterity, but also of mastery over his surroundings. Looking over the city, Iván points out that his family lives in the middle- and upper middle-class neighborhood surrounding the park; Flaco, disbelieving, motions to the tallest building in the city and beyond it, the peripheries of the city, claiming ownership of its top floors. In a heartbreaking moment, even more poignant because of Iván's oblivion, the child "proves" his story, first speaking directly to Flaco in English, reverting to the language to which he had clung in the first half of the film in order to lend credence to his claim to foreignness, and the status that his association with the United States confers upon him. In the film's final moments, Iván's linguistic strategy helps him claim a part of his identity that has always been available to him, but which he has been unable to reconcile; in so doing, he undercuts the transgressive potential of an exile identity or subjectivity, and instead reasserts himself as a product of exile, only now to prove his class location. Just as Teté had originally interpellated Iván as an ontological *gringuito* because of his adherence to English, privileging language over the physical markers of class and race, Iván now slips into a linguistic performance of identity that recognizes his otherness even as it reifies class distinction, opening up a distance from Flaco that Iván does not seem to fully realize.

Unable to resolve the different narratives Iván has constructed, Flaco reacts angrily. He twirls Iván by the legs, and the camera take on his point of view, recounting his dizzying attempts to escape and return home, focalized through the child's own unsettled perspective. At first, Flaco brings Iván to his house, where they reconcile. But when he agrees to look, one last time, for Iván's parents, Flaco sees a pamphlet his father has made in search of Iván, and his face falls in recognition. Naïvely unaware of the power of the social boundaries that he has transgressed, Iván proclaims his friendship, his connection to his erstwhile caregiver, and invites Flaco into his home. Flaco demurs, and promises to return as Iván departs. Flaco walks away, already melancholic, knowing that the relationship has been unavoidably fractured. Flaco knows he cannot transgress the social boundaries with which Iván plays, and knows that he cannot inhabit the space of Iván's home. Carefully folding Iván's picture into the pocket of his blazer, Flaco walks out of the frame and, as the image freezes, we hear the reverberations of his footsteps, which echo the unbridgeable distance between their two worlds. Iván's displacement, and his willing wandering through the city, has allowed him to build an exilic subjectivity that remains rooted in the political and social space of Pinochet's Chile, even if it is a subjectivity that sits uncomfortably at the margins of this world and, from this location, has the potential to unsettle or transform it.

CONCLUSION

Castilla's film explores the intricacies of exile and *retorno* through the prism of childhood, mapping the construction of exilic identities built in the "in-between" that connects these seemingly distinct categories. Iván's exilic journey, his itinerancy through the city, and his experiments with language, suggest, too, the transgressive potential of this subject-position, this location "on the margins," which acts as the basis from which to build a critique of, and an alternative to, a Santiago marked by the legacies of dictatorship and displacement. Castilla's lens reveals how the process of displacement and emplacement is felt most clearly in the intimate, everyday. The filmmaker's exploration of these intimate worlds, this synesthetic experience of politics, is what connects this project to my own memories of childhood and family. My memories of my grandmother help me understand how our affective worlds, understandings of self, and critical awareness are together built within very real structures of the possible. Our relationship was shaped by a distance that originally expressed itself as difference, otherness, and occasionally uncomfortable misunderstandings. It was a relationship in which our histories, our different but interconnected pasts, collapsed into synesthetic, affective connections that crossed generations. These intimate bonds were built along the routes carved by these histories of displacement, not apart from them. Iván's final words speak to this politics of the intimate and everyday: when we see him at the very end of the film, he remains an exilic subject by stubbornly hybridizing his words, speaking in tongues, in the creative practice that is Spanglish.[19] He is an exilic subject whose very presence, whose accented being, is located within the body politic, constantly threatening to destabilize the very categories upon which it is built—exile and *retorno*, insider and outsider, home and abroad, dictatorship and postdictatorship.

In so doing, Castilla's film lays the groundwork for a complex, even radical reappraisal of the assumed relationship between these seemingly stable categories. *Gringuito* presents childhood as a radically destabilizing trope, and the exilic child as a critical subject and subjectivity that can call into question how we understand the relationship between dictatorship and democracy, violence and peace, all the while underscoring the effect of almost two decades of dictatorial rule and neoliberal policy to which the editors of this volume speak. In so doing, *Gringuito* deals with deep politics that shape those figures we often deem apolitical or outside of politics—including, and especially, exilic childhood.

NOTES

1 All translations mine unless otherwise noted.

2 This is certainly a common preoccupation among films of exile. The introduction of Carolina Rocha and Georgia Seminet's groundbreaking anthology of childhood and cinema begins from the premise that "In this increasingly postnational era, children and adolescents are appropriated to mediate issues of identity and difference, history, class and gender, as well as their place in discourses that question the construct of family and nation" (Rocha and Seminet 2012, 2).

3 Verónica Cortínez has most closely studied Castilla's work. See Verónica Cortínez, "Sergio Castilla: The Emblematic Chilean Filmmaker" (2016) and Verónica Cortínez, *Cine a la chilena: Las peripecias de Sergio Castilla* (2001).

4 Hamid Naficy has coined the concept of exilic or accented cinema to outline a mode of filmmaking and cinematic practice tied to exile, diaspora, and mobility: "If the dominant cinema is considered universal and without accent, the films that diasporic and exilic subjects make are accented . . . the accent emanates not so much from the accented speech of the diegetic characters as from the displacement of the filmmakers and their artisanal production modes." In other words, Naficy's accented cinema discovers a new way of seeing rooted in this liminal, interstitial subject-position (Naficy 2001, 4).

5 "*Morena*," which translates directly as brown, or brown skinned, has long had sexualized, racialized, and classed connotations, and here takes on a particular mixture of desire and disdain.

6   "Simply stated, the child is familiar to us and yet strange, he or she inhabits our world and yet seems to answer to another, he or she is essentially ourselves and yet appears to display a systematically different order of being" (Jenks 1996, 3). This ability to reconcile apparent paradoxes renders it a particularly powerful construct, a means not only to understand youth but to trade the terms and limits of adulthood: "The child, therefore, cannot be imagined except in relation to a conception of the adult, but essentially it becomes impossible to generate a well-defined sense of the adult, and indeed adult society, without first positing the child" (Jenks 1996, 3). In this vein, see also Ariès (1962); Sokoloff (1992); James, Jenks, and Prout (1998); and Caldwell (2003). The history of childhood in Latin America is growing, spearheaded by Milanich (2009) and Premo (2005), among others. In Chile, see especially Rojas (2016) and Castillo Gallardo (2019).

7   The apparent paradox here is between being "*negrito*" (black or brown, and often non-elite) and "*gringuito*" (a loaded term but that presumes foreignness, particularly being from North America or Europe, and also whiteness). Of course, Castilla plays with Iván's paradoxical identity throughout the film, most clearly in his refusal, in English, to accept that he is "gringo," which stands alongside his refusal, also in English, to acknowledge that he speaks Spanish.

8   As we shall see, it is his ability to move from one set of linguistic and cultural codes to another that allows Iván to not only navigate the city but make it his own and, in so doing, manufacture a new, if still emergent, exilic subjectivity. José Miguel Palacios (2014) articulates one of the most compelling definitions of "exilic subjectivity": "The process of homecoming is the clearest manifestation of the particular historical, political, and cultural tensions that produce exile, which, in turn, engenders 'exilic subjectivity'—the embodiment of dialectical tensions between exiles and their nation-state, time, and history. Exilic subjectivity is that consciousness of the self that is specific to the exile experience" (153). Palacios pays special attention to the act of homecoming central to this construction, the "exilic subjectivity that switches from one language to the other, from past to present, and from one national territory to another, in order to rebuild its fragmented self in the act of homecoming" (162).

9   The freedom Iván finds in physical and social mobility is exemplified in the following scene, where Flaco pulls his cart—and Iván, joyful, mounted on top—through the dirt roads of a shantytown, while the camera follows, tracking their movement and letting the foreground blur with movement. This scene is a clear reference to the social documentary of the early 1970s, and especially *La batalla de Chile / The Battle of Chile*, which featured a similar shot, the camera following a cart in languid motion through a city suffused with political graffiti, a poetic scene Guzmán reproduces in *Chile, la memoria obstinada / Chile, Obstinate Memory* to remember the cinematographer Jorge Müller, disappeared in the first years of dictatorship. It is also a poetic

representation of the tense ties, and the limits, of Iván's social transgression. While the scene is shot enthusiastically, and Iván laughs and cries while Flaco seems to glide over the street, his weight buoyed by the weight of the cart, we remain clearly aware that it is Iván being pulled by the efforts of Flaco into his home in the shantytown.

10 For Naficy, the power of accented cinema, of the cinema of exile, diaspora, and homecoming, lies in the dialectical relationship between displacement and emplacement. "Place is a segment of space that people imbue with special meaning and value. . . . It refers not only to physical entity, however, but also to our relations to it and to our social relations within it. Most of us take for granted our place in the world and come face-to-face with it only when we are threatened with displacement. Thus, placement is tied to its opposite, displacement. . . . [And,] since place is also historically situated, displacement and emplacement have a temporal dimension—often linked to the dates of a great homelessness or grand homecoming." Iván's "homecoming" journey is a "return" to a place for the very first time, a double displacement that he attempts to resolve in his escape into the city, in his search for spatial and social emplacement (Naficy 2001, 152–53).

11 O'Hearn and Andrej Grubačić's analysis of exilic space and subjectivity is a treatise on the nature of politics "from below." The authors trace the history of these "refusals," which "once traveled on ships and lived in jungles, steppes, and mountains; today, they still live in jungles and mountains, in Zapatista and Aymara regions, but also in the urban exilic spaces of Kingston, autonomous Kurdish regions, supermax prisons, and occupied town squares" (O'Hearn and Grubačić 2016, 163). I attempt to fold exile itself into this conversation, defining it as a form of exclusion sine qua non, but also a contestatory position and practice par excellence, a form of power or agency born out of the margins, out of the peripheral or in-between places and positions engendered by exile itself. From this vantage point, exile, and the exilic are integrally cathected.

12 Ngai writes that this concept describes "a *new legal and political subject*, whose inclusion within the nation was simultaneously a social reality and a legal impossibility—a subject barred from citizenship and without rights. Moreover, the need of state authorities to identify and distinguish between citizens, lawfully resident immigrants, and illegal aliens posed enormous, political, and constitutional problems for the modern state. The illegal alien is thus an 'impossible subject,' a person who cannot be and a problem that cannot be solved" (2004, 3, emphasis in original). In Ngai's formulation, the migrant, an early articulation of illegality, is an impossible subject, a social and historical reality but a political impossibility. On impunity, the "transition," and how

official and unofficial discourse, including that of reconciliation, limit the possibility for justice even in "democracy," see Steve J. Stern (2004).

13 For Lury, curiosity is key here, fashioning the child as an agent empowered by his or her curiosity, "with its hallucinatory quality and creative mix of fact and fiction" (2005, 311). See also Sutton (2005, 356–57) and Solomon (2017, 153).

14 Here, I am drawing on José David Saldívar's synthetic analysis of borderlands thinkers, including Walter Mignolo and Gloria Anzaldúa.

15 "Thirdspace" is an exciting concept articulated, among others, by Edward Soja. Naficy, too, draws on this "organizing concept" as a means of conceptualizing the creative potential of cinematic subjects and strategies whose "own individual experiences" of exclusion and exile create a thirdspace of "alterity, creativity, and insight" (2002, 34–35).

16 The foundational transgression performed by Iván's exilic wanderings is that of childhood itself. The film's structure is built on the contrast between Jorge and Iván, where Iván's coming-of-age story, his transition into a mature, hybrid subject, dovetails with Jorge's stasis, making true the self-fulfilling prophecy he presents Camila while still in New York, that he would be childlike in his return to Chile. Hannah Kilduff (2017) suggests that the "'figure of the child'" challenges easy dichotomies that structure social thought by negotiating "between the universal and the specific, the historical and the personal and the past and the present" (8), and Castilla's film illustrates the key point that childhood scholars emphasize, that childhood cannot be understood outside of, and is often involved in, laying out the terms and limits of adulthood.

17 "Linda" translates as "beautiful," and "hermanita" as "little sister." I leave it in the original here to highlight the mixture of Spanish and English that Iván adopts here.

18 This is a subtle engagement with Stephanie Donald, Emma Wilson, and Sarah Wright's assertion that the child and childhood have been crucial to various projects of nation-state formation. "Explorations of a child's agency on-screen can push at the boundaries of film theory to create a 'new cinematic politics of childhood' in cinematic portrayals of the child's experience. Allegorically, the child can feel pressure from the past (even when that past is imaginary), and yet be called upon to also represent hopes for the future. This makes the child a powerful symbol for nations coming to terms with shifting political or social changes, both as a mode of representation to themselves and as a projection to the wider world" (Donald, Wilson, and Wright, 2017: 2).

19 On the creative potential of Spanglish, see, alongside Saldívar, Sommer (2003) and Anzaldúa (1999).

WORKS CITED

Anzaldúa, Gloria. 1999. *Borderlands / La Frontera: The New Mestiza*. San Francisco: Aunt Lute Books.

Ariès, Philippe. 1962. *Centuries of Childhood: A Social History of Family Life*. New York: Vintage.

Caldwell, Lesley. 2003. *The Elusive Child*. New York: Routledge.

Castillo Gallardo, Patricia. 2019. *Infancia / Dictadura. Testigos y actores (1973–1990)*. Santiago: LOM Ediciones.

Cortínez, Verónica. 2001. *Cine a la chilena: Las peripecias de Sergio Castilla*. Santiago, Chile: RIL Editores.

———. 2016. "Sergio Castilla: The Emblematic Chilean Filmmaker." *Radical History Review* 124 (January): 192–202.

Donald, Stephanie, Emma Wilson, and Sarah Wright. 2017. Introduction to *Childhood and Nation in Contemporary World Cinema: Borders and Encounters*, edited by Stephanie Donald, Emma Wilson, and Sarah Wright, 1–10. London: Bloomsbury Academic Press.

Gringuito. 1998. Directed by Sergio Castilla. Santiago, Chile: Amor en el Sur Ltda.

James, Allison, Chris Jenks, and Alan Prout. 1998. *Theorizing Childhood*. Cambridge: Polity Press.

Jenks, Chris. 1996. *Childhood*. London: Routledge.

Kilduff, Hannah. 2017. Introduction to *Childhood and Nation in Contemporary World Cinema: Borders and Encounters*, edited by Stephanie Donald, Emma Wilson, and Sarah Wright, 1–10. London: Bloomsbury Academic.

Lury, Karen. 2005. "The Child in Film and Television: Introduction." *Screen* 46 (3): 307–14.

Milanich, Nara. 2009. *Children of Fate: Childhood, Class, and the State in Chile, 1850–1930*. Durham, NC: Duke University Press.

Naficy, Hamid. 2001. *An Accented Cinema: Exilic and Diasporic Filmmaking*. Princeton, NJ: Princeton University Press.

———. 2002. "Making Films with an Accent: Iranian Émigré Cinema." *Framework* 43 (2): 15–41.

Ngai, Mae M. 2004. *Impossible Subjects: Illegal Aliens and the Making of Modern America*. Princeton, NJ: Princeton University Press.

O'Hearn, Dennis, and Andrej Grubačić. 2016. "Capitalism, Mutual Aid, and Material Life: Understanding Exilic Spaces." *Capital & Class* 40 (1): 147–65.

Palacios, José Miguel. 2014. "Chilean Exile Cinema and Its Homecoming Documentaries." In *Cinematic Homecomings: Exile and Return in Transnational Cinema*, edited by Rebecca Prime, 147–68. London: Bloomsbury Academic Press.

Palacios, José Miguel, and Catalina Donoso Pinto. 2017. "Infancia y exilio en el cine chileno." *Iberoamericana* 17 (65): 45–66.

Peeren, Esther. 2006. "Through the Lens of the Chronotope: Suggestions for a Spatio-Temporal Perspective on Diaspora." *Thamyris/Intersecting* 13: 67–78.

Premo, Bianca. 2005. *Children of the Father King: Youth, Authority and Legal Minority in Colonial Lima*. Chapel Hill: University of North Carolina Press.

Rocha, Carolina, and Georgia Seminet, eds. 2012. *Representing History, Class, and Gender in Spain and Latin America: Children and Adolescents in Film*. New York: Palgrave Macmillan.

Rojas Flores, Jorge. 2016. *Historia de la infancia en el Chile republicano (1810–2010)*. 2nd ed. Santiago: Ediciones de la JUNJI.

Saldívar, José David. 2012. *Trans-Americanity: Subaltern Modernities, Global Coloniality, and the Cultures of Greater Mexico*. Durham, NC: Duke University Press.

Sokoloff, Naomi. 1992. *Imagining the Child in Modern Jewish Fiction*. Baltimore: Johns Hopkins University Press.

Solomon, Stefan. 2017. "Education, Destiny, and National Identity." In *Childhood and Nation in Contemporary World Cinema: Borders and Encounters*, edited by Stephanie Donald, Emma Wilson, and Sarah Wright, 147–56. London: Bloomsbury Academic Press.

Sommer, Doris, ed. 2003. *Bilingual Games: Some Literary Investigations*. New York: Palgrave Macmillan.

Stern, Steve. 2004. *Remembering Pinochet's Chile: On the Eve of London, 1998*. Durham, N.C.: Duke University Press.

Sutton, Paul. 2005. "The *Bambino Negate* or Missing Child of Contemporary Italian Cinema." *Screen* 46, no. 3 (Autumn): 353–59.

Thomas, Sarah. 2005. "Sentimental Objects: Nostalgia and the Child in Cinema of the Spanish Memory Book." *Revista Canadiense de Estudios Hispánicos* 42 (1): 145–71.

Wilson, Emma. 2005. "Children, Emotion, and Viewing in Contemporary European Film." *Screen* 46 (3): 329–40.

14

FILMS ON LOSS AND MOURNING

Bridging the Personal and the Collective

María Helena Rueda

The film *Una mujer fantástica / A Fantastic Woman* (2017), by Sebastián Lelio, generated much interest for its portrayal of a transgender woman by a transgender actress. The film's treatment of loss and mourning received less attention. Critics who took note of the loss suffered by the protagonist merely described it as the event that occasioned the abuse inflicted on her later in the film.[1] It is not a coincidence, however, that this abuse was triggered by a death. Loss and mourning are powerful forces, reconfiguring the lives of those who experience them. They can reveal social anxieties that are normally suppressed, and instigate demands for justice or recognition. This chapter focuses on this aspect of *Una mujer fantástica* and other Chilean films that have had broad international circulation, in order to suggest that examining these films' interest in loss and mourning offers a way to understand their global impact.

Films about loss and mourning tap into widely shared human emotions and can therefore appeal to diverse global audiences. This was one reason why Lelio's film connected so well with audiences around the world and garnered an Oscar win. At the same time, this film's interest in loss draws on specifically Chilean concerns. As is well known, the Pinochet regime's repressive practices, and its brutal transformation of society, resulted in countless painful losses. Many Chilean films looked at the effects of those losses, inviting spectators to reflect on the collective mourning that ensued.[2] The concepts of loss (*pérdida*) and mourning (*duelo*) were also fundamental to discussions about Chilean culture in the postdictatorship period.[3] During that time, many scholars stressed the need to collectively mourn the losses caused by the Pinochet regime, while others saw a greater need for reconciliation.[4] Artistic production—including filmmaking—was described by some cultural critics, most notably Nelly Richard, as the place where remembering and grieving could primarily take place. I will not delve here into those debates, which have been thoroughly studied elsewhere.[5] However, by examining films associated with loss and mourning, I will show how they form a rich tapestry that both connects them to those debates and exceeds them.

The films I will examine here cross genre. Documentaries by well-known directors who went into exile after the coup, such as Patricio Guzmán's *Salvador Allende* (2004) and Carmen Castillo's *Calle Santa Fe / Santa Fe Street* (2007)—both of which I will discuss below—had a distinct national relevance. They depicted events and raised questions that specifically pertained to Chilean identity and recent history. Those films, however, were also prominently showcased abroad. In portraying experiences of loss and mourning, they delved into questions that spoke to a wide range of people and communities. Several recent fiction films from Chile also explore situations of loss and mourning. While they tend to focus on personal losses, rather than events that affected the entire society, they share with the documentaries an interest in loss and its consequences. In addition to Lelio's Oscar-winning film, I will discuss Pablo Larraín's *El club / The Club* (2015), which also deals with conflicts that result from a significant loss. The geographic and temporal settings are barely relevant to the stories portrayed in these films. They could have taken place in many different places around the world. Like the documentaries above, they have been well received outside of Chile.

In what follows, I draw a parallel between documentaries (like those by Castillo and Guzmán) that explicitly address the losses caused by the dictatorship, and fiction films (like those by Lelio and Larraín) that look at other kinds of losses. Both types of films approach loss and mourning as situations in which the personal and the collective become inextricably connected. In doing so, the films also establish a bridge between Chilean and transnational concerns. The loss and mourning faced by the people in these films are the result of localized circumstances, but are also essentially human ordeals that transcend nationality and culture. Before commenting on the films in some detail, I will review a few theories on loss, mourning, and their representation in film, which can help guide our thinking on this topic.

LOSS AND MOURNING IN CINEMA

In his 2012 book *Mourning Films*, Richard Armstrong studied cinema as a medium that is well suited for the portrayal of loss and mourning, because it is "a space in which we see someone who is no longer there" (1).[6] Armstrong argues that films on mourning take advantage of this quality of cinema to reflect on the interplay between presence and absence that characterizes the condition of mourning. They engage the spectator in an effort to make sense of the projection of an absence, much as the grieving person struggles to make sense of the lost person's presence in their life. The aural and visual character of film also makes it less reliant on words to convey meaning. Armstrong cites this as another reason why cinema might be particularly able to represent mourning, a condition that tests the limits of language. Many of the films analyzed by Armstrong rely less on dialogue and narration than on music, silence, imagery, and camera angle. He suggests that "filmed images offer more astute ways into the experience of grief than words do" (8). While his book mostly studies films from Europe and the United States, his observations also apply to Chilean films that confront loss and mourning as a subject.

All of the films I mentioned above make abundant use of the cinematic resources identified by Armstrong to convey experiences associated with loss, and Armstrong's ideas dialogue strongly with debates about memory and mourning in Chile. These films tell their stories through the strategic use of image, color, editing, and camera angle. They show things obliquely rather than directly, privileging subjective points of view. Dialogue is inconclusive, offering the spectator hints rather than explanation. Silence and music often play a larger role than conversation and commentary in conveying emotion. In both the feature and the documentary films, we are led to think that words are not fully reliable, that there is always another possible perspective. This approach connects these films to postdictatorship reflections on how the Pinochet regime led to a rupture of language.

Discussions of Chilean cultural production after the coup often referred to the "loss of words" as one of the multiple losses caused by the dictatorship. Nelly Richard borrowed the phrase from philosopher Patricio Marchant to describe a "traumatic suspension of speech" (2000, 273) caused by the violence of the dictatorship. In Richard's account, "The figures of trauma, mourning and melancholy became the emblematic figures of a certain form of critical thought of post-dictatorship" (273). Those concepts, with an acknowledged Freudian lineage, defined the dictatorship as a period linked to dramatic losses of life and meaning. Richard's main concern, echoed by others, was the risk of society as a whole falling into a permanent state of despondent melancholy due to unprocessed grief (274). To avoid such an outcome, Richard emphasized the need to process loss through mechanisms of substitution (of the lost object by its representation) and transposition (of the experience into figuration and expression)—as theorized by Julia Kristeva.

Discussing a number of fiction films made in Chile between the years 2000 and 2009, Antonella Estévez (2010) offers a different perspective on those films' approach to the melancholy of unprocessed loss. She suggests that we can find traces of this melancholy in their format, rather than in the stories they tell. In these films, including some by Lelio and Larraín, she identifies a few formal devices used to convey a melancholic affect. The first is a strong reliance on visual and aural elements. The films are also self-referential, inviting spectators to reflect on their status as artifice; that is, as mere projections of reality. Finally, they use slow rhythms that follow characters in real time and pay close attention to objects, with long takes and ample silences, offering plenty of opportunities for the perception of absence—a core feature of mourning.

Estévez acknowledges Richard's conceptualization of loss and mourning as the defining traits of the cultural scene in postdictatorship Chile, but her analysis points to an alternative option for films in that landscape. Rather than using the mechanisms of substitution and transposition favored by Richard, the films analyzed by Estévez explore the creative potential of the melancholic gaze. The directors of these films do not intend them to be part of a collective process of mourning aimed at overcoming a shared loss. The films use cinematic strategies to convey the general sense of irrecoverable loss experienced in Chile after the dictatorship. They therefore also explore the political potential of melancholy, defined by Freud as a state of mind where subjects refuse to move on from a significant loss in their lives. In Freud's view, people affected by melancholy turn their attention away from their own ego and into the world of others.

David Eng and David Kazanjian (2003) discuss the subject by reading Freud's views together with Walter Benjamin's seventh thesis on the philosophy of history. This thesis deals with the melancholy of historians when contemplating the remains of a violent past. For Benjamin, such melancholy persistently reactivates the dramatic losses suffered by a society in that past.

The melancholic observer brings the remains stubbornly back to the present, activating the possibility of creatively and politically transforming that present. In this way, Eng and Kazanjian argue, "The past is brought to bear witness to the present—as a flash of emergency, an instant of emergency, and a moment of production. In this regard, the past remains steadfastly alive for the political work of the present" (5).

Judith Butler's afterword to that same volume offers additional insight into the political potential of loss. Butler describes loss as an experience that configures social, political, and aesthetic relations. Also commenting on Benjamin's seventh thesis, and with added insight from his book *The Origin of German Tragic Drama* (1928), Butler discusses how past losses persist as ruptures in the present. Remains of that past reveal it as irrecoverable, which opens up the possibility of political agency in the present with an eye on the future. In her reading of Benjamin, melancholy stems from losses that are a result of violence against a community of human beings. Such violence "constitutes an assault on thinking," which cancels the possibility of recovery through reason (2003, 468). Those losses spectrally haunt the present, constituting the basis of what she calls "a melancholic agency" (468). Registering loss becomes the way in which the members of a collectivity see themselves as constituted by "a common sense of loss," a pathos that she calls "oddly fecund, paradoxically productive" (468).

The political potential of loss is what interests me in the Chilean films that explore it as a subject. It is an interpretation of loss that challenges the idea of mourning as a private experience. Whether they emphasize collective or personal losses, the films I have mentioned reflect on loss as an event that connects people in an awareness of common humanity. Loss is a transformational experience, projecting individuals onto a community, and redefining the past and the future. In the representation of loss, these films address this paradoxically creative and productive potential of loss as a momentous, life-altering, and revealing experience. That this community has at least the potential of being transnational is what reveals the importance of using loss to examine how these films can gain new, global intelligibility.

PRIVATE LOSSES, PUBLIC SYMBOLS

Carmen Castillo and Patricio Guzmán are among the best-known documentary filmmakers recording the memory of the Chilean dictatorship.[7] They both suffered personal losses as a result of the coup and were forced into exile. They have both made powerful films that actively engage viewers in reflections about loss, mourning, and memory. Both of them combine present-day interviews with recovered materials, avoiding the imposition of a single, authoritative version of the events they register. Their films, like other Chilean documentaries that look at personal losses resulting from the dictatorship,[8] focus their attention on those events. Their approaches differ from one another in an important respect, however. Although both act as narrators and interviewers, Guzmán's body is largely absent from his documentaries, while Castillo's is present at every moment. Castillo consistently emphasizes her personal experience, but Guzmán's own experiences have only become a more prominent part of his films in recent years.[9] This personalization of loss deepens the scope of collective political losses that went alongside more private ones.

Patricio Guzmán's *Salvador Allende* (2004) documents the life of a president whose death embodies a collective loss. The director recovers old film footage, objects, and photographs. He also shows emblematic places, often contrasting old images with new ones where those same places are either radically altered or in ruins. We see that Allende's old house has been turned into a hospice for the elderly, his former office in the presidential palace is now a hallway, several buses his government used to transport workers are rusting in a junkyard, and so on. In a present where the past has been defaced or left to rot, Guzmán looks for remnants that evoke what was once there. In one of the initial scenes, the director peels away paint from a white wall, revealing traces of an Allende-era political mural. The documentary relies on the power of ruins and remnants to elicit memory and epitomize loss and the mourning that ensues. The director shows little interest in the present Chilean landscape, which he describes as covered in a "layer of amnesia" ["capa de amnesia"].

Early in the film, Guzmán states that Allende had "incarnated the utopia of a just and free world" ["encarnado aquella utopía de un mundo más justo y más libre"]. The idea behind this statement pervades the documentary, and not only with regard to Allende himself. All the people interviewed in the film appear as now-ruined incarnations of that lost "utopia," bearing witness to the gravity of its loss. In an interview with the founders of the Valparaíso Socialist Party, we hear one of them recount the day of the coup, speculating about what they could have done to prevent it, still seemingly unable to come to terms with the loss. While he talks, the camera wanders over the faces of the other founders, highlighting their sadness and the marks of aging on their skin. The director does not interview anyone who might "incarnate" hope for social justice in the present. We learn little about the lives of the people being interviewed, other than how they were impacted by the death of both Allende and the project he represented. Nor do we learn much about Guzmán himself. Even though he provides the voice-over narration, and in some cases speaks in the first person, he makes few references to his personal story.[10] With regard to Allende, we mostly hear about his role in Chilean history. The little personal information provided is subsumed into the wider national and international story that had him as the protagonist. In a particularly telling example, Guzmán interviews the daughter of Allende's nanny, who grew up in his house and had him as a playmate in their childhood. She recalls him giving moving speeches as a young boy, as if prefiguring the charismatic politician he would become. Interviews with Allende's daughters reveal only details about his political campaigns, which often included his family. We learn almost nothing about Allende the person, outside of his role as the leader of the leftist Popular Unity (*Unidad Popular*, or UP) coalition.[11] The film's focus on landscapes and histories of loss, rather than the more affective, personal dimensions of that loss, establishes a community of mourners while glossing over the individual members of that community; even Guzmán's personal mourning for the loss of Allende is largely absent.

In Carmen Castillo's *Calle Santa Fe* (2007), by contrast, the interconnections between personal and collective experiences take center stage. The film registers Castillo's return from exile to the Santiago street where her partner, Miguel Enríquez, was killed by Pinochet's secret police. Enríquez was the leader of the Revolutionary Left Movement (better known as MIR, short for *Movimiento de Izquierda Revolucionaria*), and this documentary is also an effort to trace the history of the movement and its struggles. The film talks not only about Castillo's personal loss, but also about the losses experienced by other members of the MIR and by Chilean society as a whole. Castillo's individual process of mourning is portrayed as deeply intertwined with the collective mourning of a nation. At the start, we see footage from an old newsreel announcing Enríquez's assassination. Then we see a point-of-view shot of Castillo browsing old letters, photographs, and political pamphlets. We also hear her talk about the events in voice-over narration. Toward the end of her monologue, Castillo asks, "Can this have a meaning for anyone other than me?" ["¿Tendrá algún sentido esto para alguna persona que no sea yo?"]. This question—to herself and to her viewers—frames the documentary as an account of the dissolution of the project defended by the MIR, as experienced by people who were part of it. It also places Castillo's sense of loss at the center of the film.

Still, her documentary constructs an account of collective loss that is composed of multiple individual personal narratives, all of them nuanced and marked by contradiction. At a certain point, we see images of a trip Castillo made to Chile in 1985, thanks to a special permit granted by Pinochet to visit her father, who was seriously ill. To questions from reporters who wait for her at the airport, she responds, "I know the reunion of this family has a strong symbolic content, but I'd like to be left alone in these fifteen days, so I can be with my father and not deal with the symbols" ["Yo sé que la reunión de esta familia tiene un fuerte contenido simbólico, pero quisiera que estos quince días me dejaran estar junto a mi padre y no ocuparme de los símbolos"]. Elsewhere in *Calle Santa Fe*, Castillo recalls her own activism in exile, saying that she played the part of the "heroic widow" ["viuda heroica"], a role assigned to her by others that she now rejects. She describes her actions at the time as those of a sleepwalker consumed by a personal grief that did not fit in any single collective narrative. In this sense, Castillo's affective approach to the film ties her to others who experienced loss in different ways.

These complexities are particularly visible when Castillo questions the idea of dying for the struggle. Her reflections on the subject start when she talks to an elderly couple that lost three sons who were part of the militant resistance to Pinochet. Even while recalling the pain caused by those deaths, the couple affirms that their sons' fight was worthwhile. Reflecting on this interview, Castillo says in voice-over narration that at some point in her exile, she publicly condemned the MIR's "cult of death and sacrifice" ["culto de la muerte y el sacrificio"]. She criticizes that earlier position by saying that when she defended it, she did not consider the pride people like that couple could feel about dying for the struggle. In the following scene, she asks former MIR members if they think so many deaths were justified, and receives a range of answers. A former leader admits that asking young people to die was a mistake. Another militant thinks individual lives were lost in service of a worthwhile collective cause. A woman says that the MIR's cult of the dead made survivors feel that perhaps they were not as good as those who were killed. By presenting different meanings ascribed to the death of MIR members, Castillo invites viewers to reflect on a multifaceted vision of loss.

The film starts with a question, goes on to ask others, and proposes different, often contradictory, answers. We see the filmmaker's own thoughts and beliefs changing as the documentary progresses.[12] Even to the question about the meaning of what we are seeing, Castillo offers multiple possible answers. *Calle Santa Fe* is often interpreted as an exercise in memory. There are indeed several efforts to memorialize.[13] Perhaps the most important effort is Castillo's attempt to purchase the Calle Santa Fe house, in order to turn it into a museum. But the film is also about how past losses lead to actions that can shape the future. Castillo abandons her plans for the house after talking to a young activist who describes Castillo's defense of that space as an example of an attachment to a personal story, to the detriment of the collective one. After that conversation, Castillo decides to simply install a plaque marking the space, and goes on to show multiple instances of Miguel Enríquez's name and likeness being used as an inspiration in current struggles for social justice. We hear of people involved in present-day efforts to improve the lives of disadvantaged Chileans. A key scene shows a group of young musicians rapping about Enríquez, social injustice, and the need to work collectively to improve the future. We get the sense that the ideals articulated by the MIR are still very much alive, albeit transformed. *Calle Santa Fe* is a creative effort to project loss into a future shaped by a reflection on that loss.

Documentaries that look at the legacy of the dictatorship are in one way or another engaging the idea of loss. They evoke the lives, ideals, and projects that were destroyed by the coup, but they also look at what remains. They prove that nothing was ever completely lost, because the artifacts, memories, and ideals are still around. Engaging in a process of remembrance, recovery, and creation, these films display Judith Butler's productive and generative interpretation of mourning. Although Guzmán's documentary engages the past from a more collective perspective and Castillo's is more personal, they invite viewers to connect with the documentary subjects as humans. As such, these documentaries are relevant to many different audiences, because they transcend some—if not all—of the local affiliations that often accompany the mourning of those lost for political motives. Critics like Idelber Avelar (1999) argue that mourning for the "defeated" Left in postdictatorship contexts is inseparable from political militancy. I contend, however, that a focus on personal loss, beyond the particularities of local politics, makes these films relatable to audiences who not only might not share Guzmán's and Castillo's political leanings but may be unfamiliar with the national histories their work evokes. I would like to now turn my attention to the fiction films of Lelio and Larraín, to show how loss appears in those films.

LOSS IN CHILE'S "INTIMATE FILMS"

The directors of the two films I will discuss in this section belong to a group of filmmakers often referred to as the *Novísimos*.[14] While certain critics have stated that this generation of filmmakers is largely apolitical in nature, I would like to explore how their approach to loss encourages reflections that are indeed quite political, by engaging Butler's views on the politics of mourning, as explained in *Precarious Life* (2004):

> Many people think that grief is privatizing, that it returns us to a solitary situation and is, in that sense, depoliticizing. But I think it furnishes a sense of political community of a complex order, and it does this first of all by bringing to the fore the relational ties that have implications for theorizing fundamental dependency and ethical responsibility. (22)

For Butler, loss is an experience that highlights our connections to others, revealing our common vulnerability. While her essay focuses on violent death, she mentions that this applies to any significant loss. Feelings of vulnerability caused by loss lead to an awareness of our deep connections to others. This awareness is heightened with deaths that are particularly shocking, untimely, and life-altering, such as the ones portrayed in the films I discuss below.

Pablo Larraín and Sebastián Lelio are perhaps the two most internationally recognized Chilean filmmakers today, and they have both produced films depicting loss and mourning. The former is well known for his so-called dictatorship trilogy, comprised of *Tony Manero* (2008), *Post-Mortem* (2010), and *No* (2012), all of which confronted losses occasioned by the Pinochet regime. Lelio also touched upon questions on loss in *Navidad / Christmas* (2009), in which a young woman breaks into her deceased father's home, and *El año del tigre / The Year of the Tiger* (2011), in which an inmate escapes from prison after an earthquake only to find that his family has been killed by the accompanying tsunami. Interestingly, both directors have also made highly visible English-language films centering on loss and mourning: *Jackie* (2016), for Larraín, and *Disobedience* (2017), for Lelio.

In Larraín's *El club* and Lelio's *Una mujer fantástica*, loss precipitates both conflict and a sense of interconnectedness. A dramatic death at the beginning of *El club* exposes the dark histories of its priest characters, disrupting their relatively peaceful life in a community where the past was largely ignored. In this way, its plot connects to international audiences who might be familiar with past abuses in the Catholic Church and their consequences. Meanwhile, when Marina, the protagonist of *Una mujer fantástica*, loses her romantic partner, she also loses the comfort of a satisfying relationship and must confront the hostility of others toward her transgender body. Loss, then, becomes a way for the film to denounce discrimination against trans people. All of the characters in these films are expelled from what we assume were secure, intimate spaces, and thrown into a world where others loom large in their lives. Both films end when the characters return to a sense of stability, albeit one that is deeply transformed, now that they are awakened to the essentially social dimension of their existence.

At the beginning of *El club*, we are presented with a small group of older people, four men and a woman, who live a seemingly tranquil life in an unremarkable yellow house in a coastal town. In the opening scenes, one of the men trains a race dog on a cloudy beach, the woman sweeps the floor, a second man tends to a vegetable garden, and two others watch TV. We later learn that the house's male occupants are Catholic priests who were retired from their parishes due to wrongdoings that the church wanted out of the public eye. Father Vidal was accused of pedophilia, Father Ortega of infant abduction, and Father Silva of complicity in the dictatorship's brutalities. The oldest, Father Ramírez, suffers from dementia and no one really knows why he is there. Now they all lead secluded lives with the woman, a nun named Sister Mónica, as their guard. She makes sure that they follow strict routines and never interact with the town residents. The apparent stability of the household is disrupted by the arrival of a new priest, Father Lazcano. Soon after he meets the other priests, a homeless man who calls himself Sandokán starts howling a long diatribe at the house, describing in explicit detail how Lazcano sexually abused him as a child. The possibility of public exposure sends the house residents into a panic. Silva gives Lazcano a gun to scare the intruder away, but the priest uses it instead to shoot himself in the head in front of his victim. This dramatic scene triggers a series of events that destroy the surface calm of the house, revealing the hideous and unpunished crimes linking this private "club" to the collectivity that they had managed to keep at bay. Although Sandokán leaves the house right after the suicide, he remains a menacing presence throughout the movie. He shows up at spaces frequented by the priests and the nun, and eventually sets up camp outside their house.

Though in a deeply disturbed state, Sandokán is the only one who mourns the loss of Lazcano.[15] We learn of his intense attachment to the priest, an attachment nurtured by the latter to facilitate the abuse. This internalized dependency had prompted the adult Sandokán to compulsively stalk Lazcano, eventually leading the priest to take his own life. The suicide seems to awaken in Sandokán the complex sense of political agency identified by Butler, allowing him to implicate others in his previously private pain. Sandokán displays in every encounter with the surviving priests the profound wounds inflicted on him by the abuse, and these displays bring down the walls protecting their private world. Sandokán's mourning for the death of Lazcano is also a harangue against the impunity that Lazcano (and by extension, the other priests) enjoyed; in this sense, he disrupts the small, complicit community of priests and forces them to reckon with a larger collective. Sandokán's sense of loss, then, is able to call an entire system of complicity and silence into question.

After the suicide, the house's occupants try to regain their sense of normalcy. They agree on a relatively harmless version of the events to tell the police, recite a prayer over the body, wash away the blood with water, and conduct a low-profile burial ceremony at the local cemetery. Their fragile normalcy is challenged anew, however, by the arrival of another priest, Father García, sent by the Church to investigate the death and possibly close down the house. Described as a progressive representative of "the new Church," García interrogates each of the house's occupants about the event and also about their own pasts. All of them appear to justify their previous wrongdoings, oblivious to the pain they inflicted on others. The nun equates their highly controlled life with a form of redemption for past sins. She tells García that the priests lead "a holy life" ["una vida santa"]. The encounters with Sandokán, which relentlessly continue throughout the film, disrupt this fallacy, however, blatantly exposing the enduring pain inflicted by the church and spurring the characters into action.

When Sister Mónica hatches a macabre plot to punish Sandokán, the "progressive" priest does nothing to stop her. The nun, together with Fathers Ortega and Silva, kill all of the town's race dogs and pin the blame on

Sandokán. As the plotters anticipated, the dogs' owners assault Sandokán, leaving him badly injured. Father García cleans Sandokán's wounds and forces the priests and the nun to accept him as part of their community in exchange for not shutting down the house. In the closing scenes, Sister Mónica receives Sandokán into the house by reciting the rules he must follow. The priests change his name to Tomás, as if attempting to erase the pain inflicted on him by changing his identity. Sandokán shows them the futility of this effort by giving them a long list of the medications they will need to give him to manage his multiple physical and mental traumas. His presence will no longer allow the priests to remain detached from those that they had harmed. This ending was especially powerful, for both domestic and international audiences, given that *El club* was released at a time when the Catholic Church, in Chile and beyond, was shaken by countless revelations of abuse committed by priests. Its focus on reckoning for past losses and transgressions—some related to the dictatorship, others not[16]—was a way of making the film intelligible to international audiences.

In *Una mujer fantástica*, we also find more oblique evocations of the dictatorship. Marina's assertion of her right to say good-bye to her partner's body recalls the language used by relatives of the disappeared.[17] But there is in this film another, less obvious, connection to the dictatorship's brutality. The Pinochet regime long attempted to reconstruct society through violent mechanisms of control over the body. In this repressive campaign, heteronormativity determined which bodies had a legitimate place in society (Fischer 2016, 124–27). As was also evident in *El club*, strict parameters of maleness and femaleness were deployed to justify the repression of bodies.[18] The issue of violence against queer bodies is much more explicitly referenced in *Una mujer fantástica*.

Many critics have pointed out, accurately, that the visibility of transness in *Una mujer fantástica* comes with a certain depoliticizing of the protagonist;[19] it is through the story of loss that the film becomes more overtly political. Recently, a number of Chilean films featuring trans characters have challenged the strict paradigms of normativity inherited from the dictatorship, by shattering hetero- and cisnormative representations of the body,[20] and *Una mujer fantástica* is only the most globally visible of these films. It has probably had more viewers around the world than any other previous Chilean movie, thanks to its Oscar win. Marina's character does not really threaten societal gender norms: she is beautiful, she has a stable job as a waitress, she performs as a female opera singer, and she is involved in a loving relationship with a cis man, Orlando. Orlando's death, however, brings to the fore the repressive face of normalization. Marina is told by Orlando's family not to attend his funeral; certain bodies are simply not allowed to mourn publicly. Because mourning is a powerful force in the constitution of a community, there is much at stake in exercising control over who has access to its social performance.

Invoking loss, then, is a way for the film to condemn discrimination against Marina. In a tense scene, Marina meets her deceased lover's estranged wife. Talking about her marriage, the wife says: "We were quite normal" ["éramos bien normales"]. About the protagonist, she adds: "I think this is just perversion. . . . When I see you, I don't know what I'm seeing. I see a chimera" ["En esto hay pura perversión no más. . . . Es que cuando te veo, no sé, no sé lo que veo. Una quimera veo"]. With these comments, she affirms the heterosexual married couple as the norm and denies Marina the right to be a "normal" member of society. Such a view allows Marina to exist only as an aberration or a monster. Orlando's son makes the tacit violence of these comments more explicit, by kidnapping and brutally attacking Marina along with a group of his friends later in the film. This dehumanization adds substance to Marina's claim that participating in her partner's funeral is a "human right."[21] Albeit in a rather unsubtle way, these scenes heighten the film's denunciation of how trans people are discriminated against in Chile—a social issue that crosses national boundaries and appeals to international human rights discourse.

Spectators can either see the need to include the trans protagonist in the "normality" evoked by the cisgender characters or question the basis of normalization itself. The film seems to encourage the first approach—as some of its critics point out—but the second one is still possible. Even in its Oscar-winning, international art house format, *Una mujer fantástica* is not an easy film to classify or interpret. The director himself has called attention to how he wanted to be ambiguous about the film genre and leave plot lines unresolved. This intentional openness is an invitation for spectators to apply their own readings and draw their own conclusions. The film's historical resonance in Chile and its international appeal worked to direct attention to the movie, and with it to the plea of transgender people in the country. Daniela Vega became a powerful spokesperson for trans rights, and the film's success was crucial for the passage of a Chilean law giving transgender people the right to change their gender denomination in government-issued documents.

CONCLUSION

Stories about loss and mourning can carry profound social implications. Documentaries that look at collective losses turn to the individuals affected by them as a way to connect historical context to personal experience. Films focused on personal loss evoke historical context when characters become aware of their ties to others in the aftermath of loss. Attention to loss and mourning gives ostensibly political films a distinct personal dimension and the ostensibly personal films a strong political one. It also connects films with both national and transnational audiences, encouraging reflection on the profound collective and personal implications of any meaningful loss.

NOTES

1   See, for instance, Bradshaw (2018).

2   For an overview of Chilean films about the dictatorship that came out between 2001 and 2018, see Morales (2018).

3   After the dictatorship ended, and throughout the 1990s, there were numerous debates on this subject that continue to inform current scholarship on the legacies of the dictatorship. Cultural critic Nelly Richard played a key role in the discussions. Many contributions to the conversations appeared in the *Revista de Crítica Cultural*, edited by Richard, and were later compiled in a three-volume collection titled *Debates críticos en América Latina* (2008). Also important were a compilation by Richard and Moreiras (2001) as well as books by Moreiras (1999) and Avelar (1999), both of which dealt with the Southern Cone more broadly.

4   After Pinochet left power following the 1989 democratic elections, the victorious center-left coalition, *Concertación de Partidos por la Democracia*, governed through negotiation and compromise to avoid confrontation in a highly polarized political environment. This consensus-based approach to governance resulted in an inability to discuss the damage caused by the dictatorship, which was itself perceived by many intellectuals as a loss.

5   See, for instance, Lazzara (2006).

6   Laura Mulvey (2006), meanwhile, draws a key parallel between the decay (and necessary preservation) of celluloid, on one hand, and the "natural mortality of the human figures whose existences [film] unnaturally preserved" (17), on the other. In this sense, for Mulvey, cinema is the quintessential medium of loss, both material and human.

7   Guzmán's trajectory started with the well-known three-part documentary *La batalla de Chile / The Battle of Chile* (1976, 1978, 1979), which registered the movement that led to Allende's government and its violent dissolution. Castillo's films include *La flaca Alejandra / Skinny Alejandra* (1995), a conversation with a former leftist MIR militant who after being tortured became a collaborator with Pinochet's secret police. Both directors have made several other documentaries on the period.

8   Such films include Lorena Giachino's *Reinalda del Carmen, mi mamá y yo / Reinalda del Carmen, My Mother and Me* (2007), Germán Berger's *Mi vida con Carlos / My Life with Carlos* (2008), and Macarena Aguiló's *El edificio de los chilenos / The Chilean Building* (2010), among many others.

9   For example, in *El botón de nácar / The Pearl Button* (2015), Guzmán recalls his own memories of hearing rain tapping on the zinc roof of his childhood home.

10 Lazzara (2012) argues that the film's title is deceptive. In his view, Guzmán himself is the real subject of the documentary, and the people he interviews express his own thoughts and emotions (72). While I agree that the director exercises strong authorial control over his interviewees' statements, in my view the film is, nonetheless, still mainly about Allende as a symbol of the collective loss of a nation.

11 In contrast, the 2015 documentary *Allende mi abuelo Allende / Beyond My Grandfather Allende*, made by Marcia Tambutti Allende, a granddaughter of the former president, takes a much more personal approach. It connects Allende's loss to a network of other losses in the Allende family, including the suicides of Tambutti's brother, Gonzalo Meza, and Tambutti's aunt (Salvador Allende's daughter), Beatriz Allende.

12 For Bernardita Llanos (2013), the filmmaker's onscreen evolution is part of her configuration of a personal subjectivity in the recovery of memory. Such configuration is, in my opinion, inseparable from the documentary's reflection on loss.

13 See Jelin (2003) for a discussion on forgetfulness and negotiations between "rival memories" (6) of Latin American repressive regimes.

14 The name *Novísimos* was first used by Ascanio Cavallo and Gonzalo Maza (2010). Their influential volume included studies of twenty-one filmmakers who had released their first films in and around 2005. Barraza (2018, 16) notes that this denomination has been controversial, with some critics pointing out a lack of conceptual rigor in Cavallo and Maza's compilation. There is some consensus that this group represents an important new tendency in Chilean cinema. Carolina Urrutia Neno (2013) characterizes their work as self-conscious, ambiguous, counterhegemonic, and interested in developing alternatives to classic film realism.

15   Later in the film, García talks to Sandokán about his relationship with Lazcano. He tells the priest that Lazcano raised him. García offers his condolences and formulaically calls the deceased a good man, a saint, and a person of God. Sandokán initially concurs, but then interrupts the formulaic exchange by revealing the true nature of his attachment to Lazcano. Describing in detail how Lazcano convinced him that sex with a priest would bring him closer to God, Sandokán disrupts García's attempt to handle the situation in a detached way.

16   The reference to unpunished crimes also recalls the realities of postdictatorship life in Chile: Sarah Wright (2017) argues that the dogs' slaughter at the end serves as a symbol for the unabashed extermination of human life by Pinochet's forces. While the film's treatment of clerical sexual abuse appeals to transnational audiences, it also contains multiple elements that connect it to Chile's recent history of terror.

17   In interviews, Lelio has encouraged spectators to make this connection. Asked about the protagonist's desire to attend her partner's funeral, for instance, he said: "Saying goodbye is a human right. We know this very well in Chile, where so many people disappeared, and so many families were left without the chance to say goodbye to their beloved" (Lazic 2018).

18   During the dictatorship, dissident artists like Carlos Leppe expressed resistance to the regime through the performative display of queer bodies. Transvestism and the queering of bodies was also a fundamental form of dissent during the postdictatorship transition period. See, for instance, the work of writer/performer Pedro Lemebel. In *El club*, meanwhile, not only was Sandokán brutally beaten at the end, so was Father Vidal, the other surviving character associated with homoerotic practices.

19   Pablo Solari (2017), for example, decries the lack of complexity in the presentation of the social and moral world of the characters, who for him appear as archetypes.

20   Among these films are *Naomi Campbel* (2013) by Nicolás Videla and Camila José Donoso, *El diablo es magnífico / The Devil Is Magnificent* (2016) by Nicolás Videla, *En tránsito / In Transit* (2017) by Constanza Gallardo, and *Claudia tocada por la luna / Claudia Touched by the Moon* (2018) by Francisco Aguilar.

21   Other characters, in contrast, hold a more accepting view of Marina. Orlando's brother treats her kindly and shows sympathy for her pain—even if he ultimately accedes to the restrictions imposed by others in his family. People close to Marina, like her sister, singing coach, and restaurant boss, seem fully supportive of her gender identity.

WORKS CITED

Armstrong, Richard. 2012. *Mourning Films. A Critical Study of Loss and Grieving in Cinema*. Jefferson: McFarland.

Avelar, Idelber. 1999. *The Untimely Present: Postdictatorial Latin American Fiction and the Task of Mourning*. Durham: Duke University Press.

Barraza, Vania. 2018. *El cine en Chile (2005-2015): Políticas y poéticas del nuevo siglo*. Santiago: Ed. Cuarto Propio.

Bradshaw, Peter. 2018. "*A Fantastic Woman*. Sublime Study of Love, Loss and the Trans Experience." *The Guardian*, March 1.

Butler, Judith. 2003. "Afterword. After Loss, What Then?" In *Loss: The Politics of Mourning*. Edited by David Eng and David Kazanjian, 467–73. Berkeley: University of California Press.

———. 2004. *Precarious Life*. New York: Verso.

Castillo, Carmen, dir. 2007. *Calle Santa Fe*. Paris, France: Institut National de l'Audiovisuel (INA) and Les Films d'Ici.

Cavallo, Ascanio, and Gonzalo Maza, eds. 2010. *El novísimo cine chileno*. Santiago: Uqbar Editores.

Eng, David E., and David Kazanjian, eds. 2003. *Loss: The Politics of Mourning*. Berkeley: University of California Press.

Estévez, Antonella. 2010. "Dolores políticos: Reacciones cinematográficas. Resistencias melancólicas en el cine chileno contemporáneo." *Aisthesis* 47: 15–32.

Fischer, Carl. 2016. *Queering the Chilean Way: Cultures of Exceptionalism and Sexual Dissidence, 1965–2015*. New York: Palgrave MacMillan.

Guzmán, Patricio, dir. 2004. *Salvador Allende*. Paris, France: JBA Production, and Liège, Belgium: Les Filmes de la Passerelle.

Jelin, Elizabeth. 2003. *State Repression and Labors of Memory*. Minneapolis: University of Minnesota Press.

Larraín, Pablo, dir. 2015. *El club*. Santiago, Chile: Fábula.

Lazic, Elena. 2018. "A flamboyant film devoid of guilt: Sebastián Lelio on *A Fantastic Woman*." *Seventh Row*, February 10. https://seventh-row.com/2018/02/10/sebastian-lelio-a-fantastic-woman/.

Lazzara, Michael J. 2006. *Chile in Transition: The Poetics and Politics of Memory*. Gainesville: University Press of Florida.

———. 2012. "Remembering Revolution after Ruin and Genocide: Recent Chilean Documentary Films and the Writing of History." In *Film and Genocide*, edited by Kristi M. Wilson and Tomás F. Crowder-Taraborrelli, 67–86. Madison: University of Wisconsin Press.

Lelio, Sebastián, dir. 2017. *Una mujer fantástica*. Santiago, Chile: Fábula.

Llanos, Bernardita. 2013. "Subjetividad y memoria en Calle Santa Fe de Carmen Castillo." In *Enfoques al cine chileno en dos siglos*, 193–200. Santiago: LOM Ediciones.

Morales, Marcelo. 2018. "El cine chileno NO habla mucho del golpe y la dictadura: Catastro de películas estrenadas entre 2001–2018." *Cine Chile. Enciclopedia del cine chileno*, September 11. http://cinechile.cl/criticas-y-estudios/el-cine-chileno-no-habla-mucho-del-golpe-y-la-dictadura-catastro-de-peliculas-estrenadas-entre-2001-2018/.

Moreiras, Alberto. 1999. *Tercer espacio: Literatura y duelo en América Latina*. Santiago: LOM Ediciones.

Mulvey, Laura. 2006. *Death 24x a Second: Stillness and the Moving Image*. London: Reaktion Books.

Richard, Nelly. 2000. "The Reconfigurations of Post-dictatorship Critical Thought." Translated by John Kraniauskas. *Journal of Latin American Cultural Studies* 9 (3): 273–82.

Richard, Nelly, and Alberto Moreiras eds. 2001. *Pensar en la post-dictadura*. Santiago: Ed. Cuarto Propio.

Richard, Nelly, ed. 2008. *Debates críticos en América Latina*. Santiago: ARCIS.

Solari, Pablo. 2017. "*Una mujer fantástica*: Realismo quimérico." *El Agente Cine*, April 18. http://elagentecine.cl/cine-chileno-2/una-mujer-fantastica-2-realismo-quimerico.

Urrutia Neno, Carolina. 2013. *Un cine centrífugo: Ficciones chilenas 2005–2010*. Santiago: Ed. Cuarto Propio.

Wright, Sarah. 2017. "The Muteness of Dogs: Pablo Larraín's *El club* (2015)." *Bulletin of Spanish Visual Studies* 1 (1): 95–116.

INDEX

accented cinema, 326, 328–29, 332n4, 334n10
Acland, Charles, 111
Actores secundarios / Secondary Actors, 273–75, 287n4
aesthetic regime of art, 160
affect
    confluence between subjectivity, emotions, politics, and, 74–76
    and documentaries' introspective gaze, 71–73
    versus emotion, 96n2
    and "management of memory," 95n1
    tendencies in documentaries showing affective turn, 82–95
affiliation, transition from filiation to, 165
Aftershock, 111, 114
Agamben, Giorgio, 61
agency, of children, 326–27
Aguiló, Macarena, 12, 277–79, 288n12, 288n13
Ahn, SooJeong, 13
Al final: La última carta / "At the End: The Last Letter," 102nn34,35
Allende, Salvador, 4, 5, 269–70, 287n4, 344–45. See also *Salvador Allende*
Allende mi abuelo Allende / Beyond My Grandfather Allende, 354n11
allurement, 231, 232–34
Almodóvar, Pedro, 239n6
Altman, Rick, 108, 123n3
amateurism, 101n30
Amiga (Anwandter), 180, 182, 184, 191, 193n7
Ángel negro / Black Angel, 118–19, 122
animated film. See *Atrapados en Japón / Trapped in Japan*
Annabelle, 111
Anwandter, Alex, 177–81, 192
    Amiga, 180, 182, 184, 191, 193n7

"¿Cómo puedes vivir contigo mismo?," 184
Latinoamericana, 180, 185
"Locura," 182, 185
"Manifiesto," 184–85
musical moments in *Nunca vas a estar solo*, 186–91
music-video lyrics, songs, and iconography of, 181–86, 194n16
Rebeldes, 182–83
"Siempre es viernes en mi corazón," 184, 194nn16,18
"Tatuaje," 183, 191
Apio verde / "Green Celery," 121
Aquí no ha pasado nada / Much Ado About Nothing, 10, 58, 62–63
Aravena, Constanza, 249
archives, 301–2
Arfuch, Leonor, 305, 311n11
Armstrong, Richard, 341
art house cinema
    porous relationship between horror and, 107, 112–13
    success in, circuit, 250–51
Artsploitation, 117
Asociación de Fotógrafos Independientes (AFI, Association of Independent Photographers), 275–77
atemporality, of *Una mujer fantástica*, 251–52
Atrapados en Japón / Trapped in Japan, 293–95, 308–9
    criticisms of, 311n9
    narration of, 295
    (re)construction of father figure in, 295–301
    souvenirs and embodied experience in, 301–8, 310–11n8
auteur cinema, 34, 39–40, 249

authorship, collective, 86–90, 98n13
"auto-erasure," cinema of, 207
Avelar, Idelber, 347
Ayala, Diego, 62–63
Aylwin, Patricio, 22n8

Baby Shower, 119, 120
Baczko, Bronislaw, 173n4
Bakhtin, M. M., 166
Baldwin, James, 234
Banco del Estado de Chile, 124n7
Bank Muñoz, Carolina, 21n3, 234–35
Barraza Toledo, Vania, 9–10, 22n12, 122, 354n14
Barriga, Cecilia, 83–84, 99n21
Barry, Vivienne, 293, 295–96, 310–11n8. See also *Atrapados en Japón / Trapped in Japan*
Barry Silva, Carlos, 293–94, 295–301
La batalla de Chile / The Battle of Chile, 5, 97n10, 333n9
Bazin, André, 59, 140
belonging
    in *Gringuito*, 315, 317–19
    in international film community, 43, 45
    in *Vida de familia*, 214n11
Benjamin, Walter, 342–43
Bennett, Jane, 303
Benson-Allot, Caetlin, 121
Berger-Hertz, Germán, 294–95
Bermúdez Barrios, Nayibe, 13
Bhabha, Homi, 145
Bildungsroman, 162, 163, 164, 173, 173–74n5. See also coming-of-age stories
biographical genres, 305
Bisama, Álvaro, 169
Bize, Matías, 9, 51
Black Panther, 151–52n16
blaxploitation films, 134, 150n5
Blood Window, 114, 117
body genre, martial arts films as, 137–46
Bolaño, Roberto, 159, 161–66, 169, 172, 174n5
bolero, 179–80, 186–91
Bonitzer, Pascal, 225–26
Böttner, Lorenza, 246, 261n4
Bourdieu, Pierre, 46, 249
Bustos, Pachi. See *Actores secundarios / Secondary Actors*
Butler, Judith, 343, 347, 348

Cabello, Cristeva, 223–24, 239n6
Calle Santa Fe / Santa Fe Street, 11–12, 80, 278–79, 280–81, 288n13, 340, 345–48
Cámara de Exhibidores Multisalas de Chile (CAEM, Chilean Chamber of Multiplex Exhibitors), 15, 21n2, 123n5, 124n8
Campos, Minerva, 41
Caña, María del Carmen, 96n2
Cánovas, Rodrigo, 239n4
capitalist realism, 61, 68n18
Carmona, Alejandra, 294–95
Carreño, Rubí, 239n2
Cartas visuales / Visual Letters, 102n35
Casa Roshell, 221–24
    and disappropriation of trans culture, 236–38
    framing of, 224–29
    politics of interior and disidentification in, 229–36
Castilla, Sergio. See *Gringuito*
Castillo, Carmen
    Calle Santa Fe, 11–12, 80, 278–79, 280–81, 288n13, 340, 345–48
    films by, 354n7
    La flaca Alejandra, 80, 281
    loss and mourning in films of, 343–44
Catholic Church, 349–51
Catrileo, Matías, 210, 214n12
centrifugal cinema. See also Urrutia Neno, Carolina
    and changes in theories of Chilean cinema, 52–56
    changes regarding, 51–52
    and Fernández Almendras's centrality in Chilean filmmaking, 57–59
    and marital conflict in *Vida de familia*, 203–4
    and new realism, 59–66
    overview of, 10
    theoretical guidelines at foundation of, 55
El chacotero sentimental / The Sentimental Teaser, 7
Chan, Jackie, 152n19
Chaskel, Pedro, 83–84, 99n21
Chicago Boys, 6

childhood
  as creative social construct, 318–19, 333n6
  as destabilizing trope in *Gringuito*, 332
  in films of exile, 332n2
  as political category, 314–19
  and projects of nation-state formation, 335n18
  as understood in terms of adulthood, 335n16
children
  as agents and subjects, 326–27
  in films of exile, 332n2
  returning from exile, 313–14
  subjected to political violence during dictatorship, 288n12
Chile
  Japanese commercial and cultural exchange with, 309–10n2
  loss and mourning in, 339–40, 341–42
  as "model" country, 245
  neoliberal economic opening in, 2
  origins of economic system of, 262n5
Chilean cinema
  aesthetic experimentation in, 166
  changes in theories of, 52–56
  changing conceptions of, 37
  context of trans politics in, 247–50
  detachment of, from communities depicted in, 262–63n12
  dissociation from previous generations, 201–3
  evolution and promotion of, 15–16
  expansion and professionalization of, 33, 270–71
  film festivals and funding for, 40–41
  foreign and domestic reception of, 1–2
  formation of new corpus of, 33–34
  global aesthetic embraced by, 2–3
  history of, 3–7
  increased visibility of, 38–39
  internationalization and cultural commodification of, 16–17
  New Chilean Cinema movement, 37
  Novísimo Cine Chileno, 51, 56, 59, 66n2. See also *Novísimo* Generation
  under Patricio Aylwin, 22n8
  during Popular Unity years, 269–70
  relevance of nation-based critique for, 12–15
  renaissance in, 200
  and rise of neoliberal individualism, 262–63n12
  scholarship on, 14, 21n2
  shift of emphasis in, 62
  size and aspirations of community, 34–37
  social networks in, 36
  in twenty-first century, 8–12
Chile Films, 5, 21n5, 77, 97n8
Chile junio—1973 / June 1973 (newsreel), 289n23
Chilewood, 122, 125n17
Chinango, 143
Choi, Domin, 89–90
chronotope, 166
Chua, Peter, 140
Cinecittà studio sequences, in *Il Futuro*, 171–72
Cine de Allende (The Cinema of the Allende era), 77
Cine de hijos (Cinema made by children of the disappeared), 81
CinemaChile, 24n22, 42, 248–49
cinema of exile, 77–78, 332n4, 334n10
La ciudad de los fotógrafos / The City of Photographers, 275–77, 284, 286
class divide, in *Gringuito*, 321–22, 325, 328, 330–31
El club / The Club, 62–63, 112–13, 340, 349–51
Club Roshell, 223, 225, 227
collaboration / collective authorship, 86–90, 98n13
El color del camaleón / The Color of the Chameleon, 283–84
coming-of-age stories, 161–66. See also *Bildungsroman*
commercial horror films, 110–12, 115–16
community
  construction of horror cinema, 108–9
  and destabilization of dictatorship, 273–76
  documentaries and power of, 285–86
"community of practice," 36

Index • 361

"¿Cómo puedes vivir contigo mismo?" / "How Can You Live with Yourself?" (Anwandter), 184
Concertación de Partidos por la Democracia (Concertation of Parties for Democracy), 353n4
Consejo del Arte y la Industria Audiovisual (CAIA, National Council of Art and the Audiovisual Industry), 24n22
Consejo de Seguridad del Estado (State Security Council), 270
Consejo Nacional de la Cultura y las Artes (CNCA, National Council of Culture and the Arts), 22n8
constellated genre community, 108
consumption, construction of horror cinema community via, 108–9
contemporary fiction films, 60–66
Contreras, Manuel, 282, 289n17
Control Z, 207
Coordinadora Universitaria por la Disidencia Sexual (CUDS, University Organization for Sexual Dissidence), 263n17
El coraje del pueblo / The Courage of the People, 237
Corro, Pablo, 54, 60
Cortínez, Verónica, 325
Creative Europe program, 44
Cuban Revolution, 76
culture
    of Chilean and transnational horror cinema, 109–11, 117–18
    creation and maintenance of horror, in Chile, 113–14
    "culture of violence," 178, 193n4
    horror cinema's indications about Chilean, 121–22

Damiens, Antoine, 249, 251, 262n10
Dapena, Gerard, 107, 131
Dear Nonna, 102n35
de Certeau, Michel, 108–9, 118
Deleuze, Gilles, 225, 326
de los Ríos, Valeria, 15, 170–71
democracy, transition to
    Actores secundarios and changes in documentaries during, 273–75
    cinema during, 269–71
    La ciudad de los fotógrafos and changes in documentaries during, 275–77
    and documentaries depicting private sphere as part of public history, 277–81
    and perpetrator films, 281–84
    and trauma films, 271–72
Dennison, Stephanie, 13
Depetris, Irene, 94
Derrida, Jacques, 226–27
Destroy She Said (Duras), 231
detachment
    aesthetics of, in Latin American filmmaking, 208–12
    politics of, 22n12
de Toro, Alfonso, 160–61
Diario inconcluso / Unfinished diary, 78–79
Díaz Espinoza, Ernesto, 66n2, 131, 150n5. See also *Kiltro*; *Mandrill*; *Mirageman*
Dinamarca, Paula Yermén, 225, 259, 263n15
Dios / God, 87–89
Dirección de Inteligencia Nacional (DINA, National Intelligence Directorate), 263n14, 278, 282, 289n17
disappropriation, of trans culture, 236–38
disidentification, 234–35
displacement
    and accented cinema, 334n10
    and connection with family, 313–14
    and making of impossible exilic subject in *Gringuito*, 319–31
    and politics of exilic childhood in *Gringuito*, 315–19
di Tella, Andrés, 300–302
diversity, documentaries focused on, 84–86. See also LGBTQ+ issues and themes; queer cinema; "queer relay"; trans culture; trans film
documentaries
    affective turn in, 73
    categories of, 72–73
    centered on intimate issues, 84–86
    change in interaction between image and political power, 90–95

in contemporary Chilean cinema, 11–12
developed or finished in exile, 97n10
of ECO Communications Collective, 98n13
evolution from activist documentary to subjective turn, 76–81
and evolution in representation of trauma, 281–84
growth of and changes in, 273–77
on loss and mourning, 340
with macropolitical rhetorics turning focus onto issues of neoliberalism, 82–84
perpetrator films, 281–84, 286
with political substance in community-based conception of cinema, 86–90
private sphere as part of public history in, 277–81
relationship between politics and, 71, 74–76, 82
and sense-based approaches to political praxis, 74–76
supported by Chile Films, 97n8
tendencies in, showing continuity with previous films and reflection of affective turn, 82–95
transition to introspective gaze in, 71–72, 80–81
documentary fiction, 300
documentary victim, 81
documentary witnesses, 80
dominated, gaze of, 241n14
Donald, Stephanie, 335n18
Donoso, Camila José, 224–25, 236–38, 239n3, 259. See also *Casa Roshell*; *Naomi Campbel*
Donoso, José, 175n11, 221–22, 239nn1–3
Donoso Pinto, Catalina, 9, 202, 318
Dorfman, Ariel, 279, 288–89nn14–15
Dorfman, Rodrigo, 277–78, 279–81, 288n14
Douglas, Mary, 108
Downhill, 118
Duras, Marguerite, 231
Dyer, Richard, 134–35, 141

Easter Island, 92–94
ECO Communications Collective, 98n13
economy of space, 228–29
El edificio de los chilenos / The Chilean Building, 12, 277–79, 288n13
Edwards, Agustín, 287n4
emasculation, 134, 136, 140, 141, 143
embodied experiences
in *Atrapados en Japón*, 305–8
impact of, 72
emotion. *See* affect
Empaná de pino / Meat Empanada, 120
emplacement, and accented cinema, 334n10. *See also* displacement
En algún lugar del cielo / Some Place in the Sky, 294–95
Eng, David, 342–43
En la cama / In Bed, 9, 22n11, 51
Enríquez, Miguel, 345, 347
Espinosa, Patricia, 172
estallido social (social explosion), 17
Estévez, Antonella, 9, 54, 202, 208–9, 342
exile
and *Atrapados en Japón*, 294, 303
of Carmen Castillo, 346
children and childhood in, 332n2
and Chilean and transnational horror cultures, 110
documentaries developed or finished in, 97n10
and *Generation Exile*, 279–81
impact on children, 313–14
making of impossible exilic subject in *Gringuito*, 319–31
politics of exilic childhood, 315–19
role in documentaries, 293–95
of Vivienne Barry, 293, 301
exilic cinema, 77–78, 332n4, 334n10
exilic spaces, 320, 324–25, 334n11
exilic subjectivity, 319–31, 333n8, 334n11

Fábula, 16, 41, 42
Falicov, Tamara, 2, 13–14, 208, 251
family
displacement and connection with, 313–14
and documentaries on exile, 293–95
"national," 245

family (*continued*)
    and perpetrator films, 281–84, 286
    and politics of exilic childhood in *Gringuito*, 317–19
Fernández Almendras, Alejandro
    Aquí no ha pasado nada, 58, 62–63
    centrality in Chilean filmmaking, 57
    Huacho, 58
    Matar a un hombre, 10, 57–59
    Sentados frente al fuego, 54, 56, 57
    social issues in works of, 10
    social representation in films of, 57–59
    and transition in poetics of *Novísimo* generation, 56
Ferozz: The Wild Red Riding Hood, 213n6
festival films, 13–14, 251. See also film festivals; international film festivals
Festival Internacional de Cine de Valdivia (FICValdivia), 9, 44, 51, 159, 200, 287n5, 309n1
fictions of identity, 223
filiation, transition to affiliation from, 165
Film Commission Chile (FCCh), 24n22
film criticism, 52–55
film festivals. See also international film festivals
    exhibition of Chilean horror cinema at, 113–14, 115, 117, 125n15
    trans film and, 250
Film Map, 87. See also Mapa Fílmico de un País (MAFI, "Filmic Map of the Country")
Fisher, Mark, 61, 68n18
La flaca Alejandra / Skinny Alejandra, 80, 281
Flores Delpino, Carlos, 52–53
Fondo Nacional para el Desarrollo Cultural y las Artes (Fondart, National Fund for the Development of Culture and the Arts), 22n8
forensic gaze, 241n15
Fornazzari, Alessandro, 121–22
Fotografías / Photographs, 300–301
Foxley, Susana, 278. See also *El edificio de los chilenos / The Chilean Building*

Fragmentos de un diario inacabado / Fragments of an Unfinished Diary, 78–79
framing
    in aesthetic theory, 225–27
    in *Casa Roshell*, 227–29, 230
Francia, Aldo, 175n11
Francis, Pope, 88–89
Friedberg, Anne, 226
La frontera / The Frontier, 7
Fuguet, Alberto, 9, 51, 199, 200, 213n2
Fujino, Diane, 140
funding, 40–41, 208
Il Futuro / The Future, 159–61, 172–73
    appropriation of *Bildungsroman* imaginaries, 174n5
    narrative of formation of protagonist, 161–66
    Scherson's personal aesthetic and form-based affiliations, 166–72

Gabriela Copertari, 12
Galtung, Johan, 193n4
gaze
    in *Casa Roshell*, 229–31
    of dominated, 241n14
    forensic, 241n15
    in *El lugar sin límites*, 241n13
    in *Naomi Campbel*, 255–56
Gender Identity Law (2018), 247–48
Generation 2000, 8
Generation Exile, 279–81
Generation of 2005. See *Novísimo* Generation
genre film, 8–9. See also horror cinema; martial arts cinema
    belonging in multiple communities, 123n3
    constellated genre community, 108
glide, 231–32
global art cinema, 39–40
global audiences, and cinema of "auto-erasure," 207
globalization, cinema linked to, 3. See also international film festivals
Gómez, Sergio, 199, 213n2
Gómez-Barris, Macarena, 250, 253–54, 263n14
González, María Paz, 85–86
Goodwin, Andrew, 181
Gorbman, Claudia, 179–80, 191

Green, Kyle, 140
Green Ghost, 150n6
The Green Hornet, 134
Gringuito, 7, 314–15, 331–32
    displacement, *retorno*, and making of impossible exilic subject in, 319–31
    politics of exilic childhood in, 315–19
Grosz, Elizabeth, 228
Grubačić, Andrej, 324, 334n11
Guerrero, Manuel, 210
Guzmán, Patricio
    La batalla de Chile, 5, 97n10, 333n9
    and documentation of Allende's ascent, 4
    films by, 354n7
    loss and mourning in films of, 343–44
    role in events of dictatorship, 11
    Salvador Allende, 340, 344–46, 347–48, 354n10
    self-representational introspection of, 80–81
Guzzoni, Fernando, 62–63, 64. See also *Jesús*

Halberstam, Jack, 246, 252, 254–55, 261n3
haptic visuality, 307
Harbord, Janet, 110, 115
Hauer, Rutger, 169
Hawkins, Joan, 121
Heavenly Bodies, 134–35
Henricksen, Leonardo, 284, 289n23
Herzog, Amy, 179, 180
Hija / Daughter, 85–86
Hills, Matt, 113
Hirsch, Marianne, 11, 98n15, 285
Hjort, Mette, 34
Holroyd, Michael, 305
homoeroticism, and martial arts films, 140–42
"homosexual ghetto," 241n12
hooks, bell, 241n14
Horne, Luz, 300
horror cinema, 107–8
    Chilean, as replicating and differing from international, 111, 118–21
    Chilean films without commercial release, 114, 115t
    construction of community, 108–9
    creation and maintenance of, culture in Chile, 113–14
    engagement with other genres, 120, 124n10
    indications about Chilean national culture, 121–22
    interfacing of Chilean and transnational cultures, 109–11, 117–18
    local and international attention for, 8–9
    media coverage of Chilean, 116–17
    platforms and modes of circulation of, 113–16, 117–18, 123n5, 125n15
    porous relationship between art house cinema and, 107, 112–13
    prior to 2000, 123–24n6
    receiving support from Banco del Estado de Chile, 124n7
    short films, 124n11
Huacho, 58
human rights violations, 210–11

identity
    and cinema of "auto-erasure," 207
    disidentification and politics of interior in *Casa Roshell*, 229–36
    fictions of, 223
    Latin American sexual and gender, 223–24
    and making of impossible exilic subject in *Gringuito*, 319–31
    in McOndo's stories, 212–13n1
    and politics of exilic childhood in *Gringuito*, 316–17, 333n7
    in *Vida de familia*, 209–10, 212, 214n11
immigration, 260
"impossible" subject, 326–27, 334–35n12
Inosanto, Diana Lee, 136
intercultural film, 307–8, 311n12
interior, politics of the, 224, 229–36, 238

international film festivals, 33–34, 45–47
    and Chilean social networks, 36
    as economic hubs for international film industry, 40–41
    exhibition and circulation in, 37–40
    as hubs of world cinema, 38
    and internationalization of small cinemas, 35–36
    markets and industry spaces at, 40–43
    and neocolonial relationship between affluent nations and Global South, 208
    New Latin American Film Festival, 77
    training hubs at, 43–45
    trans film and, 250
The Iowa Review, 199
Iquique, 3
Isherwood, Baron, 108
Italian neorealism, 59, 63, 68–69n23, 171–72, 175n11
itinerancy, in *Gringuito*, 319–24, 325, 326, 333–34n9

Japan, commercial and cultural exchange with Americas, 309–10n2. See also *Atrapados en Japón / Trapped in Japan*
Jara, Mario, 202
Jara, Víctor, 180
Jenks, Chris, 318, 333n6
Jesús, 62–63, 64–65, 177, 193n2
Jiménez, Cristián, 55, 200. See also *Vida de familia / Family Life*
Jofré, Aníbal, 62–63
Johnny 100 Pesos, 7, 149n2
Jordan, Michael B., 151–52n16

Kazanjian, David, 342–43
Kelly, Jim, 134
Kilduff, Hannah, 335n16
Kiltro, 133, 139–40, 142–43, 150–51n9
Kindertotenlieder (Mahler), 178, 186–87, 189–91, 195n21
King, John, 13
Kirkwood, Julieta, 262n11
Korsgaard, Mathias Bonde, 187
Kredell, Brendan, 113

Labanyi, Jo, 296
La Moneda Palace bombing, 282
Landsberg, Alison, 272
Lane, Anthony, 254
language
    and aesthetic regime of art, 160
    and Bruce Lee's path to stardom, 136
    and performance of identity and class distinction in *Gringuito*, 330
Larraín, Martín, 68n15
Larraín, Pablo
    El club / The Club, 62–63, 112–13, 340, 349–51
    as global filmmaker, 39–40
    loss and mourning in films of, 348–49
    NO, 1–2, 3, 21n1
    social issues in works of, 10
    and transition in poetics of *Novísimo* generation, 56
Larraín, Ricardo, 7
Latinoamericana (Anwandter), 180, 185
Laub, Dori, 80
Lavanderos, Fernando, 54, 67n11
La Victoria, 259
Lazzara, Michael, 11, 354n10
Lee, Bruce, 129–30, 134, 135–36, 138–39, 141, 143, 150n4
Leiva, Elisa, 248–49
Lelio, Sebastián
    and Chilean cinema's detachment from depicted communities, 262–63n12
    as global filmmaker, 39–40
    loss and mourning in films of, 348–49
    Una mujer fantástica, 15, 69n24, 222, 239n5, 246, 251–54, 261, 263nn13–14, 339, 349, 351–52
    and *Novísimo* Generation, 9
    La sagrada familia, 51
Lemebel, Pedro, 180, 193n7, 262n6
Leppe, Carlos, 355n18
Ley de Seguridad del Estado (State Security Law), 270
LGBTQ+ issues and themes. See also *Casa Roshell*; *El lugar sin límites / Hell Has No Limits* (Donoso); *Una mujer fantástica / A Fantastic*

Woman; queer cinema; "queer relay"; trans culture; trans film
   in Anwandter music videos, 182, 184–85
   in Anwandter works, 177, 192
   and economy of space, 228–29
   "homosexual ghetto," 241n12
   and identities under term "trans," 240n8
   in popular music, 195n23
   and Zamudio archive, 177–78
Lie, Nadia, 208
light, and photosensitivity in *Il Futuro*, 162, 167
Littin, Miguel, 4, 175n11
A Little Lumpen Novelita (Bolaño), 159, 161–66, 169, 174n5
Llanos, Bernardita, 354n11
"Locura / Madness" (Anwandter), 182, 185
López, Nicolás
   Aftershock, 111, 114
   and Chilewood, 122, 125n17
Lorca, Federico García, 147
loss and mourning
   Butler on, 348
   in *Calle Santa Fe*, 345–48
   in Castillo and Guzmán films, 343–44
   in *El club*, 340, 349–51
   documentaries on, 340
   and identity in *Vida de familia*, 209–10
   in Larraín and Lelio films, 348–49
   in *Una mujer fantástica*, 339, 349, 351–52
   and Pinochet regime, 339–40, 341–42
   in *Salvador Allende*, 344–45, 347–48
   social implications of stories on, 353
   theories on and representation in film of, 341–43
love affairs, and coming-of-age stories, 164–65
Lowenstein, Adam, 121
Lübbert, Andrés, 283–84, 286, 289nn21–22
Lübbert, Jorge, 283–84

El lugar sin límites / Hell Has No Limits (Donoso), 221–22, 239nn1–2
El lugar sin límites / Hell Has No Limits (Ripstein), 239n1, 239n3, 241n13
Lury, Karen, 326–27, 335n13
Lyne, William, 150n5

Machete Kills, 148
MAFI School, 87
Magic Magic, 112–13
Mahler, Gustav, 178, 186–87, 189–91, 194n16, 195n21
Malermo, Miguel, 113
Mallet, Marilú, 78–79
Mandrill, 145
"Manifiesto" / "Manifesto" (Anwandter), 184–85
La mansión Nucingen / The House of Nucingen, 109–10
Mapa Fílmico de un País (MAFI, "Filmic Map of the Country"), 87–90, 98n14, 101n31
Marchant, Patricio, 341
Marchi, Margarita, 278, 288n13
"Maricón Zara" (Planeta No), 195n23
Marks, Laura, 307, 311n12
martial arts cinema
   as body genre, 137–38
   Lee's impact in, 129–30
   link between erotic films and, 151n10
   link between masculinity and, 134, 136, 137–46, 151n12
   and Zaror as global star, 148–49
   and Zaror's filmography and trajectory, 131–37
   and Zaror's racial malleability and global stardom, 130–31
   and Zaror's villainous and minor roles, 147–48
Martin-Jones, David, 207
masculinity, link between martial arts genre and, 134, 136, 137–46, 151n12
Matar a un hombre / To Kill a Man, 10, 57–59
Mateos, Concha, 86–87
McOndo, 199–200, 202, 212–13n1
McOndo literary movement, 199–200
media, and contextualized reality, 63–64
melancholy, 54, 55, 65, 208–9, 342–43

(Me llamo) Sebastián, 195n23
melodramatic motifs, in *Il Futuro*, 161–66
memory and memory studies, 11
    affect and management of, 95n1
    Calle Santa Fe as exercise in, 347
    documentaries as rescuing Chilean, 285–86
    and documentaries depicting private sphere as part of public history, 277–81
    and embodied experience, 305–8
    and perpetrator films, 281–84
    and photography as documentation, 276
    postmemory, 11, 12, 81, 98nn15–16, 272–73, 281–84
    presence in contemporary world, 275
    promotion of films about, 287n2
    prosthetic, 272
    transmission of, 271–72
    traveling, 299
El Mercurio, 273, 287n4
military authoritarianism, 270
Mirageman, 143–45, 151n13
Mi vida con Carlos / My Life with Carlos, 294–95
mobility
    and exilic cinema, 332n4
    in *Gringuito*, 319–24, 325, 326, 333–34n9
Molloy, Sylvia, 233
Montañez, María Soledad, 207
Mórbido, 117
Moreno, Sebastián, 275–77, 284, 286
Moulian, Tomás, 287n2
mourning. *See* loss and mourning
Movimiento de Izquierda Revolucionaria (MIR), 345–46
Una mujer fantástica / A Fantastic Woman, 15, 69n24, 222, 239n5, 246, 251–54, 261, 263nn13–14, 339, 349, 351–52
Mulvey, Laura, 140, 230, 353n6
Muñoz, José, 223
Museum of Memory and Human Rights, 210, 212, 214nn13,15
music and musical moments
    in contemporary filmmaking, 178
    in *Nunca vas a estar solo*, 179–80, 186–91

music video(s)
    impact on popular culture and mediascape, 181, 192
    lyrics, songs, and iconography of Anwandter's, 181–86, 194n16
    sequences in *Nunca vas a estar solo*, 177, 178–79

Naficy, Hamid, 294, 316, 323, 326, 328, 332n4, 334n10, 335n15
Naomi Campbel, 224–25, 246, 254–61, 263n18
Narboni, Jean, 231
Nasty Baby, 112–13, 124n10
national cinemas, 12–15, 35, 96n4
National Commission on Political Prison and Torture, 288n12. *See also* Valech Commission
National Council of Art and the Audiovisual Industry (CAIA), 24n22
National Council of Culture and the Arts (CNCA), 22n8
National Fund for the Development of Culture and the Arts (Fondart), 22n8
National Intelligence Directorate (DINA), 263n14, 278, 282, 289n17
nationalism, 130–33, 149–50n3
Nattino, Santiago, 210
Neale, Steve, 113
neoliberalism, 82–84, 99n19, 121–22, 131–33, 202
neorealism, Italian, 59, 63, 68–69n23, 171–72, 175n11
Netflix, 9, 15, 114, 146
Neustadt, Robert, 245
New Chilean Cinema movement (*Novísimo Cine Chileno*), 37, 52, 77
New Chilean Narrative, 213n2
New Latin American Cinema, 4
New Latin American Film Festival, 77
new realism, 59–66
Ngai, Mae, 326, 334–35n12
Nichols, Bill, 297, 298–99
Nightworld, 109, 110, 124–25n12
NO, 1–2, 3, 21n1
La noche de enfrente / Night Across the Street, 112–13
normativity, and transness under Pinochet, 351–52
nostalgia, 209

Novísimo Cine Chileno, 51, 56, 59, 66n2
Novísimo Generation, 8, 9, 10, 56, 57–59, 62, 201–3, 354n14
Nuevo Cine Chileno (New Chilean Cinema), 37, 52, 77
Nunca vas a estar solo / You'll Never Be Alone, 177–81
    LGBTQ+ issues and themes in, 192
    musical moments in, 179–80, 186–91
    music video sequences in, 178–79
    themes of, foreshadowed in Anwandter music videos, 181–86

Oddó Osorio, Luis, 3
O'Hearn, Dennis, 324, 334n11
Olguín, Jorge, 118–19, 120, 122
oppositional cinema, 101n31
optic visuality, 307
Orellana, Naomi, 222
Organization for Economic Cooperation and Development (OECD), 131
Orientalism (Said), 139–40
Orozco, Lissette, 282–83, 286

El pacto de Adriana / Adriana's Pact, 282–83
Palacios, José Miguel, 318, 333n8
Panizza, Tiziana, 91–94, 102n35
Parada, José Manuel, 210
Parada, Marcela, 66n3
Paranaguá, Paulo Antonio, 13
Peeren, Esther, 323
Peirano, María Paz, 16, 21n1, 262n8
performativity, as embedded in time-space, 323
Peric, Ivana, 251–52, 253
Perlongher, Néstor, 228, 240n8, 241n12
perpetrator films, 281–84, 286
Petrie, Duncan, 34
photography, 275–77
photosensitivity, in *Il Futuro*, 162, 167
Piedras, Pablo, 294
Piñera, Sebastián, 68n17, 247–48
Pinochet, Augusto
    and Chile's economic system, 262n5
    cultural production under, 5–6
    gestures to legacy of, in *Una mujer fantástica*, 253

    human rights violations under, 210–11, 214n13
    and Larraín's *NO*, 1
    and loss and mourning in Chile, 339–40, 341–42, 346–47, 349–52
    and "national family," 245
    scholarship on legacy of, 353n3
    seizes power, 5
Pino-Ojeda, Walescka, 122
Planeta No, 195n23
Play, 51, 200
Podalsky, Laura, 13, 95–96nn1–2
political documentaries, 71, 90–95
"politics of detachment," 22n12
politics of the interior, 224, 229–36, 238
"politics of transaction," 213n9
Polly, Matthew, 150n4
Póo, Ximena, 9
Popular Unity (Unidad Popular, UP), 4, 79, 269–72, 274–75
postdictatorship period, 210–12, 213n9, 214n15, 247, 259
postmemory, 11, 12, 81, 98nn15–16
postmemory generation, 272–73, 281–84
private spaces
    affect and political tension between public and, 85–86
    as part of public history in documentaries, 277–81
ProChile, 42
Propaganda, 87–88, 89
prosthetic memories, 272
Proyecto Hogares ("Project Homes"), 278, 288n13. See also *El edificio de los chilenos / The Chilean Building*
public spaces, affect and political tension between private and, 85–86
Puig, Manuel, 175n11

queer cinema, 120, 124n10
"queer relay," 249, 251, 260–61
Quintana, Ángel, 63

Ramírez Soto, Elizabeth, 14, 262n9, 278, 299, 310n7
Rancière, Jacques, 74–76, 82, 86, 91, 95, 101n30, 160, 205
Rapa Nui people, 92–93
Rara, 10–11, 62–63, 64, 65

realism. *See also* Italian neorealism
   capitalist, 61, 68n18
   new, 59–66
   return to, 59
reality, contextualized, 63–64
Rebeldes / Rebels (Anwandter), 182–83
recognition, due to international film festivals, 38–39
Redeemer, 145–46, 151n9
reenactments, 297–300
Remitente: Una carta visual / "Sender: A Visual Letter," 102n35
Renov, Michael, 72, 294
retorno
   and making of impossible exilic subject in *Gringuito*, 319–31
   and politics of exilic childhood in *Gringuito*, 315–19
Revolutionary Left Movement (MIR), 345–46
Richard, Nelly, 213n9, 340, 341–42
Ríos, Héctor, 83–84, 99n21
Ríos, Mónica, 252
Ripstein, Arturo, 180, 194n19, 239n1, 239n3, 241n13
Rivas, Adriana, 282–83
Rivas, Diego "Pitbull," 152n20
Rivera Garza, Cristina, 237–38
Rocha, Carolina, 332n2
Rodriguez, Robert, 131, 139
Rojas, Lucio, 8–9, 114, 117–18, 125n15
Rojas de Negri, Rodrigo, 277
Rome
   and *Il Futuro* as chronotype of ruin, 168–70
   and understanding transmedial movement between Latin American film and literature, 172
Ross, Miriam, 41
Roth, Eli, 122
Rueda, Amanda, 207
ruin, *Il Futuro* as chronotype of, 168–70
Ruiz, Raúl, 4, 109–10, 112–13, 175n11

Saavedra, Carlos, 9, 53
La sagrada familia / The Sacred Family, 51
Said, Edward, 139–40, 165
Saldívar, José David, 327
Salinas, Claudio, 9
Salvador Allende, 340, 344–48, 354n10

"Sandow, the Bodybuilder," 138
Sangre eterna / Eternal Blood, 122
Sanjinés, Jorge, 237
San Martín, Pepa, 10–11, 62–63, 64, 65
Savage Dog, 130, 147
Scherson, Alicia, 9, 51, 173, 200, 213n4. *See also Il Futuro / The Future; Turistas / Tourists; Vida de familia / Family Life*
Schlunke, Katrina, 94
Schneider, Arnd, 37
school occupation (1985), 274
Sciamma, Céline, 262n10
Se arrienda / For Rent, 51, 200
secondary production, 108–9, 116, 118
Sedeño, Ana, 86–87
self-representational introspection, in documentaries, 71–72, 80–81
Seminet, Georgia, 332n2
Sendero / Path, 114
sensory experiences
   impact of lived and embodied, 72
   and political documentaries, 90–95
   and unconventional approaches to political praxis in documentaries, 74–76
"sharing of the sensible," 74
Shaviro, Steven, 233
Shaw, Lisa, 13
short horror films, 124n11
"Siempre es viernes en mi corazón" / "It's Always Friday in My Heart" (Anwandter), 184, 194nn16,18
Silva, Sebastián, 112–13, 124n10
Simpson, Mark, 140
Sirk, Douglas, 239n6
Sitnisky, Carolina, 12
soap operas, and construction of Chilean manhood, 139
social capital, and international film festivals, 45–46
social imaginary, 173n4
socialism, idealized by youth, 274–75
social media
   Anwandter's presence on, 182
   Zaror's presence on, 136–37
social realism, 59–66
Solanas, Fernando "Pino," 99n19
Solari, Pablo, 355n19
Solos / Descendants, 122
Sorlin, Pierre, 109
souvenirs, 301–8, 310–11n8

space
  economy of, 228–29
  in *Il Futuro*, 166–72
Spoerer, Juan Diego, 295
Stange, Hans, 9
star(s)
  construction of, 134–35
  paradox of, 135
Stars, 134. *See also* Dyer, Richard
State Security Law, 270
Stenius, Magnus, 140
Stewart, Susan, 303
student movement, 274–75
Subero, Gustavo, 119, 120
subjectivity
  confluence between affection, emotions, politics, and, 74–76
  creation in *Atrapados en Japón*, 308–9
  and documentaries' introspective gaze, 71–73
  evolution from activist documentary to subjective turn, 76–81
  exilic, 319–31, 333n8, 334n11
  and (re)construction of father figure in *Atrapados en Japón*, 296
Sultan, 147
Sundance, 16
Sutton, Paul, 326

tactile experience, in *Atrapados en Japón*, 306–8
Tambutti Allende, Marcia, 354n11
"Tatuaje" / "Tattoo" (Anwandter), 183, 191
Teena, Brandon, 178, 193n3
Teillier, Jorge, 206, 209, 214nn10–11
Teleanálisis, 97n12
"thirdspace," 335n15
Tierra sola / *Solitary Land*, 92–94
time, in *Il Futuro*, 166–72
time-space, as grounding exilic identities, 323
Tomboy, 262n10
Tráiganme la cabeza de la mujer metralleta, 66n2
training hubs, film festivals as, 43–45
"transaction, politics of," 213n9
trans culture. *See also* LGBTQ+ issues and themes

  capaciousness of term "trans," 261n3
  disappropriation of, 236–38
  and normativity under Pinochet, 351–52
transficción, 222–23, 234, 240n7
trans film. *See also Casa Roshell*; LGBTQ+ issues and themes; *El lugar sin límites* / *Hell Has No Limits* (Donoso); *Una mujer fantástica* / *A Fantastic Woman*; queer cinema; "queer relay"
  and international notions of Chilean culture, 245–47, 261
  relationships between political stances and representations of trans people in, 250–61
  trans politics and, 247–50
Transfrontera, 223
transmediality, 160–61
trash cinema, 120, 125n16
Trauma, 117–18, 125n15
trauma
  evolution in representation of, 281–84
  and perpetrator films, 281–84, 286
  transgenerational impact of, 277–81
trauma films, 271–72
traveling memories, 299
Trejo, Roberto, 9
Tres instantes, un grito / *Three Moments, One Cry*, 83–84, 99n21
Turistas / *Tourists*, 62, 159, 213n4

Undisputed 3: Redemption, 132, 147
Unidad Popular (UP, Popular Unity), 4, 79, 269–72, 274–75
Urrutia Neno, Carolina, 10, 180–81, 202, 203–4, 354n14. *See also* centrifugal cinema

Valdés, Adriana, 100–101n29
Valdivia International Film Festival (FICValdivia), 9, 44, 51, 159, 200, 287n5, 309n1
Valech Commission, 211, 288n12
Valladares, Patricio
  Downhill, 118
  influences on, 118
  international attention for, 8
  Nightworld, 109, 110, 124–25n12
  Vlad's Legacy, 109, 110, 124–25n12

Vázquez, Angelina, 78–79
Vega, Daniela, 222, 247–48, 352
Venceremos / We Shall Overcome, 83–84, 99n21
Venkatesh, Vinodh, 96n2
Vernallis, Carol, 178, 181
Vida de familia / Family Life, 200–201, 212
    and aesthetics of detachment in Latin American filmmaking, 208–12
    as connecting to global audience, 207–8
    financial support for, 208
    symbolism of house in, 214n11
    universal applicability of, 203–6

Videla, Nicolás. See *Naomi Campbel*
Video Club, 111
Vidor, King, 239n6
Viña del Mar International Film Festival, 4, 77, 175n11
"violence, culture of," 178, 193n4
Violi, Patrizia, 297
visuality, haptic and optic, 307
Vlad's Legacy, 109, 110, 124–25n12
Volantín cortao / Kite Adrift, 62–63

Walker, Janet, 278–79
The Way of the Dragon, 136
Weber, René, 115
Wekufe: El origen del mal / Wekufe: The Origin of Evil, 121

Williams, Linda, 137
Wilson, Emma, 335n18
Winston, Brian, 81
Wong, Cindy, 44
Wood, Andrés, 7
Wright, Sarah, 335n18, 355n16

Yamaguchi, Yoshiko, 297
Yawar Mallku / The Blood of the Condor, 237
Y las vacas vuelan / And Cows Fly, 67n11
young cinema. See *Novísimo Generation*
Yu, Sabrina, 141

Zambo Dendé, 146
Zamudio, Daniel, 64–65, 69n24, 177, 182, 185, 192, 195n23
Zamudio archive, 177–78, 186, 187, 191
Zaror, Marko
    filmography and trajectory of, 131–37
    as global star, 148–49
    and link between martial arts genre and masculinity, 137–46
    mythical characters played by, 150n6
    racial malleability and global stardom of, 130–31, 137
    villainous and minor roles of, 147–48
Zilberman, Alan, 113

CONTRIBUTORS

Vania Barraza is Professor of Spanish at the University of Memphis. She is the author of *El cine en Chile (2005–2015): Políticas y poéticas del nuevo siglo* (Cuarto Propio, 2018)—which won the 2020 Harvey L. Johnson Publication Award from the Southwest Council of Latin American Studies (SCOLAS)—and *(In)subordinadas: raza, clase y filiación en la narrativa de mujeres latinoamericanas* (RIL, 2010).

Claudia Bossay holds a degree in History from Universidad Diego Portales in Chile, and a PhD in Film Studies from Queen's University Belfast, in Northern Ireland. She is an Assistant Professor in the Instituto de Comunicación e Imagen of the Universidad de Chile. Her research interests combine the history of the audiovisual medium, the historical experience of cinemagoing, and the role of female filmmakers in Chile.

Carl Fischer is Associate Professor of Spanish in the Department of Modern Languages and Literatures at Fordham University. He is the author of *Queering the Chilean Way: Cultures of Exceptionalism and Sexual Dissidence, 1965–2015* (2016), as well as articles in journals such as *American Quarterly*, *Comunicación y medios*, and *Studies in Spanish & Latin American Cinemas*.

María Angélica Franken holds a PhD in Chilean and Latin American Literature from the University of Chile and is an Assistant Professor at the Adolfo Ibáñez University. Her research interests are literature and cinema from a comparative and intermedial perspective, the construction of childhood, and migrant exchanges between Chile and Germany.

Paola Lagos Labbé holds an undergraduate degree in Social Communication, a master's degree in Documentary Film, and is a PhD candidate in Audiovisual Communication at the Universitat Autònoma de Barcelona.

She is a full-time instructor at the Universidad de Chile, where she teaches and researches on cinema, and her research interests include Latin American documentary, contemporary non-fiction films, essays, autobiographical and experimental cinema, analog, and amateur films.

Arturo Márquez-Gómez is Assistant Professor of Spanish at the University of the South. His research explores contemporary literary, audiovisual and multimedia practices in the Hispanic and Latino world through theoretical perspectives on LGTBQ issues.

Moisés Park teaches at Baylor University and holds a PhD from the University of California, Davis. He is the author of fifteen articles and book chapters, as well as the 2014 book *Figuraciones del deseo y coyunturas generacionales en literatura y cine: Eltit, Fuguet, Johnny cien pesos y Machuca*, and the poetry books *El verso cae al aula* (2017) and the bilingual *Poemas marciales* (2019).

María Paz Peirano is Assistant Professor in the Instituto de Comunicación e Imagen of the Universidad de Chile. She holds a PhD in Social Anthropology and her main line of research is on the production, circulation, and international promotion of contemporary Chilean cinema. She is the co-author of *Film Festivals and Anthropology* (with Aida Vallejo, 2017).

Mónica Ramón Ríos has published the scholarly essays *La escritura del presente* about scripts by writers, *Cine de mujeres en Postdictadura*, and edited the volume *Literaturas y feminismo*. As a fiction writer, she has published the novels *Segundos* (2010) and *Alias el Rucio* (2014–15) and the collection of short stories *Cars on Fire* (2020). She has worked in the publishing collective Sangría Editora since 2008 and currently teaches at Pratt Institute.

Jonathan Risner is an Associate Professor in the Department of Spanish and Portuguese at Indiana University Bloomington. He is the author of *Blood Circuits: Contemporary Argentine Horror Cinema* (SUNY Press, 2018) and has published articles in journals, such as *Journal of Latin American Cultural Studies*, *Hispanófila*, and *Studies in Spanish & Latin American Cinemas*.

María Helena Rueda is Associate Professor of Spanish and Latin American Studies at Smith College, where she teaches courses on Latin American literature and film. She is the author of *La violencia y sus huellas: Una mirada desde la narrativa colombiana* (Iberoamericana / Vervuert 2011) and the co-editor of *Meanings of Violence in Contemporary Latin America* (Palgrave 2011).

Camilo Trumper is Associate Professor of Latin American History at the University at Buffalo, SUNY, interested in the relationship between urban politics, the public sphere, and visual studies. His first book, *Ephemeral Histories: Public Art, Politics and the Struggle for the Street in Chile* (Berkeley: UC Press, 2016), was awarded the 2018 Best Book Award by the Historia Reciente y Memoria section of the Latin American Studies Association, the 2017 Best Book Award in the Humanities by the Southern Cone Studies Section of the Latin American Studies Association, and the 2017 Marysa Navarro Best Book Prize by the New England Council of Latin American Studies.

Carolina Urrutia Neno is Assistant Professor in the Faculty of Communications at the Catholic University of Chile. She holds a master's degree in Art Theory and a Ph.D. in Aesthetics, directs the film journal *laFuga.cl*, and is the author of the volume *Un cine centrífugo* (Cuarto Propio, 2013).

María Constanza Vergara Reyes teaches in the Department of Language and Literature at Universidad Alberto Hurtado. She specializes in contemporary Latin American literature and Chilean first-person films. She co-edited the book *Profundidad de Campo: Des/encuentros Cine-literatura en Latinoamérica* (with Betina Keizman, 2016).

www.ingramcontent.com/pod-product-compliance
Lightning Source LLC
Chambersburg PA
CBHW051535230426
43669CB00015B/2600